Postcolonial, Queer

SUNY series

EXPLORATIONS

in

POSTCOLONIAL STUDIES

Emmanuel C. Eze, editor

Patrick Colm Hogan, *Colonialism and Cultural Identity: Crises of Tradition in the Anglophone Literatures of India, Africa, and the Caribbean*

Alfred J. López, *Posts and Pasts: A Theory of Postcolonialism*

S. Shankar, *Textual Traffic: Colonialism, Modernity, and the Economy of the Text*

John C. Hawley, editor, *Postcolonial, Queer: Theoretical Intersections*

POSTCOLONIAL, QUEER

Theoretical Intersections

edited by

JOHN C. HAWLEY

STATE UNIVERSITY OF NEW YORK PRESS

Published by
STATE UNIVERSITY OF NEW YORK PRESS, ALBANY

For information, address State University of New York Press,
90 State Street, Suite 700, Albany, NY 12207

Production, Diane Ganeles
Marketing, Dana Yanulavich

Library of Congress Cataloging-in-Publication Data

Postcolonial, queer : theoretical intersections / John C. Hawley, editor.
    p. cm. — (SUNY series, explorations in postcolonial studies)
  Includes bibliographical references and index.
  ISBN 0-7914-5091-0 (alk. paper) — ISBN 0-7914-5092-9 (pbk. : alk. paper)
    1. Homosexuality—Philosophy. 2. Gays—Identity. 3. Postcolonialism. I. Hawley, John
C. (John Charles), 1947– II. Series.

HQ76.25.P67 2001
306.76'6'01—dc21
                                                                        00-051018

            10   9   8   7   6   5   4   3   2   1

for
John Sauve,
Albert Palacios,
Federico Monterroza,
and Sal and Jennifer Lauria

CONTENTS

ACKNOWLEDGMENTS

Dennis Altman, "Rupture or Continuity?: The Internationalization of Gay Identities," *Social Text* 48 (vol. 14, no. 3), pp. 77–94. Copyright 1996, Duke University Press. All rights reserved. Reprinted with permission.

Joseph Boone, "Vacation Cruises: or, The Homoerotics of Orientalism." *PMLA* (110:1): 89–107. Copyright 1995. Reprinted by permission of the Modern Language Association of America.

Gaurav Desai, "Out in Africa." *Genders 25* [reprinted in *Sexpositives: The Cultural Politics of Dissident Sexualities*, eds. Thomas Foster, Carol Siegel, and Ellen E. Berry, pp. 120–43]. Reprinted by permission of New York University Press.

Donald E. Morton, "Global (Sexual) Politics, Class Struggle, and the Queer Left." *Critical inQueeries*. (vol. 1, no. 3). Copyright by author 1997. Reprinted by permission of author.

J. K. Gibson-Graham, "Querying Globalization." *Rethinking Marxism* Spring 9.1 (1996/97), pp. 1–27.

INTRODUCTION

JOHN C. HAWLEY

Nothing can bring back the hygienic shields of colonial boundaries. The age of globalization is the age of universal contagion.
—Michael Hardt and Antonio Negri, *Empire* (136)

I slept all night soundly and woke up at seven feeling as though the whole of creation was conspiring to make me happy. I hope no doom strikes.
—Joe Orton in Tangier, *Diaries* (187)

There have been recent indications of a convergence of concerns in the fields of postcolonial and queer theory (see, for example, Patton and Sanchez-Eppler 2000, Povinelli and Chauncey 1999, Goldie 1999), but the markers for that convergence bristle with the skittish nature of their subject matters. Some queer critics at times find themselves resistant to the seemingly deeply ingrained homophobia of much postcolonial culture and discourse; many of those in postcolonial studies decry gay/lesbian studies as "white" and "elitist." This collection seeks to address that binarism and to see where it may be false and mutually destructive.

Although various of our authors address racial issues, we do not wish the reader to conclude that to be nonwhite or to live in a non-EuroAmerican nation is, perforce, to be postcolonial. Nonetheless, we do suggest that there are and have been many levels of colonization,

1

and therefore many expressions of a "postcolonial condition" throughout the world, including the West. Although the term "postcolonial" gained a footing in various discourse communities principally as a designation for literature originating in the British Commonwealth, and then expanded in the 1960s to "New Literatures in English" (see Goldie 1999), it has continued to broaden in its application and now, as Ashcroft, Griffiths, and Tiffin describe it, includes: "the study and analysis of European territorial conquests, the discursive operations of empire, the subtleties of subject construction in colonial discourse and the resistance of those subjects, and, most importantly perhaps, the differing responses to such incursions and their contemporary colonial legacies in both pre- and post-independence nations and communities" (1998: 187). What is clearly missing in this definition—an omission that threatens the viability of such a term except as a branch of Eurocentric historiography—is the role of the United States, Japan, Australia, China, and other powers in the world with major (and often imbricating) spheres of cultural and economic influence that continue the patterns of colonization established in earlier centuries by European powers. America, in particular, emblematizes the "postnational" space that Arjun Appadurai notes as uneasily engaged with "diasporic peoples, mobile technologies, and queer nationalities" (1996: 159; 174–75). Furthermore, as Leela Gandhi acknowledges, it is not just the scope of the term "postcolonial" that increasingly comes under question, but its usage and implied methodologies as well, since "its uneasy incorporation of mutually antagonistic theories—such as Marxism and poststructuralism—confounds any uniformity of approach" (1998: 3).

Any term like "postcolonial" that presumes to describe a matrix of shifting components and extreme complexity must fall short (see, for example, related discussions in Ashcroft et al, in Loomba 1998, and especially in San Juan 1998, Dirlik 1997, and Appiah 1996). But Gandhi gamely asserts that the term can at least be seen as "a theoretical resistance to the mystifying amnesia of the colonial aftermath" (4). Ania Loomba agrees that the term is useful "in indicating a general process with some shared features across the globe," but cautions that "if it is uprooted from specific locations, 'postcoloniality' cannot be meaningfully investigated, and instead, the term begins to obscure the very relations of domination that it seeks to uncover" (1998: 19). Warnings and reactions such as these suggest that one must be careful in suggesting any overarching similarities in what might more honestly be termed "post-colonialities"—site specific, while sharing a family resemblance. That resemblance often involves the revision of imposed histories and the proclamation of affiliation and identity declaration.

However, while the role of homosexual exploitation in colonial history has been well documented (see Lane 1995, Bleys 1995), the second term in our title, "queer," is at least as contentious as "postcolonial," and arguably more amorphous. Various of the authors in this collection implicitly acknowledge their preference of the earlier terminology: gay and lesbian, principally because these seem to be clearer markers of a biologically-rooted condition and of a consequent liberatory political movement that invites transnational identification (see Dennis Altman's article in this collection). Annamarie Jagose defines queer, on the other hand, as a description of "those gestures or analytical models which dramatize incoherencies in the allegedly stable relations between chromosomal sex, gender and sexual desire," and then notes its protean nature. "Institutionally," she writes, "queer has been associated most prominently with lesbian and gay subjects, but its analytic framework also includes such topics as cross-dressing, hermaphroditism, gender ambiguity and gender-corrective surgery" (1996: 3). The central tenet of queer theory is a resistance to the normativity which demands the binary proposition, hetero/homo. Pure queer theory, based on Judith Butler's antifoundationalist work in opposition to fixed identities, asserts that identity "is performatively articulated as the *effect* of regulatory regimes—a constraint queer theory attempts to transgress, subvert, and disrupt" (Cover 1999: 30). If we can speak of the difference as one of emphasis, strictly gay and lesbian discourse more typically stresses the essentialist nature of sexuality over the socially constructionist nature embodied in queer theory. Thus, one branch of queer theory can be very unsettling to gays and lesbians when it is, in Jagose's words,

> used as a way of distinguishing old-style lesbians and gays from the new, where that distinction may be registered not so much historically as variations in the understanding of identity formation but stylistically in, for example, body piercing. Or queer may be used to describe an open-ended constituency, whose shared characteristic is not identity itself but an anti-normative positioning with regard to sexuality. In this way, queer may exclude lesbians and gay men

whose identification with community and identity marks a relatively recent legitimacy, but include all those whose sexual identifications are not considered normal or sanctioned. (98)

Steven Seidman agrees that, "although many meanings circulate under
this sign, queer suggests a positioning as oppositional to both the heterosexual and homosexual mainstream" (1997: 140). Such a destabilizing of identity politics can echo the challenge postcolonial theory offers
to (perhaps the same?) group of Westerners. "The clash between the
periphery and center *within these movements*," writes Seidman, "is a
key source of postmodern thinking and politics" (113).

Jagose summarizes the troubled response of many (traditional)
gays and lesbians to this challenge as a series of questions:

> whether a generic masculinity may be reinstalled at the heart of the
> ostensibly gender-neutral queer; whether queer's transcendent disre-
> gard for dominant systems of gender fails to consider the material
> conditions of the west in the late twentieth century; whether queer
> simply replicates, with a kind of historical amnesia, the stances and
> demands of an earlier gay liberation; and whether, because its con-
> stituency is almost unlimited, queer includes identificatory cate-
> gories whose politics are less progressive than those of the lesbian
> and gay populations with which they are aligned. (3–4)

In my view, these are legitimate concerns—note, for example, the striking similarity in description between the "historical amnesia" of which
queers may be guilty, and the "mystifying amnesia of the colonial aftermath" that Leela Gandhi hopes postcolonial theory may help to counter.
Not all of these issues can be addressed (nor can any be laid to rest) in
this volume, but they must be acknowledged from the start. In addressing various postcolonial topics, this book's twelve contributors engage
queer theorizing sometimes as friend, sometimes as foe—as do the individuals whose views are analyzed in the chapters.

To further complicate the issue, despite its increasing popularity in
academic departments, queer theory resists becoming a normative *discipline*. As Jagose puts the question, "it is not simply that queer has yet to
solidify and take on a more consistent profile, but rather that its defini-
tional indeterminacy, its elasticity, is one of its constituent characteristics" (1). But it is precisely this troublesome central feature of queer the-

ory that suggests its possible utility in approaching sexualities that are less obviously binary than those in cultures in which "gay" and "lesbian" make compelling (political, public, and private) sense (see, for example, Warner 1993, 1999; Vanita 2000, Wah-Shan 2000, Green 2001). If we are to expand Gayatri Spivak's question and ask whether the *gay and lesbian* subaltern can speak, perhaps the best path to a level playing field for investigation would be a postcolonialism that humbly stays a bit out of kilter, a bit queer, and, for Westerners, a bit less garrulous.

Some scholars, of course, have made it a point to correct (counter)cultural amnesia. Teresa de Lauretis has done as good a job as anyone in quickly tracing the historical path that moved from "homosexual" to "gay," to "gay and lesbian," and on to "queer." In general, the move has involved "the effort to avoid all these fine distinctions in our discursive protocols, not to adhere to any one of the given terms, not to assume their ideological liabilities, but instead to both transgress and transcend them—or at the very least problematize them" (1991: v). As noted, the move is generally described as a protest against the binary: homosexuality/heterosexuality. "It is no longer to be seen either as merely transgressive or deviant vis-à-vis a proper, natural sexuality (i.e., institutionalized reproductive sexuality), according to the older, pathological model, or as just another, optional 'life-style,' according to the model of contemporary North American pluralism" (iii). As we shall see, this implied contesting of the North American (or European) model of "the gay life-style" plays a significant role in the chapters contained in this book, where the adoption of such Western trappings of sexual identity are seen locally as not only counternational but also elitist. Equally important to the protest is the affirmation, though. As de Lauretis notes, the queer rubric being written across this palimpsest of historical meanings conceives of male and female homosexualities as "social and cultural forms in their own right, albeit emergent ones and thus still fuzzily defined, undercoded, or discursively dependent on more established forms." Thus, their mode of functioning is "both interactive and yet resistant, both participatory and yet distinct, claiming at once equality and difference, demanding political representation while insisting on its material and historical specificity"(iii).

"Queer" acknowledges ongoing debates over the question of essentialism versus constructionism in both gay and lesbian studies, and in feminist theory, and recognizes the inadequate current knowledge of dif-

ferences between and among various gay men and women. Of special
import for this collection, the term admits this relative lack of an understanding of "practices of homosexualities and representations of same-
sex desire" as they apply to "race and its attendant differences of class or
ethnic culture, generational, and socio-political location" (viii). As with
the ongoing argument over the limitations of the term "postcolonial," so
with the debates over the terms "gay" and "lesbian," the historical
record of the usefulness of each term is celebrated while the limitations
are honestly confronted. Just as *the* postcolonial is more properly understood to be plural, so any description of same-sex desire must, in de Lauretis's words, recognize "the specificity and partiality of our respective
histories, as well as the stakes of some common struggles" (xi).

"Queer" recognizes that "gay" men and "lesbian" women may not
have very much in common, and such an acknowledgment may disrupt
notions of political solidarity. In the end, the movements may in fact have
a great deal in common after all, but this "queering" of gay and lesbian
studies is both a protest against foreclosure of possible inclusion and a
demand that the liberal (white, yuppified, Western) gay and lesbian establishment recognize the "subalterns" in its midst (Spivak: 1988; see, for
example, Almaguer 1991, Eng and Hom 1998, Foster 1991, Brandt
1999, Appiah and Gates 1995, and others). As de Lauretis notes, "perhaps, to a gay writer and critic of color, defining himself gay is not of the
utmost importance; he may have other and more pressing priorities in his
work and in his life" (ix). One might further argue that, if this racial distinction impinges on the sexual identification of nonwhite members of
Western societies, how much more so must this be the case in the rest of
the world. Some of the implications of this question play themselves out
in the orientalizing of people of color and their employment as sex workers by gay tourists (see Boone, Hayes, and others in this collection; see,
also, such studies as Mercer 1991, Povinelli and Chauncey 1999, Harper
et al. 1997, Ratti 1993, Murray and Roscoe 1998, Schmitt and Sofer
1992, Browning 1998, Prieur 1998, Herdt 1997, Parker 1999, Seabrook
1999, Blackwood 1986, Chasin 2000, and others).

As significant as race can be in such questions, the role of class in
both postcolonial and, more pressingly, queer theorizing has become
increasingly noted (Morton 1996, Hennessy 1994, Cover 1999, Kaplan
2000). What seems clear to many critics is that class is fairly consistently
ignored or downplayed as an explanatory factor in analyses of sexualities
and that queer theory, as "non-materialist," may too often focus on

"desire over needs" (Cover 29). Within traditional gay and lesbian discourse the problem presents itself in at least three ways: first, as a generally unconscious universalizing of Western sexualities (graphically shown by Elizabeth Povinelli's examples of "web sites [that] provide gay pornography to browsers where there are *hijra*, *travesti*, and *kathoeys* but no gay men" and "gay and lesbian freedom parades in Asia and Europe [that are] organized in part by men and women who have vacationed in the United States and stayed in transnationally advertised gay and lesbian bed-and-breakfasts" [442–43]); secondly, as an implied invitation to "come out" and embrace a "common" [remarkably Western] gay brotherhood and lesbian sisterhood that cuts across any nice cultural distinctions; and thirdly, as a preoccupation with "texts produced in the West and, generally, by those well-positioned in the bourgeois class" (Cover 31).

Articles like Donald Morton's, J. K. Gibson-Graham's, and Hema Chari's in this collection seek to right the balance by suggesting alternate discourses of economic exchange and, by implication, of sexuality (and sexual exchange). Morton's chapter directly confronts queer theoreticians from a Marxist point of view, underscoring what he considers to be vested interests of postmodernists (whether westerners or "migrant" intellectuals) who are situated in capitalist countries. He argues that the appearance on the historical horizon of certain "questions" (homosexuality, abortion, environmental pollution, etc.) is caused by material transformations at the level of the mode of production. Chapters such as Gibson-Graham's, also argued from a Marxist point of view but looking upon queer theory much more favorably, nicely embody Povinelli's contention that "if sex can learn from globalization and transnationalism, these schools have much to gain from critical studies of sex" (445). And Hema Chari's study of Salman Rushdie, like Morton's chapter, asks how knowledge is produced by Western capital, and how class issues can be made to supersede the (homo)sexual in such productions. Taken together, the three articles are the most direct discussion of class issues in the book, and they would seem to demonstrate that one cannot expect such a focus to be univocal in its conclusions.

THE NEW WORLD ORDER

One of the challenges consistently brought against the field of postcolonial studies is its apparent dependence on a European perspective of world history, dividing time in half much as Pope Gregory XIII once did. At the same time, one might argue that the indeterminacies implicitly celebrated in queer theorizing parallel the social and economic factors of globalization, for good or ill; both queer theory and globalization may therefore offer a more accurate framework for imagining the contemporary situation of gay/lesbian studies and postcolonial theory. Malcolm Waters describes globalization as "a social process in which the constraints of geography on social and cultural arrangements recede and in which people become increasingly aware that they are receding" (1995:3). Roland Robertson similarly characterizes it as an "increasing acceleration in both concrete global interdependence and consciousness of the global whole" (1992: 8; see, also, Wallerstein 1974, 1980, Giddens 1990, Appadurai 1996, Berman 1982), but stresses a point that has relevance for any attempt to imagine a postcolonial world from a "queer" perspective. "The very fluidity of global change," he writes, "has invited . . . nostalgia for secure forms of 'world order,' as well as a kind of projective nostalgia for the world as a home" (162). The "nostalgic paradigm" that Robertson proffers suggests an essentializing of simplified cultural histories in nations striving to assert a postcolonial (or, from a nativist point of view, pre-colonial) identity, as well as (some will argue) an essentializing of sexualities among those very "critic[s] of color" who find themselves with "more pressing priorities."

The world-system to which Robertson directs our attention in only a precursory way becomes the focus of attention for Michael Hardt and Antonio Negri, whose *Empire* describes a new form of sovereignty "composed of a series of national and supranational organisms united under a single logic of rule" which, in contrast to imperialism, "establishes no territorial center of power and does not rely on fixed boundaries or barriers. It is a *decentered* and *deterritorializing* apparatus of rule that . . . manages hybrid identities, flexible hierarchies, and plural exchanges through modulating networks of command" (2000: xii). In such a world, distinct nation-states become irrelevant; borders become a blur. Globalization, in effect, becomes queer. Nor can this sovereignty be resisted by grounding political analysis on the localization of struggles. Building their argument on Appadurai's description of the "production of locality" (Appadurai 1996: 178–99), Hardt and Negri assert that the current need is to investigate "the social machines that create and recreate the identities and differences that are understood as the local," as well as those that are known as the global, and to see them as "a regime of the production of identity and difference" (2000: 45). The local is already subsumed by the global episteme.

The process of this marginalization of the local can be ruthless. It is by now a commonplace that globalization renders nation-states increasingly irrelevant at a time that postcolonial groups are seeking to assert newly found sovereignty by building nations. But it is also a commonplace that fiction emerging from such self-identifying "new" nations often dances around themes that pit the individual against a totalizing national power that doesn't have time for individual rights. As much as nationhood may do to ward off dominant globalizing powers, as Hardt and Negri assert, the same forces are turned inward to repress internal difference. "[T]he nation becomes the only way to imagine community . . . [and] the multiplicity and singularity of the multitude are negated in the straightjacket of the identity and homogeneity of the people" (106–7). In such nation-building cultures, sexual dissidence is a distraction: you are either one of us, or you are not. Thus, conversely, "the nation-state is a machine that produces Others, creates racial difference, and raises boundaries that delimit and support the modern subject of sovereignty" (114). This production of alterity has been closely analyzed for its historical justification of the colonizing project, but it serves a similar function for those postcolonial states that seek self-definition in contradistinction to the Western powers that have "left." Moreover, both the colonizer and the postcolonized can reduce all differences to the lowest common denominator, belittling all real distinctions within a social group (such as sexual "deviance") to the simple one of not-us. Thus, in its "inclusionary" phase Empire "does not fortify its boundaries to push others away, but rather pulls them within its pacific order, like a powerful vortex" (198).

As if to respond to Appadurai's call that we "think ourselves beyond the nation" (158), in its "differential" moment Empire affirms the differences its has consumed and, "since these differences are considered now to be cultural and contingent rather than biological and essential, they are thought not to impinge on the central band of commonality or overlapping consensus that characterizies Empire's inclusionary mechanism" (199). In Hardt's and Negri's view, "the postmodernist and postcolonialist [and queer?] theorists who advocate a politics of difference, fluidity, and hybridity in order to challenge the binaries and essentialism of modern sovereignty have been outflanked by the strategies of power" (138; see also Appadurai 162). In fact, under the dynamics of corporate capital under the "Empire," the former politics of difference that Homi Bhabha celebrates as communitarian (1994: 18) has been subsumed.

The commercialization that this involves, with the proliferation of target markets based upon real or imagined difference, leads directly to the criticism brought by several of the chapters in this collection against the Americanization (though Hardt and Negri would argue that Empire is outside the control of any one nation) of gay and lesbian "life-styles" across the touristic world. Dennis Altman has elsewhere argued the point that such marketing is used as a vehicle to co-opt gay and lesbian consumers and, in the process, seemingly fix their identities (1982: 102–3). The criticism goes farther in essays such as Morton's, which focuses on the field of queer theory itself. This management of social identities becomes the clear focus of Hardt and Negri's critique, as well, when they describe the third movement within Empire as the hierarchization and management of differences under a command structure. "In our present imperial world," they write, "the liberatory potential of the postmodernist and postcolonial discourses . . . only resonates with the situation of an elite population that enjoys certain rights, a certain level of wealth, and a certain position in the global hierarchy" (156).

Thus, in the chapters that follow we are attempting to address configurations of homosexual and "queer" identity from a transnational perspective; to question the relation between hegemonic (U.S.) cultural transmissions as they intersect with indigenous or colonized formations of sexual identity; to connect cultural arrangements like sexual, racial, and class identities to the political economy of late capitalism; and to engage some of the theoretical debates around how to know these issues. In his opening chapter Dennis Altman sets forth many of the questions addressed in subsequent essays. His is a meditation on Appadurai's observation that "the modern nation-state . . . grows less out of natural facts—such as language, blood, soil and race—and more out of a quintessential cultural product, a product of the collective imagination" (1996: 161), with an implied substitution of Michael Warner's "queer planet" for the nation-state. In asking whether or not there is a universal gay identity linked to modernity, Altman does not argue a transhistoric or essentialist position, but instead questions the extent to which the forces of globalization can be said to produce a common consciousness and identity based on homosexuality. Such a topic elicits a number of questions that Altman attempts to investigate: a sense of the continuing importance of premodern forms of sexual organization; a consideration of whether the movement toward a sense of identity/community is similar or noticeably different for women; more sensitivity to class/caste divides; the persistence of different family patterns despite growing affluence and apparent westernization; the complications of the diaspora; and the interactions among developing countries themselves. As a long-established gay (as opposed to explicitly queer) writer, Altman moves with some caution into the field of queer theory, focusing more comfortably on issues that would more clearly align themselves with the postcolonial.

Among the many considerations prompted by Altman's crucial chapter are those that parallel Appadurai's observations that Americans rarely spend much time investigating the changes wrought by any other culture when it ingests the cultural products Westerners, and specifically Americans, like to identify as their own: free enterprise, supply side economics, democracy, human rights (174) and, we might add, sexual liberation. The bulk of the chapters in this book, therefore, are notably site-specific, beginning in Algeria, South Africa, or elsewhere and then suggesting a broader theoretical application of the intersection of queer and postcolonial questions that arise in the local context under discussion. Joseph Boone's study of orientalism and its ramifications for queer theory shares a good number of concerns with Chari's study of Rushdie, as Chari acknowledges. Jarrod Hayes completes the triad of chapters on roughly aligned topics. Pointing to the Algerian (French) poet Jean Sénac, the novelist Rachid Boudjedra, and various other examples, his chapter follows Altman's lead and suggests that the globalization of homosexuality might be the form taken by resistance to other globalizations. But Hayes moves more forcefully in a queer direction by pointing out that the diverse paradigms of homosexuality represented in Boudjedra's novel also resist to-date Western attempts to define and categorize "Islamic homosexualities." He raises the question as to whether, when we speak of the globalization of the hetero-homo binary, we are complicit with the flows of late-capitalism or whether we situate our analysis in resistance to it. The chapter is theoretically organized around a discussion of Altman, Stuart Hall, and the Frankfurt school of late capitalism and offers the counterintuitive proposal that the forces of economic globalization may, in fact, have homophobic effects.

Moving to Asia, Jillana Enteen and Chong Kee Tan investigate the variety of political uses to which sexually-linked terms can be put,

implying that the "universalizing" of gay terminology (condemned elsewhere in the book as hegemonically Western) in fact *can* serve a local
liberatory function. Enteen demonstrates that the development of new
interactions with the terms and stereotypes, the realignment within these
categores, enables Thais to carve out previously unavailable identification or identities that are in dialogue with contemporary situations. Tan
then shows that, while Taiwanese academics generally prefer to leverage
American queer theory to de-stigmatize homosexuality, Hong Kong's
Chou Wah-shan prefers the challenge to culture enabled by a stark portrayal of differences between Chinese and American ways of dealing
with homosexuality.

If Tan's chapter notes a growing visibility and audience for gay (or
queer) identities in Asia, Gaurav Desai's article is an attempt to contex-
tualize the lack of discourse on African sexualities in a larger framework
(see, in response, Murray and Roscoe 1998), focusing on Wole Soyinka's
Interpreters and Bessie Head's *Maru*. He is arguing for the right of
African gays to tell different stories about themselves than has been possible heretofore. But it is in any case only in the most recent years that
African writers are addressing such issues. Desai demonstrates the high
cost demanded of those who choose no longer to "pass" in a society that
may seem uninterested in posing the sort of question that queers feel a
desire to answer, despite the imposed stigma of neocolonialism leveled
against gays in Africa. One of the most influential avenues for the developing "discussion," if the term is not premature, is that of cinema (e.g.,
Philip Brooks's and Laurent Bocahut's *Woubi Cheri*, Mohamed
Camara's *Dakan*, Ingrid Sinclair's *Flame*, etc). Film studies have
assumed a leading role for some queer theorizing, and Paige Schilt's article is our collection's attempt to acknowledge that fact. Her chapter
focuses, first, on Isaac Julien's appropriation of the style and narrative
voice of the traditional BBC arts and culture documentary in order to
create a queer humanism that marginalizes the homophobia emanating
from Jamaican popular culture. Secondly, she looks at the use of religious imagery used to evoke a distinctive and disjunctive temporality for
the oppressed that problematizes the very narratives of civilization and
progress that Julien mobilizes in his critique of homophobia. In between
these two perspectives, the chapter considers the challenge that the circulation of homophobia poses to Paul Gilroy's original formulation of a
nonnationalist diasporic community constituted through creative cultural consumption—implicitly recalling Altman's essay and its consider-

ation of such a transnational queer community. William Spurlin's chapter then expands upon several of the questions prompted by Desai's and Schilt's chapters. Given broad governmental and constitutional changes that have occurred in the transition from apartheid to democracy in the "new" South Africa, including the prohibition of discrimination against lesbians and gay men, this chapter begins by examining important elisions in representations of homosexuality in historical and anthropological work. As normalizing ideologies of sexuality still persist in the region, despite juridical changes, Spurlin (re)reads same-sex relationships as subversive, insofar as they disrupt heteronormativity. His chapter challenges prevalent nationalistic claims, echoed elsewhere, that read homosexuality as a Western import. But, like Morton, Spurlin criticizes what he sees as the imperialistic gestures of queer studies that have not adequately engaged local understandings of what "queer" might mean in such a (non-postmodern) context. Finally, the chapter speaks for many of the others by addressing the strands of homophobia present in nationalistic discourses—discourses which, as we have noted above, rest on a culturally homogenous view of "the" nation and ignore the politics of sexuality as a possible site for decolonization.

The issues addressed by the individual chapters gradually suggest the complex manifestations of postcolonial problems in local discussions of emergent sexualities. In his recent survey and critique of postcolonial modes of cultural analysis, Bart Moore-Gilbert notes that "the most pressing problems which face postcolonial studies are not so much a loss of their initial impetus, or the emergence of a more critical audience than they once enjoyed, but the issues which arise from the multiplicity of historical and social contexts out of which 'the postcolonial' has emerged and the diverse cultural forms and modes of critical engagement which, consequently, it now inhabits" (188). What is most pressingly at stake, in his view, is how to theorize the broad diversity of postcolonialisms as they manifest themselves in the areas of gender, class, and sexuality. This book is an attempt to engage these issues. As Samir Dayal's thoughtful concluding chapter suggests, there are issues of justice at the heart of the topics under discussion here.

It is time that the burgeoning field of postcolonial studies addresses the effects of colonization and neocolonialism on the sexualities and sexual relations both of those designated elsewhere as subalterns, and of those whose position as members of the ruling class persisted or persists regardless of their own possibly "deviant" status within their own cul-

tures. The constructed nature of caste (once racial, now principally economic?) reflects (and often powerfully contests) much of the social interchange now controlled by access to financial and information
resources—mass media, the World Bank, the American university system. The fact that major conferences are just now beginning to turn their
attention to this nexus of social concerns suggests that there is a growing willingness to be candid and respectful of the topic in academic circles, and to recognize the issues of justice at the heart not only of gender issues related to "internationalization," but at the center of issues of
homosexuality, as well. But there is an ongoing debate over the role of
Western gays and lesbians in defining a global queerness that purports
to offer an international community whose commonalities override but
do not deny those of race and nationality. If as Waters notes, "the concept of globalization is an obvious object for ideological suspicion
because, like modernization . . . , it appears to justify the spread of western culture and of capitalist society by suggesting that there are forces
operating beyond human control that are transforming the world" (3),
then Western (or westernized) gays and lesbians necessarily must face
such "suspicion."

One reason for the general preference of queer terminology in
some of these chapters can be surmised from Steven Seidman's valorization of a postmodern approach to questions of social theory and sexual
politics. The aim of postmodernism, he writes, "is less 'the end of domination' or 'human liberation' than the creation of social spaces that per-
mit the widening of choice, the proliferation of social differences and
multiple solidarities, and expanded democratization through the deconstruction of naturalized and normalized social norms, the creation of
multiple public spheres, and so on" (Seidman 110). In the quest for the
obliteration of binarisms (such as the bipolar gender system), such openness to multiplicity and challenge to any gay unitary identity may position queer theorists surprisingly near non-Western postcolonial theorists. As Seidman notes, and as we have observed, "some people of color
have argued that a discourse that abstracts a notion of gay identity from
considerations of race and class is oppressive because it typically implies
a white, middle-class standpoint" (123). Social constructionism, in fact,
teaches us that "the gay subject invoked in subcultural discourses and
representations is seen as an historical product" (128).

But as Dayal's conclusion will show, that historical construct has a
psychological dimension that must not be allowed to be too easily sub-

sumed by social and economic movements. In this collection we are trying to advance the boundaries of knowledges about the intersections of queer theory and postcolonial theory; we are not producing a book in which everything is "settled" or "cut and dried," but are instead engaged in the kind of project that necessarily involves opening up controversial aspects of these issues for further debate. Nonetheless, if, as seems obvious, globalization is irresistible as an ultimate determinant of future social exchange, the participants shaping that future are individuals with sexualities that also intervene in the definition of a postcolonial, post-national, and perhaps "post-gay," world community.

WORKS CITED

Almaguer, Tomás. "Chicano Men: A Cartography of Homosexual Identity and Behavior." *Differences* 3.2 (1991): 75–100.

Altman, Dennis. *The Homosexualization of America, The Americanization of the Homosexual.* New York: St. Martin's, 1982.

Appadurai, Arjun. *Modernity at Large: Cultural Dimensions of Globalization.* Minneapolis: U of Minnesota P, 1996.

Appiah, Kwame A. "Is the Post in Postmodernism the Post in Postcolonialism?" In *Contemporary Postcolonial Theory: A Reader,* ed. P. Mongia. London: Arnold, 1996.

Appiah, Kwame A., and Henry Louis Gates Jr., eds. *Identities.* Chicago: U of Chicago P, 1995.

Ashcroft, Bill, Gareth Griffiths, and Helen Tiffin. *Key Concepts in Post-Colonial Studies.* London and New York: Routledge, 1998.

Berman, Marshall. *All That Is Solid Melts into Air: The Experience of Modernity.* New York: Simon and Schuster, 1982.

Bhabha, Homi. *The Location of Culture.* London: Routledge, 1994.

Blackwood, Evelyn, ed. *Anthropology and Homosexual Behavior.* New York: Haworth, 1986.

Bleys, Rudi C. *The Geography of Perversion: Male-to-male Sexual Behaviour outside the West and the Ethnographic Imagination, 1750–1918.* New York: New York UP, 1995.

Brandt, Eric, ed. *Dangerous Liaisons: Blacks, Gays, and the Struggle for Equality.* New York: New Press, 1999.

Browning, Frank. *A Queer Geography: Journeys Toward a Sexual Self*. Rev. ed. New York: Noonday, 1998.

Chasin, Alexandra. *Selling Out: The Gay and Lesbian Movement Goes to Market*. New York: St. Martin's, 2000.

Cover, Rob. "Queer with Class: Absence of Third World Sweatshop in Lesbian/Gay Discourse and a Rearticulation of Materialist Queer Theory." *ARIEL* 30.2 (1999): 29–48.

de Lauretis, Teresa. "Queer Theory: Lesbian and Gay Sexualities." *Differences* 3.2 (1991): iii–xviii.

Dirlik, Arif. *The Postcolonial Aura: Third World Criticism in the Age of Global Capitalism*. Boulder, Colo.: Westview, 1997.

Eng, David L., and Alice Y. Hom, eds. *Q & A: Queer in Asian America*. Philadelphia: Temple UP, 1998.

Foster, David William. *Gay and Lesbian Themes in Latin American Writing*. Austin: U of Texas P, 1991.

Gandhi, Leela. *Postcolonial Theory: A Critical Introduction*. New York: Columbia UP, 1998.

Giddens, Anthony. *The Consequences of Modernity*. Cambridge: Polity, 1990.

Goldie, Terry. "Queerly Postcolonial." (Special Issue on Postcolonial and Queer Theory and Praxis) *ARIEL* 30.2 (1999): 9–26.

Green, James N. *Beyond Carnival: Male Homosexuality in Twentieth Century Brazil*. Chicago: University of Chicago, 2001.

Hardt, Michael, and Antonio Negri. *Empire*. Cambridge, Mass.: Harvard UP, 2000.

Harper, Phillip Brian, Anne McClintock, José Esteban Muñoz, and Trish Rosen, eds. "Queer Transexions of Race, Nation, and Gender. (Special issue of *Social Text*). *Social Text* 52–53 15.3–4 (1997).

Hennessy, Rosemary. "Queer Theory, Left Politics." *Rethinking Marxism* 7.3 (1994): 85–111.

Herdt, Gilbert. *Same Sex, Different Cultures: Gays and Lesbians Across Cultures*. Boulder, Colo.: Westview, 1997.

Jackson, Peter A., and Gerard Sullivan, eds. *Multicultural Queer: Australian Narratives* (Special double issue of *Journal of Homosexuality*). 36.3/4 (1999).

Jagose, Annamarie. *Queer Theory: An Introduction*. New York: New York UP, 1996.

Kaplan, Cora. "Millennial Class." *PMLA* 115 (2000): 9–19.

Lahr, John, ed. *The Orton Diaries: Including the Correspondence of Edna Welthorpe and Others.* New York: Da Capo Press, 1996.

Lane, Christopher. *The Ruling Passion: British Colonial Allegory and the Paradox of Homosexual Desire.* Durham: Duke UP, 1995.

Loomba, Ania. *Colonialism/Postcolonialism.* London and New York: Routledge, 1998.

Mercer, Kobena. "Skin Head Sex Thing: Racial Difference and the Homoerotic Imaginary." In *How Do I Look? Queer Film and Video*, ed. Bad Object-Choices. Seattle: Bay Press, 1991.

Moore-Gilbert, Bart. *Postcolonial Theory: Contexts, Practices, Politics.* London: Verso, 1997.

Morton, Donald. "The Class Politics of Queer Theory." *College English* 58.4 (1996): 471–82.

Murray, Stephen O., and Will Roscoe, eds. *Boy-Wives and Female Husbands: Studies of African Homosexualities.* New York: St. Martin's, 1998.

Novoa, Juan Bruce. "Homosexuality and the Chicano Novel." In *Studies in Homosexuality*, ed. Wayne Dynes. New York: Garland, 1992: 33–41.

Parker, Richard. *Beneath the Equator: Cultures of Desire, Male Homosexuality, and Emerging Gay Communities in Brazil.* New York: Routledge, 1999.

Parker, Richard, and John H. Gagnon, eds. *Conceiving Sexuality: Approaches to Sex Research in a Postmodern World.* New York: Routledge, 1995.

Patel, Geeta, and Kevin Kopelson, eds. "Inqueery/Intheory/Indeed." (Special issue of *GLQ*). *GLQ* 2.4 (1995).

Patton, Cindy, and Benigno Sanchez-Eppler, eds. *Queer Diasporas.* Durham: Duke UP, 2000.

Povinelli, Elizabeth A., and George Chauncey. "Thinking Sexuality Transnationally." (Special issue of *GLQ: A Journal of Lesbian and Gay Studies*). *GLQ* 5.4 (1999): 439–49.

Prieur, Annick. *Mema's House, Mexico City: On Transvestites, Queens, and Machos.* Chicago: U of Chicago P, 1998.

Ratti, Rakesh, ed. *A Lotus of Another Color: An Unfolding of the South Asian Gay and Lesbian Experience.* Boston: Alyson, 1993.

Robertson, Roland. *Globalization: Social Theory and Global Culture.* London: Sage, 1992.

San Juan Jr., E. *Beyond Postcolonial Theory.* New York: St. Martin's, 1998.

Schmitt, Arno, and Jehoeda Sofer, eds. *Sexuality and Eroticism among Males in Moslem Societies*. New York: Harrington Park/ Haworth P, 1992.

Seabrook, Jeremy. *Love in a Different Climate: Men Who Have Sex with Men in India*. London: Verso, 1999.

Seidman, Steven. *Difference Troubles: Queering Social Theory and Sexual Politics*. Cambridge: Cambridge UP, 1997.

Spivak, Gayatri Chakravorty. "Can the Subaltern Speak?" In *Marxism and the Interpretation of Culture*, eds. Cary Nelson and Lawrence Grossberg. Urbana, Ill.: U of Illinois P, 1988.

Vanita, Ruth, and Saleem Kidwai, eds. *Same-Sex Love in India: Readings from Literature and History*. New York: St. Martin's P, 2000.

Wah-shan, Chou. *Tongzhi: Politics of Same-Sex Eroticism in Chinese Societies*. New York: Haworth P, 2000.

Wallerstein, Immanuel. *The Modern World-System*. New York: Academic, 1974.

———. *The Modern World System II*. New York: Academic, 1980.

Warner, Michael, ed. *Fear of a Queer Planet: Queer Politics and Social Theory*. Minneapolis: U of Minnesota P, 1993.

———. *The Trouble with Normal: Sex, Politics, and the Ethics of Queer Life*. New York: Free Press, 1999.

Waters, Malcolm. *Globalization*. New York: Routledge, 1995.

CHAPTER ONE

Rupture or Continuity?

The Internationalization of Gay Identities

DENNIS ALTMAN

> No one can deny the persisting continuities of long traditions,
> sustained habitations, national languages, and cultural geo-
> graphies, but there seems no reason except fear and prejudice
> to keep insisting on their separation and distinctiveness, as if
> that was all human life was about.
> —Edward Said, *Culture and Imperialism*

Early in 1995 posters appeared on streetposts in Manila's Malate district
advertising a new gym, with illustrations of muscular (white) men taken,
presumably, from overseas gay magazines. The posters seemed to
promise a luxurious gym/sauna of the sort found in Paris or Los Angeles, but the gym itself is in an old garage, as small and dark as the other
gyms that dot the Taft Avenue area. In the distinction between the image
and the reality lies much of the paradox of the apparent globalization of
postmodern gay identities.

Modern and *postmodern* can be used here interchangeably, for
both terms represent the rapid reshaping of extensive areas of life and

economy in previously underdeveloped parts of the world to fit the needs of Western capitalism. Most people live in an intermediate position between tradition and (post)modernity, and structures of sex and gender reflect the ambiguities and contradictions that this intermediacy imposes. I think of examples such as a Filipino anthropologist who after seven years studying in the United States still identifies with the *bakla* (effeminate homosexuals) of his native town; but also of young American street kids who bash "fags" and yet will sleep with other men for money (or sometimes, unacknowledged, with each other for affection).

It has become fashionable to point to the emergence of "the global gay," the apparent internationalization of a certain form of social and cultural identity based upon homosexuality. He—sometimes, though less often, she—is conceptualized in terms that are very much derived from recent American fashion and intellectual style: young, upwardly mobile, sexually adventurous, with an in-your-face attitude toward traditional restrictions and an interest in both activism and fashion. Images of young men in baseball caps and Reeboks on the streets of Budapest or Sao Paulo, of "lipstick lesbians" flirting on portable telephones in Bangkok or demonstrating in the streets of Tokyo—none of which are fictitious—are part of the construction of a new category, or more accurately the expansion of an existing Western category, that is part of the rapid globalization of lifestyle and identity politics, the simultaneous disappearance of old concepts and invention of new ones.

These observations do not only reflect a Western interpretation; references to "global society" are common in publications from gay groups in developing countries. (For example, the term is used in *Gaya Nusantara*, the publication of the Indonesian gay/lesbian network.)[1] There is evidence of this new gay world particularly in Southeast Asia, South and Central America, and Eastern Europe. The most obvious indicator is the development of commercial space, that is, of entertainment venues, restaurants, and shops that cater to a distinctly homosexual clientele. Both Western and non-Western experiences suggest that such space provides important opportunities for gay men and lesbians to meet and to develop social and political ties. (One of the first gay groups in Manila took its name from the Library, a bar where its first meetings were held.)

Based on the listings in the 1994–95 *Spartacus International Gay Guide*, the commercial scene seems to be expanding rapidly outside the so-called First World. The *Guide* lists each of the following places as having more than twenty commercial establishments catering to gays: Bogota, Budapest, Buenos Aires, Caracas, Istanbul, Johannesburg, Lima, Manila, Mexico City, Monterrey, Prague, San Jose (Costa Rica), San Juan, and Tangier. In addition, Brazil and Japan are listed as each having five cities with more than twenty establishments.[2] These figures—which should be regarded with some skepticism—suggest that affluence is one, but certainly not the only, factor in explaining the emergence of a commercial gay world. Note, for example, the relative overrepresentation of Latin America as against the underrepresentatiton of Chinese East Asia, which suggests that there are political and cultural factors involved.

Such crude counting, however, does not adequately emphasize the impact of Western-style consumerism, as in the growth of luxurious discos in a number of places or the development of overtly gay saunas very different from traditional bathhouses. Another significant indicator of its impact is the development of a gay/lesbian press (for example, in Mexico, Brazil, Hungary, and Hong Kong), which is almost always related closely to both a commercial world (for advertising revenue) and enough political freedom to escape censorship. But perhaps most significant is the emergence of gay/lesbian political groups.

Gay organizing has something of a history in South and Central America, with origins in the 1970s in Brazil, Mexico, and the southern cone, which were then crudely—and cruelly—repressed by the rise of military regimes, especially in Argentina and Chile (see Adam 142–43; Lumsden; MacRae; Trevisan). But such organizing has increased worldwide in the 1990s, especially in Eastern Europe and in Asia. Note, for example, the first Asian Lesbian Network, organized by the Thai group Anjaree in 1990; the first Indonesian Lesbian and Gay Congress in December 1993 attended by members of ten groups; the existence of the Progressive Organization of Gays in the Phillippines since 1992; Japanese developments around the 1994 International AIDS Conference in Yokohama and a subsequent demonstration organized by Occur, a group of Japanese lesbians and gay men; and the first organized meeting of gay-identified men in India at the end of that year (see "Anjaree"; Murphy; "Newly Out"; *Report*).

The basic question is whether these developments suggest a fundamental change equivalent to the creation of powerful gay communities with economic, social, and political clout as in North America, Australasia, and northern Europe.[3] Is there, in other words, a universal gay identity linked to modernity? This is not to argue for a transhistoric or essentialist position (à la Whitam or Boswell [see Whitam and Mahy; Boswell]) but rather to question the extent to which the forces of globalization (both economic and cultural) can be said to produce a common consciousness and identity based on homosexuality. Critics have argued that globalism and consumerism create individualism and greater life choices, which consequently lead to the emergence of Western-style identities and identity politics. As Rosaline Morris put it: "We know that the apparatus of power is different in every society and that the discourses of sex and gender differ from context to context. Yet a considerable body of critical theory persists in a mode of historical analysis— the emphatically linear genealogy—that derives from the West's specific experience of modernity" (Morris 39).

To avoid slipping into this linear genealogy we need to understand sexuality as involving the complex and varied ways in which biological possibilities are shaped by social, economic, political, and cultural structures. The argument about the reshaping of homosexualities in developing countries offers a particular way of understanding the whole fabric of the sex/gender order.[4] The contemporary world is simultaneously experiencing the creation/solidification of identities and their dissolution: we don't know yet if identities based on sexuality will be as strong as those based on race or religion. The ideas of "gay/lesbian" as a sociological category is only about one hundred years old, and its survival even in Western developed countries cannot be taken for granted.

The problem thus becomes one of finding the right balance between tradition and modernity, while recognizing that these terms themselves are vague, problematic, and politically contested; appealing to traditional moral values in many Pacific islands, for example, means appealing to imported Christian ideals which were central to the colonial destruction of existing social structures. As Allan Hanson (of New Zealand) says: "'Traditional culture' is increasingly recognized to be more an invention constructed for contemporary purposes than a stable heritage handed on from the past" (Hanson 899).

There is a constant danger of romanticizing "primitive" homosexuality, seen very clearly, for example, in the popular anthropology of Tobias Schneebaum, who writes (and presumably believes): "It was in Asmat (West Irian), however, that I felt for the first time part of a universal clan, for Asmat culture in some regions not only allowed for sexual relationships between men but demanded that no male be without his male companion, no matter how many wives he had or how many women he might be sleeping with" (Schneebaum 433).

Similarly, Western romanticism about the apparent tolerance of homoeroticism in many non-Western cultures disguises the reality of persecution, discrimination, and violence, which sometimes occurs in unfamiliar forms. Firsthand accounts make it clear that homosexuality is far from being universally accepted—or even tolerated—in such apparent paradises as Morocco, the Philippines, Thailand, and Brazil: "Lurking behind the Brazilians' pride of their flamboyant drag queens, their recent adulation of a transvestite chosen as a model of Brazilian beauty, their acceptance of gays and lesbians as leaders of the country's most widely practiced religion and the constitutional protection of homosexuality, lies a different truth. Gay men, lesbians and transvestites face widespread discrimination, oppression and extreme violence" (Steakley).

What Constitutes a "Modern" Gay Identity?

Arguing that the very idea of a homosexual/heterosexual divide only became dominant in the United States in the mid-twentieth century, George Chauncey writes: "The most striking difference between the dominant sexual culture of the early twentieth century and that of our own era is the degree to which the earlier culture permitted men to engage in sexual relations with other men, often on a regular basis, without requiring them to regard themselves—or be regarded by others—as gay. . . . Many men . . . neither understood nor organized their sexual practices along a hetero-homosexual axis" (Chauncey 65). Today, becoming "gay" is to take on a particular set of styles and behaviors. As Paul Russell's protagonist writes: "Almost through an act of will, I had made myself embrace this new identity of mine and never look back. I had gay friends. I ate at gay restaurants. I went to gay bars. I had my apartment near DuPont Circle" (Russell 231).

Chauncey's formulation is probably true for most societies, many of which are far more relaxed about homosexual behavior, at least among men, than were the pre-gay-liberation United States and Western Europe. Of Java, for example, Benedict Anderson argues that "male homosexuality at least was an unproblematic, everyday part of a highly varied Javanese sexual culture" (Anderson 278), and similar comments are often made about Bali. North African men are often claimed to regard sex with boys as totally natural.[5] There is an extensive literature suggesting that homosexual behavior—though not identity—is widespread throughout Latin America, where what is crucial is not gender but whether a man is "active" or "passive."[6]

The only possible generalization may be that there exists a far greater variety of understandings of sex/gender arrangements than tends to be recognized by official discourses. Moreover, attempts to use Western terminology—*gay people, men who have sex with men, bisexuals*—often block us from understanding the different ways in which people understand their own sexual experiences and feelings. Reporting on a discussion among gay and lesbian Asians at a recent International AIDS Conference, Shivananda Khan argued:

> There were strong cultural frameworks of "third gender" which have had a long history and many within such groups have played socio-political-religious roles in their societies. To transpose Western understandings (and subsequently HIV/AIDS prevention programs) is to destroy these social constructions and recreate them in a Western mold. Discussion revolved around moving away from gender diomorphic structures that arose from the West and talk about Alternate Genders, in other words more than two genders . . . Similarly we should be talking about lesbian identities and gay identities, should be discussing homosexualities instead of homosexuality, communities instead of community. (Khan 7–8)

In most traditional Asian and Pacific societies, there are complex variations across gender and sex lines, with "transgender" people (Indonesian *warias*, Thai *kathoey*, Filipino *bayot*, Polynesian *fa'fafine*, etc.) characterized by both transvestite and homosexual behavior. As Gilbert Herdt writes, "Sexual orientation and identity are not the keys to conceptualizing a third sex and gender across time and space" (Herdt 47). In many societies there is confusion around the terms. Different people use terms such as *bayot* or *waria* in different ways, depending on whether the emphasis is on gender or on sexuality: the terms can refer to men who wish in some way to be with women, or they can refer to men attracted to other men. Anthropology teaches us the need to be cautious about any sort of binary system of sex/gender. Niko Besnier uses the term *gender liminality* to avoid this trap, stressing that such liminality is not the same as homosexuality: "sexual relations with men are seen as an optional consequence of gender liminality, rather than its determiner, prerequisite or primary attribute" (Besnier 300).

Certainly most of the literature about Latin America stresses that a homosexual *identity* (as distinct from homosexual *practices*) is related to the rejection of dominant gender expectations, so that "a real man" can have sex with other men and not risk his heterosexual identity. As Roger Lancaster puts it: "Whatever else a *cochon* might or might not do, he is tacitly understood as one who assumes the receptive role in anal intercourse. His partner, defined as 'active' in the terms of their engagement, is not stigmatized, nor does he acquire a special identity of any sort" (Lancaster 150). Thus the *nature* rather than the *object* of the sexual act becomes the key factor.

In Western countries during the hundred years or so before the birth of the contemporary gay movement, the dominant understanding of homosexuality was predicated on a confusion between sexuality and gender. In other words, the "traditional" view that the "real" homosexual is the man who behaves like a woman. Something of this confusion remains in popular perceptions. But for most Western homosexual men it ended with the development of the gay movement at the beginning of the 1970s (although even today "drag" remains an important reminder of the idea that sexual subversion is also gender subversion). As Gail Rubin has pointed out: "Since the mid-nineteenth century there has been a slowly evolving distinction between homosexual object choice and cross-gender or trans-gender behavior. . . . The development of the leather community is part of a long historical process in which masculinity has been claimed, asserted, or reappropriated by male homosexuals" (Rubin with Butler 96).

Modern forms of homosexuality often exist side-by-side with older traditional ones, and the boundaries can appear either blurred or distinct depending on one's vantage point and ideology. Thus some homosexuals in non-Western countries seek to establish historical continuities, while others are more interested in distancing themselves, psychologically and analytically, from what they consider old-fashioned forms of homosexuality, especially those that seem based on crossgender lines. In Indonesia, for example, local men who identify themselves as gay will sometimes sharply distinguish themselves from *banci* or *waria* (terms which include effeminate men and, occasionally, masculine women[7]) but in other contexts will identify with them. The title of the Indonesian lesbian/gay journal *Gaya Nusantara,* which literally means "Indonesian style," captures this ambivalence nicely with its echoes of both traditional and modern concepts of nation and sexuality. It is often assumed that homosexuals are defined in most traditional societies as a third sex, but that as well is too schematic to be universally useful. As Peter Jackson points out, the same terms in Thailand can be gender *and* sexual categories (see Jackson).

To identify as homosexual without rejecting conventional assumptions about masculinity or femininity (as with today's "macho" gay or "lipstick lesbian" styles) is one of the distinguishing features of modern homosexuality. This new freedom is both distinctively different from any premodern formations of sexuality and intimately related to other features of modern life. Modern homosexualities are characterized by the following characteristics: (1) a differentiation between sexual and gender transgression; (2) an emphasis on emotional as much as on sexual relationships; and (3) the development of public homosexual worlds.

Homosexuality is no longer considered an expression of "really" being a woman in a man's body (or vice versa), but rather as physically desiring others of one's own gender without necessarily wishing to deny one's masculinity/femininity. These changes are played out in somewhat different forms in different cultural settings. Thus Jackson speaks of there being four or five categories of sex/gender (*phet*) in Thailand, and of the new masculinization of homosexuals so that gay men—an emerging category—are those who desire each other. Richard Parker has written of the emergence of new "systems of thought in Brazil," whereby "sexual practices have taken on significance not simply as part of the construction of a hierarchy of women and men, but as a key to the nature of every individual" (Jackson 95).

Similarly, the term *gay* suggests not only a sexual but also an emotional definition. As Christopher Isherwood once said, "You know you are homosexual when you discover you can love another man."[8] In other words, imagining same-sex relationships as the central part of one's life marks the real creation of a specific homosexual identity. We are speaking here of an emotional as much as of an erotic economy. As one (anonymous) survey of homosexuality in Pakistan put it "'Gay' implies a legitimation of a relationship that runs counter to family, and therefore gay life does not exist in Pakistan in general, or in Karachi in particular. From a practical standpoint, two lovers would find themselves without a social context. . . . Human beings do tend to develop emotional bonds, and in Pakistan these bonds either result in tragedy or unacceptable (to a Westernized sensibility) compromise to steal private moments of tenderness or sexual release."[9]

There are growing accounts of such relationships in developing countries and a move away from relationships between locals and Westerners to relations which are, at least on the surface, open and egalitarian, both in terms of unspecified role-playing and in terms of emotional (and often sexual) reciprocity. There is a clear distinction between a willingness/desire for sex between men and the creation of this desire as a central emotional lodestone. I think of a Moroccan friend who defined himself as homosexual, not bisexual, and thus consciously set himself apart from other presumed bisexual men. There is a need to examine emotional as much as sexual fantasies; the latter are likely to be polymorphous (as revealed in much sexology research) but the former are often at the same time conservative (settling down as a couple) and subversive where the couple is of the same gender; thus the enormous reaction against gay marriage or recognition of gay couples).

One might ask whose scripts are being played out as more people in developing countries adopt the idea of forming homosexual couples. This goes beyond the expression of sentiment as part of even transitory sexual transactions; "I love you" is often a necessary excuse for sex as it is for many Western teenagers. But as someone once asked me, Is the move to imagine oneself in a lasting homosexual relationship the acting out of Chinese opera or soap opera? As most societies exhibit a great deal of homosociability, and often physical affection between men, does this mean that all we are seeing is a Westernization—and perhaps a limiting—of already existing relations? The rhetorics of liberation and modernity rarely allow for the fact that each change contains a restrictive as well as a liberatory component.

A new willingness to discuss homosexuality openly has accompanied the creation of a specific "gay world," which is defined socially, commercially, and politically. With these changes has come the development of the "gay community" as a recognized part of most Western industrialized societies, in some countries enjoying a considerable degree of legitimacy and recognition by the state. In part this reflects the ideology of individual rights and fulfillment—the Jeffersonian "right to happiness" applied to sexuality. In part, too, it grows out of a recognition of pluralism and cultural diversity, which have been important factors in changing attitudes towards homosexuality in the Netherlands, Canada, and Australia. These ideas may be inappropriate in other settings, as Jackson argues they are in Thailand (see Jackson) and as Peter Fry suggests for Brazil. "The concept of the modern homosexual falls on deaf ears in a culture where homoerotic practices are highly generalized and where masculinity and femininity are regarded as more important than homo- or heterosexuality" (Fry, esp. 73).

In Brazil and Thailand, and in other (usually richer) parts of the developing world, a small elite see themselves as interconnected with a global network via groups such as the International Lesbian and Gay Association and an international commercial scene in which they participate. Others (often from similar class positions) are more critical; in the early 1980s Stephen Murray and Manuel Arboleda noted that "Mexican liberation organizations eschew the term 'gay' because their leadership do not consider Anglo gay culture to be what they aspire to emulate. They are also sensitive about 'cultural imperialism' from the north and the elitism of expensive local replicas of Anglo gay bars" (Murray and Arboleda 136). However, some of the most virulent of such critiques are themselves imported via Western conceptualizations of postcolonial and subaltern analysis.

The existence of a commercial gay world cannot be read as bringing with it the same consciousness in different societies. Is Shinjuku, the area in Tokyo with the heaviest concentration of gay bars and shops, really like the Castro in San Francisco? If not, where are the differences? There is a constant need to disentangle commercial and media images from changes in consciousness. The United States is so consumer defined that the gay movement was quickly co-opted and turned into an interest group and a niche market (with gay resistance increasingly expressed in aesthetic terms—*queer* rather than *anticapitalist*).[10] Neither the development of a political movement nor its incorporation along American lines is necessarily the outcome for other societies.

It seems clear that *some* form of gay and lesbian identity is becoming more common across the world. As gay identities increase, so the number of men having homosexual sex may *decrease*. This is suggested by one observer of India (despite a lack of distinction in his piece between identity and behavior):

> Is it any surprise then that in India you run into bellboys at hotels, men on crowded local trains, the guys in the seats next to you in the movies, all of whom are more than adequately interested in fondling

your penis? India has no gay movements and perhaps never will. There are no gay magazines; perhaps they don't need them. There are no gay bars per se; again, perhaps they are not necessary. . . . Bedding someone back home was far easier than over here. (Kim 94)

It is certainly possible that many people in developing countries, whatever their exposure to Western media imagery and consumer afflu-ence, will not adopt Western sexual identities, or that terms such as *gay, lesbian,* even *queer* will be taken up and changed much as English names are adopted in the bars of Patpong and Shinjuku. Critics have argued that "even" in the West many men who have sex with men but do not identify as gay may not be closeted (imperfect) homosexuals but may be consciously rejecting a particular identity (see Bartos). Yet many non-Western homosexuals are nonetheless attracted to a Western model, which they seek, consciously or not, to impose on their own movements. They are aided by discourses of human rights and the more specific lan-guage of AIDS/HIV (thus recognition of a gay community becomes a fre-quent demand at most international AIDS conferences). When such demands are voiced in the name of representing Asians or South Amer-icans, is it to be understood as the oppressed demanding to be heard or as a new stage of internalized imperialism? And what about those offi-cial voices from countries such as Iran or China who decry homosexu-ality as a result of "Western decadence," ignoring the rich homoerotic traditions of their own precolonial history?

Globalization and Sexual Identities

The images and rhetoric of a newly assertive gay world spread rapidly from the United States and other Western countries after 1969. Ameri-can gay consumerism soon became the dominant mode for the new gay style of the 1970s. Despite a radical gay movement born in the 1968 stu-dent riots, by the end of that decade an American-derived commercial gay world had grown up in Paris, and the Marais was a recognizable gay quarter on the model of Castro or the West Village. Looking back on notes I made on a short visit to Brazil in 1979, I find they reflect many of the issues I am now struggling with in relation to the Philippines and Indonesia: the meanings of apparent mimicry of Western forms; the role of class and age divisions in the gay world; the somewhat different public display of homosexuality in countries where the conventions of body contact are different to those we take for granted in the West (see Altman, "Down Rio").

In one sense the importation of gay style and rhetoric is part of the ongoing dominance of the so-called First World. Filipino writer Vicente Groyon III reflects all the contradictions and ambivalences at play when he writes:

> You are reading the latest copy of Interview, one of the trendy fashio-slash-lifestyle monthlies that tell you what to wear, what to talk about and how to live. You are under the impression that you belong to the world the magazine describes, and not in this tropical, underdeveloped, unstable country. You dream of escaping to this world full of perfect people, with perfect faces and perfect lives and perfect clothes and perfect bodies. (Groyon 111)

The ever-expanding impact of (post)modern capitalism is clearly redrawing traditional sex/gender orders to match the idealogy and consciousness imposed by huge changes in the economy. The impact of economic growth, consumerism, urbanization, social mobility, and improving telecommunications places great strains on existing familial and personal relations, and on the very conceptions of self with which people make sense of these arrangements. Discussions about the changes demanded by capitalism tend to fluctuate between nostalgia and celebration: what one person sees as an increase in personal liberty another may well read as the destruction of valuable traditions.

We cannot discuss the development of modern forms of sexual identity independent of other shifts, which at first glance may not be directly relevant. In the new urban industrial areas created by the much vaunted economic growth of "newly industrialized countries," large populations of young people, attracted by the prospect of jobs, have probably weakened and certainly changed their relations to their families. It will become easier for the millions of people attracted to the new boomtowns of southern China to act out gay identities; as entrepreneurs see profits to be made from catering to these new identities, the regime's ability to maintain social control will be tested. Equally, of course, the rapid economic growth of China and other East Asian economies is leading to major shifts and expansion in commercial sex work.

In a sense, globalization is capitalist imperialism writ large, and many of its features continue and perpetuate the erosion of custom, of existing kinship and villages/communities, and of once-private space in the interests of an expanding market dominated by the firms of the First World. What was once accomplished by gunships and conquest is now achieved via shopping malls and cable television. Whether this amounts to something new or merely to a speeding up of existing relations is a complex question. Robert C. Connell has noted that "European imperialism, global capitalism under U.S. hegemony, and modern communications have brought all cultures into contact, obliterating many, and marginalizing most. Anthropology as a discipline is in crisis because of this" (Connell 601).

One might describe the current debates around changing forms of homosexuality as presenting a choice between political economy, which argues for universalizing trends, and anthropology, which argues for cultural specificities. There are people with strong emotional and career investments in each camp, and whether a Thai or a Colombian argues that modernity destroys indigenous cultural forms or provides new space for sexual freedom may tell us more about their own place in the world than about what is actually happening. It is obvious that both economic and cultural forces are changing sexual regimes and the relationships between the sex/gender order and other economic and cultural structures. What is less clear is how such changes enter into the psyche. Are the luxurious saunas of Paris and Bangkok, or the emerging gym cultures of Santiago or Osaka affecting deeply held values, or are they merely superficial shifts in style?

What seems universal—even something as specific as a homosexual bathhouse or a disco—will be changed and mediated through the individual culture and political economy of each society. As Katie King argues: "We need to talk of homosexualities and therefore of various forms of 'gay.' When I now talk about 'global gay formations and local homosexualities' I am talking about layerings of maps and territories that also interact, correct, and deconstruct each other, that describe distinct and important systems of material circumstances" (King 82). But arguments for cultural specificity can sometimes lead us to forget the "systems of material circumstances" to which King refers. Thus, Anne Allison in her fascinating book about Tokyo hostess clubs argues that attempts to define things as "essentially Japanese" (and hence not comparable with other societies) ignore "politics, economics, history and class" (Allison 80).

The significant aspect of the contemporary globalization of capitalism is the growth of affluence in many countries and the corresponding greater freedom for individual choice it makes possible. Affluence, education, and awareness of other possibilities are all prerequisites for the adoption of new forms of identity, and the spread of these conditions will increase the extent to which gay identities develop beyond their base in liberal Western societies. (They are not, however, *sufficient* prerequisites, as authoritarian governments in both the Middle East and East Asia have made clear.) In turn, the development of such identities may well swamp existing homosexual/third sex cultures, as has been claimed for Indonesia, Mexico, and India.

Globalization in the form of increased travel and communication between countries similarly adds pressure to adapt to hegemonic cultural forms; while tourism plays an uneven role in the construction of new forms of homosexuality, it has clearly been crucial in such areas as the Carribean, North Africa, and parts of Asia (e.g., Sri Lanka and Bali).[11] Moreover, increasing numbers of people from Third World countries travel to the West, and this becomes another factor in cultural transmission.

But globalization is extremely uneven in its effects, simultaneously reducing and creating all sorts of shifting cultural and communal ties. As Virginia Vargas writes of Latin America:

> An incomplete and subordinate process of modernization has had an ambivalent effect, increasing the marginalization of wide social, regional and cultural sectors on the one hand, while at the same time facilitating the integration and a broadening of the horizons of those same sectors, giving rise in the past few decades to a chorus of voices coming from the latter who have been traditionally marginalized from the process of political transformation. (Vargas 145)

The problem for these voices is how to avoid speaking a language of outmoded nostalgia, how to select from the constant influx of new ideas, styles, and technologies that can be used to improve human life rather than merely reshape it to fit the demands of a global market.

The crucial question is, How do new forms of sexual identity interact with the traditional scripts of sex/gender order? Peter Jackson has argued eloquently for a continuum:

> While gayness in Thailand has drawn selectively on western models, it has emerged from a Thai cultural foundation as the result of efforts by Thai homosexual men to resolve tensions within the structure of masculinity in their society. I also maintain that the proposition that gayness in Thailand is a "western borrowing" is misplaced and overlooks the internal structuring of Thai masculinity, from which Thai gay male identity has emerged as a largely continuous development. (Jackson)

I am less convinced that this formulation applies in other countries, where there is probably more of a rupture between traditional and modern forms of gay identity. Even in the West developments vary from country to country. Vernon Rosario claims that there is a decline in gay consciousness in Paris and a return to the concept of shared citizenship (Rosario). I would argue that this has always existed (summed up in Foucault's well-known ambivalence about "coming out," an ambivalence that included both personal and political reservations).[12] A tension between claiming universal rights for individual diversity and claiming communal rights for specific groups is hardly new; few societies are likely to pursue a politically correct solution with the same zeal as Americans have. It is difficult to imagine affirmative action in hiring lesbian/gay faculty becoming a reality in equally rich societies such as Kuwait or Hong Kong.

Thus, a discussion of new or modern homosexualities needs to incorporate the following:

• a sense of the continuing importance of premodern forms of sexual organization. This is also (though less) applicable in the West: what is the film *Priscilla, Queen of the Desert* if not a return to older notions of homosex/genderfuck/drag as one and the same, a statement that embraces *both* queer *and* pre-gay-liberation formations?

• a consideration of whether the movement toward a sense of identity/community is similar or noticeably different for women. To date, several characteristics (e.g., the lower number of visible lesbians and the ambivalent relations between gay men and feminist movements in general) are very similar to those of the West, but such similarities may well disguise larger differences. There is no reason to assume that the current ideology, which constructs a common homosexuality as sufficient to embrace existing differences between women and men, will be adopted in non-Western countries.[13]

• more sensitivity to class/caste divides. The romantic myth of homosexual identity cutting across class, race, and so on doesn't work in practice any more than it does in the West. The experience of sexuality in everyday life is shaped by such variables as the gap between city and country; ethnic and religious differences; and hierarchies of wealth, education, and age. The idea of a gay or lesbian/gay community assumes that such differences can be subordinated to an overarching sense of sexual identity, a myth that is barely sustainable in comparatively rich and affluent societies (though, hardly surprising, does best in relatively harmonious settings such as the Netherlands).

• the persistence of different family patterns despite growing affluence and apparent Westernization. As Shivananda Khan suggested, "Significant numbers of gay-identified men are apparently repositories of cultural history, teachers of their nephews and nieces in the extended family, holders of family traditions, who perhaps continue to live with their parents and take care of them. . . . The unmarried son/daughter who may have developed a sexual identity, but places that role within a family structure."[14] My interviews with several apparently Westernized gay men in Manila have borne out this pattern as relevant to the Philippines, and Stephen Murray argues that it is a central factor in most developing countries (Murray, "Underdevelopment").

• the complications of the diaspora. Some homosexuals of Asian origin living in the West seem to make no distinction between their situation and that of people back home; thus the introduction to an anthology of gay and lesbian South Asian writing links together "an Indian professor at an Ivy League university, [and] a Pakistani practicing law in Vancouver" with "a married woman who must see her female lover secretly in New Delhi [and] . . . an old man who has lived out a lonely life in a rural village" (Ratti 11). While this seems to me to blur crucial differences, it is also true that some of the most potent gay influences from overseas come from immigrants, whose experiences are often reflected back to their original homelands.[15]

• the interactions among developing countries themselves. It is misleading to assume that all influences stem from the West (or the North in a somewhat different taxonomy). Thus there are ongoing and close contacts between the new gay organizations of Southeast Asia. Partly because of the resources made available through HIV programs, groups such as Pink Triangle (Malaysia), Library Foundation (Manila),

KKLGN (Indonesia), and People Like Us (Singapore) are extremely aware of and interested in each others' activities. Similar networking exists in Eastern Europe and South America.

Conclusion

The forces of global change (including HIV/AIDS and the surveillance of and interventions into human sexuality it has spawned) mean that homosexuality is increasingly interrogated.[16] This also means that some people will benefit from imposing a Western analytic model to explain sexuality; often they will be Third Worlders with a personal or professional investment in modernity. Traditionalists will respond either by denial (often because of Western-derived moralities) or by seeking to build a nationalist version of homosexuality, with romantic claims to a precolonial heritage which is seen as differentiating them from Western homosexuals. In my own conversations with homosexuals in Asia there is an ongoing ambivalence about the extent to which they are constituting themselves as part of a global identity. As Eduardo Nierras puts it, "When we say to straight people, or, more rarely, to Western gay people, 'We are like you' we must remember to add, 'only different.'"[17]

Clearly what is at work is a complex compound of tradition and modernity, themselves better understood as ideal points on an academic continuum than as descriptions of fixed realities. Gay identities may emerge in different ways and without the overtly political rhetoric of the West. I suspect that gay separatism, for example, as expressed in the creation of "gay ghettos" in major U.S. cities, is likely to be less attractive in many societies, even where the economic preconditions for it seem to exist. This becomes a test of the globalization thesis: new identities may well develop but their development is not predictable through Western experience. On the other hand, the differences are not as great as sometimes claimed (nor should we forget that Western gay life is no more monolithic than non-Western gay life). It is worth remembering Chris Berry's unspoken comment when a young Chinese man told him: "It is not possible to do whatever you want to do in Chinese culture. It's not like Australia":

> The writer didn't mention that he had never felt able to discuss his sexuality with his parents. That he knew 17–year-olds who had

committed suicide. That he had been told three out of five calls to the Lesbian and Gay switchboard were from married men. Not because he felt Eddie's Chinese situation was just the same as other people's Australian situations, but because he realized Eddie's situation was Eddie's alone. (Berry 64)

The more I see, the more skeptical I am of sharp divides between Western and non-Western experiences of sexuality, and the surer I become that we cannot discuss sex/gender structures independent of larger sociopolitical ones. We may well need a political economy of homosexuality, one that recognizes the interrelationships of political, economic, and cultural structures. Far from assuming a linear progression toward a Western-style queerness, this would recognize that the ongoing shifts in sexual identities within Western societies see the playing out of very similar tensions and factors; if we were capable of imagining Thailand or Brazil as the norm and then measuring San Francisco or Sydney against them, our sense of what is modern and traditional might be somewhat altered. Most people negotiate numerous models of identity in everyday life, and what might seem paradoxical or contradictory to the observer is no more than evidence of the human ability to constantly reshape him- or herself. Sexuality, like other areas of life, is constantly being remade by the collision of existing practices and mythologies with new technologies and ideologies.

NOTES

I am grateful to the Australian Research Council for support, and to a number of people whose ideas have helped me shape this chapter, among them Eufracio Abaya, Ben Anderson, Chris Berry, Sandy Gifford, Shivananda Khan, Peter Jackson, Laurence Leong, Alison Murray, Dede Oetomo, Anthony Smith, and Michael Tan.

    1. There is very little relevant literature on the internationalization of lesbian identities. But see Allison Murray; Took Took Thongthiraj. My own research has largely been concerned with male gay worlds in Southeast Asia, to which I have particular access; while I mention lesbians at various points, it is without any illusion of having firsthand knowledge.

    2. Christian van Maltzahn, ed., *Spartacus International Gay Guide*, 23d ed. (Berlin: Bruno Gmunder, 1994–95). This is a widely used listing of all commercial and social/political places that cater to any sort of homosexual clientele.

3. On the development of these communities, see Altman, *The Homosexualization of America* ; and Barry Adam, *Rise of a Gay and Lesbian Movement*.

4. The term is Gail Rubin's. See her "Traffic in Women," in *Towards an Anthropology of Women*, ed. Rayna Reiter; and "Thinking Sex: Notes for a Radical Theory of the Politics of Sexuality," in *Pleasure and Danger: Exploring Female Sexuality*, ed. Carole S. Vance. Compare Rosemary Pringle, "Absolute Sex? Unpacking the Sexuality/Gender Relationship," in *Thinking Sex*, ed. R. W. Connell and G. W. Dowsett.

5. For a rather uneven survey of the subject see Arno Schmitt and Jehoeda Sofer.

6. The literature on Brazil is particularly rich. See, for example, Richard Parker, *Bodies, Pleasures, and Passions*; Rommel Mendes-Leite, "A Game of Appearances: The 'Ambigusexuality' in Brazilian Culture of Sexuality," in *Gay Studies from the French Cultures*, ed. Rommel Mendes-Leite and P. O. de Busscher.

7. See Dede Oetomo and Bruce Esmond, "Homosexuality in Indonesia," English version of a paper published in Indonesian in 1990 (private communication).

8. In conversation with the author. See Altman, *Homosexual: Oppression and Liberation*, new ed., 40.

9. "Gay Life in Pakistan: An Assessment," an unsigned paper made available by the Pakistan AIDS Prevention Society.

10. This is the (perhaps overstated) argument of Donald Morton. See his "Politics of Queer Theory in the (Post)Modern Moment," *Genders* 17 (fall 1993); 121–50.

11. On gay tourism, see Aldrich, *The Seduction of the Mediterranean*; and Altman, "Encounters with the New World of 'Gay Asia,'" in *Identities, Ethnicities, Nationalities: Asian and Pacific Inscriptions*, ed. Survendri Perera.

12. This point is discussed in most of the biographies of Foucault. See, for example, David Macey, *The Lives of Michel Foucault*.

13. For a Western lesbian view of gay life in Japan that does not recognize the possibilities of these differences see Sarah Schulman, *My American History: Lesbian and Gay Life during the Reagan/Bush Years*, 241–46.

14. Private communication, 5 February 1995.

15. There is a growing literature about gay and lesbian Asians in Western countries. For an introduction to the discussion see Dana Takagi, "Maiden Voyage: Excursion into Sexuality and Identity Politics in Asian America," *Amerasia Journal* 20 (1994): 1–18.

16. On the impact of HIV/AIDS on non-Western homosexualities see Altman, *Power and Community*, passim.

17. Eduardo Nierras, "This Risky Business of Desire: Theoretical Notes for and against Filipino Gay Male Identity Politics," in Garcia and Remoto, *Ladlad: An Anthology of Philippine Gay Writing*, 199. The anthology furnishes many examples of this ambivalence.

WORKS CITED

Adam, Barry. *The Rise of a Gay and Lesbian Movement*. Boston: Twayne, 1987.

Aldrich, Robert. *The Seduction of the Mediterranean*. London: Routledge, 1993.

Allison, Anne. *Sexuality, Pleasure and Corporate Masculinity in a Tokyo Hostess Club*. Chicago: U of Chicago P, 1994.

Altman, Dennis. "Down Rio Way." In *The Christopher Street Reader*, ed. Michael Denneny, Chuck Orleb, and Tom Steele. New York: Coward McCann, 1983. 214–19.

———. *The Homosexualization of America*. Boston: Beacon, 1983.

———. *Homosexual: Oppression and Liberation*, new ed. New York: New York UP, 1992.

———. *Power and Community*. London and Philadelphia: Falmer, 1994.

———. "Encounters with the New World of 'Gay Asia.'" In *Identities, Ethnicities, Nationalities: Asian and Pacific Inscriptions*, ed. Survendri Perera. Melbourne: Meridien, 1995. 121–38.

Anderson, Benedict. *Language and Power*. Ithaca, N.Y.: Cornell UP, 1990.

"Anjaree: Towards Lesbian Visibility." *Nation* (Bangkok), 25 September 1994.

Bartos, Michael, "Community vs. Population: The Case of Men Who Have Sex with Men." In *AIDS: Foundations for the Future*, ed. Peter Aggleton, Peter Davies and Graham Hart. London: Taylor and Francis, 1994.

Berry, Chris. *A Bit on the Side*. Sydney: emPress, 1994.

Besnier, Niko. "Polynesian Gender Liminality through Time and Space," in Herdt.

Boswell, John. *Christianity, Social Tolerance, and Homosexuality*. Chicago: U of Chicago P, 1980.

Chauncey, George. *Gay New York*. New York: Basic, 1994.

Connell, Robert C. "The Big Picture: Masculinities in Recent World History."
Theory and Society 22 (1993): 601.

Fry, Peter, "Why Brazil is Different." *Times Literary Supplement*, 8 December
1995: 7.

Garcia, J. Neil C., and Danton Remoto, eds. *Ladlad: An Anthology of Philippine Gay Writing*. Pasig, Metro Manila: Anvil, 1994.

Groyon III, Vicente. "Boys Who Like Boys." In *Ladlad: An Anthology of Philippine Gay Writing*, ed. Neil Garcia and Danton Remoto. Manila: Anvil, 1994.

Hanson, Allan. "The Making of the Maori: Culture Invention and Its Logic."
American Anthropologist 91 (December 1989): 899.

Herdt, Gilbert, ed. *Third Sex, Third Gender*. New York: Zone, 1994.

Jackson, Peter. "Kathoey><Gay><Man: Sexualities in Asia and the Pacific." In
Sites of Desire/ Economies of Pleasure, ed. Lenore Manderson and Margaret Jolly. Chicago: U of Chicago P, 1996.

Khan, Shivananda. "The Naz Project (London)." *Quarterly Review* (July-September 1994): 7–8.

Kim, "They Aren't That Primitive Back Home." In *A Lotus of Another Color*,
ed. Rakesh Ratti. Boston: Alyson, 1993.

King, Katie. "Local and Global: AIDS Activism and Feminist Theory." *Camera
Obscura* 28 (January 1992): 82.

Lancaster, Roger. "'That We Should All Turn Queer?' Homosexual Stigma in the
Making of Manhood and the Breaking of Revolution in Nicaragua." In
Conceiving Sexuality, ed. John Gagnon and Richard Parker. New York and
London: Routledge, 1994.

Lumsden, Ian. *Society and the State in Mexico*. Toronto: Canadian Gay
Archives, 1991.

Macey, David. *The Lives of Michel Foucault*. London: Hutchinson, 1993.

MacRae, Edward. "Homosexual Identities in Transitional Brazilian Politics." In
The Making of Social Movements in Latin America, ed. Arturo Escobar.
Boulder, Colo.: Westview, 1992.

Mendes-Leite, Rommel. "A Game of Appearances: The 'Ambigusexuality' in
Brazilian Culture of Sexuality." In *Gay Studies from the French Cultures*,
ed. Rommel Mendes-Leite and P. O. de Busscher. New York: Harringrton
Park, 1993.

Morris, Rosalind C. "Three Sexes and Four Sexualities: Redressing the Discourses on Gender and Sexuality in Contemporary Thailand." *positions:
east asian cultures critique* 2 (1994): 39.

Morton, Donald. "Politics of Queer Theory in the (Post)Modern Moment." *Genders* 17 (fall 1993): 121–50.

Murphy, Peter. "Militancy Hits Manila." *Sydney Star Observer*, 25 August 1994.

Murray, Alison. *No Money, No Honey*. Singapore: Oxford UP, 1991.

Murray, Stephen. "The 'Underdevelopment' of Modern/Gay Homosexuality in Mesoamerica." In *Modern Homosexualities*, ed. Ken Plummer. London and New York: Routledge, 1992.

Murray, Stephen, and Manuel Arboleda. "Stigma Transformation and Reflexication: 'Gay' in Latin America." In *Male Homosexuality in Central and South America*, ed. S. Murray. New York: gai saber Monograph #5, 1987.

"Newly Out in Japan." *Los Angeles Advocate*, 4 October 1994.

Nierras, Eduardo. "This Risky Business of Desire: Theoretical Notes for and against Filipino Gay Male Identity Politics." In Garcia and Remoto, *Ladlad*.

Oetomo, Dede, and Bruce Esmond. "Homosexuality in Indonesia." Privately published, 1990.

Parker, Richard. *Bodies, Pleasures, and Passions*. Boston: Beacon, 1991.

———. "'Within Four Walls': Brazilian Sexual Culture and HIV/AIDS." In H. Daniel and Richard Parker, *Sexuality, Politics and AIDS in Brazil*. London: Falmer, 1993.

Pringle, Rosemary. "Absolute Sex? Unpacking the Sexuality/Gender Relationship." In *Thinking Sex*, ed. R.W. Connell and G.W. Dowsett. Melbourne: Melbourne UP, 1992. 76–101.

Ratti, Rakesh, ed. *A Lotus of Another Color: An Unfolding of the South Asian Gay and Lesbian Experience*. Boston: Alyson, 1993.

Report on Emerging Gay Identities in South Asia: Implications for Sexual Health. London: Naz Project, 1995.

Rosario, Vernon. "Sexual Liberalism and Compulsory Heterosexuality." *Journal of Contemporary French Civilization* 16 (1993): 262–79.

Rubin, Gail. "Traffic in Women." In *Towards an Anthropology of Women*, ed. Rayna Reiter. New York: Monthly Review, 1975.

———. "Thinking Sex: Notes for a Radical Theory of the Politics of Sexuality." In *Pleasure and Danger: Exploring Female Sexuality*, ed. Carole S. Vance. Boston: Routledge, 1984. 267–319.

Rubin, Gail, and Judith Butler. "Sexual Traffic." *differences* 6 (summer-fall 1994). 62–99.

Russell, Paul. *Sea of Tranquility*. New York: Dutton, 1994.

Said, Edward. *Culture and Imperialism*. New York: Vintage, 1994.

Schmitt, Arno, and Jehoeda Sofer. *Sexuality and Eroticism among Males in Moslem Societies*. New York: Harrington Park, 1992.

Schneebaum, Tobias. *Where the Spirits Dwell*. New York: Grove, 1988.

Schulman, Sarah. *My American History: Lesbian and Gay Life during the Reagan/Bush Years*. New York: Routledge, 1994.

Steakley, Sereine. "Brazil Can Be Tough and Deadly for Gays." *Bay Windows* (Boston), 16 June 1994.

Takagi, Dana. "Maiden Voyage: Excursion into Sexuality and Identity Politics in Asian America." *Amerasia Journal* 20 (1994): 1–18.

Thongthiraj, Took Took. "Toward a Struggle against Invisibility: Love between Women in Thailand." *Amerasia Journal* 20 (1994): 45–58.

Trevisan, Joao. *Perverts in Paradise*. London: Gay Men's Press, 1988.

van Maltzahn, Christian, ed. *Spartacus International Gay Guide*, 23rd ed. Berlin: Bruno Gmünder, 1994–95.

Vargas, Virginia. "Academics and the Feminist Movement in Latin America." In *Making Connections*, ed. Mary Kennedy, Cathy Lubelska, and Val Walsh. London: Taylor and Francis, 1993.

Whitam, Frederick, and Robin Mahy. *Male Homosexuality in Four Societies*. New York: Praeger, 1986.

CHAPTER TWO

Vacation Cruises; or, The Homoerotics of Orientalism

JOSEPH BOONE

Why the Orient seems still to suggest not only fecundity but sexual promise (and threat) . . . is not the province of my analysis here, alas, despite its frequently noted appearance.
—Edward Said, *Orientalism* (188)

So we had sex, or at least I lay and allowed him to fuck me, and thought as his prick shot in and he kissed my neck, back, and shoulders, that it was a most unappetising position for a world-famous artist to be in.
—Joe Orton in Tangier, *Diaries* (174)

Perhaps nowhere else are the sexual politics of colonial narrative so explicitly thematized as in those voyages to the Near and Middle East recorded or imagined by Western men. "Since the time of the prophet," one of these texts proclaims, "fabulous Araby has reeked of aphrodisiac excitement" (Edwardes and Masters 175). With various shades of prurience and sophistication, similar sentiments echo throughout the writings of novelists, poets, journalists, travel writers, sociologists, and ethnographers whose pursuit of eros has brought them, in Rana Kabbani's phrase, "to the Orient on the flying-carpet of Orientalism" (*Passionate Nomad* x). For such men, the geopolitical realities of the Arabic Orient become a psychic screen on which to project fantasies of illicit sexuality and unbridled excess—including, as Malek Alloula has observed, visions of "*generalized perversion*" (95) and, as Edward Said puts it, "sexual experience unobtainable in Europe," that is, "a different type of sexuality" (190). This appropriation of the so-called East in order to project onto it an otherness that mirrors Western psychosexual needs only confirms the phenomenon that Edward Said calls "Orientalism" in his book of that name.[1]

But exactly what others are being appropriated here? Despite Alloula's italicizing of the word *perversion*, despite Said's carefully ambiguous rendering of the phrase "a different type of sexuality," both Alloula's and Said's analyses of colonialist erotics remain ensconced in conspicuously heterosexual interpretative frameworks.[2] In contrast, the epigraph from Joe Orton's diary makes explicit an aspect of the vacation agendas of many male tourists that remains unspoken in most commentaries on colonial narrative: namely, that the "sexual promise (and threat)" that Said attributes to the Orient is for countless Western travelers inextricably tied to their exposure abroad to what has come to be known within Western sexual discourse as male homosexual practice (188).[3] Whether these homoerotically charged encounters figure as a voyeuristic spectacle—that is, as one more "exotic" item the tourist views from a distance—or as a covert goal of the traveler's journey, the fact remains that the possibility of sexual contact with and between men underwrites and at times even explains the historical appeal of orientalism as an occidental mode of male perception, appropriation, and control.

The number of gay and bisexual male writers and artists who have traveled through North Africa in pursuit of sexual gratification is legion as well as legend: André Gide lost his virginity on the dunes of Algeria in 1893 (where Oscar Wilde served as his procurer two years later), and E. M. Forster on the beaches of Alexandria in 1916. Morocco has also served as a mecca for the gay and bisexual literati vacationing in North Africa—many clustered around Tangier's famous resident Paul Bowles— to say nothing of the nonliterati, those celebrities of ambiguous sexual persuasion ranging from Mick Jagger to Malcolm Forbes.[4] Many heterosexually identified men have traveled to the Arabic Orient in pursuit

of erotic fulfillment as well, but even these adventurers have had to confront the specter of male-male sex that lurks in their fantasies of a decadent and lawless East; such encounters put into crisis assumptions about
male sexual desire, masculinity, and heterosexuality that are specific to
Western culture. In the following pages I hope to address the way in
which the public and personal texts produced by both straight and non-
straight travelers are implicated in a colonizing enterprise that often
"others" the homosexually inscribed Arab male, a condition that
obtains, albeit with differing valences and contexts, whether that
"other" is perceived with dread or with desire. Simultaneously, in nearly
all these texts, the imagined or actual encounter with exotic otherness
engenders profound anxieties about one's authority to narrate: the
threat of being "unmanned" by the attractive yet dangerous lure of a
polymorphous Eastern sexuality that exceeds representation is echoed in
many Western writers' fears, in face of such excess, of never writing
again.

To delineate more precisely these discursive manifestations of displaced and discovered homoeroticism, this chapter investigates three
categories of occidental (and not so accidental) tourists whose writings
eroticize the Near and Middle East. First, it looks at heterosexually identified writers whose transformation of Egypt's perceived sexual bounty
into a symbol of polymorphous perversity engenders their obsessive fascination with, and often anguished negotiation of, the homoerotic. Second, it examines the homoerotic undertow in representations of life on
the desert, where masquerading as the foreign other, sadomasochistic
desires, and gender ambiguities uneasily collide. Third, it turns to the
gay male enclaves established in the African Mahgreb since the beginning of the twentieth century, in order to consider the implications of the
colonially sanctioned tradition of male prostitution for various narratives of gay self-affirmation. Driving and binding all of these homoeroticizing strands of orientalist narrative are a series of interrelated
sociopolitical, psychosexual, and aesthetic issues: the practice and economics of empire, perceptions of race, the collusion of phallocratic and
colonial interests, constructions of sexual "deviance," questions of narrative authority, crises of representation. Because of the number of
texts—biographical, autobiographical, personal, fictional—canvassed in
the following pages, highlighting one topos over another is at times necessary, partly but not solely because of space limitations. Working by
pastiche, letting the heterogenous strands of my analysis contribute to

the illumination of a subject that is necessarily multifaceted and hybrid, rather than forcing each strand to illustrate every aspect of an emerging overview, seems an effective strategy with which to forestall the classic colonizing—indeed scholarly—move of defining each part in name of an already assumed whole.

In tracing the trajectories outlined above, my own narrative aims to traverse and unsettle, even as it provisionally inscribes, a number of imposed boundaries—not the least those separating "West" from "East" and "heterosexual" from "homosexual." What follows is written as part of the growing academic discipline of gay and lesbian studies, whose boundaries I hope to push by showing how contingent and Western its conception of "homosexuality"—as an identity category, a sexual practice, and a site of theoretical speculation—often proves to be when brought into contact with the sexual epistemologies of non-Western cultures, particularly when encounters of "East" and "West" are crossed by issues of colonialism, race, nation, and class. Taking a cue from Homi K. Bhabha's formulation of the continually "unfixing" propensities of the colonial stereotype, I present a series of collisions between traditionally assumed Western sexual categories (the homosexual, the pederast) and equally stereotypical colonialist tropes (the beautiful brown boy, the hypervirile Arab, the wealthy Nazarene)—collisions that generate ambiguity and contradiction rather than reassert an unproblematic intellectual domination over a mythic East as an object of desire. For many white gay male subjects, that object of desire remains simultaneously same *and* other, a source of troubling and unresolved identification *and* differentiation. It is precisely in the space opened by this gap that a critique of orientalist homoerotics may usefully locate itself and begin the work of dismantling those paradigmatic fictions of otherness that have made the binarisms of West and East, of heterosexuality and homosexuality, at once powerful and oppressive.[5]

Re(Orient)ing Sexuality

As the categories outlined above suggest, the imagined terrain of male desire that I am mapping out has very real geographic coordinates. Stretching from the North African countries of Morocco, Algeria, and Tunisia to Egypt and thence to the Syrian-Arabic peninsula, this vast territory, whose ethnic and cultural diversities have over the centuries been tenuously linked by a common language and shared Islamic faith,[6] also corresponds to what Richard Burton, in the Terminal Essay of his 1885–86 translation of the *Thousand Nights and a Night*, dubbed the "Sotadic Zone." Within this zone, as Burton argues for fifty-some pages of exacting if dubious detail, sodomy, or "what our neighbors call *Le vice contre nature*," "is popular and endemic, held at worst to be a mere peccadillo, whilst the races to the North and South of the[se] limits . . . as a rule, are physically incapable of performing the operation and look upon it with the liveliest disgust" (10: 177, 179). What Burton labels a "popular and endemic" Sotadic *practice* might more properly be called a "popular and endemic" *stereotype* of Eastern perversity, one firmly wedged within the dominant Western imagination.[7]

By documenting this tradition of "Eastern" sodomitic "vice," Burton offers a theory important less for its accuracy than for its frankness in articulating a widespread perception that had hitherto been filtered through codes of vague allusion. Readers of John Hindley's English translation of *Persian Lyrics* (1800), for instance, are informed that "the disgusting object[s]" of these love poems have been feminized "for reasons too obvious to need any formal apology" (33), without his offering—or feeling it necessary to offer—any further explanation of what such "disgust" might signify. In his classic study of modern Egyptian life (1833–35), Edward W. Lane also draws on the trope of disgust to avoid making explicit the sodomitic antics performed on the streets of Cairo by a trickster and boy assistant: "several indecent tricks which he performed with the boy I must refrain from describing; some of them are abominably disgusting" (391). And yet despite this aura of unmentionability, one can find textual evidence of a fascination with the Near and Middle East's rumored homoeroticism scattered through commentaries that reach back to the Crusades.[8] By 1780 Jeremy Bentham could dispassionately write, "Even now, wherever the Mahometan religion prevails, such practices seem to be attended with but little dispute" (1: 175; see also Crompton 111).

In this light, Said's failure to account for homoerotic elements in orientalist pursuits is a telling omission. Said's theorization of orientalism has invaluably served to draw scholarly attention to the discursive paths whereby the Arabic Orient has come to represent "one [of the West's] deepest and most recurring images of the Other" (1). The threatening excess of this otherness, Said argues, has most often been gendered as feminine and hence sexually available so that it can be penetrated,

FIGURE 2.1   An example of Western colonialist fantasy disguised as anthropological study, this anonymous photograph, *The Captives* (c. 1930), purports to take the viewer into the forbidden world of the Near Eastern male brothel. But the presence of various studio props connoting "enslaved exoticism" (the arranged drapery, manacle, rope, conch shells) belies the photograph's claim to authenticity. (L'amour bleu: *Die homosexuelle Liebe in Kunst und Literatur des Abendlandes*, ed. Cecile Beurdeley [Berlin: Gmünder, 1988] 244/Reproduced by permission of Edita Companie, Lausanne.

cataloged, and thus contained by the "superior" rationality of the Western mind (40, 44, 137–38). Such metaphors for the West's appropriation
of the East are at the very least implicitly heterosexual. But as a close
analysis of several specific Western experiences and representations of
the Near East reveals, that which appears alluringly feminine is not
always, or necessarily, female. A telling example of this reversal of
expectation, as I have argued elsewhere, can be located in Said's analysis of the notebooks and journals that Gustave Flaubert kept during his
voyage to Egypt in 1849–50 (see "Mappings" 80–81). Said focuses on
Flaubert's heady account of his affair with the professional female
dancer Kuchuk Hanem. For Said, Flaubert's transformation of Kuchuk's
materiality into an occasion for poetic reverie in his diaries forms a paradigmatic example of the mechanisms of orientalism: the masculinized,
penetrating West possesses for its own purposes the East's fecundity,
gendered as female in Kuchuk's "peculiarly Oriental" (187) sensuality.
Yet Said overlooks the crucial fact that the first exotic dancer to catch
Flaubert's eye is not the female Kuchuk but a famous *male* dancer and
catamite. "But we have seen male dancers. Oh! Oh! Oh!" exclaims
Flaubert in a letter to his best friend as, with barely contained excitement, he details Hasan el-Belbeissi's lascivious pantomine, (semi)female
garb, and kohl-painted eyes. This description in turn leads Flaubert to
discuss the practice of sodomy among his Egyptian acquaintances
("Here it is quite accepted. One admits one's sodomy") and thence to
confess his own attempt to "indulge in this form of ejaculation" at the
local bath (83).

Some of the most blatantly heterosexual examples of orientalism—
ranging from nineteenth-century travelogues to pseudoscientific surveys
of "Eastern" sexual customs—reveal a similar proximity to the homoerotic.[9] Likewise Sir Richard Burton, a serious if amateur student of orientalism, opens the boundaries of his *textual* body to a destabilizing
pressure when he addresses the subject of desire between men in the Arabic Orient. For example, in his introduction to the *Nights* Burton begins
with a phallic metaphor that bestows on his translation a specifically
male body. Prior bowdlerized editions, he says, have "castrat[ed]" the
tales, producing only "ennui and disappointment" in the reader—rather
than, we are to assume, their original phallic vigor—whereas his aim is
to "produce a full, complete, unvarnished, copy of the great original"
(1:xii, iii). The means by which Burton seeks to restore the text to its
"uncastrated" manhood, however, proves quite curious (xii); he pro-

ceeds to adorn it with footnotes, annotations, and appendices whose copiousness rivals the primary text, creating a proliferation of multiple (one might argue, as Sandra Nadaff does, feminine) sites of textual pleasure that threaten to explode the complete and contained male body he has assigned his translation. Primary among these supplements, moreover, is the Terminal Essay, whose lengthy fourth section is dedicated to *le vice contre nature*. Burton announces his intention to display this subject—again note the implicit maleness of the figure—"in decent nudity, not in suggestive fig-leaf" in order to establish once and for all the prevalence of sodomy in the Arab Muslim world (10: 178). The "unvarnished," uncastrated, male body assigned to the text in the introduction, here exposed "in decent nudity" and without the proverbial "fig-leaf," has become a sodomitic subject in both senses of the phrase.

Moreover, like the language used to frame this discussion of Near Eastern sodomy, the contents of the Terminal Essay work against Burton's anthropological and orientalist predilection to contain and classify his subject. As his inquiry into sexual relations between men broadens, so too the initially circumscribed Mediterranean belt (10: 201) wherein the vice is said to flourish keeps expanding eastward—till, by the conclusion of the essay, it encompasses the Far East and the continents of the precolonized Americas. As East spins back into West, Burton is forced to confirm *le vice*'s growing presence even in "our modern capitals, London, Berlin, and Paris" (10: 213), although he has earlier set the West off-limits, claiming that the northern European races are "as a rule . . . physically incapable of performing the operation" (10: 179). Burton's definition of sodomy collapses in contradiction and repeats in its global uncontainability the operation that his notes perform on a textual level, exposing the sanctity of the male body's claim to uncastrated completeness as another masculinist myth. Or to put it another way, as long as Burton can maintain an anthropological pose, he does not mind parading the non-European homosexual subject of the *Nights* in "decent nudity"; but when he must envision himself as a reader, one whose authority over its contents yields to vicarious participation in the fictions being relayed, he finds himself restoring the "fig-leaf" beneath which he has previously declared himself willing to glimpse. For many Western men the act of exploring, writing about, and theorizing an eroticized Near and Middle East is coterminous with unlocking a Pandora's box of phantasmic homoerotic desire, desire whose propensity to spread without check threatens to contaminate, indeed to reorient, the heterosexual "essence" of occidental male subjectivity.

FANTASIZING THE "DELIGHT . . . AND INFAMY OF THE EGYPTIANS"

Of all the regions of the Near East, Western writers most readily came to associate ancient and modern Egypt with the spreading "contagion" of homosexuality. Curiously, Egypt's reputation as "that classical region of all abominations," in Burton's phrase, (10:194) has proved to be an irresistible draw to the literary ambitions of a score of occidental writers from Gerard de Nerval and Flaubert to Lawrence Durrell and Norman Mailer—writers intent on producing texts as gargantuan as their (hetero)sexual appetites. In these writers' prose the dazzling spectacle of Cairene and Alexandrian streetlife is transformed into an emblem of the psyche's overflowing polymorphous desires. As such, it becomes a convenient screen on which to project fantasies of illicit, unbridled eroticism. In *Colonizing Egypt,* Timothy Mitchell has forcefully shown how such psychological projections onto Egypt's seeming otherness derive from a general Western representational tendency to treat all things Egyptian—including Egyptian visitors to Europe—as objects on display, as exhibition pieces, whose "carefully chaotic" arrangement has been orchestrated solely to satisfy the "isolated gaze" of a European viewer (1, 9). Experiencing Egypt's curiosities as panoramas and tableaux depends, of course, on the illusion of some ineffable but inviolate boundary dividing spectator and spectacle, subject and object, self and other. However, despite the strategic mystification of foreign otherness at work in this process, Egypt's historical positioning as a conduit *between* East and West, Europe and Africa, the familiar and the foreign, has meant that, contrary to expectation, it has never functioned just or simply as the Occident's other. Rather, as Antonia Lant suggests, Egypt has come to represent in the Western imagination an intermediate zone, "a foothold, a staging point," that signifies liminality and indeterminacy itself (98). As the realm of nonfixity, moreover, it has become a ready-made symbol for that interior world of the polymorphous perverse that its Western visitors find uncannily familiar and, as an effect of repression, unimaginably estranging.

Colonized as other but never susceptible to total differentiation from or appropriation by the West, Egypt in its exotic appeal thus presented the occidental tourist with an unsuspected challenge. Hence the note of hysteria infiltrating the late eighteenth-century *Travels* of C. S. Sonnini, a former engineer in the French navy, who pauses in his narrative to lament

[t]he passion contrary to nature . . . [that] constitute[s] the delight,
or to use a juster term, the infamy of the Egyptians. It is not for
women that their amorous ditties are composed. . . . [F]ar different
objects inflame them. . . . This horrid depravation, which, to the dis-
grace of polished nations, is not altogether unknown to them, is
generally diffused all over Egypt: the rich and poor are equally
infected with it. (1:251–52)

Part of the horror is that this "inconceivable appetite" "is not altogether
unknown" to civilized Europe: if the Egyptian vice knows no class ("rich
and poor are equally infected by it"), can it be expected to respect the
boundaries of colonizer and colonized? Thirty years later, a similar
image of unchecked infection appears in Lane's *Manners and Customs
of the Modern Egyptians* when the Victorian author addresses, with
characteristic understatement, this aspect of Egyptian "immorality." "A
vice for which the Memlooks . . . were infamous," Lane writes of the
Ottoman rulers, "was so spread by them in [Egypt] as to become no less
rare here than in almost any other country of the East." Here, Egypt is
the victim of contagion, the Turks are the culprits, and, one assumes
(since Lane asserts that "of late years *it is said* [the vice has] much
decreased"), the civilizing machinery of British empire is the solution
(304; emphasis added). Once again, aspersions of "unnatural" sexuality
become markers of larger, competing colonial interests.

This mythicizing of the sheer magnitude of Near Eastern "vice" is
not unrelated to a Western obsession with the genital size of Egyptian
men that filters into even the driest orientalist discourse. For while the
figure of the effeminate Asiatic—embodied, for instance, in the trans-
vestic dancer—represents one face of orientalist homoerotic fantasy, its
reverse image, that of the hypervirile, mythically endowed sheikh holds
equal currency in orientalist homoerotic discourse. Thus Burton in his
Personal Narrative of a Pilgrimage to El-Medina and Mecca (1893)
argues that members of "the Nilotic race, although commonly called
'Arabs'," are more closely related to African blacks because of the size
of their sexual organs (2:83); that this information is buried in a footnote—one written in Latin, no less, to ward off the nonspecialist—
would seem to indicate that what is at stake here is a certain European
male anxiety or sense of inadequacy that needs to be kept under wraps.
That white, male subjectivity is the real issue underlying this prurient
obsession with indigenous body parts is made even more blatant in the

link between racial stereotype and sexual perversion made in Jacob Sutor's *L'Amour aux Colonies* (1893), published under the pseudonym Dr. Jacobus X. An army surgeon posted to various French outposts, Sutor claims that his clinical experience has proved beyond a doubt that the Arab, "an active pederast, is provided with a genital organ which, for size and length, rivals that of the Negro" (298), and, in a similarly sensationalist tone, he adds that "with such a weapon does the Arab seek for anal copulation. He is not particular in his choice, and age or sex makes no difference" (300). If foreignness, genital endowment, and sodomy are of a piece for Sutor, so too do exoticism and excess come together to form the more clearly homoerotic frisson of Allen Edwardes' survey of Eastern eroticism. "As hitherto noted, the penile proportions of the Egyptians were as notorious as their promiscuity," he states as fact, then proceeds, with more than a touch of prurience, to describe bas-reliefs that depict "Nilotic peasants and labourers with their loin-clothes" hoisted "to reveal fleshy genitalia"; elsewhere he records the ."impressive sight" presented by orgies of "round-robin sodomy" in the Egyptian hamman (*Jewel* 207), where "well-proportioned" nude bath-boys service willing customers of all classes (246). The guise of orientalist scholarship clearly gives Edwardes leeway to express a surfeit of subconscious homoerotic fantasy.

In a like manner, the autobiographical and literary productions of Flaubert and Durrell—which I discuss in greater depth elsewhere ("Mappings")—transform Egypt into a landscape of unbridled libidinal desires, a landscape in which same-sex activity is conspicuously highlighted. Figuratively exploring such "foreign" terrain may give these writers an excuse to inhabit textually a fantasy of sexual otherness their heterosexual identities must otherwise disavow, but these imaginative ventures into alien territory only highlight the problematic, indeed unstable, construction of Western discourses of masculinity under the sign of the phallus. And for both Flaubert and Durrell the fantasized projection of sexual otherness onto Egypt eventually occasions a crisis of writing, of narrative authority, when the writing subject is confronted by such imagined sensual excess.

Bombarded on his arrival in Egypt by "such a bewildering chaos of colours [and sound] that [his] poor imagination is dazzled as though by continuous fireworks" (79), Flaubert quickly embraces the exotic otherness of Egypt as a source of artistic inspiration and sexual gratification. Part of these general "fireworks"—which I have already men-

FIGURE 2.2   Egypt's historical positioning as a meeting point between Europe and Africa, the familiar and the foreign, lends itself to racial and homoerotic codings in George Quaintance's *Egyptian Wrestlers* (1952), where the pharoah's court provides the context for a spectacle of gay erotica pitting two virile, loin-clothed slaves—one African, one Aryan—against each other in a taboo embrace. (*The Art of George Quaintance: Catalogue of the Fifty-Fourth Exhibition of the Janssen Gallery*, ed. Volker Janssen [Berlin: Janssen, 1989] 33. Reproduced by permission of Janssen-Verlag, Berlin.)

tioned—is the erotic dance of the "marvellous Hasan el-Belbeissi," whose talent at putting "additional spice into a thing that is already quite clear in itself" injects into Flaubert's correspondence and diaries a stream of homoerotic banter and speculation that becomes a source of titillation and eventually the spur to experimentation without radically disturbing the writer's heterosexual self-definition (note the cavalierness with which Flaubert writes "Here . . . it is spoken of at table. Sometimes you do a bit of denying, and then everyone teases you and you end up confessing" [84]).

Simultaneously, however, the possibilities unlocked by this flirtation with Egyptian sodomy become the source of a subliminal anxiety linked to Flaubert's literary ambitions. Having traveled to Egypt in search of creative inspiration, Flaubert expresses his writerly potential in metaphors of heterosexual reproduction ("but—the real thing! To ejaculate, to beget the child!" [199]), and conversely expresses his despair at not having realized his literary goals in images of nonreproductive sexual play (198–99); in such instances he subtly figures the exotic otherness of sexual perversion as the threat of erasure, the negation of artistic vitality or sap, when "the lines don't come" (see "Mappings" 102). For all Flaubert's openness to his Near Eastern experiences, then, his encounter with foreign homosexuality triggers an uneasiness about what it means to be a writer *and* a man; in consciously striving to become one of the West's great writers, Flaubert subconsciously regards his narrative authority as equivalent to, and dependent upon, a sexual authority associated with Western codes of heterosexual potency.

A similarly disabling equation of sexual aberration and writerly debilitation haunts Durrell while stationed in Egypt during World War II. "Love, hashish, and boys [are] the obvious solution to anyone stuck here for more than a few years," he writes Henry Miller from Alexandria in 1944, a few months later adding, "One could not continue to live here without practising a sort of death—hashish or boys or food" (Wickes 190, 195).

A parallel "sort of death" faces Darley, the narrator-protagonist of the *Alexandria Quartet*. Confronted with Alexandria's dazzling yet benumbing spectacle of sensual excess—"the sexual provender that lies at hand is staggering in its variety and profusion," Darley confesses upon his arrival with envy and some fear—this would-be writer experiences a breakdown that is both sexual and textual, finding himself equally unable to write or "even to make love" (1:4, 11). Darley's feel-

ings of impotence and inadequacy, compounded by Justine's betrayal,
increasingly lead him to doubt his "manhood." In turn these doubts trig-
ger a flood of hitherto repressed memories and events that implicate him
in an expanding web of homosexual desire and panic. The welling up of
these taboo desires is made possible largely by the psychodramatic resonances that Egypt has come to assume in Darley's psyche and Durrell's
fiction, its mythic landscape transformed into an emblem of the fragmented, anarchic terrain of the component instincts through which the
questing writer must pass on his way to artistic manhood. Ironically,
only when Darley has purged himself of all expressions of polymorphous play and perversity can he break through the writer's block that
has plagued him for four volumes and emerge on the last page of the
Quartet as a productive writer and successful heterosexual lover.

     In light of these displacements it is fascinating to look at Durrell's
letter equating the enjoyment of "hashish or boys or food" with "death"
of the self. For Durrell follows this comment with a description of the
"wonderful novel on Alexandria" he has just conceived, "a sort of spiritual butcher's shop with girls on the slab" (2: 196). Underlying this
inspiration of the written text of the *Quartet* as a heterosexist fantasy of
girls as meat to be devoured glimmers the converse fear of sodomy
("boys") as an ultimate indulgence in passive pleasures (like drugs, like
food) that spell a "sort of death" to active, or "masculine," artistic
(pro)creativity. The homoerotic fantasies unleashed by Durrell's projection onto Egypt of the "dark tides of Eros" (185) within every psyche
generate a crisis of masculine subjectivity that compels the author to
Promethean efforts to contain the very desires on which his exploration
of foreign otherness depends. To a lesser degree, the same paradox over-
whelms Flaubert's exploration of Egyptian sensuality. In the process,
what I am calling "the homoerotics of orientalism" threatens to become
another name for Occidental homophobia.

DRESSING DOWN THE DESERT ANDROGYNE

While writers like Flaubert and Mailer locate their visions of a sexualized, mythic Near East in the sheer spectacle and stimulation of Egypt's
infinite variety, the homoerotic impulse infiltrating occidental visions of
the Arabic Orient also manifests itself in adventurers who search out the
nomadic life of the desert and who embrace ascetic solitude rather than

profusion. Seeking to blend into their surroundings by taking on the apparel of the Bedouin, such figures have historically tended not merely to attempt to possess but, more important, *become* the desired other. Putting on "Arab drag," as it were, provides the desert androgyne with a disguise that allows for the play of sexual and gender ambiguity, which, coupled with a persistent misogyny, issues forth in a more complicated modality of homoerotic desire that is sometimes expressed in puritanical asceticism and sublimation, sometimes in sadistic outbreaks of violence, and sometimes in swooning surrender to the desert's harsh beauty. In the process these desert androgynes transform their short lives into the subject of scandal and eventually the stuff of myth—a status that may overshadow but cannot eclipse the specific scenarios of Empire and colonialism that make possible their legendary romances with the desert.

This blend of sexual repression, homosexual yearning, and sado-masochistic surrender finds quintessential expression in T. E. Lawrence, the century's most famous icon of the thrill and contradictions of assuming Arab dress. Costuming in desert gear was foremost for Lawrence a means of "quitt[ing] me of my English self," of attempting to become the other rather than the colonizer. At the same time he admitted that he "could not sincerely take on the Arab skin: it was an affectation only" (30). This contradictory doubleness—which Marjorie Garber links to psychic transvestism (304–09) and Kaja Silverman to the "double mimesis" of psychic colonialism (17–19)—characterized all aspects of Lawrence's life, including the powerful if elusive homoerotic strain that he writes into *The Seven Pillars of Wisdom*, the official story of his engagement in the Arab revolt of 1914–18. The homoerotics of this epic tug in two directions: toward an impossibly idealized Bedouin homosexuality and toward its nightmarish opposite, utter degradation—conditions that both pivot on the simulations and dissimulations of dress and disguise. The first strain is proclaimed in chapter 1, as Lawrence frankly addresses the "strange longings" that blossom in the "virile heat" of the desert as his youthful Bedouin followers "slake one another's few needs in their own clean bodies." The passion of "friends quivering together in the yielding sand with intimate hot limbs in supreme embrace," Lawrence continues, is but "a sensual co-efficient of the mental passion which was wielding our souls in one flaming effort" (28). An erotic ideal thus finds its reflection in a political ideal that, under the sign of male-male love, tenuously combines British colonial

FIGURE 2.3   While T.E. Lawrence's famous white robes were part of his self-contained image of ascetic masculinity, this photograph, appearing in Lowell Thomas's *With Lawrence in Arabia* (London: Hutchinson, 1924), purports to offer evidence of Lawrence's participation in a more ambiguous form of boundary crossing: "Lawrence occasionally visited enemy territory disguised as a gipsy woman of Syria," Thomas's caption reads. (Courtesy of the estate of Lowell Thomas and Hutchinson Co., London.)

interests and the movement toward Arab sovereignty. This idealizing strain is continued in the story of the Bedouin lovers Daud and Saad—"an instance," Lawrence writes approvingly, "of the eastern boy and boy affection which the segregation of women ma[kes] inevitable" (244). Finally, this idealization of love between men is set forth as the raison d'être of Lawrence's participation in the Arab conflict in the volume's Dedicatory Poem, "To S. A.," which begins "I loved you, so I drew these tides of men into my hands. . . . To earn you Freedom." Again, the sexual ideal coexists with and as an expression of the political goal.

Most biographers agree that the dedication refers to Sheikh Ahmed, otherwise known as Dahoum, the fourteen-year-old waterboy with whom Lawrence became infatuated on his first extended stay in the Middle East. Onto this constant companion Lawrence projected an idealized vision of the Arabic race as pure, simple, and untainted by European culture. The determination with which Lawrence set out to construct Dahoum as an ideal other mirrors the determination with which he willed his own self-image into being, confident that through sheer self-mastery he could "mak[e] himself," in his biographer's words, "a perfected and refined instrument" (Mack 97, 86). One by-product of such discipline was Lawrence's puritanical sublimation of his homosexual inclinations. Yet in renouncing the flesh, Lawrence also set himself up for a vicious return of the repressed, which in *Seven Pillars* takes the form of the nightmarish inverse of the text's representation of idealized male bonds: the brutal rape he claims he endured when taken prisoner by the Turks at Der'a and the psychologically devastating loss of self-mastery that violation signified for him. These two faces of homosexuality have assumed unmistakably ideological valences in Lawrence's psyche: the Arab freedom fighters whose cause he has undertaken engage in "clean" sex, while the Turks—also Britain's foes—are "beastly" rapists (28, 452).

But for all the detail with which Lawrence represents his humiliation and degradation—exhibitionistically offering his bloodied body to his readers as textualized spectacle—what actually happened at Der'a remains lost in what biographers agree to be Lawrence's inability to distinguish between fact and fantasy. After telling how he spurned the Turkish bey's "fawn[ing]" sexual advances, Lawrence reports being taken into the hall by the bey's soldiers and repeatedly beaten, lashed, and sodomized (452). Yet it is indicative of the narrative's confusion that Lawrence's descriptions of torture and sexual abuse become indistinguishable: in the nightmarish *fear* of sexual contact that forms the mirror inverse of Lawrence's idealization of homoerotic relations, submitting sexually and being tortured become one and the same fantasy.[10] What emerges is Lawrence's guilt for having surrendered his vaunted self-mastery to the mastery of another; for him the threat of anal penetration subconsciously signifies a loss of will that in turn signifies a loss of self.

The incredible narrative projections of fear and desire that arise from Lawrence's contemplation of one man's penetration by another are usefully explained by Leo Bersani in his influential essay, "Is the Rectum a Grave?" Bersani argues that phallocentric culture promotes a powerfully subliminal equation between passive anal sex—which represents the breakdown of bodily boundaries—and a shattering of the male ego that is tantamount to psychic death. For underlying the cultural prohibition against being penetrated by another man is the irrational fear of dissolution of the very boundaries of the self—a notion that, as Bersani shows, relies on a specifically *modern* and *Western* conception of the ego as a contained and integral fortress. "That night the citadel of my integrity [was] irrevocably lost," Lawrence concludes the published account of the Der'a rape (*Seven Pillars* 456); and, in a private explanation to Charlotte Shaw in 1924, he confesses, "[T]o earn five minutes respite from . . . pain . . . I gave away the only possession we are born into the world with—our bodily integrity" (*Letters* 47–48).

This specifically male fear of the loss of corporeal integrity and ego boundaries cannot be separated from a concurrent desire to experience sexual surrender, as Bersani also makes clear: the desire that is given expression in Lawrence's evocation of "the delicious warmth, probably sexual, . . . swelling through [him]," as he is brutally kicked and then whipped in the groin (*Seven Pillars* 454). This experience forces on Lawrence the humiliating knowledge that he can allow himself to experience sexual pleasure only if pain and coercion are part of the scenario—his resistance has to be whipped out of him, by a force external to himself—for he has now become, in Silverman's terms, the "feminine" rather than "reflexive" masochist (35). And Lawrence becomes conscious of this hitherto repressed knowledge precisely through his psychodramatic projections *onto* the Middle East of his attraction to and terror of sexual surrender *as* feminizing.[11]

Lawrence's masochism marks his subsequent relation to writing. He obsessively rewrites the Der'a incident from 1919 to 1925, elaborat-

ing and revising its details, just as he obsessively revises the unruly manuscript of *Seven Pillars*: it has become a text that is out of control, a text
that he cannot master. This crisis in narrative authority reenacts the loss
of bodily integrity and sexual control that Lawrence has grafted onto the
experience of his rape. One result is that Lawrence increasingly
expresses disgust towards the act of writing in terms that conflate authorial and biological functions: "I can't write . . . since creation . . . is only
a nasty vice. You have to be very eager-spirited to overcome the disgust
of reproduction" (Mack 423). Ironically, this metaphoric association of
textual production and sexual reproduction demonstrates Lawrence's
subliminal allegiance to the phallocentric model that inhibits him sexually: a model whose assumed link between masculine "potency" and
successful literary production has been noted in Flaubert and Durrell.
Hence, as the fantasized site of male prowess, of spermatic reproduction, the *textual* body that arouses Lawrence's "disgust" mirrors the
self-disgust he expresses in *Seven Pillars* toward what he now terms his
"soiled"—because mastered—sexual body. And he now equates the
"rankling fraudulence" of this body with his "daily posturing in alien
dress": desert drag no longer serves as an adequate vehicle for mediat-
ing his homoerotic urges. For the desublimation of his homosexuality
through masochistic degradation not only curtails the idealized fantasy
of "clean" Bedouin sex but also forces him to see in his role in "the
national uprising of another race" as a "fraud" perpetuated by English
interests (*Seven Pillars* 514). The man who has traveled to the Arabic
desert filled with confidence, privately transforming himself into the foreign other he wants to be (and to have) while publicly transforming himself into the heroic liberator of the land of his desires, returns home to
England in self-defeat. Having failed to become the colonial object of his
desire, Lawrence settles, ironically, for a pale imitation: psychic existence as a mastered subject, in thrall to an "imperial" notion of masculine will that transforms his homosexual yearnings into what he sees as
a "feminine" surrender for which he can only punish himself in rites of
degradation and self-abnegation.[12]

The Tourist Trade in Boys

Not all imaginative travelers to the Near East remain so resigned as
Lawrence or so resistant as Durrell to the homoerotic pulsations fueling

many occidental visions of Near and Middle Eastern sexuality. For over a century, numerous gay and bisexual men have journeyed to Arabic North Africa to discover what they already suspect is there: a colonized Third World in which the availability of casual sex is based on an economics of boys. A case in point is Algeria. Seized by the French in 1834, this country became a popular cruising site for Gide, Wilde, Alfred Douglas, Ronald Firbank, and many other homosexual men of means by the century's end.[13] During the first two decades of the twentieth century, however, Algeria's reputation for gay tourism was superseded by that of the French-Spanish colony of Morocco. Tangier's as an International Zone by Western interests from 1923 to 1956 played an important role in this shift by encouraging suspect activities ranging from international monetary speculation and a black market in drugs to underage prostitution.[14] This atmosphere inevitably nurtured a reputation for sexual permissiveness, to the point that behaviors unthinkable in much of Europe and America became local badges of honor. Writing in the 1950s, William Burroughs sums up the appeal of Tangier as a haven for those gay, bisexual, and otherwise sexually marginalized Anglo-American artists and intellectuals whose desires were a source of persecution back home: "The special attraction of Tangier can be put in one word: exemption. Exemption from interference, legal or otherwise. Your private life is your own, to act exactly as you please. . . . It is a sanctuary of non-interference" (50).

Given the reality of homosexual persecution that drove a number of Europeans and Americans to settle in Tangier,[15] I do not mean to undervalue the degree to which these enclaves created self-affirming communities impossible elsewhere or to overlook the degree to which these expatriate colonies, however privileged in their trappings, sometimes allowed for the emergence of desires and practices that resisted the dominant Western erotology of romantic coupling. But the "sanctuary of non-interference" that Burroughs applauds depended on certain historical and economic factors of Western colonialism that perpetuated degrees of exploitation potentially as objectionable as the experience of marginalization and harassment that sent these Western voyagers abroad in the first place. Sex for sale provides an obvious but far from simple example. As Alfred Chester notes, "[I]t is traditional in Morocco to pay for sex," and although the Westerner may find the price nominal, "to the Moslem it can be enough to live on—and when it is, there is no escaping the fact that, however gilded it is by tradition, prostitution is

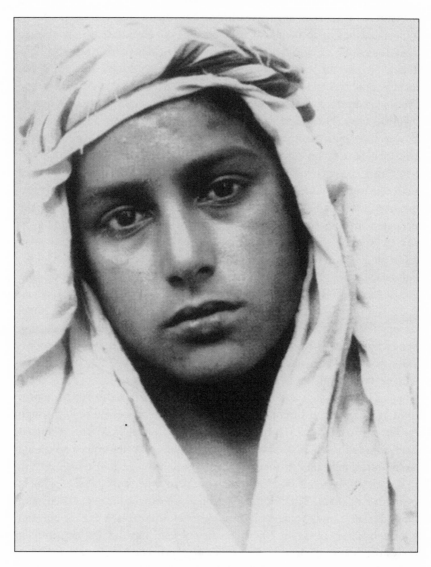

FIGURE 2.4   Best known for his photographs of nude Italian boys of North African origin striking various Hellenic poses, Wilhelm von Gloeden capitalizes on the orientalist motif of the beautiful Arab boy in his portrait series "Ahmed, 1890–1900," which was reproduced as tourist postcards. (Collection Lebeck. Reproduced by permission of Agfa Foto-Historama, Cologne.)

taking place." Chester then wickedly adds, in reference to the vaunted primacy of ends over means in Moroccan men's sex practices, "What makes it adorable to people at either end of the banknote is that, though the Moslem is an employee, he really and truly loves his work" (225). There maybe more than a grain of truth in Chester's final turn of phrase: local economies of Moroccan sex may latch onto, participate in, and even exploit exploitative Western practices in complex and unpredictable ways. "Love" of work, however, does not erase the dynamics of power that many employers would rather believe their "employees" consider mere technicalities of the trade. The novelist Robin Maugham, a longtime Tangier resident, anecdotally sums up the political subtext of such tensions in relating an incident that occurred right after the granting of Moroccan independence in 1956. Harassed during a walk by the persistent propositions of a young boy, one of Maugham's companions snaps, "Oh do go home," to which the boy replies, "*You* go home, you go home . . . and don't come back to *my* country" ("Peter Burton" 145; emphasis added). In a colonial context, what and where *is* "home," and whose "home" is it?

Within this tradition of gay occidental tourism, Gide's 1902 novel of sexual discovery, *L'immoraliste* is paradigmatic, relentlessly disclosing beneath its veneer of reticence a narrative of homosexual—and specifically pederastic—awakening.[16] The text opens with the protagonist Michel confessing to a group of friends summoned from France the story of his marriage and near fatal honeymoon trip to an Arabic world that, as a scholar of orientalism, he has hitherto possessed only through books. Almost dying in Tunis from a tubercular attack, Michel is nursed back to health in Algeria, where he undergoes a voluptuous awakening to life intimately tied to the exotic foreign landscape that envelops him in its "richer, hotter blood" and penetrates to "the most . . . secret fibers of my being" (52). The Nietzschean dialectic of freedom versus culture, body versus mind, that evolves as Michel embraces a life of sensual abandon barely covers the homoerotic subtext that the text continually teases the reader to decode. The first clue to this coded subtext is Gide's representation of Michel's gaze, which keeps uncovering, in brief flashes, the naked limbs of Arab boys and youths beneath their loose clothes. A second, related clue to Gide's gay subtext is the sheer procession of pubescent boys who pass through Michel's quarters or whom he encounters on his walks during his convalescence. A third clue lies in Michel's growing obsession with masks, deceit, and concealment—an obsession, in effect, with the homosexual art of passing and getting away with it. A fourth clue involves Gide's manipulation of Michel's language, so that the words always seem on the verge of saying something other than what they ultimately reveal.[17] That the reader is being actively solicited to decode the "open secret" of such passages is spelled out in an aside in which Michel compares himself to a text—specifically, to a palimpsest beneath whose "more recent" layers the scholar digs to find the "more precious ancient text," that of the repressed self (51).

But the possibility of leading (and writing) a double life, coupled with Michel's growing recognition of his latent desires, breeds profound ambivalence, for, in a complex process of internalization that amounts to a fetishizing of the closet, Michel's psyche translates *secret* desires into necessarily *criminal* ones. The ultimate measure of Michel's "criminality" becomes his neglect of Marceline, whose health has declined as his has improved, and whose death Michel guarantees by forcing her to return with him to North Africa, the scene of his homoerotic awakening: symbolically her death ensures that Michel can live a free man. But to be free translates for Michel into utter immersion in sensual self-gratification at the expense of other selves. "I am afraid that what I have suppressed will take its revenge," he tells his auditors, and then, in a revelation withheld till the novel's final lines, we learn of Michel's pederastic relationship with the Kabyl child Ali, whose caresses, "in exchange for a few sous," are "what keeps me here more than anything else" (170–71), sunk in torpid surrender to inner passions projected outward onto the African landscape. "This climate, I believe, is what's responsible for the change. Nothing discourages thought so much as this perpetual blue sky. Here any exertion is impossible, so closely does pleasure follow desire" (170).

The disturbing conflation that this conclusion effects between homoerotic surrender and the lure of North African otherness points to the unconscious colonialism involved in Gide's projection of a narrative of gay awakening onto the Near East. First, Michel's awakening depends on the orientalist move of equating the Near East almost solely with the body and surfeit: for Michel, North Africa can *only* be apprehended sensually, leaving no room for art or intellect. "Art is leaving me, I feel it," says Michel, then adds, "[but] to make room for . . . what?" (163; Gide's ellipsis). Second, Michel's awakening depends on his refusal to see the *actual* foreign others who serve as embodiments of his desire as anything other than objects: boys, once Michel realizes he desires

them, form an endless chain of anonymous, available bodies, the means
to *his* awakening and never subjects of their own stories or desires.

The economic underpinnings of this exchange in boys as objects of
Western consumption, only hinted at in Gide, are made explicit in Joe
Orton's diary account of his and Ken Halliwell's sexual escapades in
Tangier in 1967. Orton's diary, in fact, owes its inspiration to his agent's
suggestion that he start a "journal *à la Gide*" (Lahr 12) of his travels.
The Morocco entries emulate Gide with a vengeance, recording the constant stream of youths trooping in and out of Orton's Tangier flat. The
flat, however, is not all that is paid for: Orton takes as a given, indeed
as a source of stimulation, the fact that you get what you pay for and
pay for what you get in terms of Tangier trade, and he records with cyn-
ical humor the bargaining that undergirds sexual pleasure in Morocco.
Who could want more, he sardonically muses, than "the [daily] company of beautiful fifteen-year-old boys who find (for a small fee) fucking with me a delightful sensation"? (187).

A corollary of the occidental tourist's fantasy that all boys are
available for the right price is the assumption that they represent interchangeable versions of the same commodity: (nearly) underage sex. The
number of identically named Mohammeds that Orton meets thus
becomes a running joke in his diary ("His name, inevitably, was
Mohammed" [193]), and, to keep his schedule of assignations from
becoming hopelessly muddled, Orton begins to distinguish among these
boys by assigning them farcical surnames: Mohammed I; Mohammed
Yellow-Jersey; Mohammed Gold-tooth. What may be humorous in the
abstract is, of course, dehumanizing in reality, for such typecasting only
reinforces the boys' anonymity and dispensability.[18] Tellingly, it is the
one Mohammed who attempts to assert his individuality—proudly
declaring to Joe and company that he is off to Gilbratar to make a life
for himself, with a legitimate job—against whom Orton turns, belittling
the youth's ambition as bourgeois careerism and claiming, to top it off,
that he's a bad lay. Not coincidentally, it is also this Mohammed who
has asserted his subjectivity by complaining to Orton, "You give me
money, yes—but me want *l'amour*. Me like you. Me want *l'amour*"
(174). L'amour, of course, is the one item missing from the vacation
cruise packet Orton has signed up for.

As gay adventurer in Tangier, then, Orton manifests the contradictions of the colonialist abroad; he hates and mocks the general run of
tourists for ruining "*our* town" (187), while at the same time he depends

on the hierarchy of (moneyed) white man / (purchased) brown boy to make his own vacation a success. This doubleness repeats itself in the contradiction between Orton's courageous rebellion against sexual orthodoxy (exemplified in his enjoyment of sex for its own sake) *and* his basic phallocentrism (categorizing each boy he has sex with as a "very valuable addition to my collection" [186]). Finally, this appropriation of the East manifests itself, albeit more subtly, on the level where sexual and textual pleasures combine for Orton. For his diary entries, as a record of conquests meant to keep the excitement going, become yet one more means of possessing the foreign other, but now as textual image rather than physical body. Note, for example, the point of view from which Orton recounts one particularly steamy encounter: "At [that] moment with my cock in his arse the *image* was, and *as I write still*, is, overpoweringly erotic" (207; emphases added). If Orton does not manifest the anxieties of textual and sexual authority or the loss of the desire to write present in many male writers' homoerotic negotiations with the Near and Middle East, it may be due to the fact that his embrace of a gay identity is strong enough to allow him to reassert the coupling of writerly authority and male potency that has always characterized phallocentric discourse—only now, ironically, in the name of homo—rather than heterosexual pleasure.

The continuities represented by Gide's and Orton's responses to the North African trade in boys are played out in numerous Western narratives written by gay or bisexual men.[19] In contrast, the Moroccan storyteller Mohammed Mrabet's *Love with a Few Hairs* (1967) dramatically recasts the plot of *L'immoraliste* from the perspective of the "kept" Arab boy: here the sexual object—also named Mohammed—becomes the subject of his *own* story, a story which renders the Westerner, or Nazarene, the anonymous other.[20] The very first sentence of Mrabet's tale— "Mohammed lived with Mr. David, an Englishman who owned a small hotel near the beach"—introduces the kept boy theme matter-of-factly, indeed as a fact of life. The reader next learns that "only [one] thing about Mohammed's life . . . [had] made his father sad . . . during the four years he had been living with Mr. David." Any expectation that the father's problem may involve the propriety of Mohammed's having maintained a sexual relationship since the age of thirteen with a man the father's age is quickly deflated: the vice that disturbs the father is not sex but alcohol abuse: "One day soon you'll be getting married. Do you want your wife and children to see you drunk?" (1). Here the structural opposition is between drinking and marriage, *not* between marriage and a pederastic relationship, for in the narrative that immediately unfolds—the story of Mohammed's ill-fated infatuation with and unhappy brief marriage to a girl named Mina—the sexual relationship with Mr. David hovers uninterrupted in the background, in a stratum of Tangier life proximate to, but held at a distance from, the present story of "love with a few hairs"—a reference to the magic potion Mohammed procures to make Mina love him.

The text's opening also spells out the economics of the occidental trade in boys, but from a Moroccan perspective. The family, it is clear, looks on Mr. David as a benefactor who periodically brings Mohammed's father "gifts" that the father can then sell on the black market (2). This understood exchange, whereby Mohammed is passed from father to paternal lover, is only one in a chain of monetary exchanges that Mrabet depicts as structuring all facets of Moroccan life. Within this framework, the Western tourist's guiding principle of promiscuous sexual consumerism—you get what you pay for—gives way to the more pervasive local economy of barter and exchange. Sex, as a result, becomes Mohammed's most effective bargaining chip, both in manipulating Mr. David for the money needed to finance his marriage and in maneuvering to stay in Mr. David's good graces despite the marriage. Here Mrabet's artistry is at its most subtle, as carefully placed variations on the sentence, "That night Mohammed slept with Mr. David," become telling signals to the current economic and emotional pressures of Mohammed's adjacent heterosexual love life: when he is in need of money or unhappy, he knows where to go and what to do. In this recasting of the Gidean fantasy from the perspective of the indigenous subject, it is fascinating to note the virtual *anonymity* that surrounds Mr. David as an individual: we never even learn whether "David" is his given name or his surname. Whatever Mohammed's degee of seemingly real affection for Mr. David, he ultimately sees his benefactor as indistinguishable from the other Nazarenes hanging out in Tangier, and this perspective dramatically reverses the dynamics of otherness that rule in Gide and Orton.

Yet Mrabet's demystification of the colonialist fantasy of the trade in boys coexists with his acceptance of the misogyny and sexism that marks many of the Western narratives discussed here. This contiguity between Eastern and Western sexism is most pronounced in the collusion of Moroccan male culture and Mr. David's occidental cohorts in supporting Mohammed's scheme to get his marriage annulled by treating Mina so badly she'll beg to be let go. In fact the entire logic of the plot works to demonstrate the correctness of Mr. David's admonition "Don't trust any woman," which in turn reinforces Mina's expendability in the story's economy of desire (177). While Mr. David accepts Mohammed's bisexuality as a given, he also encourages the boy to maintain a *string* of girlfriends, rather a single relationship. It is Mohammed's ultimate acceptance of the logic of this suggestion that forms Mrabet's conclusion: a reformed Mohammed moves back in with Mr. David, "ha[s] other girls but [does] not let himself love any of them," and therefore lives happily ever after (196). The text's erasure of Mina is finalized when, years later, Mohammed reencounters her on the way to visit his father (who, having opposed Mohammed's marriage to Mina, had estranged himself from his son). After escaping her, Mohammed hurries, in the text's last line, "quickly [on] to his father's house" (198). The closing words thus reestablish the alignment *between* father and Mr. David, *between* Eastern and Western patriarchy, that also opened the narrative, proving that *fathers* know best: "You should be like the Englishman," Mohammed's father scolds him in the novel's opening scene, "He doesn't go out into the street drunk" (2). And one of the last things we learn about Mohammed is that he now rarely drinks—he has not only become a "good" Muslim like his religiously observant father, but also a mirror of his respectable Western lover.

The previous pages have traced a number of crossings over hypothetical borders or divisions: East/West, female/male, homosexual/heterosexual, colonized/colonizer, among others. What I hope this chapter's negotiation of these categories has demonstrated is that, as the line between these terms blur, neither the dichotomies which these pairings purport to describe nor the hierarchical arrangements they are meant to enforce prove to be so apparent. In particular, by gridding the geographical and sexual oppositions—West/East, hetero/homo—onto and across each other's axes, I have attempted to call attention to the sexual and textual politics that complicate so many Western men's "journeys," both real and imagined, to a homoeroticized Near and Middle East. In those accounts of orientalism that assume the heterosexuality of the erotic adventurer, for example, we have seen how the confrontation with the specter of homosexuality that lurks in Western fantasies of Eastern decadence destabilizes the assumed authority of the tourist as distant,

uncontaminated spectator. In those narratives where the occidental traveler, by virtue of his homosexuality, is *already* the other, we have seen
how the presumed *equivalence* of Eastern homosexuality and occidental
personal liberation may disguise the specter of colonial privilege and
exploitation encoded in the hierarchy of white man/brown boy. And in
reading Mrabet against Gide and Orton, we have not only seen how the
other other's story unsettles the assumed hierarchy between
colonizer/colonized, but also how, despite this political critique, a com-
plicitous equivalence *between* East and West may *re*establish itself under
the aegis of patriarchy, precisely when the tension between the hierarchy
male/female becomes palpable. This return to the gender binary on
which sexual hierarchy within patriarchy is based serves as a reminder
that the story of many Western men's encounters with the Near East,
whatever these tourists' putative sexual orientations, has also been the
story of a crisis in male subjectivity—the crisis that *is*, by definition,
occidental masculinity itself. Every rereading of this story may help us
re-orient our perception of the complex undercurrents created by those
fantasized geographies of male desire that depend on, even as they dis-
claim, the homoerotics of an orientalizing discourse whose phallocentric
collusions and resistant excitations this chapter has just begun to
uncover.

Notes

This chapter has benefited greatly from the responsive audiences it met at UC-
Berkeley; the Humanities Center at UC-Davis; The Conference on Literary The-
ory held at Georgetown University; UC-Riverside's first "Unauthorized Sexual
Behaviors" Conference; and the University of Southern California's "Life of the
Mind" series. Thanks are also due to Earl Jackson, Ed Cohen, Lee Edelman,
David Roman, Hilary Schor, Jim Kincaid, Jonathan Strong, and Scott Elledge for
their insightful comments, as well as to Karen Lawrence, Parama Roy, Sandra
Naddaff, Emily Apter, Nancy Paxton, Greg Mullins, and Michael Lucey for
sharing ideas, work, and citations from their related projects.

　　1. By "Orient" Said means the Near and Middle East; for insightful critiques of the ways in which Said's terminology unintentionally produces a uni-
fied entity all the more easily dominated by a discursively all-powerful West, see
Mani and Frankenberg; Bhabha; and Sharpe. Likewise while I attempt to make
my use of the terms *West* and *East* as specific as possible, it is impossible not to

generalize at times; I hope the context of my statements make clear when I am using these rhetorical markers as shorthand for much more complex geographic and psychological realities.

2. While Alloula's phrase occurs in a chapter titled "Oriental Sapphism," his interest lies in the heterosexual male viewer for whom these images of lesbian love in the harem are created Said's sidestepping of the homoerotic dimensions of this "promise (and threat)" is not unique; see the way in which Kabbani raises the specter of homoeroticism only to subsume it into the sexuality of the oriental woman (*Europe's Myths* 80, 81). Homosexual practice in the British empire is addressed by Ronald Hyam, who notes that "the empire was often an ideal arena for the practice of sexual variation" (5–6); however, his exclusive focus on official British guardians of empire, coupled with his dismissal of feminist criticism, limits his usefulness in analyzing the sexual politics of colonialism. The most thoughtful examination of the homoerotic subtexts in Western visions of the Arabic Orient is Marjorie Garber's chapter, "The Chic of Araby."

3. Here terminology becomes, if not a problem, a reminder that defining "the homosexual" as such is very much a Western enterprise While male-male sexual practice is plentiful in Muslim culture, there is no Arabic word equivalent to the English *homosexuality*. The closest approximation is the classical Arabic *liwat*, which designates an act of sodomy performed on, or by means of (not with) a boy (Schmitt 5, 9–11).

4. These literary-artistic vacationers and sojourners have included, among others, Jean Genet, Tennessee Williams, Joe Orton, William Burroughs, Allen Ginsberg, Gregory Corso, Ronald Firbank, Robin Maugham, Angus Stewart, Rupert Croft-Cooke, Michael Davidson, Harold Norse, Truman Capote, Alfred Chester, Ned Rorem, and Roland Barthes.

5. In conceiving this project, I am mindful of Jenny Sharpe's warning that "It might well be argued that studies [written within an authorizing Western discourse on] the domination of dominant discourses merely add to their totalizing effects" (137); my presentation attempts to avoid this trap as much as is possible by focusing on an aspect of colonialist discourse—sexuality between men—that itself remains relatively "unauthorized" in those "totalizing" discourses to which Sharpe refers If this investigation owes much to the critiques of European colonialism that have followed in the wake of Said, its gendered analysis is endebted not only to queer theory but also to those many feminist analyses that have engaged issues of colonialism; see Sharpe; Abu-Lughod; El Saadawi; Mernissi; Shaarawi; Lowe; and Woodhull, as well as Spivak's and Mohanty's analyses of the intersections of Western feminist and Third World criticism. I do not focus on same-sex activity between women in this essay, but lesbianism within the harem has also been the subject of much orientalizing commentary since Montesquieu's *Persian Letters*; see the critiques offered by Behdad;

Alloula; Croutier. For an account of how some European women have appropriated iconography of the harem to encode lesbian desire, see Apter's "Gender
Trouble."

6. The Arab world that I subsume under the rubric "Arabic Orient" follows, loosely, the definitions unfolded in Lewis, who traces the historical emergence of an "Arab" identity that resides as much in a common language, a
shared religious faith, and a loose confederation of multiple, often highly vari-
able cultures and nation-states as in a single ethnicity or nationality.

7. Conversely, this is not intended to deny the practice or specificity of
sexual relations between males in many strata of Muslim Arabic society. A number of historical factors have influenced the prevalence and (to Western perception) relative tolerance of same-sex love within the nonetheless predominantly
heterosexual cultures of the Arabic Orient: the Prophet's "relative indifference"
to male homosexuality, reflected in stipulations in the Koran that make its legal
prosecution highly unlikely (Daniel 40); the general celebration of all male sexual pleasure in Islamic cultures; the tendency to measure sexuality in terms of
activity and passivity rather than solely in terms of gender; the medieval Persian
tradition of pederasty; the latitude offered by sociocommunal codes of propriety
and discretion (see Bouhdiba 100–4, 119, 140–42, 200–10; Daniel 40–42;
Schmitt, esp. 7; Foucault 191–92; Schmitt and Sofers).

8. For reports of thirteenth- and fourteenth-century testimony, see
Boswell 281–82, and Daniel 62 on Jacques de Vitry's propagandistic *Oriental
History*, William of Ada, and Friar Guillaume Adam. For seventeenth- and eigh-
teenth-century accounts of the frequency of male-male sexuality in the Near and
Middle East, see Rycaut on Turkey (1668); Covel on the Levant (1670–79); and
Sonnini (1780) and Denon (1801) on Egypt just before and during the
Napoleonic invasion.

9. For further examples of this phenomenon, see my analysis of Hector
France's 1900 travelogue, *Musk, Hashish, and Blood* in "Framing the Phallus"
and my reading of the "adult" film *Sahara Heat* in "Rubbing Aladdin's Lamp."

10. Lawrence's collapse of the distinctions between sexual contact and
rape should be taken not as a general comment on the physical or psychic abuse
experienced by rape victims but as an example of the fantasies engendered by a
specifically male cultural fear of being penetrated anally.

11. After Lawrence returned home to England, the masochistic desires
awakened by this shattering of will no longer had to masquerade in Arab dress.
For the final ten years of his life, which he spent in England, the former hero of
the desert campaign established an elaborate ritual of birchings to repeat his
original surrender while punishing himself for the very pleasure that this pun-
ishment stimulated. (According to one anonymous eyewitness, Lawrence stipu-

lated that "the beatings be severe enough to produce a seminal emission"). See Mack 433; and, for corroboration, D. Stewart 244, 275; Maugham *Escape* 104.

12. Space limitations prevent me from tracing the homoeroticizing possibilities of donning Arabic dress through their many subsequent permutations. But one might consider—as Garber has done in another register (309–22, 325–26, 335)—the alternately misogynistic, masochistic, homoeroticizing, feminizing, and orientalizing valences attached to Rudolph Valentino's two screen performances as "the Sheik," that ultimate "heterosexual" love-god; or one might ponder the homoerotic current that persists even when, as in the case of Isabelle Eberhardt, the white "man" in Arab drag turns out to be a woman; or the frisson that Paul Bowles exploits when Kit Moresby's Arab captor disguises her as an Arab boy in *The Sheltering Sky*. The pathos of all these instances is that the Western subject—real or fictionalized—can imagine male homosexuality only as a total surrender to surfeit, passivity, or violation (desired rather than, as with Lawrence, both desired and feared), because the command to yield takes the decision, the agency, out of one's hands. That is, by attempting to become part of a culture whose fatalistic creed is summed up in the saying *mektoub* 'it is written,' the occidental tourist recasts "deviance" as part of an immutable decree beyond individual or authorial control.

13. It is no coincidence that the decade that saw the creation of the pathological category *homosexual* intensified the search for non-European outlets, such as Algeria, for sexual energies increasingly persecuted within Western culture.

14. The phrase *underage prostitution* begs further definition, as does the subsequent use of the term *boys*. Many writers who describe their sexual odysseys to the Near and Middle East use the term *boy* to refer to any male youth from adolescence to late teens and even early twenties. Indeed, the myth of "younger is better" is so potent a part of gay tourist lore that some of these travelers pretend to be engaging in "underage" sex even when they are not. But for those men whose desires are definitionally pederastic, pubescent and prepubescent boys, especially Riffian lads who have come down from the mountains to eke a living in the city, are by several accounts readily available. Within a Near Eastern perspective, the term *underage sex* carries little or no meaning and little of the sense of taboo or moral condemnation that it bears within Western constructions of sexuality as an "adult" activity; a child, particularly one of the peasantry or working class, is never a sexual innocent, indeed is a practicing adult from the time he takes to the streets on his own. See A. Stewart's and Davidson's pederastic narratives, as well as Rossman's survey of the North African "pederast underground" (100–102, 116–21).

15. For example, scandals and prison sentences forced both the respected journalist Michael Davidson (169–81) and novelist Rupert Croft-Cooke to leave England for Morocco.

16. For a report of Gide's similar sexual initiation in Algeria, see his auto-biography, *If It Die* (267–69; 303); for an analysis of the colonialist underpin-nings of this account, see Michael Lucey ("Gide Writing" 30; "Consequence" 182, 185).

17. Apter identifies the rhetorical strategy whereby the gap in Michel's sentences "prefigure" an "unstated subtext of homoeroticism" as *anacoluthon* (*Gide* 113–15).

18. Since part of the Moroccan vacation fantasy has to do not simply with availability but youth, Orton's other means of differentiating among his prospects is to assign an age to each (a "very attractive fifteen-year-old boy," "a quite nice looking boy of seventeen," "a very pretty boy of about eleven" [174, 184, 209). And yet, so strong is the myth that younger is better, we find Orton scaling down his original estimates: thus Mohammed, "a very beautiful sixteen-year-old boy" at the beginning of the 9 May entry is "about fifteen" by 25 May and has become "fourteen" by 11 June (160, 185, 207).

19. Examples include Maugham's *The Wrong People* (1964), Norse's "Six for Mohammed Riffi" (1962–63), Stewart's *Tangier: A Writer's Notebook* (1977), Chester's "Glory Hole: Nickel Views of the Infidel in Tangiers" (1963–65), Croft-Cooke's *Exiles* (1970), *Scott Symon's Helmet of Flesh* (1986), *and Aldo Busi's Sodomis in Eleven Point* (1992).

20. Transcribed and translated from the Moghrebi by Bowles, Mrabet's text also illustrates an ironic "payoff" of the colonial trade in boys; for Bowles not only worked indefatigably for the past three decades to secure publication and recognition for numerous Moroccan writers but also made handsome pro-tegees like Mrabet into favored male companions. The implicit power dynamic of Western patron/Moroccan artist underlying these "literary collaborations" thus participates in and complicates the erotic transactions described in this essay. Another narrative told from the point of view of the "kept" Moroccan boy is Layachi's *Life Full of Holes*.

WORKS CITED

Abu-Lughod, Lila. *Veiled Sentiments: Honor and Poetry in a Bedouin Society.* Princeton: Princeton UP, 1986.

Alloula, Malek. *The Colonial Harem.* Trans. Myrna and Wlad Godzich. 1981. Minneapolis: U of Minnesota P, 1986.

Apter, Emily. *André Gide and the Codes of Homotextuality.* Stanford, Calif.: Stanford French and Italian Studies, 1987.

———. "Female Trouble in the Colonial Harem." *Differences* 4:1 (Spring 1992): 205–24.

Behdad, Ali. "The Eroticized Orient: Images of the Harem in Montesquieu and His Precursors." *Stanford French Review* 13 (1989): 109–26.

Bentham, Jeremy. *Works of Jeremy Bentham.* Ed. John Bowring. 1838–43. 11 vols. New York: Russell, 1962.

Bersani, Leo. "Is the Rectum a Grave?" *AIDS: Cultural Analysis/Cultural Activism.* Ed. Douglas Crimp. Cambridge: MIT P, 1987. 197–222.

Bhabha, Homi K. "The Other Question . . . Homi K. Bhabha Reconsiders the Stereotype and Colonial Discourse." *Screen* 24 (1983): 18–36.

Boone, Joseph A. "Mappings of Male Desire in Durrell's *Alexandria Quartet.*" *Displacing Homophobia.* Spec. issue *South Atlantic Quarterly* 88 (1989): 73–106.

———. "Framing the Phallus in the *Arabian Nights*: Pansexuality, Pederasty, Pasolini." *Translations/Transformations: Gender and Culture in Film and Literature.* Proceedings of the Literary Studies East and West Conference. Ed. Cornelia Moore and Valerie Wayne. Honolulu: U of Hawaii P, 1993. 23–33.

———. "Rubbing Aladdin's Lamp." *Negotiating Lesbian and Gay Subjects.* Ed. Monica Dorenkamp and Richard Henke. New York: Routledge, 1995.

Boswell, John. *Christianity, Social Tolerance, and Homosexuality.* Chicago: U of Chicago P, 1980.

Bouhdiba, Abdelwahab. *Sexuality in Islam.* London: Routledge, 1985.

Burroughs, William S. *Interzone.* New York: Viking, 1989.

Burton, Sir Richard, trans. and ed. *The Book of the Thousand Nights and a Night: A Plain and Literal Translation of the Arabian Nights Entertainments.* Burton Club ed. 10 vols. London: n.p. 1885–86.

———. *Personal Narrative of a Pilgrimage to Al-Madinah and Meccah.* 2 vols. New York: Dover, 1964.

Chester, Alfred. "Glory Hole: Nickel Views of the Infidel in Tangiers." *Head of a Sad Angel: Stories, 1953–1966.* Santa Rosa: Black Sparrow, 1990. 217–31.

Covel, John. "Dr. John Covel's Diary (1670–79)." *Early Voyages and Travels in the Levant.* Ed. J. Theodore Bent. London: Clark, 1893. 101–287.

Croft-Cooke, Rupert. *The Verdict of You All.* London: Allen, 1974.

Crompton, Louis. *Byron and Greek Love: Homophobia in Nineteenth-Century England.* Berkeley: U of California P, 1985.

Croutier, Alev Lytle. *Harem: The World Behind the Veil*. New York: Abbeville, 1989.

Daniel, Marc. "Arab Civilization and Male Love." 1975–76. *Gay Roots: Twenty Years of Gay Sunshine: An Anthology of Gay History, Sex, Politics, and Culture*. Ed. Winston Leyland. San Francisco: Gay Sunshine, 1991. 33–75.

Davidson, Michael. *The World, The Flesh, and Myself*. 1962. Reprint, London: GMP, 1985.

Denon, Vivant. *Travels in Upper and Lower Egypt*. 2 vols. New York: n. p., 1803.

Durrell, Lawrence. *Alexandria Quartet*. 4 vols. New York: Pocket, 1957–1960.

Edwardes, Allen. *The Jewel in the Lotus: A Historical Survey of the Sexual Culture of the East*. New York: Julian, 1959.

———. *Erotica Judaica: A Sexual History of the Jews*. New York: Julian, 1967.

Edwardes, Allen, and R. E. L. Masters. *The Cradle of Erotica*. New York: Julian, 1963.

Flaubert, Gustave. *Flaubert in Egypt: A Sensibility on Tour*. Trans. and ed. Francis Steegmuller. Chicago: Academy Chicago, 1979.

Foucault, Michel. *The Uses of Pleasure*. 1984. New York: Vintage, 1986.

France, Hector. *Musk, Hashish, and Blood*. London: n. p., 1900.

Garber, Marjorie. *Vested Interests: Cross-Dressing and Cultural Anxiety*. New York: Routledge, 1992.

Gide, Andre. *If It Die . . . : An Autobiography (Si le grain ne meurt)*. Trans. Dorothy Bussy. New York: Random, 1935. Trans. of *Si le grain ne meurt*.

———. *The Immoralist*. 1902. Trans. Richard Howard. Reprint, New York: Vintage, 1970. Trans. of *L'immoraliste*.

Hindley, John. *Persian Lyrics, or Scattered Poems from the Diwan-i-Hafiz*. London: Harding, 1800.

Hyam, Ronald. *Empire and Sexuality: The British Experience*. Manchester, England: Manchester UP, 1990.

Kabbani, Rana. *Europe's Myths of Orient: Devise and Rule*. Macmillan, 1986.

———, ed. *The Passionate Nomad: The Diary of Isabelle Eberhardt*. Boston: Beacon, 1987.

Lahr, John. "Introduction." *The Orton Diaries*. New York: Perennial, 1986. 11–31.

Lane, Edward William. *An Account of the Manners and Customs of the Modern Egyptians*. 1833–35. Reprint, London: Alexander, 1898.

Lant, Antonia. "The Curse of the Pharoah; or, How Cinema Contracted Egyptomania." *October* 59 (1992): 86–112.

Lawrence, T. E. *Seven Pillars of Wisdom: A Triumph*. 1926. Reprint, London: Penguin, 1963.

———. *T. E. Lawrence: The Selected Letters*. Ed. Malcolm Brown. New York: Norton, 1988.

Layachi, Larbi. *A Life Full of Holes*. Trans. Paul Bowles. New York: Grove, 1982.

Lewis, Bernard. *The Arabs in History*. Rev. ed. New York: Torchbooks-Harper, 1960.

Lowe, Lisa. *Critical Terrains: French and British Orientalisms*. Ithaca, N.Y.: Cornell UP, 1991.

Lucey, Michael. "The Consequence of Being Explicit: Watching Sex in Gide's *Si le grain ne meurt*." *The Yale Journal of Criticism* 4 (1990): 174–92.

———. "Gide Writing Home from Africa, or From Biskra with Love." *Qui Parle* 4.2 (Spring 1991): 23–42.

Mack, John E. *A Prince of Our Disorder: The Life of T. E. Lawrence*. Boston: Little, 1976.

Mailer, Norman. *Ancient Evenings*. Boston: Little, Brown, 1983.

Mani, Lata, and Ruth Frankenberg. "The Challenge of *Orientalism*." *Economy and Society* May 1985: 174–92.

Maugham, Robin. *Escape from the Shadows*. New York: McGraw, 1973.

———. "Peter Burton Interviews Robin Maugham." *The Boy from Beirut and Other Stories*. San Francisco: Gay Sunshine, 1982. 109–60.

Mernissi, Fatima. *Beyond the Veil: Male-Female Dynamics in Modern Muslim Society*. Bloomington: Indiana UP, 1987.

Mitchell, Timothy. *Colonizing Egypt*. Cambridge: Cambridge UP, 1988.

Mohanty, Chandra Talpade. "Under Western Eyes: Feminist Scholarship and Colonial Discourses." *Third World Women and the Politics of Feminism*. Ed. Mohanty, Ann Russo, and Lourdes Torres. Bloomington: Indiana UP, 1991. 51–80.

Mrabet, Mohammed. *Love with a Few Hairs*. Trans. Paul Bowles. 1967. San Francisco: City Lights, 1986.

Naddaff, Sandra. *Arabesque: Narrative Structure and the Aesthetics of Repetition in* "The Thousand and One Nights." Evanston, Ill.: Northwestern UP, 1991.

Orton, Joe. *The Orton Diaries*. Ed. John Lahr. New York: Perennial-Harper, 1986.

Rossman, Parker. *Sexual Experience between Men and Boys: Exploring the Pederast Underground*. New York: Association, 1976.

Rycaut, Paul. *The Present State of the Ottoman Empire*. London: Starkey, 1668.

El Saadawi, Nawal. *The Hidden Face of Eve: Women in the Arab World*. London: Zed, 1980.

Said, Edward. *Orientalism*. New York: Vintage, 1979.

Schmitt, Arno. "Different Approaches to Male-Male Sexuality/Eroticism from Morocco to Usbekistan." Schmitt and Sofers, eds. 1–24.

Schmitt, Arno, and Jehoeda Sofers, eds. *Sexuality and Eroticism Among Males in Moslem Societies*. New York: Harrington Park, 1992.

Shaarawi, Huda. *Harem Years: Memoirs of an Egyptian Feminist*. London: Virago, 1986.

Sharpe, Jenny. "Figures of Colonial Resistance." *Modern Fiction Studies* 35 (1989): 137–55.

Silverman, Kaja. "White Skin, Brown Masks: The Double Mimesis, or, With Lawrence in Arabia." *Differences* 1.3 (1989): 3–54.

Sonnini, C. S. *Travels in Upper and Lower Egypt*. Trans. Henry Hunter. 3 vols. London: Stockdale, 1807.

Spivak, Gayatri Chakravorty. *In Other Worlds: Essays in Cultural Politics*. New York: Routledge, 1988.

Stewart, Angus. *Tangier: A Writer's Notebook*. London: Hutchinson, 1977.

Stewart, Desmond. *T. E. Lawrence*. New York: Harper & Row, 1977.

Sutor, Jacob [Dr. Jacobus X]. *Untrodden Fields of Anthropology: Observations on the Esoteric Manner and Customs of Semi-civilized Peoples*. 2 vols. Paris: Librairie de Medecine, Folklore et Anthropologie, 1898. Trans. of *L'Amour aux Colonies*.

Wickes, George. *Lawrence Durrell-Henry Miller: A Private Correspondence*. New York: Dutton, 1963.

Woodhull, Winifred. "Unveiling Algeria." *Genders* 10 (1991): 112–31.

CHAPTER THREE

Queer Resistance to (Neo-)colonialism in Algeria

JARROD HAYES

"[T]u es belle comme un comité de gestion . . ." [You are as beautiful as a self-management committee . . .] This, perhaps the most famous line in Algerian poetry in France, was written by the openly gay *pied noir* poet Jean Sénac on the occasion of Che Guevara's visit to a self-managed shop in the newly liberated Popular and Democratic republic of Algeria (*Citoyens de beauté* 15).[1] Officially classified as French by the colonial bureaucracy, Sénac always refused to consider himself as such. An ardent Algerian nationalist, he was an advisor to the Minister of Education under the Ben Bella government until its overthrow by Boumediène in 1965. In a later poem, "Constatract," which appeared in the posthumously published collection *dérisions et Vertige* containing a number of homoerotic poems, he rewrote the famous line: "Nous continuerons d'aimer/ De transcrire/ De tu es belle comme une rose/ A tu es beau comme un comité de gestion" (91). [We shall continue to love/ To transcribe/ From you are as beautiful as a rose/ To you are as beautiful as a self-management committee.] Though the new line has the same English translation, in the French it is distinguished by an important difference: the adjective "beautiful" has been changed from the feminine "belle," presumably to agree withe the understood antecedent "Algeria" (femi-

79

nine in French), to the masculine "beau," to agree this time with an
unnamed man (or, more likely, adolescent). The new line itself describes
the transformation of a cliché of romantic hetero love (you are as beautiful as a rose) into a revolutionary expression of gay desire (you are as
beautiful as a self-management committee). In addition, the well-known
expression of revolutionary enthusiasm (you [f.] are as beautiful as a
self-management committee) has also been transformed into, has
become a source of, an articulation of homosexual desire (you [m.] are
as beautiful as a self-management committee). Or perhaps the first version was already the second one in drag, and homosexual desire had
been a source of Sénac's revolutionary enthusiasm all along.[2]

The field of Lesbian and Gay Studies was preoccupied for many
years by the debate between so-called social constructionists and essen-
tialists. Presumably (and often social constructionists were the ones who
defined essentialism, since few scholars would ever self-identify as essen-
tialists), the latter believed that homosexuals and perhaps even gays and
lesbians had existed throughout history. The former asserted that homosexuality, like sexuality in general in Michel Foucault's paradigm, was a
modern construct, linked with the social, political, and economic transformations of the nineteenth century, when the terms "homo-" and
"heterosexuality" first appeared.[3] However, in the context of a wider
interdisciplinary discussion of transnationalism, late capitalism, multinational corporations, and economic globalization, it has become more
fashionable of late to speak of a so-called globalization of the modern
construct of homosexuality, which previously, was considered to be
uniquely Western. Whereas the model of gay identity that is supposedly
spreading like wildfire is often assumed to take the Stonewall rebellion
as its origin, the example of Sénac demonstrates that other insurrections
(in this case the Algerian one) can also serve as an origin of a politicized
lesbian or gay identity. In addition, this globalization of the hetero/homo
binary (since there can be no heterosexuality without homosexuality, the
globalization of the one cannot come without that of the other) is often
considered to flow (as if naturally) from economic globalization. However, when we talk of a "globalization of the hetero/ homo binarism,"
do we not assume too quickly that the same forces that create the globalization of heterosexuality also simultaneously produce the globalization of homosexuality? Put differently, the globalization of sexuality
may be as much a product of the much earlier colonial project as of late
capitalism, and contrary to the arguments of some homophobic versions

of nationalism, colonialism worked in part through an imposition of heterosexuality, not homosexuality. Likewise, anticolonial resistance sometimes took the form of a resistance to colonial heterosexuality, that is the form of an anticolonial homosexuality. In a Foucauldian understanding of Power, which recreates (sometimes recuperates) the possibilities of resistance to itself, making a distinction between a would-be imported homosexuality and a homosexuality *qua* resistance to an imported *heterosexuality* may seem pointless. But in a context where many nationalist discourses use the supposedly imported nature of homosexuality as a basis for exclusion from and marginalization (even extermination) within the Nation, such a distinction is worth making.

What the example of Jean Sénac and others taken from the Algerian context suggests is that, in this move to have what was previously considered to be uniquely Western and modern sweep across the face of the earth, the increasing conformity of same-sex desire to the so-called Western paradigm, might have as much to do with a resistance to neocolonial, late capitalist economic expansion, as with something imported by it. These examples also suggest that both social contructionist accounts of "non-Western" same-sex eroticism and accounts of the globalization of Western homosexuality equally rely on the same colonial (and now neocolonial) fantasies of the absolute otherness of the colonized person (or, in colonial discourse, the "native"). Most Western accounts of non-Western sexualities have more to do with defining Western sexuality than with describing, in this case, a so-called Islamic difference. So when, before the popularization of globalization, constructionist scholars claimed there was no such thing as homosexuality in the "Islamic world," they assumed that in the "West" there was. They in fact produced the obviousness of the existence of the Western hetero-homo binarism and naturalized it as something that could be assumed. One could also say that they produced an Islamic difference in order to *create* a Western homo-hetero binarism. (For theoretical models of this production of difference, one might consider Edward Said's account of "Orientalism" as a Western discourse that invents the Orient, or Homi K. Bhabha's notion of hybridity, the particular manifestation of colonial authority that produces cultural difference in order to be able, in turn, to discriminate against it.)[4] In that they assume the same constructionist difference, which is supposedly overridden by the forces of globalization, accounts that argue for the globalization of the "hetero-homo binarism" also risk sharing the same project.

In "Global Gaze/Global Gays," Dennis Altman describes "the emergence of a western-style politicized homosexuality in Asia" (417), often in conjunction with the arrival of international AIDS prevention campaigns. Two recent conferences signal a similar interest in the globalization of "Western-style" homosexuality: a panel entitled "The Globalization and Contestation of the Hetero-Homosexual Binarism" at the Inaugural Symposium of the Sawyer Seminar on Sexual Identities and Identity Politics, which occurred at the University of Chicago, 18–19 October 1997, and "Queer Globalization/Local Homosexualities: Citizenship, Sexuality, and the Afterlife of Colonialism," sponsored by the Center for Lesbian and Gay Studies 23–25 April 1998. What both titles have in common is a certain affinity with Stuart Hall's influential essay, "The Local and the Global: Globalization and Ethnicity," which is an important influence for discussions of sexual globalization. Further consideration of Hall's paradigm of globalization might also help us nuance certain assumptions in many such discussions. Hall first distinguishes between two types of globalization by associating the first, of the colonial sort, with England as a colonial power (one might also consider how France might fit into this paradigm), and the second, of the neo- or postcolonial—even postmodern—sort, whose paradigm is represented by the U.S. In his discussion of globalization, what he calls "the local" introduces a huge complication, for it is a site of resistance. The title of the first conference cited above, while affirming the existence of a globalization of Western-style sexualities (i.e. the hetero-homo binary that defines them) suggests, like Hall, that there is also a resistance to this globalization. The second title associates Hall's global/local binary with another, queer/homosexualities. It also associates "queer" with globalization and the more modern (and therefore less postmodern) "homosexualities" with the local, which in Hall's account, marks the resistance of "traditional" cultures to the forces of globalization. The second title implies that "traditional" forms of same-sex sexual behavior are capable of resisting more "Western" ones, which further suggests that the proponents of globalization may be borrowing social constructionist accounts of what constitutes "Western homosexuality" without questioning them. (Paradoxically, in the second title, "queer" has replaced "homosexuality" as a uniquely Western construct, and "homosexuality" has become the general term for any indigenous same-sex sexual behavior.) While in the first title, homosexuality (along with heterosexuality) is globalized, in the second, traditional forms of homosexuality resist sexual globalization. I, however, would suggest not only that "traditional" forms of same-sex sexual behavior resist globalization, but also that what has been called the globalization of homosexuality (suggested by the first title) is itself a form of resistance. In other words, resistance to globalization affects each half of the hetero/homo binary unequally; it is in fact the homo that resists the hetero globalizing moves of late (and not-so-late) capitalism. An alternative interpretation of the second title might argue that the notion of globalization should itself be queered, a possibility whose exploration is the task of this essay.

At this point, I should perhaps clarify that I do not think the "globalization of the hetero-homo binarism" is not a helpful concept. "Global" is not the same as "universal"; the "hetero-homo binarism" may be more and more global, but it is far from universal, both in North Africa (or the Maghreb) and the "West." Likewise, certain aspects of the "hetero-homo binary" may not be all that new in the Maghreb; that is, they may have existed in Maghrebian society before the globalizing trends of late capitalism. As Stephen O. Murray and Will Roscoe point out, most constructionist accounts of "Islamic homosexualities" imply a narrative of sexual progress: "Despite their pessimistic post-humanist disavowals, social constructionist accounts still evoke a history of homosexuality as a progressive, even teleological, evolution from premodern repression, silence and invisibility to modern visibility and social freedom" (*Islamic Homosexualities* 5). Such narratives of progress, which combine economic development and sexual evolution in their own interesting way, assume that Muslims, to put it bluntly, are sexually underdeveloped. In a parallel way, I think it would be very easy to make the same assumptions in articulating the "globalization of the hetero-homo binarism." This globalization, corresponding as it does to the economic flows of late, multinational capitalism, implies its own narrative of progress. Again, I want to stress that I am not in favor of junking this narrative; I merely want us to consider what is at stake in the articulation of such paradigms: who benefits from them, who does not.

Altman avoids many of the dangers of current discussions of globalization by carefully questioning the clichés of what constitutes "traditional" Asian same-sex desire in Western studies of the region as well as the so-called differences between Western and Asian "homosexualities." He also points out that the emergence of a new style of homosexuality has not pushed out the more "traditional" one. In *Epistemology of the Closet*,

Eve Kosofsky Sedgwick also "show[s] how issues of modern homo/het-
erosexual definition are structured, not by the supersession of one model
and the consequent withering away of another, but instead by the relations
enabled by the unrationalized coexistence of different models during the
times they do coexist." Rather than proposing alternatives to Foucault's
paradigm shift she attempts to "denarrativize" his "valuable narratives"
with the aim "to denaturalize the present, rather than the past—in effect,
to render less destructively presumable 'homosexuality as we know it
today'" (47–48). Sedgwick's approach is particularly helpful in a consideration of current discussions of the globalization of homosexuality,
because "past" and "present" here could also be read as "Western" and
"non-Western." It is also important for us to render less destructively presumable homosexuality (and heterosexuality for that matter) as we know
it in the West. How many accounts, for example, of what is often called
"egalitarian homosexuality" (i.e. homosexuality as we know it in the
West) can also account for butch-femme, tops, bottoms, femme tops,
butch bottoms, S/M, drag kings and queens, transies, etc.?

In "Race, Sexual Politics, and Black Masculinity," Kobena Mercer
and Isaac Julian have described how the construction of modern Western sexualities coincided with a colonial project:

> Historically, The European construction of sexuality coincides with
> the epoch of imperialism and the two inter-connect. Imperialism
> justified itself by claiming that it had a civilising mission—to lead
> the base and ignoble savages and "inferior races" into culture and
> godliness. The person of the savage was developed as the Other of
> civilisation and one of the first "proofs" of this otherness was the
> nakedness of the savage, the visibility of his sex. This led Europeans
> to assume that the savage possessed an open, frank and uninhibited
> "sexuality"—unlike the sexuality of the European which was con-
> sidered to be fettered by the weight of civilisation. (106–7)

Likewise, when Deleuze and Guattari described "oedipalization" as a
part of colonization, they pointed out that colonialism attempted to
impose its own set of family values on colonized peoples by taking away
the extended family's political and economic functions:

> The colonizer says: your father is your father and nothing else, or
> your maternal grandfather—don't go taking them for chiefs; you

> can go have yourself triangulated [te faire triangular] in your corner, and place your house between those of your paternal and maternal kin; your family is your family and nothing else; [social] reproduction no longer passes through those points [ne passe plus par là], although we rightly need your family to furnish a material that will be subjected to a new order of reproduction. . . . To the degree that there is oedipalization, it is due to colonization. . . . (168–69; 199 in the original)

For concrete examples of colonialist family values, one need only think of the treatment of "sodomites" by *conquistadores* in the New World, or, in the Algerian case, French attacks on Algerian kinship structures through a systematic dismantling of precolonial property structures, as described by Marnia Lazreg in *The Emergence of Classes in Algeria.*

The two most recent Western studies of what researchers have chosen to label "Islamic homosexualities" are insufficient to account for the multiple manifestations of same-sex desire in Maghrebian literature, and are, if not directly contradicted by Maghrebian studies on sexuality, at least shown to be only partial accounts.[5] These two studies are *Sexuality and Eroticism among Males in Moslem Societies* edited by Arno Schmitt and Jehoeda Sofer, and *Islamic Homosexualities* by Stephen O. Murray and Will Roscoe. Schmitt writes, "But in these societies there are no 'homosexuals'—there is no word for 'homosexuality'—the concept is completely unfamiliar. There are no heterosexuals either" (5). Although Murray and Roscoe "challenge the dominant, Eurocentric model of gay/lesbian history and the implicit, occasionally explicit, assertion in many social constructionist accounts that contemporary homosexuality is somehow incomparable to any other pattern (or that there are no other patterns)" (5), although they have articulated a much more helpful account of "Islamic homosexualities" (which definitely pluralizes Schmitt's paradigm), they have assumed that, first of all, there is such a thing as "Islamic homosexualities" and that there is something that sets "Islamic homosexualities" apart from "non-Islamic homosexualities" other than the religion of their practitioners. (For purposes of comparison, one might think of how useful a book entitled "Christian homosexualities" would be.)

Schmitt has based his argument that "there are no 'homosexuals'" in the Arab world on the fact that "there is no social role of man-wants-to-fuck-male-and-wants-to-get-fucked-by-another-male," i.e., there is no Arabic word for men who both fuck and get fucked (5–6). Murray counters, "[T]his is hardly surprising. I do not know of such a verb in English or any other language" ("The Will" 33). Presumably, however, Schmitt means words like "gay" or "homosexual" which do not distinguish between active and passive partners. Writing in French, as many Maghrebian writers show, makes it easy to get around this supposed shortcoming of Arabic, and there is no absence of homosexuals in Maghrebian novels. In addition, Schmitt's argument ignores the fact that, for example, the French use of "gay" and "homosexual" (which are of Anglo-American and German origins respectively) has never been used to argue that homosexuality is somehow intrinsically foreign to French culture. The Moroccan writer Abdelhak Serhane, however, shows that even if one ignores the shortcomings of Schmitt's argument, it can still be proven false. In *Messaouda* (1983), Serhane not only provides a representation of "egalitarian homosexuality," but he also seems to contradict Schmitt's argument head on. *Messaouda*'s narrator describes homosexual incidents from his childhood as follows:

> Dans ce vast terrain réservé aux ordures chrétiennes, nous nous masturbions collectivement ou bien, à la limite de notre délire, nous violions de force l'un d'entre nous; le plus jeune ou le plus faible. Quand les forces étaient égales, nous procédions tout simplement à la *nouiba* (à chacun son tour). (133–34)
>
> [In this vast area reserved for Christian rubbish, we masturbated together and even, at the height of our frenzy, raped one of the group—the weakest or the youngest. If we were all equally matched we simply did the *nouiba* (one by one). (106–7)]

Though the novel is written in French, a language that Schmitt argues has plenty of words to describe "egalitarian homosexuality," none of these words seems to suffice for the narrator, who chooses an Arabic one in its place. Though the glossary of Arabic words (for which the translator thanks Paul Bowles) appended to the English translation of the novel defines "nouiba" as an explicitly sexual term ("homosexual act in which each of the two partners sodomizes the other, in turn" [154]), the Algerian writer Assia Djebar uses the word in the title of her film *La nouba des femmes du Mont Chenoua* and has described it as having a double meaning, that of a musical term in Andalusian music and of a group conversation in which participants take turns speaking.[6] So while "nouiba," as used by Serhane, may not quite be the word that would satisfy Schmitt's requirements, particularly since it is used here to apply to boys and not adults, it does question Schmitt's assertion that the notion of "egalitarian homosexuality" is totally foreign to Muslim societies. If Murray's assertion that no other language has a word for both fucking and getting fucked is true, Maghrebian dialects of Arabic may be the unique ones that do.

One of the clichés in many Western accounts of homosexuality in the "Islamic world" is that Arab and/or Muslim men find homosex more available with foreigners (especially Western tourists). Schmitt writes:

> In the eyes of the orientals [n.b.!] even many European male tourists appear to be feminine; their white, soft skin and polite urban behavior make them less virile. To bugger "whites" is psychologically especially attractive because, on the one hand, they represent the rich, strong, exploiting West, and, on the other hand, they are strangers, i.e., weak and "helpless."
>
> Normally the oriental youth or man gets paid for these "services"—with cash, food, entry fees, or gifts. The tourist even offers the possibility of getting buggered without "anybody" knowing about it. ("Different Approaches" 20)

The supposed attraction of Muslim men towards Westerners as described by Schmitt actually has more to do with defining physical beauty as white than with describing why sex with Western tourists is such a predominant paradigm of same-sex encounters. Not only does he not consider the colonial and neocolonial implications of many if not most of these encounters, but he also ridicules any anticolonial critique that the "Orientals," as he calls them, might articulate.

One finds similar preoccupations in the commentary of Jerry Zarit:

> Western gay men, like Western technology, filled a need in rapidly developing Iran. . . . [Iranians] had lived deprived lives for centuries, but now they were suddenly made aware of their frustrations. Westerners had a combined sexual, economic, and political appeal for Iranians. Because Western gay men provided the often needed secrecy (being an outsider who did not know the language

and could not blab to friends and family) and availability (after all,
someone had to take the scorned feminine role), they fitted in very
nicely. If they had light hair and skin, all the better, for these features
were in high demand. (59)

Again, the author constructs himself not only as an object of desire, but
also of beauty, more beautiful than the "natives," and he projects this
racist aesthetic hierarchy onto the psyches of Iranians. The West, in this
account, brings progress and modernity to Iranians, and one mode of
this civilizing mission is homosexual intercourse. For the author, then,
homosex with the "natives" plays an important role in the narrative
progress that constitutes the West's civilizing mission, and therefore,
(neo-)colonialism; it is, in short, part of the white man's burden.

Like Zarit, Gianni De Martino, derives his "scholarly" observations on "Islamic homosexuality" from his own sexual experience with
Muslim men: "Moroccans often tell you that homosexuality is only due
to the foreigners and that 'scarcely a handful' of local young men engage
in it—imitating the tourists. Later you find out that sodomy is very common. . . . It is common for a young man to prostitute himself for a movie
ticket, a few nickels, or a small gift. Tourist homosexuality simply fits
into this traditional pattern without changing it a lot" (25). For De Martini, homosexual tourism is justifiable in Morocco because it merely fits
into a practice that exists already. In "Sleeping with the Natives as a
Source of Data," Stephen O. Murray comments on such descriptions of
same-sex encounters in other cultures:

> [I]t seems to me very dangerous to extrapolate from the sexual
> experiences of a foreigner in a culture to the ordinary cultural
> understandings and behaviors there. Leaving the discussion of
> ethics to others, I raise this as a point of epistemology to those sup-
> posedly "understanding" homosexuality by their own sexual expe-
> riences in other societies (particularly impoverished ones). From
> experiences with young persons experimenting outside their usual
> world, foreigners easily overestimate the sexual role flexibility *in* a
> culture. Being in a foreign society, and in "intimate contact" with
> one or more natives, alien observers may not realize that their sex-
> ual partners in a significant sense are not playing by the usual rules
> of their sexual culture. Rather than penetrating the mysteries of
> another culture's sexual lifeways, both may be outside their own
> cultures in an *interculture*. . . . The decultured unreality of such

cross-cultural sexual encounters does not provide reassurance about the reality of interrogation about sexual behavior or sexual identity. (49–50)[7]

While I would question the notion that sex with a tourist, for a "native," is somehow less authentic, Murray correctly points out that the two partners in such an encounter will or may have completely different interpretations or understandings of the act.[8]

The above accounts all imply that Muslims are incapable of what many Western scholars have labeled "egalitarian" homosexuality, i.e., the kind of same-sex sexual behaviors that distinguish the modern West from other geopolitical and historical contexts. Many such scholars rely on a sort of typology to distinguish between various manifestations of same-sex sexual behavior. In *The Construction of Homosexuality*, for example, David F. Greenberg writes, "It is useful in discussing homosexuality to distinguish several different forms on the basis of the relative social statuses of the participants . . . —*transgenerational* (in which the partners are of disparate ages), *transgenderal* (the partners are of different genders), and *egalitarian* (the partners are socially similar). A fourth pattern [exists], in which partners belong to different social classes" (25). This vocabulary is precisely the tool by which a non-Western difference has been produced in social constructionist discourses and one need not be a social constructionist or Foucauldian to use such a typography.[9] Murray and Roscoe's essays perhaps rely on this typology even more than Schmitt and Sofer's anthology. As in many Western accounts of "Islamic" or Arabic homosexualities, Murray and Roscoe draw on several paradigms to conceptualize a so-called Islamic difference, the European medieval concept of sodomy (which also appears in Islamic theological discourses, as Schmitt points out so thoroughly) and the Greek institution of pederasty. Like sodomy, the paradigm of cross-generational models of homosexuality such as pederasty describes a sexual identity based not on a hetero/homo binary, but on an active/passive one. According to Roscoe, in fact, "Islam inherited from the civilizations of this region [from the Mediterranean to insular southeast Asia] both *status-differentiated* patterns of male homosexuality and *gender-defined* alternative roles for non-masculine males whose sexual partners were usually other males" ("Precursors" 55). The model of pederasty ("status-differentiated") shares with sodomy ("gender-defined") the notion that a man can be masculine as long as he is the active partner. It is the passive partner who is more associated with the feminine and whose sexuality, in the case of an adult citizen, is non-normative. In the Greek model, this passive role was degrading to free adult citizens, which therefore left slaves, boys, foreigners, and of course women to fill the position.[10] Within the sexual act one is thus forced to note the number of coinciding hierarchies concerning gender, class, age, and inclusion in the political formation of the city-state.

One finds a similar coincidence of hierarchies in representations of same-sex sexual behavior in the postindependence Algerian novel by Rachid Boudjedra, *La répudiation* (1969), which contains some of the most explicit representations of homosex to date in Algerian literature in French.[11] When adult fishermen make love with boy cigarette vendors, when the narrator has his buttocks fondled by unemployed dock workers at the beach in exchange for swimming lessons, is molested by an older man who masturbates in front of him at the community oven, and gets fucked (this time with his own consent) by the Qur'anic school master, the same "transgenerational," "transgendered," and "status-differentiated" hierarchies are at work. Thus, the novel might seem to confirm the clichés of Western accounts of "Islamic homosexualities." There is, however, a minor complication, the narrator's brother Zahir. In one scene, the whole family watches in amazement as Zahir fucks a buddy on the rooftop terrace. Zahir is also in love with his Jewish teacher, *heimatlos* (meaning "without a homeland" in German), who is labeled by the novel as homosexual, a word that occurs a number of times in *La répudiation*. The diverse paradigms of homosexuality represented in Boudjedra's novel therefore resist to-date Western attempts to define and categorize "Islamic homosexualities." In addition, the "Western-style" homosexual character Zahir appears long before contemporary discussions of homosexual globalization. According to Schmitt, Zahir should not exist; he also directly contradicts Murray's account of "Islamic homosexualities." In "The Will Not to Know: Islamic Accommodations of Male Homosexuality," Murray, using as one example the requirement in Islamic law of four credible, adult male eyewitnesses to prosecute for sodomy, argues that "there is a common Islamic ethos of avoidance in acknowledging sex and sexualities. . . . Usually in Arab and other Islamic societies, everyone successfully avoids public recognition (let alone discussion!) of deviations from normative standards—sexual or other" (14–15). While Murray's description may apply to certain official discourses (orthodox Muslim, fundamentalist opposition, ruling nation-

alist), it obviously cannot account for a great portion of Maghrebian literature in French (as well as a number of works written in Arabic),
which offers good examples of a counterdiscourse to precisely the dominant paradigm Murray describes. While Murray takes odds with some
aspects of more unabashedly procolonial Western accounts of Islamic
homosexualities (such as Schmitt's), his description of a "will not to
know," which he supposedly penetrates,[12] is not so different from
Schmitt's, De Martini's, and Zarit's discussion of the secrecy that sex
with foreigners supposedly allows for Muslim men. In fact, Murray displays a will to know that is quite similar to Schmitt's in the latter's
explicit declaration that the knowledge his study provides will be helpful to other tourists: "This collection . . . should be of benefit to anybody
in contact with Arabs, Turks, or Persians—be it as a tourist in Moslem
countries, a social worker 'in charge' of immigrants, or just as a friend
of an immigrant" ("Preface" xiv). In spite of major differences between
Schmitt's and Murray and Roscoe's collections, I think that they share
this common project of the production of Western homosexuality. Murray does not consider how one might find this will not to know strikingly similar to what "we" call the closet, as characterized by the "open
secret" in Eve Kosofsky Sedgwick's formulation, which makes *me* wonder how much the closet has influenced his thinking on "Islamic homosexualities," or conversely, how much he has exaggerated this supposed
Islamic difference. In defiance of Murray's "will not to know," Boudjedra's narrator directs a very heterosexual "will *to* know" at his brother.
In spite of a number of childhood digressions, the narrator tries to assert
his own heterosexuality in contradistinction to his brother's sexuality,
which he attempts to understand through a strongly pronounced will to
know his (homosexual) other.

     In addition, the novel's sexual politics are also decidedly anticolo-
nial. The narrator's father Si Zoubir, or "Mr. Prick" in Arabic,[13] a rather
wealthy merchant, is the personification of an indigenous elite's collaboration with French colonialism as well as of its role in neocolonial
oppression. He is friends with all the French judges before the revolution, a member of the Secret Members of the Clan (an obvious representation of the FLN), who resemble the colonizers more and more after
the revolution that brings them to power, and he increasingly becomes a
fundamentalist critic of the Secret Members. Thus the novel not only
associates the post-independence elite with the former colonizer in a
Fanonian way, but also predicts the collaboration between the ruling

elite and fundamentalists in a rather uncanny way. Zahir, in his hatred
for his own father, is also the main site of resistance to neocolonialism,
and the novel's politics associate sexual resistance with a postindependence critique of neocolonialism and fundamentalism. The novel was
published in 1969, the same year as the Stonewall uprising, which is
often cited as an origin of a global lesbian and gay movement. Yet one
can find, in the same year, and even earlier, representations of queer
resistance in Algerian culture.

In an article that appeared in the 1996 Lesbian and Gay Pride issue
of *Le Monde*, an Algerian artist writing under the pseudonym of Anis
described an aborted attempt to organize a lesbian and gay movement
in Algeria in the late 1980s in the context of a newly acquired freedom
of the press and multiparty system. While he did not say so directly, Anis
implied that the collaboration between the quasi-military governing
elite, what some have called the *mafia politico-financière*, and its
increasingly violent fundamentalist opposition foreclosed the possibility
of a lesbian and gay movement modeled on the Algerian feminist organizations that were actively resisting changes in the family code. As
Sénac's example foresaw, the Algerian lesbian and gay movement
described by Anis would not have been an imitation of the American one
but would have been firmly situated in Algeria's revolutionary history; it
would have been one form of resistance to both the postindependence
elite and its fundamentalist opposition in the tradition established by
Boudjedra. Many Algerian intellectuals and other commentators have
also suggested a similar collaboration and have argued that the austere
economic policies of the World Bank and the IMF created a situation
that made the fundamentalist party's promises attractive to many Alge-
rians. Rather than bringing homosexuality to Algeria, therefore, the
forces of economic globalization may actually have homophobic effects.

In addition to thinking about how the U.S. may or may not be
exporting its model of lesbian and gay identity politics, I would thus
urge us to also consider how its neocolonial economic policies may actually prevent the organization of *local* lesbian and gay movements such
as the one that *could* have happened in Algeria. The film *Bab-el-Oued
City*, directed by Merzak Allouache, which describes fundamentalist
intimidation in the Algiers neighborhood by the same name, is *about*, if
nothing else, a political analysis of the current Algerian situation. In
addition to the analyses of other intellectuals mentioned above, which
the film seems to support, *Bab-el-Oued City* also suggests that one

source of empowerment for the fundamentalist opposition came from Algerian volunteers in Afghanistan returning to Algeria. We are currently seeing the fruit of the U.S.-armed opposition to the Soviet-supported government in Afghanistan, and one could also consider what the climate might now be like there for sodomites, lesbians, gays, drag queens and/or other queers. We *have* seen what it has been like for adulterers. *Bab-el-Oued City* suggests that part of those American-supplied arms have found their way back into Algeria. Rachid, one member of the neighborhood gang of fundamentalist vigilantes, brags to schoolboys about his valor on the field of battle in Afghanistan. The gun he describes using, the Kalashnikov, is also the one the gang refers to when speaking of the future armed conflict (that, alas, is already an actuality in Algeria).

It is precisely after the bragging scene that Rachid takes leave of his audience to spy on Boualem, the novel and film's protagonist, whose theft of the Mosque loudspeaker (because the Imam's sermons were depriving him of sleep) sets off the cycle of violence depicted in the narrative. Boualem has arranged a rendezvous with Yamina, sister of Said, leader of the fundamentalist gang. Rachid witnesses Yamina's removal of her headscarf at Boualem's request and reports the entire incident to Said. Said, the self-appointed police of public morality, is also a sex police. He enforces the veiling and seclusion of his sister, and with armed force he expels from the neighborhood a single woman living alone. Yet this woman's space, whose parameters are enforced by men, is also the space of a resistance that is also sexual. In secrecy, women read Harlequin romances, watch soap operas (in defiance of Said's opposition), and gossip. It is the space where women are entertained by the queeny imitations by Didine, who knows all the lines of American soap operas by heart. In the novel, it is also the space where Lynda, the enterprising woman who rents out all these romances, and Aïcha engage in a passionate lesbian affair (which the film only hints at).

The West has no monopoly (to use an economic term) on homosexuality. This might seem to be an argument in favor of the globalization of homosexuality, but Sénac, Boudjedra's novel, Anis's essay, and *Bab-el-Oued City* raise the question as to whether, when we speak of the globalization of the hetero/homo binary, we, too, are complicit with the flows of late-capitalism or whether we situate our analyses in resistance to it. Does arguing for globalization mean articulating an argument that maintains globalization is already happening, one that argues in favor of making it happen, or one that makes it happen, so to speak, through its discursive production of a difference that must precede the erosion of difference implied in the notion of globalization. I would suggest that these three possibilities are, in fact, inseparable. For to say that there is "globalization of the hetero-homo binarism" assumes that this binarism can already be used to describe us. U.S. queer activists might therefore more appropriately look to the tropes of queer resistance to colonialism, neocolonialism, and postindependence nationalized oppression in Algerian cultural politics for sources of inspiration for a renewed antiimperialist queer politics rather than always assuming the history of U.S. lesbian, gay, bisexual, transgender, and/or queer resistance holds a monopoly on inspiration for a global queer politics.

NOTES

I would like to thank Ross Chambers, Nancy K. Miller, and Francesca Canadé Sautman for their readings of this material and their helpful suggestions.

1. A *pied noir* is a person of French (or European) descent born in Algeria. Sénac's mother was Spanish, and his father's origins are uncertain.

2. For a biography of Sénac, see Péroncel-Hugoz.

3. For the most complete account of the social constructionist/ essentialist debate with regards to sexual orientation, see Stein. Foucault elaborated his paradigm in *La volonté de savior*. Some scholars have pushed back the date or have found "roots" for modern homosexuality in previous periods (see, for example, Trumbach). For the strictest social constructionist account along these lines, see Halperin, *One Hundred Years of Homosexuality*, whose title speaks for itself.

4. See Said, *Orientalism*. For Bhabha's definition of hybridity, see "Signs Taken for Wonders" 112–116.

5. For Maghrebian accounts, see Bouhdiba, Chebel, and Serhane.

6. She explained the term in an untitled lecture given at the 1997 ALA conference (see Works Cited).

7. This essay is a review of Joseph Itiel's *Philippine Diary: A Gay Guide to the Philippines* (San Francisco: International Wavelength, 1989).

8. I owe this formulation to discussions with Randolph Trumbach.

9. I would not accuse Greenberg of using his typology to this end. Because of its wealth and diversity of examples, his study clearly demonstrates

that the practices of same-sex sexual behavior throughout history and across cultures always exceed such frameworks. For a more in-depth discussion of typologies see Donaldson and Dynes. For Dyne's own vehement anti-constructionist position, see "Wrestling with the Social Boa Constructor."

10. The bibliography on this question is extensive. See Halperin, Dover, Greenberg 141–51, Winkler, and the later volumes of Foucault's *Histoire de la sexualité,* for some examples.

11. Elsewhere, I have analyzed this novel extensively with close readings of many of the passages referred to here. I shall not repeat those analyses here, but instead refer the reader to "Approches de l'homosexualité et de l'homoérotisme chez Boudjedra, Mammeri et Sebbar," "Rachid O. and the Return of the Homopast," and "Homosexuality (Un)veiled."

12. N.b. his use of the word "penetrate" to describe what does not happen when one "sleeps with the natives" ("Sleeping with the Natives" 50, quoted above).

13. Abdel-Jaouad 22–23.

WORKS CITED

Abdel-Jaouad, Hédi. "'Too Much in the Sun': Sons, Mothers, and Impossible Alliances in Francophone Maghrebian Writing." *RAL* 27.3: 15–33

Allouache, Merzak. *Bab el-Oued.* Trans. Angela M. Brewer. Boulder. Colo.: Reinner, 1998.

Altman, Dennis. "Global Gaze/Global Gays." *GLQ* 3 (1997): 417–36.

Bab-el-Oued City. Dir. Merzak Allouache. Algeria/France, 1994.

Bhabha, Homi K. "Signs Taken for Wonders: Questions of Ambivalence and Authority under a Tree in Delhi, May 1817." *The Location of Culture.* London: Routledge, 1994. 102–122.

Boudjedra, Rachid. *La répudiation.* Paris: Denoël, 1969.

———. *The Repudiation.* Trans. Golda Lambrova. Colorado Springs: Three Continents, 1995.

Bouhdiba, Abdelwahab. *La sexualité en Islam.* Paris: Presses Universitaires de France, 1975.

Chebel, Malek. *L'esprit de sérail: Mythes et pratiques sexuelles au Maghreb.* Paris: Payot, 1995.

Deleuze, Gilles, and Félix Guattari. *L'anti-Œdipe.* Paris: Minuit, 1972.

——. *Anti-Oedipus: Capitalism and Schizophrenia*. Trans. Robert Hurley, Mark Seem, and Helen R. Lane. Minneapolis: U of Minnesota P, 1983.

De Martino, Gianni. "An Italian in Morocco." Trans. Arno Schmitt. Schmitt and Sofer, 25–32.

Djebar, Assia. Untitled lecture. African Literature Association Conference. East Lansing, Mich., 18 April 1997.

Donaldson, Stephen, and Wayne R. Dynes. "Typology of Homosexuality." Vol. 2 of *Encyclopedia of Homosexuality*. Ed. Wayne R. Dynes. New York: Garland, 1990. 1332–37. 2 vols.

Dover, K. J. *Greek Homosexuality*. 1978. Reprint, Cambridge: Harvard UP, 1989.

Dynes, Wayne R. "Wrestling with the Social Boa Constructor." *Forms of Desire: Sexual Orientation and the Social Contructionist Controversy*. Ed. Edward Stein. New York: Garland, 1990. 209–38.

Foucault, Michel. *Histoire de la sexualité*. 3 vols. Paris: Gallimard, 1976–84.

Greenberg, David F. *The Construction of Homosexuality*. Chicago: U of Chicago P, 1988.

Hall, Stuart. "The Local and the Global: Globalization and Ethnicity." *Dangerous Liaisons: Gender, Nation, and Postcolonial Perspectives*. Ed. Anne McClintock and Ella Shohat. Minneapolis: U of Minnesota P, 1997. 173–87.

Halperin, David. *One Hundred Years of Homosexuality and Other Essays on Greek Love*. New York: Routledge, 1990.

Hayes, Jarrod. "Approches de l'homosexualité et de l'homoérotisme chez Boudjedra, Mammeri et Sebbar." *Présence Francophone* 43 (1993): 149–80.

——. "Rachid O. and the Return of the Homopast: The Autobiographical as Allegory in Childhood Narratives by Maghrebian Men." *Sites: The Journal of 20th-Century/Contemporary French Studies* 1.2 (1997): 497–526.

——. "Homosexuality (Un)veiled." Chapter 3 of *Queer Nations: Sexual Subversions of National Identity in Maghrebian Literature in French*. Chicago: U of Chicago P. Forthcoming.

Lazreg, Marnia. *The Emergence of Classes in Algeria: A Study of Colonialism and Socio-Political Change*. Boulder, Colo.: Westview, 1976.

Mercer, Kobena, and Isaac Julien. "Race, Sexual Politics, and Black Masculinity: A Dossier." *Male Order: Unwrapping Masculinity*. Ed. Rowena Chapman and Jonathon Rutherford. London: Lawrence and Wishart, 1988. 97–164.

Murray, Stephen O. "Sleeping with the Natives as a Source of Data." *Society of Lesbian and Gay Anthropologists' Newsletter* 13 (1991): 49–51.

———. "The Will Not to Know: Islamic Accommodations of Male Homosexualities." In Murray and Roscoe 14–54.

Murray, Stephen O., and Will Roscoe, eds. and intro. *Islamic Homosexualities: Culture, History, and Literature.* New York: New York UP, 1997.

Péroncel-Hugoz, Jean-Pierre. *Assassinat d'un poète.* Marseille: Editions du Quai/Jeanne Laffite, 1983.

Roscoe, Will. "Precursors of Islamic Male Homosexuality." In Murray and Roscoe 55–87.

Said, Edward W. *Orientalism.* New York: Vintage, 1978.

Schmitt, Arno. "Different Approaches to Male-Male Sexuality/Eroticism from Morocco to Usbekistan." In Schmitt and Sofer 1–24.

———. "Preface." In Schmitt and Sofer xiii–xiv.

Schmitt, Arno, and Jeheoda Sofer, eds. *Sexuality and Eroticism Among Males in Moslem Societies.* New York: Haworth, 1992.

Sedgwick, Eve Kosofsky. *Epistemology of the Closet.* Berkeley: U of California P, 1990.

Sénac, Jean. *Citoyens de beauté.* Charlieu: Bartaville, 1997.

———. *dérisions et vertige.* Arles, France: Actes Sud, 1983.

Serhane, Abdelhak. *Messaouda.* Paris: Seuil, 1983.

———. *Messaouda.* Trans. Mark Thompson. Manchester, England: Carcanet, 1986.

———. *L'amour circoncis.* Casablanca: Eddif, 1995.

Stein, Edward, ed. *Forms of Desire: Sexual Orientation and the Social Constructionist Controversy.* New York: Garland, 1990.

Trumbach, Randolph. "The Birth of the Queen: Sodomy and the Emergence of Gender Equality in Modern Culture, 1660–1750." *Hidden from History: Reclaiming the Gay and Lesbian Past.* Ed. Martin Bauml Duberman, Martha Vicinus, and George Chauncey Jr. New York: Penguin, 1989. 129–40.

Winkler, John J. *The Constraints of Desire: The Anthropology of Sex and Gender in Ancient Greece.* New York: Routledge, 1990.

Zarit, Jerry. "Intimate Look of the Iranian Male." In Schmitt and Sofer 55–60.

CHAPTER FOUR

TOM, DII AND *ANJAREE*

"Women Who Follow Nonconformist Ways"

JILLANA ENTEEN

Anjaree is the only Thai organization specifically targeting women who love women. Headquartered in Bangkok, it has members throughout Thailand, providing information, encouraging community formation, and sponsoring social events for Thai women who love women. In Thai, *Anjaree* means "women who follow nonconformist ways." Despite the organization's entrenchment among Thailand's women who love women—it has existed for over a decade and boasts a membership of over five hundred—its founder, spokesperson, and leader, Anjana Suvarnananda complains that she is at a loss for words, in Thai and in English, that adequately describe her identity as a woman who loves women following nonconformist ways. At the Sixth International Conference for Thai Studies, she presented a new Thai word that she created, *yingrakying,* hoping it will circulate as a new word for women "who have erotic feelings or love feelings for other women." While Anjana often invokes the word lesbian when portraying herself and members of her organization to *farang* (Westerners), she avoids the term if given the opportunity to describe the site specific situation in Thailand.[1] When speaking in Thai and to Thai people, she resists using the word lesbian. Though widely understood, many Thais, including those involved in women-centered relationships, consider it vulgar and derogatory. When talking to Thais, Anjana employs and revises the commonly used Thai words for women who love women. Rather than perpetuating the use of these established terms and the stereotypes that accompany them, Anjana addresses the changing situations of Thai women who love women. At this meeting she stated: "We are not sure if this [new] term will go down well or if this will be the term we stick to or not. We are in the process of building our own culture and terminologies" (Suvar-nananda "Lesbianism").

The motivation to formulate a new word is partially attributable to Anjana's experience with cultures outside Thailand. She spent time studying at the Hague, had access to Western ideas, and speaks almost fluent English. These extensive experiences inform her attempts to affect community formation by broadening the community's way of conceptualizing itself and its individual members. *Yingrakying* literally means "woman-loves-woman" in Thai, originating from the phrase currently *en vogue* with Western women-centered organizers and academics: "women who love women." Rather than adopting the English word and using it in Thai in the manner the word lesbian was employed, Anjana reformulates this phrase in order to match her own intentions through translation and transformation.[2] In this case, knowledge of the English language and *farang* ideas become tools rather than models for linguistic community formation. Her word becomes a strategy for interaction and community building that encourages shifting the way women imagine themselves according to changing circumstances. *Yingrakying* is more than a convenient new word to name something heretofore ignored—it signals an awareness of the effects of a global Western-based movement that is personalized for this increasingly outward looking Thai community.

By considering, as the editors of the special issue of *Social Text*, entitled "Queer Transexions," hold, "the interrelations of sexuality, race, and gender in a transnational context," I attempt "to bring the projects of queer, postcolonial, and critical race theories together" (Harper et al. 1). In the past decade feminist, sex, and gender theories have addressed the erasure of specific bodies in terms of race and class of individuals located in the West.[3] Even more recently, work has begun that extends this theorizing beyond Western culture and location and retheorizes according to localized situations.[4] Hence the notion of sexual identity is being complicated, but universalized assumptions of identity formation are still frequently applied unproblematically to non-Western cultures. As Dennis Altman explains, "It has become fashionable to point to the emergence of 'the global gay,' the apparent internationalization of a certain form of social and cultural identity based on homosexuality" ("Rupture" 77). While this "global gay" image is being produced by both the West and the East, and its embodiment can be seen at times in Bangkok, an international gay/lesbian is a fictive construction that has no literal embodiment, nor is it manifest in all social, political, and cultural contexts. Rather than mapping Western histories and theories unproblematically onto Thai bodies, new explanations based on the situations in Thailand must be devised. Examining the shifts in identity formation by a group of women existing in the heretofore geographic and sexual margins reveals the effects of the "globalization" of information and economies. Arjun Appadurai asserts that "[t]he new global cultural economy has to be seen as a complex, overlapping, disjunctive order that cannot any longer be understood in terms of existing center-periphery models."[5] He proposes that the relationship between five terms, or landscapes, that he creates establishes a framework for looking at these global cultural flows (*Modernity* 33).

Peter Jackson, Rosalind Morris, Thook Thook Thongthiraj, and Dennis Altman practice expanding the ways in which global and local cultures in Thailand are understood, reevaluating the usefulness of using Western theories of identification to describe Thai notions of sexuality. They look specifically at Thai history and chart changing representations of sexualities in response to cultural events. This chapter extends this work, examining the shifting positions of women in Bangkok over the past decade as a result of increasing opportunities for education and financial stability. It presents varied and conflicting accounts by *yingrakying* that delineate previously available positions, and then shows how Anjana and *Anjaree* suggest new possibilities through the creation of words and communities.

Anjaree's function as a social club where women could meet women provided the impetus for my increasing involvement during my tenure of research in Bangkok. I initially joined *Anjaree* for social reasons, having learned about it from another American woman living in Thailand. The Thai women who loved women that I knew who were not members of *Anjaree* were either friends from my previous stay in Thailand or friends of friends. I conducted interviews in May, June, and October 1996. Some of the examples cited occurred while socializing during the eight months previous to my decision to consider these inter-actions part of my research. Most contemporary ethnographic research combines these formal and informal procedures and methods for gath-ering information. While Carol, an American researcher who con-tributed to this study, asserts that socializing, pursuing relationships, and creating unusual or startling situations by asking abrupt questions or purposely violating Thai practices is integral and productive to her work, I employed more formal procedures, acquiring most of my infor-mation through interviews that took place, for the most part, in English. As I will explain in the section of this essay called "English Effects," using English for the interview processes encouraged the women to speak about identity and sexuality in ways that would not occur in a Thai language setting. Many Bangkok Thais, especially the young mid-dle class, associate English use with prosperity, the influx of daring new ideas, and an increased number of ways to articulate sexualities and gen-ders. Because English functions as a second language, it can provide a sense of freedom.

The position of *yingrakying* in Thailand has changed concurrently with the rest of Thai society, particularly Bangkok, over the last decade. Between 1986 and 1996, Thailand had one of the world's fastest grow-ing economies, producing a high volume and variety of export products which generated a per capita income that increased exponentially. Pros-perity had the largest impact on Bangkok residents, creating a burgeon-ing middle class. The majority of the members of this new middle class are college educated and have access to information from around the world via uncensored Internet access, imported entertainment and aca-demic media, and a large influx of *farang* tourists as well as those from other parts of Asia.[6] As a result, they possess an increasingly interna-tional outlook that is reflected in their tastes and consumption. Mobile phones, Western-made cars, and Western name brand clothing are pos-sessions *de rigeur* for Bangkok professionals. Not only are Western products consumed, but also "ideas, ideologies and politics" (Pasuk and Baker 409) from outside of Thailand.[7] However, while some practices and expectations changed to reflect increasing prosperity and exposure, many of Thailand's traditional societal values remained.

One societal custom that conformed to the increasing need for educated, middle class expertise was women's participation in business.

In addition to managing family finances, Thai women have often been entrepreneurs and salespeople. In accordance with previous Thai practices, women often fill the increasing demand for economic expertise. In the past decade, many women have entered the middle-class workforce, enjoying the broadening opportunities for education and individual economic security. As a result, marriage, the Thai presses repeatedly report, is no longer the primary concern of women in their twenties and thirties. Many women are opting for career success, job stability, and comfortable salaries before marriage and motherhood. Middle-class women, single, in their twenties and thirties, economically independent and educated, make up a large, visible part of the population of Bangkok women who love women.

Tom and Dii

The most common words to describe Thai women who love women, Tom and Dii, appeared about twenty years ago. Tom comes from the English word "tomboy" and Dii from the word "lady." These terms roughly coincide with the English terms butch and femme, respectively, when referring to lesbian positionings; however, they are neither mere imitations of their English derivatives nor of American descriptions of butch/femme dynamics.[8] While one woman who studied Women's Studies in the United States believes that the positions of Tom and Dii accent and prescribe normative Thai gender roles to a greater extreme than heterosexual relationships, most women assert that these positions serve to specifically illustrate and circumscribe the desires and roles of Thai women who love women.[9]

Altering English terms to name these distinctly Thai identities conforms to the Thai habit of adopting English words where no Thai word exists. For example, in the nineteenth century, when a couple was involved romantically, they would declare themselves married. No registration was required, but marriage was premised on a man's financial commitment in return for a woman's running a household and remaining sexually faithful. Over time, having "boyfriends" and "girlfriends" became possible social relationships that acknowledged interest yet did not entail specific commitments, and a new word emerged. The Thai word is *faen*—derived either from the English word "friend" or "fan." The meaning of this Thai word, however, does not directly reflect either

English referent. Rather, it named a situation occurring for which there were no preexisting lingual referents. Similarly, the Thai word *farang* comes from the French word "français," yet the Thai use the word *farang* to refer to most non-Asians, especially Europeans and Americans, in Thailand.[10] Anjana's attempt to coin a new word follows this same pattern, where, as Mikhail Bakhtin describes, words carry traces from their pasts and incorporate the changing histories of the use they receive: "language, for the individual consciousness, lies on the borderline between oneself and the other. The word in language is half someone else's. It becomes 'one's own' only when the speaker populates it with his own intention, his own accent, when he appropriates the word, adapting it to his own semantic and expressive intention" (23). These words are significantly altered in the process of cultural translation, yet they still retain traces of their original meanings. Rather than imitation or replication, the use of this word illustrates what Mary Louise Pratt terms "transculturation" whereby "members of subordinated or marginal groups select and invent from materials transmitted by a dominant or metropolitan culture" (Pratt 36). *Yingrakying* resonates differently in Thai than "women loving women" does in English: these terms have not been strung together before and consequently do not directly reflect the people and organizations that promote equal rights and acceptance for women loving women. Instead, this past is translated, and the history changes.[11]

Like the meaning of the terms Tom and Dii, their positions neither replicate/imitate Western butch/femme constructions nor do they exist entirely in isolation from Western forms of desire and societal positioning. The presence of intermediary or mutated positions is often overlooked in scholarship about gender and sexuality in nondominant cultures.[12] Recognizing this, Will Roscoe critiques scholarship about "gay" Native Americans that simplifies the depiction of Zuni genders instead of analyzing the ways in which they do not conform to a male/female binary. "Underlying these statements," he explains, "are assumptions about cultural change based on an either/or opposition of 'traditional' and 'assimilated'" (194). Rather than viewing Tom and Dii in this either/or framework, I will delineate many of the perceived parameters and particularities. Not only are the many kinds of same-sex relationships between women in Bangkok not contained by the terms Tom and Dii, the qualifications and definitions provided by the women I interviewed about what constitutes being Tom and Dii contrast and contradict rather than forming a consistent portrayal.

Although the explanations about what designates Tom and Dii dissent, certain patterns emerge. For example, fashion is the most frequently cited visual indicator of Toms. Men's style shoes, flip-flops or sandals on their feet, Toms wear large polo shirts or oxford cloth shirts tucked into loose jeans of assorted colors. Their hair is short, straight, and styled in a manner that does not require curling or drying when wet. Toms do not carry handbags or purses, but they do wear mobile phones and pagers, which signal their middle-class status, as well as car keys hanging from their beltloops or pockets, a practice otherwise reserved for Thai men. Under their shirts, they wear undershirts instead of bras, and they tend to keep their shoulders hunched slightly forward so as to diminish the appearance of curves. Despite what seem to be clearly coded visual clues signaling class-stratified positions and particular gendered practices, the Thais I interviewed did not always rely on outward appearances as clues when asked to describe Toms. Conformity to a style of dress or appearance may be provided as examples that mark them as Toms, but they do not do so conclusively.

"Active" is another consistent adjective evoked in relation to Toms. When asked to define Tom and Dii, Pari, a *yingrakying* who previously considered herself a Tom, said that a Tom usually takes the "active" role during sex and "does not let another woman see her body or her breasts or whatever." Hiding their bodies, even during sex, "they wear tank tops [as opposed to bras or nothing]; they are active," she states. Susan, an American researching gender in Thai politics, has had several relationships with Thai women and asserts that mainstream Thai society thinks: "If you're seen as a Tom, that defines your sex in a certain way." She believes that there is a stereotypical set of assumptions that a general member of Thai society, if they attempted to sexualize the position, would assume, including that "This person would be active in bed." Carol asserts that "people associate Toms with sexuality. It has a clear sexual meaning to the outside." For her, coding oneself as Tom through appearance is not merely a fashion statement or dislike for gender conventions; it marks one sexually. However, she also finds that the "active" role of Toms is not limited to sex acts; Toms were also "active" by controlling the emotional tenor of the relationship: "how intense things are, how emotional things get." This has occurred in her own relationships with Toms as well as in other relationships she has observed. While not necessarily the initiators of relationships, Toms are described as active in controlling the sex, emotional tenor, and level of commitment.

Several Thai women agree that Toms are "active," yet resist the extension that being Tom includes a sexualized component. They insist that young women who live with their families are rarely imagined as sexual beings unless they are involved with a man. Female friends often spend large amounts of time together including passing the night in each other's beds, and the display of emotional intimacy does not lead family members to suspect sexual activity. One woman recounted that her mother found out about her involvement with a woman through a friend. Despite the mother's disapproval of the relationship, she did not admonish her daughter for inviting her girlfriend to her bedroom to spend the night. Sharing a bed did not offend her mother, the daughter reports, because the relationship carried no sexual connotations in her mother's imagination. This same mother would object to a man merely entering her daughter's bedroom. Desire between women is frequently overlooked despite seemingly clear indicators, because the interaction between women is not thought of as sexual.[13]

Imitating men is frequently described as an aspect of being Tom. When Pari perceived herself as a Tom, she tried to imitate men. Another Tom, Pui, who is college educated, in her thirties, living in Bangkok, and financially independent, gives the following definition for Tom:

> [A] woman who loves to see herself and tell herself she is a man is Tom. . . . A Tom will not accept herself as a woman although the truth is, and then she can't be a man too but she has to be somebody, so Tom is what she can be. Tom copy man's rule because she thinks she is, so they act like a man in almost everything—love pretty women, sexy or lady; always say 'pom' [I, masc. sing] and 'krab,' [masculine tag to denote politeness], short hair, men's clothes.

Refusing to enact the roles prescribed for women, and unable, yet wishing, to be a man marks the position of Tom for Pui. She uses masculine linguistic cues and is attracted to women who embody current dominant Thai notions of feminine beauty. Pui sees the Tom as a tertiary, pejorative position, but it is the only identity available to a woman "who thinks she is" a man. While some Toms describe themselves as better able to provide for the women they love than Thai men, Pui imagines herself as an inferior imitation of a man. Consequently, her relationships tend to be with Diis that are married or engaged, and she expects and accepts to take second place and eventually be deserted. The desire to be a man is the extreme position for a Tom, one that many women without a Tom community most often describe.

Having sex or having a girlfriend is also not a defining feature of being Tom. Throughout Thailand, the women I interviewed concurred: Toms are not defined by Dii companionship. In fact, Toms frequently form their own communities and networks of friendships without including Diis. Carol stresses community identification rather than sexual actions: "Toms are in a community together, and it extends to their sexual life" and not the other way around. While community formation is also not a requirement to being Tom, Toms often form social groups ranging in size from two to six or seven. These groups spend their free time together—in restaurants, bars, or taking weekend trips. My informants consistently mentioned Toms they knew that had no girlfriends. Most of these women socialized with other Toms; however, other Toms focused on their relationships with Diis and spent their time with their girlfriends. Frequently Dii girlfriends are included in the social events. However, it is rare that a Dii not involved with a Tom remains a part of the social group.

These Tom communities are often premised on an unspoken agreement not to discuss their sexual identies or desires. For example, one group of Toms that I encountered, only one of whom is a member of *Anjaree*, had never talked about whether or not they were Toms before I began associating with them. They all dressed accordingly and looked the part, and they socialized with each other, but they never overtly divulged their own desires. The woman who was a member of *Anjaree* had asked me not to reveal her participation to the others. When I later asked her why, she said she was not sure they were Tom, even though, several years before, three of them had both pursued the same Dii. For some reason, she did not make the assumption, despite the visual clues and their shared object of desire. Yet Toms often speculate about the existence of other Toms. A frequent topic of conversation is whether someone is a Tom or not, though the question is almost never directed at its subject. For example, at restaurants my friends frequently speculate whether servers are Toms. Despite hair, clothes, and mannerisms that are stereotypically Tom, the conversation keeps returning to speculation: "I think she's a Tom. Do you? Yes, I definitely think she's Tom."[14] A lot of attention goes to classifying strangers, yet conclusions are rarely drawn, and questions are not asked, even among friends. Community

formation is thus often premised on silence about desire and identification among members, displacing self-revelation with assertions about
those outside the circle. José Muñoz terms these "survival strategies"
disidentification, the practices by "minority subject[s] . . . in order to
negotiate a phobic majoritarian public sphere that continuously elides or
punishes the existence of subjects who do not conform to the phantasm
of normative citizenship" (4). Through the process of disidentification,
these women are able to form bonds without exposing themselves to
potential persecution.

When a woman is involved with a Tom, she is considered to be a
Dii, but this is neither a permanent, nor fixed, position. A Dii conforms
to the mainstream image of Thai femininity and, in fact, any woman in
Thailand could be Dii. Diis are often involved with men in addition to
their Tom partners. Both the families of Diis and Toms whom I interviewed assume that majority of Diis will eventually get married and have
children, as motherhood is described as, and generally assumed to be,
the position most powerful and desirable for a Thai woman. Diis take
the "woman's role" in the relationship following a code for dress, manner and gestures, and nurturing. During sex, "Diis lay back and enjoy.
They cuddle and things. Making love is only one way" (Pari). Passivity
during sex is not necessarily the "woman's role" in heterosexual relationships, yet it is built into the Tom/Dii continuum, partially because of
the position of Toms as active and partially because many Toms refuse
to expose their bodies, wishing not to reveal feminine attributes. The
sexual role of Diis was described as passive or receptive by all the Toms
and Diis with whom I came into contact.

In heterosexual Thai society, men normally initiate contact. However, in the Tom/Dii scenario, a Dii can initially be "more flirty" and
"that's acceptable." Because Diis are not visually coded, any woman is
"fair game" to a Tom for a possible relationship (Susan). That is why initial contact is often left to Diis. According to Anjana, there are no established symbols that "allow erotic messages and interactions between people," such as pink triangles or rainbow colors. This may account for the
acceptability of their initiations: "A Tom is like a moving target. Diis can
identify you" (Suvarnananda Personal). These initial contacts can occur
in locations where Toms and Diis are known to frequent, but they also
occur in the workplace or at any number of places where people mix.
Thus this acknowledgement that Diis initiate contact contradicts the
insistence that Toms cannot be identified by appearance. If Diis approach

Toms, they are making assumptions about their sexuality based on visual codes. Diis are considered even less visible than Toms, marked only, according to some, when they are accompanied by Tom partners. Because their identity is not considered fixed or primary, community formation is even more difficult than for Toms. Carol remarked that she has only seen community formation among Diis at *Anjaree* functions. Pari, Mao, and other women I interviewed point out that some Diis are entrenched in traditional family relationships: "someone married, has kids, decides I've just fallen in love with a Tom" (Pari). In these instances, Toms normally spend a lot of time with the entire family, including the husband. They may take the kids out, be included on family trips, and become involved in many of the family's activities. In most cases, the presence of a Tom does not cause suspicions or jealousy, because, as I have suggested, these relationships may not be marked as sexual.

Although *Anjaree* members frequently cite the organization's unique position in the realigning of identities, Tom and Dii positions are transformed by women outside of *Anjaree* as well. Pari stated that many other women do not fit into the Tom/Dii scenario, calling these women "another category" of "people who don't necessarily have to put the role on themselves." "I know other Thai women who have this feeling of another category. Some of them don't label themselves as lesbians, they just have relationships with women." According to Pari, most of these women have had some type of contact with Europe or the United States—through study, travel, or work. They are also older, normally in their thirties: "They know who they are and don't need to act out any-more." Carol was asked by a Tom during a conversation in Thai with a group of Toms and Diis who were not members of *Anjaree* if she was a Tom or a Dii. She replied: "'I'm 60% Dii and 40% Tom because I'm a little bit lazy. I like to get it more than I like to give it.'" She recounts their surprise: "They were just shocked. One woman said, 'I can't believe you said that, no Thai would ever say that. We all think that but no one would actually say it.'" One Tom present announced: "I can be a Tom or a Dii, too." She seemed attracted to the idea that it would be possible to express that, but I don't think she felt comfortable saying that to her Thai friends. This interchange illustrates that *Anjaree* members are not unique in their efforts to rethink their positions, but because it requires reimagining and realigning oneself vis-à-vis one's friends, family, and society, the process is facilitated by the presence of others who are similarly reconfiguring themselves.

Overall, Toms are not defined by their actions, communities, or desires. They are Toms because of the way they look: yet determining this look is not fixed. Even a Tom cannot be sure that another woman is a Tom. Yet there is a fascination in discovering this, among both women in this community and in mainstream Thai society. Diis, on the other hand, are defined in their relations to Toms. Any woman can be a Dii, as long as she is with a Tom. Without a Tom, her position is not secure. Toms together are imaginable, although their positions must eventually shift, but not Diis. While Toms are described as active, they cannot always control the tenor of the relationship because Diis, especially those who have joined the heterosexual economy, have other partners outside of this dynamic—whether boyfriends, potential boyfriends, or husbands—to consider. The ambiguous and conflicting descriptions that I have discussed do not form a coherent picture: Toms are seen but not seen, sexually marked but invisible, and Diis cannot exist without Toms but they initiate contact with active, yet inconclusively visible Toms.

"NONCONFORMIST WAYS"

Lek, an *Anjaree* member and organizer, who wrote her Masters thesis about Tom and Dii identities, contends that you can no longer define them as static categories, but rather positions on a continuum. She states,

> For my thesis, I found out that there are many kinds of Tom and many kinds of Dii. Extreme Tom and Diis try to imitate their lifestyle like a heterosexual couple. They don't have the chance to see that they can have another style of relationship. Because they are socialized in a heterosexual family, they take this kind of a relationship. They have a couple in the same gender.

Lek has had a long term relationship with a *farang* lesbian and no longer considers herself strictly Tom or Dii. Rather, she believes other Tom and Diis would also change their identities if they were exposed to alternatives: "If they have the chance, I believe some of them would change." *Anjaree* is one place where this chance is offered.

One member asserted that the increasingly varied positionings between the poles of Tom and Dii described by some women was limited to members of *Anjaree*: "*Anjaree* is an exception, where people want to be more ambiguously defined." She attributed this to the class and level of education achieved by the members—although there are *Anjaree* members around the country who receive the organization's newsletters, most of the women that attend social events are middle-class, financially stable, single women living in Bangkok. A woman who attended *Anjaree*'s monthly event at the Bangkok cafe targeting gay clientele, *Utopia*, enumerated what makes the members of *Anjaree* different from what she "normally sees": the number of women present at the events, the age of the active members, and the class of women in attendance. Furthermore she stated: "All of the lesbians I know who participate in nongovernment organizations are activists who don't express themselves through certain styles of dress or hairstyles. *Anjaree* has opened up a space for another kind of identity that is neither Tom nor Dii. You can look like an ordinary woman or not, you can dress up or not, you can take care of your hair or leave it" (personal interview). Attracting this older clientele that includes many grassroots nongovernment organization activists, this *Anjaree* function showcased more than Toms and Diis. *Anjaree* membership engenders a new kind of community that is larger and more inclusive in terms of age and class. Diverse representations of *yingrakying* are in the process of consolidating.

While Anjana supports members who wish to redefine their identities, she does not directly promote it. The majority of members still identify themselves as Tom or Dii, but an increasing number no longer feel that they belong in the one of these two categories. They consistently use Tom and Dii constructions, however, in their explanations of how they imagine themselves, positioning themselves somewhere in between or combining stereotypical features of both. The continued use of Tom and Dii to describe positions that do not adhere to the ways in which these categories have been constructed illustrates a dearth in the number of words available to these women to define themselves. While the terms lesbian or women who love women may seem viable alternatives, Thai women continually resist using them when characterizing themselves. While most women employed Tom and Dii exclusively to describe Thai women loving women when speaking in English, some women would use the word lesbian when talking about a group; this may be because they did not know alternative words. Only one woman I interviewed reported that she was a lesbian, but she also located her identification within the Tom and Dii dynamic.

Anjana believes that her identity does not represent other Thai women in same-sex relationships. Because of her tenure at the Hague and her extensive contact and involvement with women from Western, as well as non-Western, cultures, Anjana describes her experiences and identification as atypically Thai. All of her serious relationships have been with Western women, and she does not place herself in either the Tom/Dii or Western lesbian categories. Attempting to describe her position, she uses the existing, ineffectual vocabulary, stating that while she is neither Tom nor Dii, "I am more in the Dii category. I was pushed into this category because everyone wanted me to be in one or the other. I couldn't make a choice" (personal interview). Anjana frequently discusses the difficulties she has imagining herself with the available vocabulary to *Anjaree* members, providing a model for other women to construct and question their identities in relation to their individual experiences.

Providing an environment conducive to reimagining one's sexual identity is only one of *Anjaree*'s projects. Anjana and other members of the administration envision *Anjaree*'s primary goals as follows: community building; providing members with resources and information so that they do not feel abnormal, isolated, or alone; and offering support and advice to women who write letters of inquiry to the newsletter, *Anjaree Sarn*. Because a substantial number of members do not belong to the middle class or live in Bangkok, they may not have contact with other *yingrakying* or access to information about Tom and Dii identity construction. For working-class women and those who place themselves strictly within the Tom/Dii dynamic, *Anjaree* provides opportunities to form liaisons both written and social by publishing a newsletter that encourages members to read, write, and respond to others' writings and organizing social events where women can meet. Writing plays an important role in establishing friendships: the newsletter is filled with letters encouraging responses and social events always conclude with address swapping. I consistently received letters from women I met at *Anjaree* events.

Despite *Anjaree*'s quickly augmenting membership, women frequently write that they feel that they are, according to Anjana: the only woman who loves women "in the world or in Thailand." Since this role is manifesting itself differently than in the past, Anjana believes that many women have no examples or role models, and they can't ask for advice from their parents. Toms in many parts of Thailand can create bonds through *Anjaree Sarn*, writing about the problems they face, conflicts and confusions, as well as asking for pen-pals. Writing from a distance, they are able to participate in the construction of new kinds of identities and form communities beyond the boundaries of their towns and villages without physical displacement.

ENGLISH EFFECTS

In addition to organizing and leading social events, setting up organizational meetings and delegating tasks, coordinating the publication of the newsletter, publicizing the organization, and keeping track of the increasing number of members, Anjana expends significant time and effort linking Thai women to international lesbian communities. She has shared efforts and information with international organizations that work to promote community building and communication at the international level as well as supporting efforts by and speaking on behalf of organizations that link lesbian rights with human rights. She has organized two Bangkok-based international forums (1990 and 1997) that focused on women who love women in Asia. Patiently answering any questions, even those that are hostile or homophobic, Anjana has provided over one hundred interviews to Thai and international journalists, researchers, and academics both inside and outside of Thailand. One reason why Anjana consistently serves as the sole voice of Thai women loving women is her ability to speak English and provide explanations using English language conventions. Often these conventions stand in stark contrast to the ideologies of "Thai-ness" found in numerous spheres of Thai society and culture.

Traditional Thai identity, or "Thai-ness," is promoted in Thailand by many sources. Most families, schools, and temples teach Thai children from a very early age to see themselves as part of their extended family, community, and nation, encouraging acceptance of duties and obligations to family, society, royalty, religion, and each other. Membership and commitment to these intersecting groups, not the sense that one is an individual possessing certain rights and freedoms, is described in introductions to Thailand from every source: guidebooks, cultural introductions to Thailand, and material developed by the Tourist Authority of Thailand (TAT).[15] In much of mainstream Thai society, tolerance exists for actions as long as they are not outspoken, inviting reactions; the practice of verbally coming out is considered unnecessary, undesirable, and specifically Western by Thai women who know of the process. Respectful behavior in Thailand includes not telling the truth rather than saying something that would offend the listener or disrupt societal expectations. Expressing dislike or discomfort of outspoken political interventions such as protestations against homophobia or human rights assertions, these women similarly do not want to speak out about their nontraditional identities or nonmainstream actions.

Increasingly, however, English language representations enact outspoken examples that run counter to Thai conventions. Images of sex and sexuality, as well as enunciations of desire or identity, originate from Hollywood, Western advertising firms or other non-Thai sources. Global communications have provided access to the English language, and as a result, Western ideas. Both imported and Thai-produced goods and services reflect interests in trends and practices that occur outside of Thailand's borders. Professor Doctor Suwatana Aribarg explains the Thai practice of silence in a 1995 interview: "'Homosexuality is inherent in every culture, every society. It's not a result of Western influence as some say.' Homosexuality may be less of an open presence in Thai society . . . because 'Thais regard sexuality as an embarrassing matter that shouldn't be openly discussed or flaunted'" ("Seen"). However, as a result of the prevalence of Western products and ideas, sex and sexualities in the Western sense have become subjects sanctified for scrutiny and discussion. English thus provides a medium where Thai practices of silence about sexuality and desire can be broken. Dennis Altman emphasizes that communication affects the way in which women construct their identities: "Clearly, Asians who adopt lesbian/gay identities are conscious of and in part molded by these western examples. In both North America and Europe gay liberation grew out of the counter-culture and other radical movements, particularly feminism. To some extent, this is also true of the developing gay worlds of the south, but more significant is the global explosion of communications" ("Global" 426). Many of the women I interviewed found it much easier to discuss their identifications and desires in English than in Thai, and many of my Thai friends preferred confessing desire to me than to their other Thai friends.[16] Anjana imagines herself and her organization in accord with English language conventions when she describes sexual actions or decries homophobic practices.

Many of the Toms and Diis in Bangkok who are not members of *Anjaree* do not know of the organization; some are reluctant to get involved. At least ten middle-class women living in Bangkok with whom I discussed *Anjaree* showed no interest; women whom I regularly socialized with refused to attend an event sponsored by *Anjaree*. These women provided a variety of reasons for their reluctance: no time, enough friends and/or social events, no interest in meeting strangers with unknown backgrounds, no interest in community building, fear of meeting the members, fear of being discovered participating in such an outspoken organization clearly premised on sexuality. Aligning oneself with an organization premised on sexuality violates Thai norms requiring silence about sexual practices, so *Anjaree* was considered taboo by women who perceived it as sexuality based. These women, like Pui, whom I quoted portraying herself as an inferior imitation of a man, are more likely to locate themselves squarely within the established categories. In contrast to this, women who have had more exposure to Western imagery and ideas as well as those proficient in English often engage in the process of changing identifications in order to relate their specific situations. While this engagement is in dialogue with exposure to non-Thai ideas and the English language, it does not merely duplicate these sources. Instead, these experiences offer a means to redefinition that does not directly violate Thai values put forth and embedded in the Thai language. English provides the distance necessary for reevaluation, not the models for replication. Anjana insists that she has reevaluated her position as a result of being involved with *farang*, living and traveling in Western countries, doing extensive research about Western feminist theories, and establishing international dialogues; she has not become a lesbian per se, but has realigned herself and encouraged other *yingrakying* to do the same. Her strategies reflect her recognition that she locates herself as a member of a population that may benefit from dialogue with other women who love women outside of Thailand. She also recognizes that entering this forum may lead to the sublimation of local concerns. Local conditions are her primary focus; yet her knowledge of external practices informs her actions and the advice she gives to *yingrakying*.

I do not mean to assert that all Thai-*farang* interactions lead to changes in the way one imagines oneself; conflicts and confusions may reduce one's possibilities for self-depiction. Lek, for instance, highlights the extensive difficulties she encountered during her relationship with a *farang* woman: "different language; different way to interpret;

culture and many factors." She states that her *farang faen* "didn't understand her kiss." In addition, "[i]t takes many energies to explain things to a different culture." Her relationship also confounded her friends and family: "[m]y friends asked why I want a *farang faen*? Thai people still have communication problems—how can people from two different cultures get along?" She feels that her *faen* was very different from her and did things that were sometimes unacceptable to Thais. For example, when they moved into a new apartment, there was a video/radio shop nearby. This shop would play their movies and music so loud that it disturbed them in their apartment down the street. Her *faen* went to the shop and demanded that they reduce the volume. This assumption that one individual's comfort was worth disrupting what appeared to be a compatible society as well as the boldness she displayed by scolding a stranger was inconceivable according to Thai values. Despite Lek's shock and disapproval of her *faen's* actions, she did internalize certain aspects of it. Our interview took place in a restaurant where the music grew progressively louder. At one point, Lek asked the waitress to turn down the music. As Lek had already explained, this presumption of individual rights is surprising and unconventional by Thai social standards. However, she did not comment on her actions, nor did she act as if she had just done something out of the ordinary. While she clearly resists changing the ways she identifies herself as a result of this relationship, the residue of her interaction creates conflicts between her actions and those she describes as accepted Thai values and mores. Her speaking about the relationship while refusing to accept her Western *faen's* assumptions creates opportunities for discussion, critique, and resistance, whether by expanding notions of identity, community, or the processes of disidentification, or resisting those of outsiders.

The emergence of women who speak about and reimagine *yingrakying* opens up new avenues in which to think of Thai women who love women articulating their multiple desires and identifications. The proliferation of new interactions with the terms and accompanying stereotypes of Tom and Dii, or the realignment identities within and beyond these categories as practiced by members of *Anjaree*, enables *yingrakying* to carve out previously unavailable identifications and identities that are in dialogue with their contemporary situations. The increasing number of outlets, such as writing in English or opportunities to write for the press and the Internet, encourages women to participate in conversations about how they imagine themselves and construct their identities, translating *farang* and other concepts, and updating Tom and Dii to make them meaningful to their own situations.

Notes

I would like to thank Anjana Suvarnananda, Varaporn Chamsanit, and "Pui" for their time, influence, and patient explanations Bruce Robbins and Anthony Alessandrini generously provided valuable editorial advice. My debt to Alexander Weheliye is greater than can be expressed in this brief space.

1. I follow the Thai practice of using first names when referring to Thais and last names when referring to Westerners. Rather than employing western words to note the many places where information, ideas, and people originate, I will use the Thai word *farang* (as a noun, both singular and plural and as an adjective). Thais have specific words to denote the race or ethnicity of other Asians: Chinese, Japanese, Koreans, Laotians. South Asians, who have lived in Thailand for several centuries and have acted as trading partners with Thailand far longer are referred to as *khon khek*, or guests. Since the word *farang* is evoked constantly in Bangkok and throughout Thailand, I will employ this term rather than a non-Thai word to describe these people in Bangkok, as it affects how these groups of people are imagined by Thais and by themselves in Thailand.

2. When discussing the women of Anjaree, I will henceforth utilize Anjana's term. However, when discussing Thai women who love women in general, I will evoke this phrasing frequently employed by researchers of women's sexuality.

3. See Cheryl Wall's collection, *Changing Our Own Words*; Abena Busia and Stanlie James's *Theorizing Black Feminisms*; Gayatri Spivak's *In Other Worlds* and *Outside in the Teaching Machine*; and sections of Judith Butler's *Bodies that Matter*. The following collections discuss the necessity for site specificity in terms of how feminism should be constituted, but spend little time exploring the specific nature of sex, gender, and sexualities: the collection *This Bridge Called My Back* edited by Cherrie Moraga and Gloria Anzaldua; *Feminist Genealogies, Colonial Legacies* edited by Chandra Mohanty and M. J. Alexander; *Third World Women and the Politics of Feminism*, edited by Chandra Talpade Mohanty, Ann Russo, and Lourdes Torres; and Kumari Jayawardena's *Feminism and Nationalism in the Third World*.

4. See, for example, Herdt's edited collection *Third Sex, Third Gender*; Martin F. Manalanson IV, "(Dis)Orienting the Body: Locating Symbolic Resistance among Filipino Gay Men"; and Ana Maria Alonso and Maria Teresa Koreck, "Silences: 'Hispanics,' AIDS, and Sexual Practices."

5. Appadurai's *Modernity at Large* (1996) does not push past anecdotal evidence, nor does it display the rigorous analysis he called for in his 1990 essay "Disjuncture and Difference in the Global Cultural Economy." Instead, much of the book consolidates earlier essays. A version of the essay which does not rise to his own challenge appears as the foundation for his second chapter.

6. With each of these sources of information comes a multitude of agendas that affect presentation. For example, while the Thai government does not restrict Internet access, sites on the Internet are launched for specific purposes that inform the inclusion and presentation of data. These sites might be designed to create desires for consumption, form certain types of international gay communities with shared agendas, create women centered and/or feminist communities, change political policies, initiate friendships, etc.

7. For a thorough account of the economic and cultural changes in Thailand during this decade, see Pasuk Phongpaichit and Chris Baker's two publications: *Thailand's Boom!* and *Thailand: Economy and Politics*. Since the time of my research, the Thai economy has taken a drastic turn for the worse. The baht, Thailand's monetary unit, was no longer valued according to a "basket" of currencies (the largest of which was the U.S. dollar). Floating freely in international currency markets resulted in a drastic, unforeseen devaluation. As a result, the I.M.F. began a bailout in December 1997.

8. See Sue Ellen Case "Toward a Butch-Femme Aesthetic" and Joan Nestle's *The Persistent Desire: A Femme-Butch Reader*.

9. Varaporn Chamsanit believes that the Tom and Dii dynamic highlights the way in which masculinity and femininity are enacted. Her assertion follows that of Judith Butler about butch and femme positions: "The replication of heterosexual constructs in non-heterosexual frames brings into relief the utterly constructed status of the so-called heterosexual original" (31).

10. Western gender models, educational systems, and city infrastructures also have a history of being interpreted by Thai rulers and applied to Thai citizens. David Wyatt describes some of the mandates of King Vajiravudh, explaining how they reflected what he saw as strategies for Thai modernity during his sojourn in the West:

> One of the most persistent themes in [King Vajiravudh's] writings might be termed modernity—that is, encouraging, even exhorting, people to act and live as modern people did in the West. He introduced surnames and coined names for hundreds of families; he refashioned the flag of Siam . . . he introduced the first national holidays . . . he promoted team sports, particularly soccer football; he worked to improve the status of women by encouraging them to

mix socially with men and by arguing for monogamy in place of widespread Siamese polygamy; and he was an ardent supporter of modern education. (228)

"Modernity," according to Wyatt, is the strategic term King Vajiravudh used to promote his adaptations of Western practices. The king coined surnames, yet he did not require Thais become Smiths or Jones. Similarly, the national holidays reflected Thailand's commemoration of their kings by celebrating the day they died rather than, following Western practices, celebrating leaders' birthdays.

11. Recently, academic and nongovernment organizations around the world have begun to employ two standardized terms for homosexuals: men who have sex with men and women who love women. These terms reflect an astounding gender bias: men in same sex relationships have sex while women share love. These increasingly acceptable terms utilized by people involved in battles for equal rights and acceptance still employ terminology and imagery that interpolates women as emotional and men as sexual. I would like to thank Louisa Schein for pointing this out to me.

12. Two essays by Dennis Altman, "Global Gaze/Global Gays" and (in this collection) "Rupture or Continuity?" are strong examples that work against this practice, attempting to analyze specific details about nonheterosexuality in several Asian countries. See also Ana Maria Alonso and Maria Teresa Koreck's essay, "Silences," which explains how "the use of the terms 'homosexuality,' 'bisexuality,' and 'heterosexuality' with reference to Mexico is rather misleading . . ." (115). Instead, the authors seek to analyze sexual identities in relation to their specified cultural, historical, and political contexts.

13. This is similar to what Carroll Smith-Rosenberg describes in *Disorderly Conduct*. In nineteenth-century America, women could express intimacy both verbally and in writing without arousing suspicions about physical intimacy.

14. Pui at a Thai restaurant in New York City.

15. See Denis Segaller, *Thai Ways*; William J. Klausner, *Reflections on Thai Culture*; and Robert and Nanthapa Cooper, *Culture Shock! Thailand*.

16. Other researchers in Thailand such as Susan and Carol concurred that their Thai informants and friends expressed similar ease in expressing these issues in English.

Works Cited

*Note: In the body of this chapter, I follow the Thai custom of referring to authors by their first names after introducing their full names. In the Works Cited, however, I have alphabetized all the authors according to MLA conventions.

Alonso, Ana Maria, and Maria Teresa Koreck. "Silences: 'Hispanics,' AIDS, and Sexual Practices." *The Lesbian and Gay Studies Reader*. New York: Routledge, 1993. 110–126.

Altman, Dennis. "Global Gaze/Global Gays." *GLQ: A Journal of Lesbian and Gay Studies* 3.4 (1997): 417–436.

———. "Rupture or Continuity? The Internationalization of Gay Identities." *Social Text* 48 (Fall 1996) 77–94.

Appadurai, Arjun. "Disjuncture and Difference in the Global Cultural Economy." *Public Culture* 2.2 (1990): 1–24.

———. *Modernity at Large: Cultural Dimensions of Globalization*. Minneapolis: U of Minnesota P, 1996.

Bakhtin, Mikhail M. *The Dialogic Imagination: Four Essays*. Ed. M. Holquist. Tr. C. Emerson and M. Holquist. Austin: U of Texas P, 1981.

Busia, Abena, and Stanlie James, eds. *Theorizing Black Feminisms*. New York: Routledge, 1993.

Butler, Judith. *Gender Trouble: Feminism and the Subversion of Identity*. New York: Routledge, 1990.

———. *Bodies that Matter: On the Discursive Limits of "Sex."* New York: Routledge, 1993.

Case, Sue Ellen. "Toward a Butch-Femme Aesthetic." *Lesbian and Gay Studies Reader*. Ed. Henry Abelove, Michele Aina Barale, and David M. Halperin. New York: Routledge, 1993. 294–306.

Carol (Name Changed). Personal Interview. 10 May 1996.

Chamsanit, Varaporn. Personal Interviews. March 1996–April 1998.

Cooper, Robert, and Nanthapa Cooper. *Culture Shock!: Thailand*. 2nd ed. Portland, Ore.: Graphic Arts Center Publishing, 1990.

Harper, Phillip Brian, Anne McClintock, José Esteban Muñoz, and Trish Rosen. "Queer Transexions of Race, Nation, and Gender: An Introduction." *Social Text 52/53* Vol 15. Nos. 3 and 4: 1–4.

Herdt, Gilbert, ed. *Third Sex, Third Gender: Beyond Sexual Dimorphism in Culture and History*. New York: Zone, 1994.

Jackson, Peter. *Dear Uncle Go: Male Homosexuality in Thailand*. Bangkok: Bua Luang, 1995.

Jayawardena, Kumari. *Feminism and Nationalism in the Third World*. London: Zed, 1986.

Klausner, William J. *Reflections on Thai Culture*. Bangkok: The Siam Society Under Royal Patronage, 1993.

Lek (name changed). Personal Interview. 13 May 1996.

Manalanson IV, Martin F. "(Dis)Orienting the Body: Locating Symbolic Resistance among Filipino Gay Men." *Positions* 2:1 (1994): 73–90.

Mohanty, Chandra Talpade, and M. J. Alexander, eds. *Feminist Geneologies, Colonial Legacies, Democratic Futures*. New York: Routledge, 1996.

——, Ann Russo, and Lourdes Torres, eds. *Third World Women and the Politics of Feminism*. Bloomington: Indiana UP, 1991.

Moraga, Cherrie, and Gloria Anzaldua, eds. *This Bridge Called My Back: Writings by Radical Women of Color*. Watertown, Mass: Persephone, 1981.

Morris, Rosalind C. "Three Sexes and Four Sexualities: Redressing the Discourses on Gender and Sexuality in Contemporary Thailand." *Positions* 2.1 (1994): 15–43.

——. "Educating Desire: Thailand, Transnationalism, and Transgression." *Social Text* 15.3/4 (1997): 53–79.

Muñoz, José Esteban. *Disidentifications: Queers of Color and the Performance of Politics*. Minneapolis: U of Minnesota P, 1999.

Nestle, Joan, ed. *The Persistent Desire: A Femme-Butch Reader*. Boston: Alyson, 1992.

Pari (name changed). Personal Interview. 15 Oct. 1996.

Phongpaichit, Pasuk, and Chris Baker. *Thailand: Economy and Politics*. Oxford: Oxford UP, 1995.

Phongpaichit, Pasuk, and Chris Baker. *Thailand's Boom!* Chiang Mai, Thailand: Silkworm, 1996.

Pramoj, Kukrit. *Si Phaendin (Four Reigns)*. Book One. Trans. Tulachandra. Bangkok: Duang Kamol, n.d.

Pratt, Mary Louise. "Arts of the Contact Zone." *Profession* 91 (1991) 33–40.

Pui (name changed). Series of Interviews and e-mail correspondence.

Roscoe, Will. "Was We'Wha a Homosexual?: A Native American Survivance and the Two-Spirit Tradition." *GLQ* 2(3) 1995: 193–235.

"Seen Through the Eyes of Thai Parents." *Bangkok Post* 21 June 1995: 31.

Segaller, Denis. *Thai Ways*. 3rd ed. Bangkok: Post Books, 1993.

Smith-Rosenberg, Carroll. *Disorderly Conduct: Visions of Gender in Victorian America*. New York: Oxford UP, 1985.

Spivak, Gayatri Chakravorty. *In Other Worlds: Essays in Cultural Politics*. New York: Routledge, 1988.

——. *Outside in the Teaching Machine*. New York: Routledge, 1993.

Susan (name changed). Personal Interview. 17 May 1996.

Suvarnananda, Anjana. "Lesbianism: A Social Problem?" Sixth International Conference of Thai Studies (Chiang Mai, Thailand) 16 Oct. 1996.

——. Personal Interview. 16 Oct. 1996.

Thailand in the '90s. Rev. ed. Thailand: National Identity Board, 1995.

Thongthiraj, Took Took. "Toward a Struggle against Invisibility: Love Between Women in Thailand." *Amerasia Journal* 20.1 (1994): 45–58.

Wall, Cheryl, ed. *Changing our Own Words: Essays on Criticism, Theory, and Writing by Black Women*. New Brunswick, N.J.: Rutgers UP, 1991.

Wyatt, David K. *Thailand: A Short History*. 2nd ed. New Haven, Conn.: Yale UP, 1984.

CHAPTER FIVE

Transcending Sexual Nationalism and Colonialism

*Cultural Hybridization as Process
of Sexual Politics in '90s Taiwan*

CHONG KEE TAN

In 1992 the first homosexual student organization, Gay Chat, came into being on the campus of Taiwan's premier tertiary institute, National Taiwan University. A year later, the movie "Wedding Banquet" burst onto the scene winning international acclaim. These and other events suggest not just the emergence of gay and lesbian identities in Taiwan, but more interestingly, the extent to which American gay and lesbian culture influences this process: The flyer that an organizer of Gay Chat handed to me did not talk about how they finally managed to persuade university officials to approve their application but about Stonewall and what that riot meant to the American movement in 1969. The cross-cultural screen romance in "Wedding Banquet" is followed by a real-life gay wedding of a Taiwanese writer and his American boyfriend in Taipei in June 1996. One could perhaps read such American and European influences as indicative of Western homosexual colonization and interpret any deviation from the Western model as postcolonial resistance. However,

I would argue instead that Taiwan has demonstrated the limits of post-colonial theory for theorizing sexuality. Indeed, hidden behind these two events is a process of hybridization that has so far not been adequately discussed.

I must be careful and point out here that I use "hybridization" to mean something a little different from how Homi Bhabha uses it. I feel that Bhabha's notion of hybridization focuses too much on the colonizer and theorizes it merely as a process that subverts an external colonizing force.[1] While acknowledging that hybridization does have this effect, I want to also emphasize how it enables a creative renegotiation of local cultural norms. At the same time, I must likewise be very careful when talking about culture in conjunction with homosexuality. Studies influenced by social constructionism have a tendency to first define a geographical space (usually in the form of a nation-state) and then assume that the differences in sexuality uncovered therein are a result of different cultural constructions.[2] To avoid the pitfall of slipping from biological determinism to cultural determinism, or sidelining the larger question of how such effects of national sexualities are reproduced through social, political, and economic interactions, the study of the seemingly "always already" culturally constructed differences in human sexuality might well benefit from a fuller understanding of the intervention of agency in the seemingly impersonal forces of cultural construction.[3] More concretely, I want to pose this question: how does the Taiwanese gay and lesbian movement negotiate between local circumstances and concerns on the one hand and an American homosexuality with its associated model of gay and lesbian rights movement on the other without becoming either xenophobic or merely derivative?

I must first caution against overstatement on the global influence of "American homosexuality" and presupposition that soon, all "gays" and "lesbians" will converge in some middle ground and become all alike. For a start, there is no singular American homosexuality—it is fractured by geography, race, gender, class, and so on. Furthermore, there is no reason to expect that just because some Taiwanese and San Franciscans employ similar vocabulary or relationship models, then these words and models must carry the same personal or social significance, or that they will function in the respective societies in similar ways. We do not find in Taiwan a pristine Taiwanese homosexuality but a confluence of local and imported conceptions, underpinned by economic, social, and political systems, producing distinct and sometimes conflicting hybrid models of what (homo)sexuality "is."[4]

Such conflicting constructions of sexual identity can coexist and shape lived experience under different circumstances in unexpected ways. On the other hand paying lived experience due attention could also inform a more nuanced understanding of prevailing constructions. Understanding the relations will enable the introduction of agency to an account (only a very preliminary one will be attempted here) not only of how cultural construction can shape lived experience but also how it can be shaped by lived experience through collective agency. I will demonstrate, using observations of the rise of Taiwanese gay and lesbian discourse in the 1990s, that the relations between theory and lived experience, as well as between different cultures, are not unidirectional but mutually interacting. This mutual interaction will both constrain and enable the assumption of certain sexual positionalities and the mobilization of certain forms of sexual politics. I would ask what sorts of spaces competing theories open up and what other possibilities they have foreclosed, as well as how on-the-ground experiences of activists caused them to amend their received notions and model of activism from the U.S. I will first provide an analysis of three events to substantiate my claims about hybridity and demonstrate how they represent three positionalities from which gay and lesbian subjects negotiate and transcend the polemics between sexual nationalism and sexual colonialism.

PUBLIC HEARING

A legislator (somewhat equivalent to an American senator), Mr. Yan, convened a public hearing on human rights for homosexuals on 28 December 1993 in response to demands by academics and homosexual groups that a sexual preference clause be added to the draft of an antidiscrimination bill. This hearing marked the most broad-based collaborative effort to de-stigmatize homosexuality by securing legislative protection from the state. Apart from generating some media coverage, however, the result was seen as quite a dismal failure.[5]

Reading through the proceedings, one is struck by the similarity of its language with past and current debates in the U.S. The academics who testified expounded on queer theories and almost all the proponents quoted American developments as models to be emulated. Even the formal procedure itself, a public hearing, was modeled after the U.S., where a senator would chair the hearing and various spokespersons would be called to testify. These are important points to note because the American experience provided Taiwanese with a forum (public hearing), a model (civil groups negotiating with the state), and a language (human rights) to articulate their demands. Most importantly, the American gay and lesbian rights movement provided a new perspective for Taiwanese homosexuals to look at themselves and their sufferings not as perversities and individual misfortunes but increasingly as a collective social injustice.[6]

The similarity ended there, however. Unlike American public hearings, the proceedings were not published by the state; instead, a homosexual group—*Tongzhi Workbench*—edited and printed it themselves by relying on private donations.[7] Another striking fact is that there were no self-identified gays and only one or two self-identified lesbians present. Gay and lesbian organizations asked their gay-friendly heterosexual friends to speak on their behalf, but these spokespersons could only say so much as a friend or as a mere reader of prepared statements.[8]

Taiwanese gays and lesbians did not come forward to speak or be counted during the public hearing because of the high level of social stigma, and hence they were unable to force the state to recognize homophobia as a reality of daily life either through extensive data on systematic discrimination or through compelling first-hand personal accounts. Under such circumstances, using the language of human rights in the abstract allowed officials to also stay in the abstract by claiming that there is already formal equality in the law and to continue ignoring the fundamental problem of society's (and their own) prejudices.[9]

Although this public hearing might appear as failed mimicry, in its geographical displacement it was already functioning towards a different goal and fulfilling a different objective. This engagement with the state achieved something very substantial: the fact that it solicited and obtained an official platform to voice such concerns showed that there is indeed political space for sexual politics in Taiwan. Consequently, instead of being demoralized after this failed attempt, the gay and lesbian rights movement took off. If the appeal to add a "sexual preference" clause had been met with police raids of bars and parks and strong official condemnation, the Taiwanese movement would probably not be as vibrant as it is now.[10] I would note in passing that generally, theorists such as D'Emilio who postulate that capitalism created the "conditions that made possible the emergence of a distinctive gay and lesbian identity" tend to focus only on the economic and social conditions of emergence, taking for granted, since the subject of their inquiry tends to be either the U.S. or Europe, the equally important political condition that is a major concern in many Asian countries.

The arena of engagement in Taiwan has since shifted from the state to the mass media. From 1994 onwards, more progressive papers frequently feature gay and lesbian news and articles. A regular column on homosexuality in *China Times* is placed in the family section right next to the children and teenage section on the same page. It tries to whittle away at parents' homophobia by showing the effect of its injustice on young people and to prevent homophobia in youths by making homosexuality familiar and nonthreatening.[11] This has not happened in supposedly more liberal America, perhaps because of less demand and more organized resistance, but it was among the earliest gains in Taiwan.

Publication of *G&L*

To publish a magazine for profit is a commercial activity, and contemporary activists and writers in Taiwan are always mindful of the danger of inadvertent collusion or outright selling out.[12] Despite such embarrassments, many readers warmly welcomed this first commercial gay and lesbian magazine. The first issue sold 19,000 copies, quite a phenomenal success. I will now examine this magazine more closely and describe how agency intervenes in the construction of pop gay and lesbian culture.

G&L has many articles on fashion and personal care, trying basically to import (reproduce) the gay consumer culture so well known in the U.S. There are also articles on gay and lesbian horoscopes, music, films, travel, books, organizations, personal ads, and naked models, covering a wide expanse of gay and lesbian subculture. The magazine is well aware of its social reality: an island nation whose inhabitants are still largely rather ignorant of what being gay and lesbian means. It features interviews with famous people and gets them to talk about their experience of coming to such self-identifications and their subsequent negotiations with their families, faiths, and careers. In short, besides providing consumption models, it also provides role models. For many of its readers, this magazine is the first time they had ever read anything explicitly written about homosexuality for people who feel they are homosexuals. It becomes their guide to the gay and lesbian world. Within this niche, the logic of activism has negotiated with the logic of commercialism a path beyond simple resistance or co-option. Purists might object that they are only using each other, but it is nonetheless mutually beneficial, and the biggest group of beneficiaries are young gays and lesbians.

However, if one looks carefully at the gay subculture that *G&L* covers, one would find that a good part of it is Western and Japanese. Is it not then a vehicle of sexual colonization? I would argue that colonization is probably not an accurate term here. A more appropriate term is "hybridization." The magazine acts as a discerning producer that selectively features successes in equal rights movements worldwide. Editorial agency intervenes at this stage. The readers write in to tell the magazine what they want, to tell each other what they think, and are themselves discerning consumers who select among the competing cultural constructions of homosexualities on offer those elements that can be combined with family cohesion (a very important consideration for Taiwanese) and other personal needs. Thus, a Taiwanese homosexuality emerges through the collective agency of the editors and readers. Such a hybrid combining Chinese, Japanese, and Western elements is unlike anything found in China, Japan, or the West. It is uniquely Taiwanese.

KUER BBS

The establishment of an (by now) extensive gay and lesbian computer network in Taiwan is another landmark event. Whereas the previous two events operate under the presumption that the common (*tong*) goal (*zhi*) is to de-stigmatize homosexuality, discourse within *kuer*[13] BBS tends toward determined marginality. The people who post on these BBSes are almost entirely university undergraduates and graduates, some of them published writers and researchers on gay and lesbian topics. Hence, opinions expressed within such BBSes are the thoughts of a part of the movement's educational elites. I will analyze a debate on male lesbians to illustrate how *kuer* is an internalization as well as a deconstruction of American queer politics.[14]

The first post that started this debate is by "dora," a "straight male" who admits that he dislikes women who wear skirts, high heels, or lace but is attracted to women who most resemble butch dykes. He mused about male lesbianism but his musing did not go down well. This reaction from "Android" is one such example:

> Bisexual, male lesbian . . . could help us become more diverse . . . but they could also be smiling assassins from the enemy. Are they friends or foes, we will have to see.
>
> Of course theoretically male lesbian is part of *kuer*, but based on my subjective emotion, I feel that a male lesbian is similar to a heterosexual man . . . sexuality wise they have it much easier than a gay man.

"dora" gives his perspective:

> I have never denied my identity as a heterosexual male, but I dislike saying: "I am a straight man" because on the one hand it is always confused with compulsory heterosexuality and on the other I also need to re-think my gender and sexual identity. However, I still keep saying it because most of the time, no one (I refer to men here) cares about your ambiguity, all they want is a clear statement in the form of "I am so and so" . . . I do not want to put myself in any politically radical position, although I am strangely respectful and admiring of activists. That is why even when my own uniqueness has been silenced in a *tongzhi* or feminist discourse, I have never complained. So I do not know why my existence still causes so much consternation?

"AntiChrist" sums it up thus:

> [T]he whole unspeakable/unspoken resentment [of male lesbian] must be represented through a set of seemingly self-righteous positions in which queer functions as an institution of exclusion and emotional outburst but reconstituted as theoretical . . . prohibition of any form other than the most orthodox gay centralization.

What is interesting here is not the fluency with theoretical positions but where this mimicry fails and the fact that when the mimicry is most incomplete, is also when it is most politically potent. More about this later.

The second thing to note is that within this group, the question of identity (Who gets to name oneself in a certain way? Who is a friend? Who is the enemy?) is often much more emotionally invested, and for good reasons. "AntiChrist" characterized it as prejudice from a position of strength. One can also read it as insecurity from a position of weakness with respect to heterosexual normality. Insecurity about one's identity is often a sign of the identity's fragility, and it is precisely this fragility that paradoxically empowers individual agencies to act, fashioning it. *Kuer*'s borders are fluid and require constant interrogations, definitions and re-definitions. Is male lesbian a *kuer*? It depends on whether he is for or against our cause. What is 'our' cause? It depends on who 'we' are, because *Kuer* is not *tongzhi* and hence does not assume that all have the same cause. But who are 'we'? 'We' are people who identify as *kuer*. This seemingly cyclic reasoning might seem futile at first glance, but it is this constant instability that allows an inscription of Western notions of queerness within a local context of *kuer* in a cyclic sequence of selective appropriations, thus enabling agency and opening up a path for the queer individual to resist Althusserian interpellation into a homosexual subject.[15] This resistance takes place at two fronts. The first and fairly obvious instance is represented by "dora" who self-consciously subverts the heterosexist and patriarchal status quo by rewriting male heterosexuality as lesbianism. The other, represented by "Android," who balks at admitting a male lesbian as *kuer*, is an untheorized resistance to the imported American queer model.[16]

The hesitance of "Android" gestures towards a rethinking of inclusiveness. From their hesitance to their embracing of sexual majorities such as "dora," Taiwanese *kuers* have demonstrated that they are already fashioning their own code of ethics. This ethics emphasizes cohesion instead of difference and comes with real possibility of inclusion. When another group of *kuers* decided to set up their own server in 1997, "dora" was one of the prominent members. Their departure from strict political correctness allows them to avoid the internal squabbling that has dogged some American groups, where white men are known to resent the inclusion of minorities, and minorities likewise resent their sometimes patronizing acceptance. One cannot be sure what inclusion means when it is automatic under the sign of political correctness. Resisting complete mimicry of the American queer model saves *kuers* from some amount of hypocrisy.

Kuer's advantage rests on their double resistance. They resist American over inclusiveness, and they resist indigenous hetero/homo interpellation by selectively appropriating American cultural capital. In other words, competing interpellations and competing cultural constructions do not simply just 'add up.' Instead they opened the space for agency, and this agency is central to the way cultures hybridize.

In the American formulation, "queer" is like freedom: difficult to say what it 'is' but easy to know what it is 'not.' And this 'not' creates an us/them divide around which to rally internal cohesion and outward action. "Queer" has, however, another us/them divide that is based not on political correctness but on academic chic. *Kuer* comes from American queer theory and within it is embedded similar divisions. Consequently, there will be those *kuers* who take certain poststructuralist assumptions as dogma, and cast all those who question them as the naïve essentialist enemy, resulting at times in all out flame wars. I myself was once the target of a joint attack on the newsgroup tw.bbs.soc.motss for daring to suggest that Judith Butler's gender theory does not take sufficient account of the body even in *Bodies That Matter*. Such mimicry results in an orthodoxy that encourages conformity and punishes dissent, and becomes a liability in a movement whose survival depends on adroit flexibility. We cannot assume that people will only appropriate what is best for them. In this case, the lure of academic chic proves too strong to resist.

The relationship between theory and practice is not one engendering the other. Western queerness was not simply imported as a theory and then engendering local mimicry, nor did local practices give rise to entirely indigenous theoretical understanding. Instead, all four—indigenous and foreign theories and practices, ever risking interpellation and through the intervention of agency, reproduce many nuances of a national sexuality.

Concluding Remarks

The rise of a gay and lesbian discourse in Taiwan today is a process of cultural negotiation. This negotiation is twofold: between contemporary and traditional values, and between indigenous and foreign theories and practices. Both paths did not involve one culture crudely replacing or dominating the other but subtle hybridizations. From its humble begin-

nings of mimicry, the resulting cultural hybridity is not a bad copy of
any 'original' but a demonstration of the fluid possibilities of sexual politics and an indirect challenge to ideological stand off between queer
radicalism and gay conservatism such as what we see in the U.S. today.

This gay cultural hybridity is so far still unstable, although if and
when the backlash against homosexuality escalates, this instability
might coalesce into more concrete political positions like the American
gay conservative/queer radical divide. For example, what would happen
when young urban gay and lesbian discourse encounters older rural
working-class lesbians; or Fukkienese, Hakka, and aboriginal, identity
discourse?[17] If and when this begins to happen, to speak of a hybridized
Taiwanese homosexuality would also function as a warning not to fall
too easily back onto stock positions of ideological polemics. So far, there
are some sporadic reactions but no sign of any groundswell backlash.
There are some signs, however, especially in the various BBSes, of a gay
orthodoxy and a tendency to scurry to the trenches at the slightest challenge.

In this chapter, I have sketched how as the Taiwanese homosexual
discourse emerges and a simplistic copying of American models fell by
the way side, three hybrid positions emerged. Such a typology is naturally only a description of ideal types, not an exhaustive account of reality.[18] It also did not give an account of the considerable influences from
Hong Kong, Japan, and increasingly, even China. However, I hope
through this short discussion, I have begun to make the case for thinking about non-Western sexuality through the framework of cultural
hybridization.

NOTES

1. See Homi Bhabha "Sings Taken for Wonders: Questions of Ambivalence and Authority Under a Tree Outside Delhi, May 1817" *Critical Inquiry*
vol. 12 no. 1, 1985.

2. This is not to say that the cultures of different nation-states do not
have their own unique characteristics, but that national cultures taken as a
whole tend to have transnational components that cannot be easily mapped onto
any contiguous geographical space.

3. This is different from saying that sexuality is "chosen," as I hope will
become clear when I develop my argument.

4. Although I have tried to cast a wide net gathering different homosexual discourses in this chapter, all that I could find is still strongly dominated by the voices of young, urban, middle-class educational elite. One must hence not generalize the discussions here to other segments of the Taiwanese population. The whole picture is far more complex.

5. See *ZiLi WanBao* 29 Dec. 1993, *LiBao* 29 Dec. 1993 for news reports, *LianHeBao* 30 Dec. 1993:11, *ZiLi ZaoBao* 22 Jan. 1994:19, *ZiLi WanBao* 19 Jan. 1994:14 for readers' letters and articles and *AiBao* no. 2 "Exposé of homosexual rights public hearing" for one typical assessment.

6. Margaret Cruikshank made a similar point in *The Gay and Lesbian Liberation Movement* about the "sixties' civil rights and later the women's movement" unmasking "the necessity of war . . . the inferiority of Blacks or the inferiority of women" as "prejudices of a ruling elite rather than as verifiable accounts of reality," thus providing the model for gays and lesbians to organize. "Sustained protest did not begin until large numbers of homosexuals began to see that the prejudices against them were neither natural nor inevitable" (62).

7. In political literature, *"tongzhi"* (literally, "common goal") means "comrade" and was the all-purpose revolutionary term of address during Mao's China. It was also used by Dr. Sun Yat-sen in the early twentieth century to address his comrades for the overthrow of the Ching dynasty. It has now been appropriated as a translation of the English word "queer" to suggest a new cause of equality for Chinese sexual minorities and becomes a clarion call for homosexuals to unite under a new purpose and boldly soldier on.

8. For example, Han, a straight woman and president of the National Taiwan University gay men's group carefully made clear before her speech that: "This collective statement from various homosexual groups that I will read does not represent all homosexuals, and I likewise do not represent these groups" (Proceedings 1).

9. As one of the participating lesbian groups, *Between Us*, later said: "The human rights argument might also obscure the problem of structural power imbalance. Using the principle of freedom and equality for all, a heterosexual social system that has most of the power can say: 'Neither should homosexuals undermine the rights of others. If you shout out homosexuality, are you not also undermining the rights of heterosexuals?'" (Proceedings 39).

10. Although Taiwan now portrays itself as a champion of democracy, political repression such as the White Terror and 228 Massacre, not to mention the legacy of martial law which was lifted only in 1987, are all still fresh in contemporary memory. The 228 Massacre is the name given to the aftermath of the national Taiwanese protest against the corrupt government of Chen Yi, appointed governor of Taiwan after the defeat of the Japanese in 1945. After a

few people were killed by Chen Yi and a national protest threatened the government, Chiang Kai-shek sent in troops and declared martial law. The subsequent "cleansing of the countryside" left tens of thousands dead, injured, or missing. The White Terror is a period of martial rule after the 228 Massacre where an unknown number (the highest estimate is about 120,000) of people were imprisoned and killed and tens of thousands more exiled. The exact period of the White Terror is not clearly demarcated but is generally agreed to have lasted about thirty years from 1947 to the 1970s.

11. This approach, interestingly, ties in with the one that Marshall Kirk and Hunter Madsen championed in their book *After the Ball*. There has never been any reference to them or their ideas in Taiwan, however. The similarities and differences between these American neoconservatives and Hong Kong and Taiwanese advocates of the non-confrontational approach is a subject that deserves a full and separate treatment.

12. For example, as Luci Hung writes in "Between the Lace and the Whip: The Flow of Lesbians' Desire as Disclosed in Contemporary Taiwanese Fiction": "What about the possibility of the grotesque being stripped of all subversive power and absorbed into the system as sensational spectacle? For queers intending on counter-attack, this danger of de-politicized containment is a trap that demands constant vigilance" (76).

13. *Kuer* is another translation of "queer" It tends generally to denote resistance to mainstream culture and a deliberately pariah stance that aims for subversion. In contrast, *tongzhi* tends to denote more reformist tendency.

14. The debate was in part inspired by Jacquelyn Zita's "Male Lesbians and the Postmodern Body." Zita focused on the theoretical problem of a postmodern gendering of the body, whereas the Taiwanese students focused on identity politics.

15. The interpellation of individual as subject might be taken as a given, but *what kind* of subject is still up for grabs. The move I made here with respect to sexuality is similar to the one made by Teresa de Lauretis with respect to gender, where she leverages Wendy Hollway's work "Gender Difference and the Production of Subjectivity" in the book *Changing the Subject* (See especially pg. 6 and 15–16 in Technologies), in her essay "Technologies of Gender" in her book of the same title.

16. One might demur that the second resistance is merely accidental, but that would amount to dismissing out of hand not yet theorized choices as unfit for theoretical inquiry, thus missing an opportunity to a more nuanced theoretical understanding.

17. See my PhD. dissertation, especially the section on the Taiwanese writer Ling Yan in Chapter Two for a fuller discussion. Fukkienese is a Chinese

ethnic group from the Fujian province in Southern China. The Fukkienese immigrated in large numbers to Taiwan, starting probably in the seventeenth century. During the Nationalist Party's (KMT) martial rule under the leadership of Chiang Kai-shek, Chinese population in Taiwan were defined as *benshenren* (native Taiwanese) and *waishenren* (Mainland immigrant). Waishenren were those immigrants who came to Taiwan in the late 1940s, during the civil war where Chiang Kai-shek's KMT lost to Mao Tze-dong's Chinese Communist Party (CCP). Chiang himself was a waishenren and he banned the use of pre-existing languages in Taiwan in favor of Mandarin. After the death of Chiang Kai-shek and his son who succeeded him as president, resistance to this language policy grew in tandem with the dislike of KMT martial rule. Fukkienese identity became one of the focal points of indigenous discourse whose politics were hostile to the KMT. Current Taiwanese president, Chen Shui-bian, is from the Democratic Progressive Party (DPP). This is a party with strong roots in the Fukkienese movement.

Hakka is a Chinese ethnic group with the unfortunate distinction of often being marginalized in Mainland China. The Hakka probably started immigrating to Taiwan in the seventeenth century together with the Fukkienese. They comprise about 11% of the Taiwanese population today. In Taiwan, where the Fukkienese identity is often conflated with the Taiwanese identity, the Hakka claim to being Taiwanese is again being marginalized. Recently, the DPP government in Taiwan has made some efforts in acknowledging the Hakka language and identity.

An Aboriginal is an inhabitant of Taiwan before the arrival of others such as Chinese and Dutch. They are believed to be Polynesian in origin. There are about eleven different tribes in Taiwan today with the Amis and Paiwan tribes being the most populous, The other tribes are: Taroko, Tayal, Bunun, Puyuma, Tsou, Saisiat, Thao, Rukai, and Yami. During its rule, the KMT government had appropriated large tracts of Aboriginal land and various tribes had been forcibly relocated to make way for mining and industrial land use. Displaced Aboriginals often end up in the cities as unskilled labor. A policy of forced assimilation was also put in place and the use of indigenous Aboriginal languages banned. Recently, there has been a resurgence of Aboriginal discourse and identity and a movement to re-claim aboriginal rights.

18. A word about what I mean by "reality" here. The "reality" of categories like "homosexual" comes from people's identification and investment in the effect of sexuality, i.e., in a discourse that uses the biological sex of one's object of desire (as opposed to race, age, etc.) as the axis of sexual classification. The "reality" of my "homosexual positionalities" comes from the accuracy with which I have described and analyzed their sexual and cultural politics based on this effect of sexuality. None of them has anything to do with the "reality" of "is there 'really' such a thing as 'homosexuality' or 'sexuality'"?

WORKS CITED

Althusser, Louis. "Ideology and Ideological State Apparatuses (Notes Towards an Investigation)." In *Lenin and Philosophy and Other Essays*. New York: Monthly Review Press, 1971.

Bhabha, Homi K. "Sings Taken for Wonders: Questions of Ambivalence and Authority Under a Tree Outside Delhi, May 1817." *Critical Inquiry* vol. 12, no. 1, 1985.

Cruikshank, Margaret. *The Gay and Lesbian Liberation Movement*. Routledge, 1992.

de Lauretis, Teresa. *Technologies of Gender: Essays on Theory, Film and Fiction*. Bloomington: Indiana UP, 1987.

D'Emilio, John. "Capitalism and Gay Identity." In Ann Snitow, Christine Stansell, and Sharon Thompson, eds., *Powers of Desire: The Politics of Sexuality*. New York: Monthly Review Press, 1983.

Hung, Luci. "Between the Lace and the Whip: The Flow of Lesbians' Desire as Disclosed in Contemporary Taiwanese Fiction." *Chung Wai Literary Monthly* 25.1:60–80, June 1996.

Kirk, Marshall, and Hunter Madsen. *After the Ball: How America Will Conquer its Fear & Hatred of Gays in the 90's*. New York: Doubleday, 1989.

Tan, Chong Kee. "Re-negotiating Transcultural Sexuality: The Deployment of Homosexual Eroticism and Prejudices in Taiwanese Fiction 1960–1997." Ph.D. dissertation. Stanford University, 1998.

Tongzhi Gongzuofang. "A Date With Anti-discrimination: Proceedings of the Public Hearing on the Advancement of Homosexual Rights." No dates. Taipei, Taiwan.

Zita, Jacquelyn N. "Male Lesbians and the Postmodernist Body." *Hypatia* 7:4:106–127, Fall 1992.

And the following Taiwanese newspapers and journals:

AiBao

China Times

G&L magazine

Isle Margin. Issue 10 (Queer issue), Jan. 1994 & Issue 14 (Sex and Nation), Sept. 1995.

LianHe Bao

LianHe WanBao

LianHe ZaoBao
Taiwan LiBao
ZhongShi WanBao
ZiLi WanBao
ZiLi ZaoBao

CHAPTER SIX

OUT IN AFRICA

GAURAV DESAI

At one point in Wole Soyinka's novel *The Interpreters,* the African-American homosexual[1] Joe Golder, who incidentally also happens to be a historian of Africa, attempts to discuss indigenous African homosexuality with the Nigerian journalist Sagoe: "Do you think I know nothing of your Emirs and their little boys? You forget history is my subject. And what about those exclusive coteries in Lagos?" Sagoe gesture[s] defeat. "You seem better informed than I am. But if you don't mind I'll persist in my delusion" (Soyinka 199). In this brief encounter, Soyinka dramatizes the hitherto dominant narrative of attempts at discussing alternative African sexualities. Typically an "outside"[2] observer, with motivations which are probably too overdetermined to be clearly delineated, ventures into the vexed territory of studying alternative sexualities in a given culture; typically, again, an "insider" says "Leave us alone. We are not interested in talking about these things and it's really none of your business." At an impasse—suspicious of the historically ethnocentric renderings of non-Western sexualities as "primitive"—the "insider" prefers to draw attention away from any nonnormative sexual practices; at the risk of not being offensive, at the risk of not being unethical, the "outsider" exits. Some necessary questions continue to remain unasked.

In this troubled exchange, however, it is not entirely clear where
the moral high ground lies. Just as Western feminism finds itself in a
"nervous condition" vis-à-vis its negotiations with non-Western practices such as incision and clitoridectomy,[3] an antihomophobic politics
finds itself unable to open up gay-affirmative spaces without running the
risk of being culturally insensitive. And yet, if no "culture" is so monolithic, so homogeneous, as to be fully recuperable within a singular sexual, aesthetic, economic, moral, or epistemic order, if "culture," that is,
always exceeds the limits it seeks to set for itself, then what divides the
"culturally sensitive" from the "culturally insensitive"? Could sensitivity to the needs and desires of *some* subjects mean risking insensitivity
to the needs and desires of others? If so, to which subjects and voices
must such a politics pay heed?

By drawing on a variety of texts—some literary, some historical,
some anthropological—I want, in this chapter, to join hands with those
African(ist)s[4] who are interested in opening up a space for considerations of African sexual practices in all their fluid forms. In particular I
am interested in the ways in which literary works interpellate issues of
sexual normativity and transgression. I open with the general problematics surrounding scholarship on nonnormative African sexualities and
show the discursive continuities in the arguments from colonial to postcolonial times.[5] I then proceed to read Bessie Head's short novel *Maru*
against the grain of existing scholarship, which insists on reading it as a
traditional heterosexual romance. I suggest that my alternative reading
of the novel is enabled by, and hopefully in its own small way contributes to, the work of those who are currently struggling to open up
the discourses of alternative African sexualities both within and without
the continent. I follow the seminal work of Chris Dunton whose essay
"'Wheyting be Dat?' The Treatment of Homosexuality in African Literature" remains the single most comprehensive treatment of the subject
to date, and the more recent work of Rhonda Cobham on the integral
relationship between sexual and national identities in the writings of
Nuruddin Farah.[6] While Cobham's work, in its critical interrogation of
the construction of masculinity, is most directly relevant to my own
reading of *Maru*, my interest in Dunton's essay is rooted in the larger
question of the conditions of possibility of literary interpretations.

Through critical readings of a variety of African literary texts written since the 1950s, Dunton argues in his essay that with few exceptions,
African writers tend to present homosexuality monothematically.

Homosexuality is, in these texts "almost invariably attributed to the detrimental impact made on Africa by the West," and consequently "the function that it plays in the text's larger thematic and narrative design is restricted and predictable" (Dunton 422). While Dunton's argument is indeed confirmed by the numerous critical readings of these texts written since the 1960s, the issue of *where* the blindness lies—on the part of the authors or on the part of the critics—is one that needs greater scrutiny. If, as reader-response theorists would have us believe, texts are as much the product of the interpretive practices of readers as they are the product of authorial intentions, then could the supposedly monothematic treatment be a product not of authorial agency but rather of the critic's interpretive limitations?

Consider the case of Joe Golder. Joe, the professor of African history with whom we began this chapter, has consistently been read in the critical literature as Soyinka's emblem of everything that is wrong with a Western-based, romanticized Afrocentricity. This critical reading emphasizes Joe's alienation from his Nigerian colleagues who read him as a doubly foreign person—not only is he an American but also one who engages in sexual practices unknown (at least so far as these interpreters are concerned) in indigenous Nigerian society.[7] Joe Golder becomes in this reading an impotent (because homosexual) character who can only poach upon African subjects (such as the young boy Noah) and be the cause of destruction. Read in this manner, the character of Joe Golder confirms Chris Dunton's thesis: he is presented as no more than a scaffold for the larger narrative thematic so that consistent with the dominant theme of the novel, this particular "interpreter," much like his Nigerian counterparts, is unable to be a productive force in the newly independent society. Like philosophers, Joe and his friends can interpret the world but cannot change it. Yet, is there a different Joe Golder in this text who remains to be heard? A Joe Golder who is not predictably lecherous and filled with vice?

In one episode in the novel, the young boy Noah jumps off a balcony to his death, the narrative suggesting that his death is caused by Joe's sexual advances. The unfortunate incident is read by most critics as Soyinka's last straw in his rebuke of Golder. Thus Derek Wright writes "(Noah) is subsequently left at the *mercy* of the *neurotic* American quadroon Joe Golder, whose attraction to blackness is *more sexual than racial* and whose *inevitable* homosexual advances result in the boy's death" (Wright 122; italics mine). Let us note immediately that the sup-

posed *inevitability* of sexual desire and a forthcoming solicitation when
a homosexual man finds himself in the company of a young boy speaks
more perhaps to the critic's interpretive assumptions and cultural imaginary than to the actual unfolding of the narrative. For there is sufficient
reason to believe that Golder doesn't quite understand why the boy
jumps to his own death, especially since he has assured him that he
would not touch or harm him.

What is clear in the narrative, and what is rarely addressed by critics, is the double bind that Joe consistently finds himself in—on the one
hand, he *does* want people to know about his sexual preferences and to
be proud of his homosexual identity (as is evident in the exchange with
Sagoe), and yet on the other, he hopes that he is not reduced to *just* being
a desiring and lecherous body by society, read by his friends, that is, as
a foreign parasite whose sole purpose is to prey upon the Nigerian men.
Read from Joe's point of view, his implication in Noah's death is less a
product of his direct actions than it is of his perceived identity. Much
like the famous Marabar Cave scene in Forster's *Passage to India,* the
victimization is more the effect of a larger social imaginary than of an
actual sexual offense. If to the British, Aziz can be read as no other than
the emblem of a desiring Muslim India, then to the Nigerian interpreters, Joe Golder, too, emerges as a dangerously desiring body. But
while Aziz, by the end of Forster's novel and in most literary criticism,
is exonerated of his alleged crime, Golder remains to this day in the criticism of this text, the homosexual—and therefore—the accused.

Herein, then, lies Joe Golder's tragedy—attempting to escape both
the homophobia within the African American community at home and the
insistent hypersexuality ascribed to the black man by the larger predominantly white American society, Joe finds that in Africa, too, he is no more
than a sexual body. Yet, if the possibility of this reading is left open by the
narrative, it is one that few critics have pursued. Instead, the critics *replay*
the textual tragedy in their own criticism. So, for instance, in Wright's
reading, Joe emerges as an odd man, a "neurotic" whose identification
with the black race, for what it's worth, is "more sexual than racial."

While a more detailed reading of Joe Golder is best left for another
occasion, I want to reiterate that it is precisely in addressing his simultaneous negotiations of racial and sexual identities that Soyinka presents
Golder as a profoundly sympathetic character. Golder is an individual
who has had to claim actively at least two identities that continually
threaten to escape him—he is at once a light-skinned black man capable

of "passing" as a white man and a homosexual capable of passing as straight. His choice not to pass—his choice to reaffirm at once two identities not only at odds with the hegemonic order of things but also, more importantly, at odds with one another—is a choice that must sober even the most unsympathetic of readers. Furthermore, Joe's decision to study African history and his move to Nigeria, despite its potentially romanticizing implications, is presented by Soyinka as his continual attempt to negotiate the different demands placed upon his identities. Like DuBois, Joe has continually been confronted with a "double consciousness, (the) sense of always looking at one's self through the eyes of others, of measuring one's soul by the tape of a world that looks on in amused contempt and pity" (DuBois 8). He comes to Africa hoping to erase at least one, if not both, of these sources of difference. He fails.

It is significant in this context that Soyinka presents us a Joe armed with a copy of James Baldwin's *Another Country*. For here is the suggestion that Golder is not some singular oddity but one with a legacy. Just as Baldwin, a gay black man, felt unable to find a home in the United States and thus sought Paris, Golder too seeks to find a different home in Nigeria. In this new African context, however, Joe Golder is unable to connect either emotionally or physically and remains desperately lonely. Golder then, is a character full of pathos if not tragedy, living through the experience of a transcendental homelessness, of belonging nowhere. To heighten this sense of pathos, towards the end of the novel, Soyinka has Joe Golder sing "Sometimes I Feel Like a Motherless Child," a song whose performance profoundly increases the sense of alienation already being felt by the other Nigerian protagonists. It is important to note that Soyinka's choice of this song is not innocent but draws upon the very same James Baldwin who has affected Joe's life. In his *Notes of a Native Son*, Baldwin, reflecting upon the distance between the African and the African American writes:

> [The African American] begins to conjecture how much he has gained and lost during his long sojourn in the American republic. The African before him has endured privation, injustice, medieval cruelty; but the African has not yet endured the utter alienation of himself from his people and his past. His mother did not sing "Sometimes I Feel Like a Motherless Child" and he has not, all his life long, ached for the acceptance in a culture which pronounced straight hair and white skin the only acceptable beauty. (Baldwin 122)

Soyinka's tragic vision then, appropriates this song from the African-
American tradition to now include the predicament of a postcolonial
nation-state in Africa. Rather than providing a supportive and inviting
space for the alienated African American, the postcolonial nation-state
too joins hands in the tragic condition.

THE EMERGENCE OF A DISCOURSE

I have focused on the character of Joe Golder not so much in the interests of promoting him to a heroic type but instead to ask a basic question in the history of literary interpretations. If indeed Joe can be read in
a sympathetic manner today (indeed, if as some of my students suggest
he could not be read as anything *but* tragic), then how do we account
for the fact that he has never so far been read as such? The answer, I suggest, has less to do with any intentional malice on the part of critics than
with the nature of critical discourse itself and the contingencies of its
production. Simply put, just as literary genres have their histories, so
does the genre of criticism, and critical discourses like any other have
rules of exclusion and inclusion. Until these rules, both internal as well
as external to the discourse, realign themselves to open up different conditions of possibilities, certain kinds of claims remain unthought, or if at
all thought, remain unintelligible and unallowable within the dominant
discourse.[8] Or, as Michel Foucault puts it, for a claim to be considered
true, it must first be "within the truth."[9] What causes realignments
within the field of discursive legitimacy is a multiplicity of factors—
some relatively external to the discourse, such as political revolutions,
others relatively internal to it, such as sheer boredom with existing models of explanation on the part of participants. Most often, of course, the
various contingencies work together to form new conditions of possibility and new intellectual configurations. Thus, with the simultaneous
growth of gay and lesbian political activism in Africa, and the emergence
of gay and lesbian studies as legiti mate foci for scholarly research, we
find ourselves today in the midst of such a process vis-à-vis the discourse
of African sexuality. As such, the times are both politically and intellectually exciting.

In addressing the limits and the stakes involved in this newly emergent discursive field, it is important to note the complicated issue of the
relationship between anticolonial politics, gay-lesbian liberation, and

the politics of feminism. If we are embarked on a space-clearing project, the desire to keep it antihomophobic, feminist, and anticolonial at the same time is one that I share and uphold, but it is important to state that the specific lines of alliance between these three nodes will for now have to remain undetermined. While one may expect to find a continuity between certain political positions, such as between feminism and anti-homophobia for instance (since both share the project of being critical of patriarchy), these continuities are not natural but rather contingently forged. And if such forging is to take shape in the threshold of a colonial landscape, it is always susceptible to the overdeterminations of "race" and "nation."

Take for instance, the seminal work of Ifi Amadiume on the changing construction of gender in Nnobi society. In her work, Amadiume shows how the institution of woman-to-woman marriages in precolonial Nnobi society suggests that there existed in this society a certain fluidity in the gender-sex system so that biological sex did not necessarily determine social gender. Amadiume's compelling insight is that the relative reification and indeed "naturalization" of sex-gender roles that one observes in more contemporary times among the Nnobi was not a precolonial legacy but rather a direct consequence of British colonial practices aimed at regulating the possible gender options available for Nnobi women. In other words, by drawing on a precolonial social institution in which women could marry other women and play the social role of husbands, Amadiume shows that things were not always as they seem today in Nnobi society. Gender roles were not easily tied to biological sex, and individual women did indeed have social possibilities that they have no more. So far, her argument is an important historical corrective to those who tend to either essentialize women or to essentialize patriarchy. But the force of Amadiume's argument is lost in her consideration of sexual practices. For having demonstrated gender mobility in precolonial society, Amadiume proceeds to insist that the phenomenon of women marriages should not be misread as any kind of institutionalized lesbianism. Such a reading, which Amadiume suggests has been carried on primarily by black lesbians in the West, can only result from the interpreter's "wishes and fantasies," and ultimately reveals nothing more than her "ethnocentrism." Furthermore, she suggests that such a reading would be "shocking and offensive to Nnobi women" (Amadiume 7) for whom lesbianism remains a foreign practice.

While Amadiume's cautionary remarks are indeed ones that any reader must pay heed to, the precise *argument* made in defense remains elusive—for surely while Amadiume is probably correct in suggesting that contemporary Nnobi Women would find any hints of lesbianism "offensive,"[10] her own greatest insight that colonial practices severely disturbed precolonial *gender* possibilities resulting in a different normatization of gender roles may also *potentially* lend itself to sexual practices. In other words, could it be that just as British colonialism radically changed the gender possibilities available to women, it may also have instituted and regulated sexual practices so that "offense" at the thought of lesbianism may be precisely the ideological mark of such intervention? Or to put it differently, can we be reasonably sure that through a historical change in which gender seems to be transformed so much, sexuality could have gone unaffected? *We cannot yet be sure*—more research would have to be done to answer this question, and indeed it may well turn out that Amadiume is right in suggesting that sexual practices were always resolutely heterosexual among the Nnobi.[11] But to silence the question through accusations of ethnocentrism and offense seems an unfortunate way to deal with an uncomfortable question. An unquestionable and unquestioning nativism is no satisfactory response to even the most pervasive ethnocentrism.

My point in singling out Amadiume's work is to show how even the most sophisticated feminists and the most engaging critics of patriarchy can nevertheless lend themselves to a theoretical silence or even downright hostility when issues of homosexuality are raised. But this hostility we must note, is, at least in our case, not unconnected to the complex problematics of cultural difference and race that are always informing such accounts. For if Amadiume's anger is directed towards black lesbians primarily in the West who, it would seem, bring their false desires to bear upon a resolutely heterosexual Africa, then the *hors texte* of this encounter is surely the earlier voice of Frantz Fanon.

It is Frantz Fanon who in *Black Skin, White Masks* provides what for many has become the classic position on the relation between Africa, the West, and homosexuality. Fanon's double move consists not only of associating white racism with homosexuality—as in the statement "the Negrophobic man is a repressed homosexual" (Fanon 156)—but also simultaneously insisting that no indigenous homosexuality exists in Africa. Fanon suggests that while transvestism may occur among some Martiniquans, these men lead normal sex lives and can "take a punch like any 'he-man'" (Fanon 180, note 44). In Fanon's account then, homosexuality becomes associated on the one hand with racism and colonial oppression, and on the other with effeminacy. In a context in which the black man's sexuality is read simultaneously as excessive as well as castrated, homosexuality comes into focus here, as Lee Edelman suggests, "only as the conflictual undoing of one man's authority by another; it signifies that is, only as a failed, debased, or inadequate masculintiy—a masculinity severed from the ground of its meaning in a phallic 'possession' betokening one's legitimate status as a subject" (Edelman 54). To be sure, at a historical moment when civilized, normative sexuality was read as one located in the monogamous, heterosexual family, and primitive sexuality in a whole host of what are read as abnormalities and "perversions," it is understandable that Fanon would wish to dissociate Africa from the "primitive"—the sexually "perverse." But as Diana Fuss notes, it is unfortunate that "Fanon does not think beyond the presuppositions of colonial discourse to examine how colonial domination itself works partially through the social institutionalization of misogyny and homophobia" (Fuss 36). Could it be that a particular form of heteronormativity was a necessary accomplice to the workings of colonial authority?

If in Fanon's framework nationalist struggle must depend on a simultaneous insistence on the creation of a productive black male subjectivity, a subjectivity that is, which does not allow itself to be symbolically "castrated" through any association with homosexuality, it is not clear that this strategy necessarily speaks to all the experiences of all the subjects within the newly forming nations. Not only does this normative order dictate the sexual construction of masculinity, it also, through the extension in which the demands of race supersede those of gender and sexuality, begins to dictate the sexual lives of women. It is thus that we find in Adrienne Rich's seminal essay "Compulsory Heterosexuality and Lesbian Experience" a letter from a Mozambican woman in exile:

> I am condemned to a life of exile because I will not deny that I am
> a lesbian, that my primary commitments are, and will always be to
> other women. In the new Mozambique, lesbianism is considered a
> left-over from colonialism and decadent Western civilization. Les-
> bians are sent to rehabilitation camps to learn through self-criticism
> the correct line about themselves. . . . If I am forced to denounce my
> own love for women, if I therefore denounce myself, I could go back

to Mozambique and join forces in the exciting and hard struggle of
rebuilding a nation, including the struggle for the emancipation of
Mozambiquan women. As it is, I either risk the rehabilitation
camps, or remain in exile. (Rich 240)

Unlike in the contemporary West then, where one may well postulate a
lesbian continuum in the midst of a radically discontinuous male
homosocial/sexual existence, in colonial-nationalist and postcolonial
Africa one often finds both the male as well as female continuums disrupted. Thus, in such a context, just as the national struggle often takes
precedence over the women's movement, so it is that the construction of
an insistent heteronormativity begins to threaten any existing alternative
sexual practices. It is in this sense that one could argue that at least in
some African contexts, it was not *homosexuality* that was inherited
from the West but rather a more regulatory *homophobia*.

The Heteronormative Ideal: Reading Bessie Head's *Maru*

If we want to understand the workings of homophobia and the active
curtailment of any nonheterosexual desire it engenders, we may find it
productive to turn to Bessie Head's 1971 novel *Maru. Maru*, as I suggested earlier, has been read by most critics as a romantic tale in which
human love triumphs over the banalities of racial prejudice. While
through the character of the Masarwa woman, Margaret, Bessie Head
pays a considerable amount of attention to the thematics of race, I want
to propose that a more productive reading of the novel suggests that it
is concerned not only with racial identity and racism but also, and perhaps more significantly, with (hetero)sexual identity and sexism.[12]

What exactly constitutes "sexual" as opposed to any other kind of
desire will have to remain an open question in our reading, since that in
many ways is a question that the narrative attempts to negotiate. For, if
Head's novel is about the circulation of desire between the four major
characters, Maru, Moleka, Dikeledi, and Margaret, it is not always clear
in which direction the desires flow. We may discern at least two triangular relationships in the novel: the first being the rivalry of Maru and
Moleka for Margaret and the second being the unspoken and indeed
unacknowledged rivalry between Dikeledi and Margaret for Moleka.
But the nature of these two triangular relationships is different insofar

as the relationship between the two men over the woman is fraught with a violent tension which leads to murderous intentions at least in Moleka, whereas the relationship between the two women, while occasionally tense, is never seriously put in jeopardy over their simultaneous desire for the same man.

I propose that the most interesting and dramatic moments in Bessie Head's novel pertain not to the heterosexual desires of the characters but rather to their anxieties about their own homosocial relationships. It need be remarked that it is precisely the homo*social* as opposed to the homo*sexual* configuration of these relationships that mark this text as an apt account of the advent of a particular kind of heterosexual normativity in African contexts. Published in 1971 at a time when Christianity had already done its work in rendering any sexuality other than heterosexual monogamy as sinful and immoral, at a time when the colonially inherited legal discourses in many African states had already labeled as deviant and criminalized any sexuality not conforming to the norms of the heterosexual family, and at a time when the discourse around homosexuality was thematized consistently in African literature as a purely Western phenomenon, Bessie Head's *Maru* marks the moment of the ambivalent triumph of heteronormativity.

If precolonial sexualities in various African contexts could indeed incorporate a whole range of acts, which may plausibly be read as "homoerotic" or "homosexual" in retrospect, they were never really labeled as such. In such a context then, the continuum between men's sexual relations and men's social bonds need not have been disrupted. But as Michel Foucault suggests of the European context, the emergence of a discourse around such activities also led to a regulation of these activities, and this meant that any such precolonial continuums of male or female desires would, in colonial and postcolonial times, have to be radically disrupted. Bessie Head's *Maru* is a text that explicitly thematizes this rupture. In other words, it is precisely the *impossibility* of imagining a continuum of sexuality both between men and between women[13] that this text seeks to mark. To be sure, I will suggest that Head's narrative surreptitiously points to the ambivalence of that rupture and thus renders the will to heteronormativity unstable. Yet it is important to understand that at the most manifest level heteronormativity is what the novel is about.

The most obvious instantiation of this claim may be found in the growing friendship between Dikeledi and Margaret. Their meetings are filled with a love and affection which profoundly marks both the characters. On one such occasion, when Dikeledi offers to lend Margaret a spare bed that she has at home, Margaret is provoked to think through the nature of their friendship: "Margaret looked up, startled. Their friendship was too unfathomable to her, as though she could not make an effort to analyze her feelings towards Dikeledi and it would drift on and on like this, continually getting into deep water" (Head 86).

Margaret Cadmore then, who, after considerable thought has refused to pass as a "colored" woman and has insisted on naming her own racial identity, finds that her feelings for Dikeledi are those which she cannot name.[14] The imagery suggests that the relationship between the two women is dangerously deep—thus "unfathomable"—and indeed is headed towards "deeper water." If by the end of the novel, the two women are seen to so profoundly love and affect one another that they end up increasingly becoming like each other, then at this still early point they both feel uneasy about their mutual feelings. While Margaret's response is to ponder unsuccessfully over their relationship, Dikeledi we are told immediately "dives" not into the unfathomable waters of their growing love, but rather into a packet of Marmite sandwiches and simultaneously into private thoughts about Moleka—and how else are we to read her ludicrous thoughts about Moleka's kisses ("Moleka's kisses taste like Marmite sandwiches. Moleka's kisses taste like roast beef with spicy gravy. Moleka's kisses . . . ," 87) than as the conventional response of what may well be recognized as a "compulsory heterosexuality?" How else are we to read them other than as performative utterances which in the face of a dangerously homoerotic tenderness insist: "I want Moleka." "I desire Men"?

While Dikeledi is having these thoughts, Margaret we are told "half-consciously" picks up a pencil and sketches her. This is an important moment because it completes a particular flow of desire that continually structures the same-sex relationships in the novel. Here then we have a scenario in which Dikeledi performs an act that establishes her affection towards Margaret; Margaret senses their growing affection with a little unease; Dikeledi displaces any sexual or erotic component of their relationship onto Moleka; and finally, Margaret half-consciously attempts to reclaim Dikeledi.

A similar structure is in effect in the relationship between the two male protagonists Moleka and Maru. The narrator suggests that "the clue to Moleka and Maru lay in their relationship with women" (34).

What follows is a classic Girardian drama: Maru and Moleka become rivals for the love of Margaret in which, as Eve Sedgwick puts it, "the choice of the beloved is determined in the first place, not by the qualities of the beloved, but by the beloved's already being the choice of the person who has been chosen as rival."[15] For while Moleka at least has a brief encounter with Margaret before he decides that he loves her, Maru simply follows suit without any such meaningful exchange with Margaret. As Sedgwick suggests in her own readings of such structures, it is important to recognize that in such an erotic rivalry, "the bond that links the two rivals is as intense and potent as the bond that links either of the rivals to the beloved" (Sedgwick 21). Indeed, in the case of Bessie Head's novel, it is clear that the bond between these two friends-turned-rivals far exceeds any bonds they establish with the female characters. For as the narrator notes: "When had Moleka and Maru not lived in each other's arms and shared everything? People said: 'Oh Moleka and Maru always fall in love with the same girl.' But they never knew that no experiences interrupted the river and permanent flow of their deep affection" (33). Moleka was devoted to the light in Maru's's eyes which he could see from across the room and even when "thousands of people noted the dramatic impact of Moleka, . . . he would always cast his eyes across the room to see if all was well with Maru" (34).

Not only is this homosocial relationship, like that between the women, the cause of some unease, it is also responsible for Moleka's crisis. If Moleka senses at some level that his love for Margaret results in his increasing alienation from Maru, he also discovers that his newfound love, along with his loss of Maru, leaves him temporarily impotent. He has, we are told, "suddenly forgot[ten] everything about making approaches to a woman" (76). As though to spatially map the flow of desire, Head presents us with a Moleka who, at one point starts off to visit Margaret, is distracted, and "unconsciously" we are told, "his feet (take) him in the direction of the house of Maru" (79). Moleka stands outside Maru's house for over two hours watching him through the window, and by the end of the evening he is described as a changed man who has had a chance of reflecting upon the nature of his love. "He was Moleka," the narrator suggests, "but with something added" (80).

What is important to note then, is that while Bessie Head gives abundant evidence for a strong, loving relationship between the two male protagonists, that relationship can only be explicitly recognized by them within the limits of a nonerotic, asexual friendship. If what we witness here is a classic example of the workings of heterosexual normativity in which the bodies of women become the objects of exchange within a patriarchal sexual economy, then the characters themselves cannot be allowed to fully partake of this knowledge. Thus it is important that when the relationship between Maru and Moleka undergoes a crisis in the face of a potential heterosexual alliance with a woman, only the omniscient narrator has the privilege of making the links. For were the crisis to be acknowledged directly by the characters as a crisis of their own love for each other, it would at the same time mean that they would have to acknowledge the deeper structure of the continuum of same-sex desire.

The question of whether the continuum is or is not experienced by the characters is crucial not only to understand the possibilities of homoerotic desire in the text but also to address the important issue of the misogyny of the text. We are told that none of the relationships that either Maru or Moleka have had in the past with women have been productive or fruitful. On the contrary, they are quite definitely harmful to the women—the "victims" we are told, "exploded like bombs" (35). Furthermore, when Moleka is unable to take out his anger directly on Maru, he plans to sexually molest Maru's sister Dikeledi to provoke his anger. Here, Moleka's displacement of his violent feelings towards Maru onto Dikeledi is entirely in keeping with the larger gendered structures of the novel. In this case, rather than using the body of the woman as the space where a homosocial love can be displaced, it is used as the battlesite for declaring war. I want to suggest that while it is the case that the relationship between male homosexuality and patriarchal interest cannot be calculated independently of the specific context of occurrence, in this particular case, it is not *homosexuality* but rather a *homophobia* that directs such misogyny. For homophobia is precisely the name of the insistent rupture of the homosocial/sexual continuum that makes it necessary for the bodies of women to be exploited as the terrain for resolving the intimate matters between men.[16]

In such a context, then, Margaret's dream, which by all critical accounts is the focal point of the heterosexual narrative, becomes increasingly ambiguous. In her dream Margaret sees herself in the midst of a field full of daisies covered by a cloudy sky:

> I looked up again and a little way ahead I saw two people embrace each other. I stared quite hard because they were difficult to see.

Their forms were black like the house and the sky, but again, they were surrounded by this yellow light. *I felt so ashamed, thinking I had come upon a secret which ought not to be disclosed, that I turned and tried to run away.* Just then a strong wind arose and began to blow me in the direction of the embracing couple. I was terrified. They did not want anyone near them and I could feel it. I dropped to the ground and tried to grab hold of the daisies to save myself from the strong wind. At that moment I opened my eyes. (103, italics mine)

When Dikeledi sees the drawing that Margaret makes based on her dream, we are told that she immediately recognizes at least one of the two in the embrace—it is her brother Maru. She is horrified by what she sees and turns to Margaret: "'You frighten me,' she said, her eyes wide and startled. 'Why?' Margaret asked. 'Do you always see things like that?' Dikeledi asked" (104). If, as most critics read this dream, it is nothing more than Maru's plan for securing Margaret's love through dream projection, and if it is nothing more than a vision of what is to come in real life—a union between Maru and Margaret depicted very much in a similar setting, the house, daisies, clouds, and all—then why is Dikeledi horrified upon hearing Margaret's account and seeing its depiction? And more importantly, why the sense of the secret that is best not disclosed? And further, if Margaret is the *intruder*, if she is the unwelcome observer of the embrace, then who exactly is Maru embracing?

If the embrace is indeed, as I am suggesting here, an embrace between the two men, a secret embrace, a taboo embrace, then it becomes important to realize that the dream, which after all is supposedly projected by Maru, becomes the vehicle of his desire to reclaim Moleka. And like all the other same-sex flows in the narrative, this one too occurs without the full knowledge of the actor. Thus if Margaret's effort to reclaim Dikeledi is to sketch her in what remains a semiconscious secretive gesture, if Moleka's feet "unconsciously" take him to Maru's house, then the homoerotic embrace in this dream too is an *unconscious* projection on Maru's part.

Bessie Head's narrative works on three levels corresponding to three different orders of knowledge: those of the characters, narrator, and the readers. The simultaneous workings of these three orders is precisely what make *Maru* so powerfully a novel about the construc-

tion of heteronormativity. For *Maru* is not just some seemingly innocent tale of boy meets girl but rather a complicated account of what it
means to become a man through the pursuit of a woman. It is a morality tale of the regulation of desire through socially sanctioned channels
and about the importance of regulating any excessive homosocial
desire. As such, the three orders of knowledge are important—if the
characters' order of knowledge represents the confused and indeed
fluid flow of desire, the narrator's knowledge provides a more reflexive and regulatory structure. For it is the narrator's role to ensure that
the homosocial relations are indeed recognized by the reader as such,
and once recognized, are shown to be actively curtailed. But the project of heteronormativity cannot end by merely suppressing homosocial desire—for it to work it also must seek to regulate the discourse
of sexuality itself. And it is here that the third order of knowledge in
the novel, which, as a silent knowledge that by definition no narrator
can provide, reopens the question of what can be said and what must
remain silent in a heteronormative world.

It is the third order of knowledge that explains why, while in every
other case the narrator has eagerly stepped in to elucidate the nature of
the homosocial relationships, at the important moment when Margaret
discloses her dream, the narrator is nowhere to be found. The work of
interpreting the embrace is left entirely to the reader. For while the
rhetoric seems to suggest the homosexual possibility, the specific
imagery of the dream links it to the fairy-tale ending of the narrative in
which the couples are "properly," that is "heterosexually," paired off
with Maru marrying Margaret and Moleka marrying Dixeledi.

To understand the possibility of the encoding of a silent knowledge
in the narrative is to understand that the triumph of heteronormativity
is at best provisional. For while the novel can only explicitly articulate
the "truth" of the heterosexual ending, it leaves the possibility of homosexual difference in place. Thus, while in Margaret's dream the homosexual embrace is threatened by the gathering "pitch black clouds," the
same clouds ominously gather over the skies in the final scene of the heterosexual coupling.[17] And just as in the dream the embrace is disturbed
by Margaret's arrival, so it is that Maru and Margaret continue to be
disturbed by the force of Moleka's presence in their lives. To make the
link between these two scenes even more explicit, Head writes of the
now married Maru: "He wanted a flower garden of yellow daisies,
because they were the only flowers which resembled the face of his wife

and the *sun of his love*" (1). The daisies that reappear here from the dream remind Maru not only of his wife Margaret but also of Moleka— for it is he who has been described earlier as the "sun around which spun a billion satellites" (58), a "sun" who is played off in the narrative against the moonlike Maru.

It is thus that Bessie Head's novel, ostensibly about race, racism, and problematics of racial passing, becomes a novel about sexuality, sexism, and the problematics of sexual passing. Head's project is to mark the construction of heteronormativity in postcolonial African cultures and to mark the sites of alternative sexual knowledges, which in such an order must remain unheard. By showing us the constructed rather than "natural" order of heteronormativity, Bessie Head allows us to reopen and rethink our investigations about the existence of a variety of sexual practices in precolonial, colonial, and indeed postcolonial Africa.

FROM SHAKA TO EVITA

Over the past few years, historical and archival research on African sexualities has pointed to several practices that challenge the invention of Africa as resolutely heterosexual.[18] For instance, in his study *The Construction of Homosexuality*, David Greenberg records the following African practices:

1. The *mugawe*, the religious leader of the Kenyan Meru who wears women's clothing and adopts women's hairstyles is often a homosexual and sometimes marries a man (Greenberg 60).

2. Among the Angolan Kwayama, some male diviners wear women's clothing and become secondary spouses of men whose other wives are female (60).

3. South African Zulu diviners are usually women but about ten percent are male transvestites (60).

4. Homosexuality associated with male-to-female gender change without necessary religious connotations has been documented among the Nandi, the Dinka, the Nuer, the Konso, the Amhara, the Ottoro, the Fanti, the Ovimbumbdu, the Thongo, the Tanala, the Bara, the Wolof, the Lango, the Iteso, the Gisu, and the Sebei. For some of these peoples the transvestite role was institutionalized, in others probably not (61).

5. Some Nandi women of Kenya have been recorded to have lesbian affairs for the first time as adults (66).

6. Lesbian affairs were virtually universal among unmarried Akan women of the former Gold Coast (now Ghana). Whenever possible, the women purchased extra large beds to accommodate group sex sessions involving perhaps half a dozen women (66).

7. Homosexual relations are common among Nyakusa boys who leave the main village with their age-mates to form a new village on the outskirts (68–69).

What all these examples[19] suggest is that even if we were to allow for a fair amount of "ethnocentrism" on the part of anthropologists who may have, as we saw Amadiume suggest earlier, "read into" the various African societies their own sexual desires, it still leaves the scales relatively unturned.[20] The question at this point, for most scholars, is not whether or not indigenous alternative sexual practices have existed or continue to exist in Africa, but rather, how one understands their historical emergence, the conditions of (im)possibility for identity formations based on these practices and in particular the relationship of these identities to racial and national identities.

This is not to suggest that the project is an easy one. The question of how one talks about "homosexuality" or "bisexuality" in precolonial Africa remains a complicated one, not only because of the historical interpellation of sexual issues within racial schemas, as we have seen in Fanon, but also because the very categories "homosexual" and "bisexual" have come today to take on a cultural and sociopolitical meaning that they could not possibly have had in precolonial African cultures. It is sobering in this context to note, as David Halperin and Jonathan Katz among others have done, that the category of "homosexual" and its supposed opposite "heterosexual" are relatively recent Western inventions (see Halperin; Katz). While the many sexual acts performed ever since the Greeks may, in retrospect, arguably be placed under the rubric of either of these categories, the force of these conceptual categories remains recent and only of dubious use in considering older periods. Furthermore, as John D'Emilio reminds us of the American context, industrialization and capitalism were necessary preconditions for the mobilization of a "gay identity," and it follows that in contexts such as colonial America or precolonial Africa, where industrialization and capitalism had yet to make their full impact, no such identity formation could take place (D'Emilio). Yet, as Greenberg's work shows, it is important that neither the inadequacy of the terms, nor our own inability to fully understand sexual *identities* in the premodern West or in precolonial Africa should lead us to the false conclusion that therefore there were no sexual *acts* performed between members of the same sex.

While the idea that homosexuality is a Western perversion only brought to Africa with colonial contact is one that continues to have appeal among a great number of Africans, it is one that is being actively challenged today by sexual minorities around the continent. Simon Nkoli, an important South African gay activist, suggests that for him the most difficult aspect of "coming out" as a black man in South Africa was the rejection that one felt from one's own ethnic community as well as the racism inherent in the white gay community. For Nkoli, the project has been to simultaneously attempt to build crossracial coalitions within South Africa's multiracial gay community as well as to speak out against homophobia in the black African communities (Patron).

Nkoli's struggle, like that of many contemporary black African gay activists across Africa, is a struggle over representation. And as is often the case in such struggles, it is a dual process being on the one hand a search for political representation, civil liberties, and the rights of equal protection under the law, and on the other, for the right to re-present the community in a sympathetic frame, to tell different stories[21] than the ones that have been told about it in history, in the hopes of preparing for better times to come.

The fight for gay liberation in Africa is bound to be a difficult one. But there are signs to show that it will not be fruitless. South Africa's march from Shaka to Evita is one indication of the possibilities for change. With its newly formulated constitution, South Africa became the first nation in the world to specifically name gays and lesbians as deserving equal protection and unprejudicial treatment under the law. Thus today, out of Africa come the reforms which make it more livable to be out in Africa, and indeed one hopes in the rest of the world.

NOTES

1. While at one point in the novel Joe Golder is referred to as being "queer" (236), the term is not used here as it is in contemporary gay politics in

the United States. I choose to use the term "homosexual" here because it more accurately conveys the reading of Golder in the newly independent Nigerian context of the novel. As often is the case in such situations, the choice of categories for the intellectual historian is complicated—should one use the word "queer" and insist upon its different signification in the Nigerian context, or should one, instead, shy away from the term, so heavily overdetermined by its contemporary American connotations, and choose a term that currently has relatively less political valence? While the term "queer" is quite appropriately used in discussions of some of the more recent events unfolding in South Africa and elsewhere in sub-Saharan Africa, I find that it is of limited value in claiming it for a 1960s context. Yet, this is a terminological issue in much need of debate.

2. The quotes are meant to remind us of the always ambiguous relation between any inside-outsider by virtue of nationality (American) but insider by virtue of "race." Indeed Joe's search is precisely for a better negotiation of this inside-outside position. The fact that Joe Golder is an academic is also of relevance here because it too sets up a familiar dichotomy—that between academic or "bookish" knowledge and lived or "experiential" knowledge. This dichotomy, while speaking to the earlier polarity between the inside-outside, also looks towards yet another polarity—homosexual versus heterosexual. While in practice all these dichotomies are indeed in flux, my argument is that foundational discourses, whether Eurocentric or nativist, whether from the political left or political right, rigidly uphold the dichotomies, thereby rendering dialogue impossible.

3. See Alice Walker and Prathiba Parmer for an elaboration of how this problematic works.

4. Elsewhere, I have argued for the use of this term as a more inclusive category than either "African" or "Africanist." In this earlier scenario, the term "African" is usually meant to authenticate a subjective or experiential knowledge, while the term "Africanist" is used, either pejoratively or arrogantly, to describe a "learned" (or "bookish") knowledge. But knowledges are neither so easily divided nor is it the case that even if they were, anything would *necessarily* follow from this "experiential" knowledge and those of "bookish" knowledge, hence resuming dialogue without erasing tensions.

5. "Why 'Africa' as opposed to the various different cultures of the continent?" is a question that is often asked in African(ist) circles. As indicated in note 1, the level of abstraction used in any discussion is always a factor, among other things, of previous discourses on the subject. Since the usual claim is that homosexuality is "un-African" rather than "un-Ibo" or "un-Hausa" or "un-Gikuyu," I have found it best, in my counterargument, to stick to the level of abstraction encountered in this claim. Similarly, since historical time periods, whether measured in relation to colonialism (precolonial, post-) or to any other

schema, are *not* typically factored into these discussions, I have not attempted in any significant way to address them here. It is precisely in these directions (of ethnic and historical specificity) that future scholarship on African sexualities must find its way. As an early effort, I have chosen to retain a wider angle on these matters.

6. See Chris Dunton and Rhonda Cobham.

7. Thus for instance, Femi Ojo-Ade writes about Golder, "He is a strange person, full of contradictions and self-hatred" (748).

8. One could cite several examples of this vis-à-vis the discussion of homosexuality in African(ist) literary criticism. In addition to the example of Joe Golder, the most obvious instantiation of such limitations is the criticism surrounding Yambo Ouologuem's *Bound to Violence* (1968; reprint, London: Heinemann, 1971). In this novel, just about every sexual relationship except one is "bound to violence"—we are presented with incest, bestiality, voyeurism, and rape. Furthermore, none of these sexual encounters are ever presented as loving or tender ones. The one exception is the relationship between Raymond Kassoumi and the Frenchman Lambert. While this relationship is by no means perfect, Ouologuem treats it as a loving relationship and insists on its tenderness. The novel, in other words, leaves open the possibility of reading this same-sex relationship between a black man and a white man as somehow sidestepping the inherent violence of the other relationships. Problematic though its implications might be, critics have chosen to silence the question by suggesting instead that Ouologuem's portrayal of tenderness and love here is either simply a flaw on his part, or else is not inconsistent given the homosexual nature of the relationship. In other words, this latter claim is based on the argument that the relationship is presented no differently from the others in the novel since the *homosexual nature of the relationship itself* is proof positive of the unnaturalness and violence.

9. Michel Foucault, "Appendix: The Discourse on Language," in *The Archaeology of Knowledge* New York: Tavistock, 1972), 224. One of the external readers of this essay felt that this discussion of Michel Foucault would be familiar to most readers of *Genders*. While shortening and revising it to some extent, I have nevertheless chosen to retain it here. As a writer, I have wanted to be able to write the essay not only for an audience interested primarily in the study of gender and sexuality and only secondarily in African studies, but *also* (and perhaps more politically importantly) for an audience of Africanists who may not otherwise turn to a journal such as *Genders*. If there is to be a dialogue between both these communities, certain ideas taken for granted by each, but not intimately familiar to the other, must be rehearsed. I feel that the discussion of the production of discourse on African sexuality is thus crucial in such a context.

10. I suggest that it is not enough, in a critical enterprise, to stop an analysis as soon as one encounters such barriers. While being sensitive to that which causes "offense," we need to ask: How does one historicize this condition of being offended? My argument parallels Joan Scott's skepticism of the category of "experience" as the ultimate grounding for historical claims. One has to attempt to understand how "experience" comes to be experienced as such, and the same is true of "offense." See Joan Scott.

11. It may be useful to note here that while I have not been able to locate any other reference to the presence or absence of lesbianism among the precolonial Nnobi, there are indeed records indicating that other African societies having similar institutional set-ups did not preclude lesbian possibilities. Thus Melville Herskovits, "A Note on 'Woman Marriage' in Dahomey," *Africa* 10:3 (1937): 335–41 suggests that while lesbianism may not always be a factor in such alliances, it sometimes may be. On the other hand, it is clear that even institutions based on heterosexual norms leave a certain amount of space for homosexual activities. Thus Evans-Pritchard reports that lesbianism was practiced by women in some polygamous Azande households. Also of note in this context is Evelyn Blackwood's more comprehensive survey of the construction of lesbianism in anthropological discourse (Evelyn Blackwood, "Breaking the Mirror: The Construction of Lesbianism and the Anthropological Discourse on Homosexuality," in David Suggs and Andrew Miracle, eds., *Culture and Human Sexuality: A Reader* (Pacific Grove, Calif.: Brooks/Cole, 1993), 328–40. Gill Shepherd's article on homosexuality in Mombasa (Gill Shepherd, "Rank, Gender, and Homosexuality: Mombasa As a Key to Understanding Sexual Options," in Pa Caplan, ed., *The Cultural Construction of Sexuality* (New York: Tavistock Publications, 1987), 240–70, Renee Pittin's article on lesbian sexuality in Katsina ("Houses of Women: A Focus on Alternative Life-Styles in Katsina City," in Christine Oppong, ed., *Female and Male in West Africa* [Boston: George Allen, 1983], 291–302), and Judith Gay's article on "Mummies and Babies" (" 'Mummies and Babies' and Friends and Lovers in Lesotho," in David Suggs and Andrew Miracle, eds., *Culture and Human Sexuality: A Reader* (Pacific Grove, Calif.: Brooks/Cole, 1993), 341–55, all cast lesbian relations in a significantly different light of economics, rank, prestige, and possibilities of upward mobility. I am aware of the dangers of using any one African society as metonymic for the whole of Africa. My listing of these instances from other African societies is not meant to make any claims about the Nnobi themselves. It is rather to counter the often articulated *generalized* claim that homosexuality is alien to Africa.

12. It is important to remark here that the many ambiguities and tensions in the novel are all the more effective not so much in relation to what the narrative explicitly thematizes but rather in relation to that which is necessarily left unsaid. My reading of *Maru* draws upon Deborah McDowell's reading of Nella

Larsen's *Passing* in which, as McDowell suggests, the thematization of *racial* passing belies the more dangerous terrain of *sexual* passing. (See, Deborah McDowell, "'It's Not Safe. Not Safe at All': Sexuality in Nella Larsen's *Passing,*" in Henry Abelove, Michele Aina Barale, and David Halperin, eds., *The Lesbian and Gay Studies Reader* [New York: Routledge, 1993], 616–25). While Head's novel is written in a sociocultural context quite different from that of the Harlem Renaissance, she may be seen to share with Larsen a similar concern: How does one write about the possibilities of alternative sexualities in black cultures without adding fodder to existing primitivist stereotypes? How does one escape normative sexuality without betraying the "race"?

13. Unlike the Western lesbian continuum, this text, racially coded, divides it too.

14. Remember here that this is a three-tiered structure—"whites" on top, "coloreds" in the middle, and "blacks" at the bottom. While Margaret is "black," she can pass as colored and is indeed on occasion advised to do so. She remains steadfast in her "black" identification.

15. Sedgwick, 21. See also Rene Girard, *Deceit, Desire and the Novel: Self and Other in Literary Structure,* trans. Yvonne Freccero (Baltimore, Md.: Johns Hopkins University Press, 1972).

16. In her essay "The Traffic in Women," Gayle Rubin suggests that the sexual division of labor is rooted not in biology but rather in the desire to distinguish clearly between what are dangerously fluid gender identities. Further, by erasing the feminine in men and by erasing the masculine in women, sexual desire is also channeled along heterosexual parameters. Rubin writes, "The sexual division of labor is implicated in both aspects of gender—male and female it creates them, and it creates them heterosexual. The suppression of the homosexual component of human sexuality, and by corollary, the oppression of homosexuals, is therefore a product of the same system whose rules and relations oppress women."

17. The novel opens at the end and what follows is an extended flashback. To make matters simple, I treat this opening sequence as though it were placed at the ending of the novel, since this is indeed where the narrative ends.

18. Above, I use the phrase "from Shaka to Evita" loosely to mark some of the changes that have taken place in discourses of African sexuality. Shaka, the celebrated Zulu king, was in many accounts read to be a repressed homosexual with expansionist tendencies. Much like the discussions surrounding Nazi Germany, fascism, and homosexuality, the argument made was that Shaka's expansionist tendencies were rooted in his repressed homosexuality. One advocate of such a claim was the anthropologist Max Gluckman (see Daphna Golan, *Inventing Shaka: Using History in the Construction*

of Zulu Nationalism [Boulder, Colo.: Lynne Rienner, 1994] for an account). Thus the rise of the Zulu nation was problematically read in the light of a disordered sexuality. The marker "Evita" is a more contemporary one and refers to the white drag queen who has publicly performed for Nelson Mandela and other black South African Nationalist leaders. Here is a new South Africa which is willing to officially celebrate rather than repress nonnormative gender performativity. (For an account, see Liz Sly, "South Africa's New Laws Give Gays Foothold on Freedom," *The Times Picayune* [New Orleans], October 9, 1994, A-25).

19. See also Tade Akin Aina, "Patterns of Bisexuality in Sub-Saharan Africa," in Rob Tielman, Manuel Carballo, Aart Hendricks, eds., *Bisexuality and HIV/Aids* (Buffalo, N.Y.: Prometheus, 1991), 81–90; Mike Coutinho, "Lesbian and Gay Life in Zimbabwe," in Tielman Hendricks and Van der Veen, eds., *The Third Pink Book: A Global View of Lesbian and Gay Liberation and Oppression* (Buffalo, N.Y.: Prometheus, 1993), 62–65; Edward Evans-Pritchard, "Sexual Inversion among the Azande," *American Anthropologist* 72 (1970): 1428–34; Gordon Isaacs and Brian McKendrick, *Male Homosexuality in South Africa: Identity Formation, Culture, and Crisis* (Oxford: Oxford UP, 1992); Dunbar Moodie (with Viviene Ndatshe and British Sibuyi), "Migrancy and Male Sexuality in the South African Gold Mines," in Martin Bauml Duberman, Martha Vicinus, and George Chauncey Jr., eds., *Hidden from History: Reclaiming the Gay and Lesbian Past* (New York: New American Books, 1989), 411–25.

20. I am aware that many Africanists resist precisely such theorizing, especially as it is done here, with recourse to anthropological models. Anthropology—perhaps with good reason—has been seen to be an enemy of the people in the colonial context, and for this reason, I *begin* with the literary discussions and then *end* with the anthropological. Conceptual ones. Rather than structuring the essay so that the literary material glosses the anthropological, I have chosen to use the anthropological material as a gloss on the literary. In other words I am saying, "look, we can see these sexualities at work in these literary texts, and so on, and *by the way* the anthropologists *also* confirm these observations" *rather than*, "the anthropologists say this and here is the literary evidence." If this is a rhetorical strategy, it is no less invented in attempting to critique the hierarchical orders of knowledge exchanges across disciplines than it is in simply winning over an audience.

21. Or, in this case, more appropriately, the ability to historicize the silences. See, in particular, Matthew Drause, ed., *Invisible Ghetto: Lesbian and Gay Writing from South Africa.* (Johannesburg: Congress of South African Writers, 1993), and Mark Gevisser and Edwin Cameron, eds., *Definite Desire: Gay and Lesbian Lives in South Africa* (New York: Routledge, 1994).

WORKS CITED

Amadiume, Ifi. *Male Daughters, Female Husbands: Gender and Sex in an African Society.* London: Zed, 1987.

Baldwin, James. *Notes of a Native Son.* Boston: Beacon, 1955.

Cobham, Rhonda. "Misgendering the Nation: African Nationalist Fictions and Nuruddin Farah's *Maps.*" In *Nationalisms and Sexualities*, ed. Andrew Parker, Mary Russo, Doris Summer, and Patricia Yaeger, 42–59. New York: Routledge, 1992.

D'Emilio, John. "Capitalism and Gay Identity." In *The Lesbian and Gay Studies Reader*, ed. Henry Abelove, Michele Aina Barale, and David Halperin, 467–76. New York: Routledge, 1993.

DuBois, W. E. B. *The Souls of Black Folk.* Intro. by John Edgar Wideman. 1903. Reprint, New York: Vintage, 1990.

Dunton, Chris. "'Wheyting be Dat?' The Treatment of Homosexuality in African Literature." *Research in African Literatures* 20:3 (Fall 1989): 422–48.

Edelman, Lee. *Homographesis: Essays in Gay Literary and Cultural Theory.* New York: Routledge, 1994.

Fanon, Frantz. *Black Skin, White Masks.* New York: Grove Press, 1967.

Foucault, Michel. "Appendix: The Discourse on Language." In *The Archaeology of Knowledge.* New York: Tavistock, 1972.

Fuss, Diana. "Interior Colonies: Frantz Fanon and the Politics of Identification." *diacritics* 24:2–3 (Summer–Fall 1994): 20–42.

Greenberg, David F. *The Construction of Homosexuality.* Chicago: U of Chicago P, 1988.

Halperin, David. "Is There a History of Sexuality?" In *The Lesbian and Gay Studies Reader*, ed. Henry Abelove, Michele Aina Barale, and David Halperin, 416–31. New York: Routledge, 1993.

Head, Bessie. *Maru.* London: Heinemann, 1971.

Katz, Jonathan. "The Invention of Heterosexuality." *Socialist Review* 90:1 (1990): 7–34.

Ojo-Ade, Femi. "Soyinka's Indictment of the Ivory Tower." *Black American Literature Forum* 22:4 (Winter 88):748.

Patron, Eugene. "Out in Africa" (Interview with Simon Nkoli). *Advocate*, no. 616, Nov. 17, 1992. 44–48.

Rich, Adrienne. "Compulsory Heterosexuality and the Lesbian Experience." In *The Lesbian and Gay Studies Reader*, ed. Henry Abelove, Michele Aina Barale, and David Halperin.

Rubin, Gayle. "The Traffic in Women: Notes on the 'Political Economy' of Sex." In *Toward an Anthropology of Women*, ed. Raina R. Reiter, 157–210. New York: Monthly Review Press, 1975.

Scott, Joan. "Experience." In *Feminists Theorize the Political*, ed. Judith Butler and Joan Scott, 22–40. New York: Routledge, 1992.

Sedgwick, Eve Kosofsky. *Between Men: English Literature and Male Homosocial Desire*. New York: Columbia UP, 1985.

Soyinka, Wole. *The Interpreters*. 1965. Reprint, London: Heinemann, 1970.

Walker, Alice, and Prathiba Parmer, eds., *Warrior Marks: Female Genital Mutilation and the Sexual Blinding of Women*. New York: Harcourt Brace, 1993.

Wright, Derek. *Wole Soyinka Revisited*. Boston: Twayne, 1993.

CHAPTER SEVEN

Queering Lord Clark

*Diasporic Formations and Traveling Homophobia
in Isaac Julien's* The Darker Side of Black

PAIGE SCHILT

The opening shot of Isaac Julien's 1993 film *The Darker Side of Black* begins at the peak of a hill and sweeps downwards, slowly taking in first elevated tropical vegetation, then distant—almost abstract—urban lowlands, and finally stopping at the sea. When a British voice announces "Kingston, Jamaica," the combination of sound and image suggests that this is the imperial British gaze surveying its territory. As Mary Louise Pratt has noted, such panoramic views were a familiar trope of eighteenth- and nineteenth-century European travel writing. Depictions of a receptive and depopulated landscape, void of any returning gazes or signs of resistance, constructed an innocent and essentially passive mastery of the landscape that legitimized European presences in foreign lands and disassociated observation from the violence of "conquest, conversion, territorial appropriation, and enslavement" (Pratt 39). In Julien's text, however, the fictional innocence of visual mastery is immediately interrupted by references to the slavery imposed by the British and its legacy of violence. When the narrator observes that "this is a place where the mem-

ory of slavery remains close to the surface of life," the fantasy of dominance encoded in the promontory view is relinked to the actual relations
of power that authorized and were authorized by imperialist knowledge-
gathering expeditions. Moreover, references to music and dance as powerful responses to "terror and brutality" emphatically locate culture and
resistance within the dehumanized visual landscape.

This initial moment, which both invokes and complicates imperialist tropes of cross-cultural representation, prefigures a tension that
structures the entire film. As the title suggests, *The Darker Side of Black*
explores the circulation of violence, homophobia, sexism, and religious
fundamentalism through the musical cultures of the African diaspora.
But in spite of the film's diasporic orientation, Jamaican dance-hall culture and Jamaican rappers remain at the center, particularly in the film's
meditation on homophobia. On one level, this focus on Jamaican music
as a powerful source for diasporic communities in the U.S. and Britain
is unremarkable; it follows the trajectory laid out by Paul Gilroy in
'*There Ain't No Black in the Union Jack*,' a book to which *The Darker
Side of Black* is clearly indebted. Gilroy identifies Rastafari ideology and
reggae music as powerful inspirations for diasporic musical experimentation and political identities.

But while the film's relation to Gilroy's formulation of diaspora is
crucial to my own analysis, I would like to consider *The Darker Side of
Black*'s focus on Jamaica from two other perspectives. The first is Julien's
appropriation of the style and narrative voice of the traditional BBC arts
and culture documentary in order to create a queer humanism that marginalizes the homophobia emanating from Jamaican popular culture. The
second is the use of religious imagery to evoke a "distinctive and disjunctive temporality of the oppressed" that problematizes the very narratives of civilization and progress that Julien mobilizes in his critique of
homophobia (Gilroy, *Black Atlantic* 212). In between these two perspectives, I'd like to consider the challenge that the circulation of homophobia poses to Gilroy's original formulation of a nonnationalist diasporic
community constituted through creative cultural consumption.

QUEERING LORD CLARK

Julien created *The Darker Side of Black* for the innovative BBC-2 program, *Arena*, but the film recalls a more established breed of BBC pro-

gramming, the arts and culture documentary, which is perhaps best personified by Sir Kenneth Clark's thirteen-part series, *Civilisation*. These films often mix history and ethnography with art history, archeology, and natural science, and they tend to deal with macrocultural units, such as "Africa" or "Western Civilization." Because they are commissioned for television, they aim to engage a nonspecialized audience. The word "amateur," however, is suggestive not just of the intended viewers of these films, but also of the modes of knowledge represented by narrators like Sir Kenneth Clark, Jacob Bronowski, and Sir Basil Davidson. These figures, each of whom narrates his own BBC documentary series, recall the ideal of the broadly educated gentleman-scholar that preceded the emergence of the specialist in late nineteenth- and early twentieth-century science. In contrast to the effacement of authorship in traditional documentary films, these author/narrators are frequently in the frame, stumbling around ruins or navigating a market or a museum. Moreover, the narrators are often less linear and more lyrical than the typically informative documentary narrator; at one point in *Civilisation*, for example, Kenneth Clark recites a fragment of Old English poetry as if it were his own.

In the tradition of the personal essay, the narration of this kind of arts and culture documentary frequently touches on individual tastes and experiences; both Clark's *Civilisation* and Bronowski's *Ascent of Man* are subtitled "A Personal View." This subtitle should not, however, be taken as a qualification of the universality of the authorial vision. According to essayist and critic Philip Lopate, "the supposition that there is a certain unity to human experience" is the foundation of the private revelations that have distinguished the personal essay since Montaigne (xxiii). This humanistic assumption, still clearly discernible in twentieth century televisual essayists, has historically been profoundly ambivalent in its effects. For Enlightenment thinkers like Montaigne, a belief in the fundamental similarity and equality of the human family provided the basis for a critique of ethnocentrism. But a belief in the theoretical universality of human experience does not necessarily dislocate European culture's position as the pinnacle of that experience. Humanism can ironically provide the ideological basis for imperialism as a mission of education and enlightenment, a charity mission for the human family's less developed branches. Thus, humanism may potentially legitimize the cultural imperialism necessary for the economic efficiency of imperialist ventures and the political security of colonizing powers (Wallerstein 82–83).

Kenneth Clark's *Civilisation* is profoundly bound up with humanism's contradictory implications. Indeed, the history of the concept "civilization" illustrates something of the shifting position of humanism in modern Western thought. In *Colonial Desire*, Robert J. C. Young suggests that the term has historically signified both a teleological sense of universal human perfectibility and a cultural/racial category defined by what it is not. For many Enlightenment thinkers, "civilization" was conceived as a process of economic, social, and rational development. While European societies may have represented the culmination of this process, civilization was theoretically available to all. "Though linear and hierarchical, such a view generally considered any hierarchy as a temporary one, merely a difference of stage at the present which could be transformed through education, not a constitutive basis of difference for all time" (Young 32). Even in the eighteenth century, however, this nonexclusive understanding of civilization coexisted with a notion of civilization as defined by its opposite: barbarity. Young quotes Pye's 1783 poem "The Progress of Refinement," in which civilization is invoked as that which the "savage mind" lacks and as the very motor of colonization. In the nineteenth century, different stages in the process of civilization, once understood as steps in a universal economic or intellectual process, came to be identified with static racial or cultural categories. By the century's end, "civilization" had become so identified with the projects of European imperialism that it no longer maintained any of its relativistic sense, and "liberal anthropology sought to discriminate between culture and civilization, and to use the former to describe the 'savage' and 'barbarian' cultures that civilization had come to destroy" (Young 43).

Clark's 1969 series brings together all of the contradictory resonances of this historically overdetermined idea. As a story of European progress, *Civilisation* begins with the cultural vacuum left by barbarian invasions and proceeds to chronicle the great achievements of Western culture as a response to unnamed contemporary events that threaten a "loss of human civilization" on par with the destruction of Rome (Vol. 1, "The Skin of Our Teeth"). Anticolonial struggles, immigration, and student or worker protests are never mentioned, but there is clearly a sense that Europe is threatened by difference, both external and internal. Civilization is figured both in relation to what it is not (Clark grounds his provisional definition of civilization in a comparison between the Apollo Belvedere and an anonymous African mask) and as progressive stages, such as "material stability" and "humanitarianism." Slavery and industrial exploitation are represented as aberrations in a history of moral, intellectual, and aesthetic progress. However, by the last program, uncontrolled material-technological progress and too-vehement sociopolitical beliefs have emerged as new threats to civilization. Clark ends with a reading of the famous lines from Yeats's "The Second Coming," but then counters with footage of well-scrubbed white students, full of "conviction" (no passionate intensity here), pouring out of the doors of East Anglia University. The film thus manages to convey a future of continued progress for a civilization implicitly defined by what it excludes. The last shot of the series shows waves breaking against a rocky cliff, an image that suggests both the threat of ignorant armies and the steadfast presence of European civilization.

In *The Darker Side of Black*, Isaac Julien appropriates this essayistic, universalizing tradition of cultural representation for his own ends. The narration reproduces the polished and elite pronunciation that has come to personify the BBC. In *The Darker Side of Black*, however, this voice of cultural authority is deployed with a difference: it works to articulate a black, gay subject position. Although it is self-avowedly "queer," this self-referential voice is not deployed to communicate the partiality and historical situatedness of its point of view. Rather than emphasizing specificity, Julien strategically appropriates the form of the traditional essay, "where the authorial 'I' speaks to and on behalf of a presumed collectivity" (Nichols, *Blurred Boundaries* 8). In *The Darker Side of Black*, the presumed collectivity is queer. The first-person narration coexists with interviews with black gay men in Jamaica, the U.S., and the U.K.; footage of Jamaican cruising areas; and tableaux allegorizing the persecution of gay men and lesbians. All of these elements combine to give visibility and voice to the very subjects marginalized by homophobic discourses and practices. Julien uses the humanistic tradition of the documentary essay to denaturalize homophobia by surrounding it with a normalizing context of black gay voices and images.

The film's discursive marginalization of Jamaican homophobia is nowhere more evident than in its representation of Buju Banton, the teenage author of the notoriously homophobic song "Boom Bye Bye." The video for "Boom Bye Bye" popularized an extended index finger and a cocked thumb as a gun-like gesture of antigay hatred. In *The Darker Side of Black*, Buju Banton first appears in close-up, pouting and preening for the camera. Banton's lips are moving, but instead of his words, we hear the narrator: "This boy here, playing with his locks, laughs when asked why feelings of hate animate his songs." The paternalistic tone and the localizing movement of the sentence work to isolate the homophobe, to construct him as an unusual specimen, almost a curiosity for the viewer to study. Ethnographic filmmaker Jeff Todd Titon has commented that this kind of voice-over interpretation of images "is more the direct equivalent of a book, and while it still seems acceptable in television specials about the wonders of the animal kingdom, its rhetorical conventions raise the now familiar stench of racism and colonialism when the film's focus is on human beings" (Titon 92). While I disagree with Titon's assertion that voice-over narration is necessarily more manipulative than other conventions (like editing), there's no denying that the voice-over imposed on Banton's silenced image creates a kind of "Wild Kingdom" effect. When Banton's voice is heard, his Jamaican dialect is paraphrased in subtitles that emphasize his strangeness. Although many of the Jamaicans interviewed for *The Darker Side of Black* speak in dialect, Banton is the only one whose speech is subtitled. The imposition of the voice-over and the translation effected by the subtitles have two results: on the one hand, they mute the voice of homophobia, subordinating it to the voice of the narrator and the other voices who speak without apparent mediation. On the other hand, this blatant gagging highlights questions of who can speak and who can be heard. In the encounters that follow, both Banton and the narrator address questions of "voice."

When Banton finally speaks, he asserts, rather ominously, that his song is not an incitement to violence but rather "a warning." His words are followed by newspaper clippings and personal narratives that suggest an increase in homophobia and a rise in homophobic violence. Several Jamaicans testify to the severity of homophobia on the island. Their statements culminate with a chilling reference to a not too-distant past when men accused of homosexual acts were beaten to death in broad daylight. The film cuts to a shot of dark, reflective water, and we hear the narrator at his most lyrical and personal: "In the face of death, we long for closeness." The camera then moves to a sea-side location, where very intense sunlight seems to mute all color. The narration identifies this unmarked landscape as a cruising area and focuses the narrative on questions of voice: "Cruising the harbor, all the men are silent. When they turn to Buju, he says. . . ." The film cuts to Banton in a seaside setting very much like the harbor of the moment before. The effect of this matching is to relocate

Banton in the queer context of the harbor, to surround him with queerness. Banton's words seem almost to react to this recontextualization. He
begins by associating himself with a monolithic national voice, but then
reconsiders and offers a more "democratic" vision of his place in
Jamaican society: "I am the voice of Jamaica. I am one of the voices. One
of the many, many, many, many voices." The narrator intervenes in this
representation of national harmony, pointing out that "this voice of
Jamaica silences other voices."[1] The narrator goes on, however, to articulate his own pluralistic vision: "One day, queer Jamaican voices will have
their own songs. Until then, songs of hate will be heard."

This interchange is followed by the remarks of Rex Nettlewood, a
professor from the University of the West Indies, who dismisses Banton
with a quote from Corinthians: "When I am a child, I speak as a child."
When Banton appears again, he is talking about his husky voice, which
makes him sound older than he is, as an inheritance from his father. We
hear the interviewer, presumably Isaac Julien himself: "So, in a way,
you're singing with your father's voice." Banton's facetious reply and a
scoffing laugh highlight the existence of tension between interviewer and
hostile interviewee. The camera cuts to a man on the beach, looking out
to sea, and the voice-over continues: "What does Buju the man say that
Buju the child could not? All I hear are the waves." These lines contradict St. Paul's developmental logic by suggesting that there is a paucity
of "more mature" Jamaican alternatives to Buju Banton's homophobic
message. The dominance of this message in the Jamaican cultural context is emphasized again as the camera pans across the water:

> If Buju doesn't speak with his father's voice, perhaps the Law of the
> Father speaks through Buju. And this law says to me, "the mascu-
> line integrity of this down-pressed race requires your death. You
> shall die so that this race may live."

Through the use of the first-person pronoun, the narrator represents
himself as the target of homophobic violence. In doing so, he creates a
tension between the authoritative voice of the narrative, constructed as
queer, and the voice of patriarchal authority, which speaks through the
homophobic lyrics of Buju Banton. But this tension does not necessarily
undermine the narrative voice, because Julien's reading of the Law of the
Father constructs patriarchy itself as the site of a lack that must be
shored up through the oppression of others.

Julien's skillful manipulation of voice and image constructs Buju Banton as childish, inarticulate, and brutish. This "savage" image is positioned within a discourse of black gay visibility and in relation to the complex, urbane, queer voice of the narrator. The starkness of the contrast evokes conventional distinctions between civilization and savagery, which, while they are unquestionably effective as a means of marginalizing Banton's voice, are problematic for their potential to resituate Jamaica within imperialist narratives about nature and history. The distinctions introduced in the film's representation of Buju Banton are reinforced by the film's self-conscious play with interview settings. The conventions surrounding the use of background space in documentary interviews normally "provide verification of the role or status of the interviewee" (Nichols, *Ideology and Image* 203). Jeff Titon emphasizes the familiarity of these conventions:

> Professors sometimes appear in [documentary] films, usually dressed in suits and ties, seated in their offices with bookshelves behind them, thus donning the mantle of academic authority as they explain something in the film. But this kind of scene long ago moved from a convention to a cliché, and many viewers skeptical of experts or clichés or both react negatively to so naked and obvious a display of authority. (92)

The Darker Side of Black does not participate in these conventions for the representation of academic authority. Instead, most academics and other "experts" from the U.S. and Britain are interviewed in front of bright, patterned screens. Others are shown with a painting or an architectural detail like a cornice in the background. The lighting is highly artificial, and the space in which the interviewees are positioned is extremely shallow. The effect of these strange settings is comic: gestures and other mannerisms are magnified. The interviewees seem to be parodying themselves. If conventionally constructed "expert" settings raise questions about who has the authority to make definitive statements about a particular culture, these less readable settings may, by stripping experts of some of their authoritative identity and rendering them in a highly playful manner, function to diminish the apparent distance between the experts and the popular culture they discuss.

On the other hand, Jamaican interviewees are represented in much more conventional ways. They are both more likely to be filmed in naturalistic settings *and* more likely to be filmed in nature settings. Dance-hall DJ Shabba Ranks is the only Jamaican who is positioned in a bla-tantly artificial setting with a patterned background. Other Jamaicans are interviewed in typically "tropical" settings with the ocean, palm trees, or even a swimming pool behind them. Even when Jamaicans are interviewed indoors, they tend to be filmed in front of a window that reveals a bit of palm tree or a view of the beach. The effect of the dif-ferential treatment of Jamaican interviewees is to emphasize their differ-ence from interviewees in the U.S. and Britain and to identify them more strongly with nature. The positioning of participants lines up along an evolutionary continuum, with "civilized" speakers from the U.S. and Britain more likely to appear in obviously technologically enhanced set-tings and "primitive" Jamaicans more likely to appear in nature. This representation of Jamaicans as closer to nature may play into pre-exist-ing stereotypes that construct Jamaicans as primitive and Other by U.S. and British standards: e.g., Jamaica as quaint and static, as in the once ubiquitous advertising slogan, "Come back to Jamaica." It is true that British and U.S. audiences are not monolithic and that a negative, West-ern perception of nature may have been inverted and valorized by African diasporic communities as a way to resist racism (Mercer 108–109). This positive reading of nature may be constrained, however, by the narrative voice, which so clearly evokes European notions of refinement and universality, and articulates a positive vision of enlight-ened Western pluralism. It is also true that the very presence of Jamaican intellectuals in the film may work to disrupt understandings of Jamaica as primitive or unsophisticated. Nevertheless, the different interview set-tings do work to maintain a sense of difference between Jamaican intel-lectuals and intellectuals in the U.S. and Britain. Thus, the civilized/sav-age distinction that the film evokes in order to condemn homophobia in Jamaican popular culture spills over, at times, into the representation of Jamaica as a whole.

"Tracking the Music on its Global Circuit . . ."

Julien's rhetorical marginalizing of Jamaican homophobia is paralleled by his representation of diasporic cultural circulation. In Julien's narra-tive of transnational music culture, the work of rappers like Buju Ban-ton and Shabba Ranks travels to new contexts in the U.S. and Britain, where homophobic messages can be more effectively resisted and refused. Just as Buju Banton was resituated in the context of the harbor, Julien situates the homophobia of the Jamaican music industry in the context of empowered metropolitan consumers. Julien expresses the idea that these consumers can transform and contain the messages emanating from Jamaican popular culture in an interview with John Savage:

> Julien: I think first the question of how a record like 'Boom Bye Bye' is received in the gay and lesbian communities both in New York and London is about the problems of the international commodification of dance-hall music. If they want to intervene in the world markets of pop culture, those artists have to go to America and Britain. . . . And what they are finding is that there is a certain limit to those markets and there are certain things one can say and certain things one can articulate that are not going to be tolerated outside their own country (Jamaica) because those queer groups are in different positions and make trouble and contest them. They then have to realise a limit both in the marketplace for them and also in terms of civil rights and a bill of rights in America, things which gays and lesbians don't have in Jamaica where homosexuality is still illegal. (Savage and Julien 8)

In this exchange, Julien is literally discussing the United States and Britain as economic markets for pop culture, but there is also a suggestion of the liberal, pluralist "free marketplace of ideas" in which competition and exchange power a movement toward greater truth. Here, and in *The Darker Side of Black*'s representation of U.S. consumers, Julien articulates a theory of consumption that has much in common with Paul Gilroy's formulation of diasporic cultural consumption as a public sphere in which new, syncretic identities are forged and complex experiences expressed. As I mentioned above, *The Darker Side of Black* echoes Gilroy's narrative of postwar black musical cultures, in which Jamaica is identified as one (nonoriginal) point of origin for black musical cultures in the U.S. and Britain. But while Gilroy focuses on the way complex, enabling ideologies like Rastafarianism are exported and transformed across the diaspora, *The Darker Side of Black* focuses on the movement of sexism and homophobia in contemporary black cultures. Within the project of rhetorically marginalizing homophobia that I have described, metropolitan diasporic communities take on utopian qualities, and the power of consumption is figured as containment as well as dialogue.

In '*There Ain't No Black in the Union Jack*,' Gilroy's effort to rethink black British culture outside of ethnically and nationally absolute models is organized around two main nodes. On the one hand, he emphasizes the politically enabling effects of cultural circulation. As oppositional sites for the formation of both race and class identities, black British musical cultures suggest, in a way that race or nation-based politics cannot, how the traditions of the African diaspora have been assimilated into British culture, "even as their presence redefines the meaning" of Britishness (155). Gilroy contextualizes Jamaican reggae and American soul, hip-hop, and R&B traditions in terms of the various traditions' interactions with one another and in terms of their appropriation and use by blacks in Britain. These cultural forms, once commodified and exported, become powerful conduits for political ideologies. Thus, American soul and hip-hop records "exported to Europe the idea that black communities in the inner city . . . could define themselves politically and philosophically as an oppressed 'nation' bound together in the framework of the diaspora by language and history" (184). Similarly, reggae music from the Caribbean communicated the "Pan-African, Ethiopianist ideology" (187) that became the basis for new articulations of Afro-British identity. In the aftermath of the decline of the Jamaican reggae scene, and under the influence of U.S. rap music, black British musicians were able to rearticulate these diverse heritages into cultural forms that responded to the exigencies and specificities of British life, particularly the competing, but not necessarily exclusive, claims of race, class, and national belonging.

In Gilroy's formulation, black British musical cultures are remarkable not just for their ability to express complex cultural experiences, but also for the implicit and explicit critiques of capitalism that they embody. Thus, the other node of his reexamination of expressive culture is consumption. Gilroy identifies the sound system as the foundation of a musical culture that privileges the conditions of consumption over the conditions of production. Sound systems revolve around recorded music rather than live performances. Records are transformed by the verbal and combinatory artistry of MCs and DJs in the dance-hall. Occasionally musicians who make records for these venues "anticipate and invite the supplementation of their original artistic effort" by producing a lyric-less version of a song. In such situations, "Consumption is turned outwards; no longer a private, passive, or individual process, it becomes a procedure of collective affirmation and protest in which a new authentic public sphere is brought into being" (210). This communal creativity, which works to deny the authority of the commodity form and challenges the separation between performers and consumers, is exemplified by the sound system, but it may also be discerned in other black musical forms that feature improvisation, discursive combination, and culturally coded modes of address (213–214). According to Gilroy, it is not just the diasporic political ideologies incorporated into syncretic black British musical forms that create the basis for new identities. The "dialogic rituals" in which these forms are consumed "symbolize or even create community" (214). Consumption, like cultural circulation, is an essential, traditionally unrecognized, factor in the formation of antiracist social movements in contemporary Britain.

For Gilroy, the hybrid forms of black musical cultures provide an alternative to absolutist notions of identity and nationhood. As I have tried to stress, the explicit messages and ideologies expressed in these forms are only one aspect of this alternative public sphere. While the songs themselves may offer models of black identity and community, those identities are negotiated in dialogic rituals of circulation and consumption. Thus, explicit messages of purity, authenticity, and originality may be in tension with the hybrid processes of circulation and transformation in which the music is consumed. In focusing on one particular homophobic message, Julien specifies this tension and points out the limited extent to which exclusionary ideologies of black authenticity can be destabilized by processes of creative cultural consumption.[2] In lyrics like "homeboys don't condone nasty men," "Boom Bye Bye" certainly promulgates an ideology of black identity. However, in calling for the violent annihilation of gay men, the song obviously excludes certain audiences from "the specific mechanisms of identification and recognition" through which new forms of dialogic identity could be constructed (*Black Atlantic* 102). Thus, while the film remains close to the reactions and responses of black consumers in diasporic locations, and while it maintains Jamaica as a source of musical forms and political ideologies, its representation of diasporic markets necessarily focuses less on reappropriation than on refusal.

In light of Julien's focus on the circulation of homophobia, the construction of Jamaica as a source of musical forms and ideologies takes on new valences. In highlighting the worldwide currency of Buju Banton's gun gesture, the film suggests that increased homophobic violence in Britain and the U.S. results from the global exposure of "Boom

Bye Bye." British writer David Dibosa, for example, explains that in the wake of the song, "The experience I have had is to face homophobia, which I have had to face before, but on the sharp end, where people have actually used the symbol of the gun pointed at my head." Another interviewee narrates the tension that the song has provoked between Jamaican communities and gay communities in New York City. These moments suggest that the movement of homophobia in the diaspora is largely uni-directional: from the margins to the metropolitan center.

Julien's representation of the U.S. suggests that metropolitan consumers are able to resist and even regulate homophobia. In the U.S. context, *The Darker Side of Black* focuses on the band Brand Nubian, who are members of the Muslim fundamentalist group Five Percent Nation. The film features interviews with Brand Nubian and clips from the video for their homophobic song "Punks Jump Up to Get Beat Down." But rather than surrounding Brand Nubian with silent gay cruising areas, the film juxtaposes them with Donald Suggs of the Gay and Lesbian Alliance Against Defamation (GLAAD) of New York. In an obvious counterpart to Buju Banton's claim to be the voice of Jamaica, Suggs talks about the importance of not letting one group, adolescent boys, speak for the entire black community. He describes the media campaign that GLAAD waged to contain Brand Nubian's paean to gay bashing. According to Suggs, GLAAD was also able to foil Jamaican rapper Shabba Ranks's scheduled appearance on *The Tonight Show* by publicizing his homophobic views. The focus on GLAAD's actions constructs the U.S. as a location where diverse voices can speak and contest homophobia. At times, Julien even seems to elide the existence of homophobia in the U.S. Although the film interrogates Brand Nubian's homophobia, interviews with Chuck D. and Ice Cube do not touch on homophobic lyrics in their own songs. The Disposable Heroes of Hiphoprosy is the final U.S. band that the film features. Julien focuses on their song "The Cycles of Violence," which uses hip-hop conventions to articulate a critique of homophobic labeling.

The suggestion of the U.S. as a utopian site for black queer consumers is reinforced by a voice-over:

> Tracking the music on its global circuit: Saturday night in downtown Manhattan, a bangee boy [rough ghetto youth] and his boyfriend give a homeboy [local youth] face [challenge him]. 'We're here, we're black and queer—get over it,' they tell him. The home-

boy turns to them, makes his hand into the shape of a gun, and fires. The bangee boy replies, 'It's not me you want to kill, but yourself that you see in me.' Somewhere, behind every homey exterior lies a homo interior.

This scene alludes, both visually and thematically, to Jennie Livingston's 1991 film *Paris Is Burning*. Livingston's film is largely structured around definitions of terms and categories from black and Latino drag ball culture. In a sequence that investigates the elusive meaning of "realness" in ball culture, one of the ball announcers defines "bangee boy realness" as "looking like the boy that probably robbed you a few minutes before you came to Paris's ball." Later he defines a "bangee girl" as "one that can hang out with the roughest and the toughest." Julien's juxtaposition of "bangee boy" and "homeboy," terms which represent a difference of degree rather than an absolute opposition, reinforces the narrator's explicit message about the slipperiness of sexual identity, as does his play on "homo" and "homey." Here again, metropolitan homophobia is linked to a Jamaican origin through the gesture of the gun. But this commentary suggests that in the "global circuit" queer voices talk back to homophobia. The voice-over is articulated over footage of a New York street at night. In contrast to the stark Jamaican harbor, in these shots everyone seems to be colorfully, exuberantly gay: boys wearing bright, primary colors hold hands and vogue down the sidewalk. Friends greet each other with kisses. In the midst of this queer world, the fictional bangee boy echoes the narrator's queer universalism. In this world, queerness is the norm, homophobia the pathology.

Julien's representation of U.S. consumers "talking back" to homophobia has an attractive utopian element. However, there are problems with locating that vision of utopia in the metropolitan space of the U.S. As I have suggested, Julien's attempt to deal with the circulation of explicitly homophobic ideologies exposes the limits of strategies of reappropriation and dialogue. Thus, the consumer politics that he features in the section on GLAAD are the politics of the boycott and the media campaign rather than the practices of the sound system. But in spite of Julien's representation of the U.S. as a pluralistic space where diverse voices contest each other, neither the literal marketplace nor the marketplace of ideas is level, and there are limits to how and when queer voices, or queer consumers, can be effective. Within the U.S., gay men and lesbians have recently gained attention as a sizable consumer niche, a trend that has resulted in new advertising support for gay publications and a new range of gay-oriented products and services. However, this kind of consumer power has not necessarily translated into political power in other realms. In their introduction to *Homo Economics: Capitalism, Community, and Gay and Lesbian Life,* Amy Gluckman and Betsy Reed note that in 1993, at the height of the "gay marketing moment," "nineteen initiatives around the nation to repeal progay legislation or to institute anti-gay policies passed, while not one local or statewide legislative effort on behalf of gays prevailed" (xvii). Closer to the realm of consumption that is *The Darker Side of Black*'s purview, between 1995 and 1997, fundamentalist Christian groups have twice waged successful consumer campaigns to stop local television networks from airing antihate public service advertisements created by the group PFLAG (Parents and Friends of Lesbians and Gays). And in 1998, New York Mayor Rudolph Giuliani introduced zoning laws which threaten the queer businesses that sustain much queer public culture. As Lauren Berlant and Michael Warner have pointed out, conservatives "flagrantly contradict their stated belief in a market free from government interference" when the maintenance of heteronormativity is at stake (563).

Furthermore, by locating his vision of queer utopia in a U.S. metropolitan space, Julien may play into developmental narratives that position the West as the culmination of political and social progress. To make this point is not to suggest that any critique of postcolonial homophobia is cultural imperialism. It is merely to suggest that critiques of homophobia might not want to rely on oppositions between the enlightened West and the backwards provinces that have traditionally underwritten cultural imperialism. Such a strategy is particularly problematic when homophobia continues to structure political, economic, and social institutions in the United States.[3] In the following section, I discuss Julien's reappropriation of a biblical iconography of persecution and redemption as an alternative strategy for critiquing homophobia that potentially enables identifications across geographic distances.

DISTINCTIVE TEMPORALITIES

Cineaste: Obviously you are quite aware of the ethnographic element in documentary. Do you think your film completely eschews ethnography?

Julien: In terms of the 'black Atlantic,' geographical distances are being dissolved by electronic reproduction, global capitalism, the locations of record companies, and so on. In MTV's global village, which we inhabit, we take for granted how certain things are produced and consumed as commodities. The film shows that but, I think, also reverses it by showing the context of the diaspora as a whole. I don't know if it is successful enough in crossing ethnic and national boundaries but we wanted to engage with all diasporan cultures involved because the diverse effects of how music is received in the different geographical locations were important to our project. (qtd. in Grundmann 31)

As I have discussed it up to this point, *The Darker Side of Black* remains implicated in two contradictory indications of Enlightenment understandings of civilization. The first is a universalizing humanism that paradoxically defines itself in relation to an uncivilized Other. The second is a narrative of Western-style progress, which is most evident in the film's representation of differences between margin and metropolis. In exploring the film's treatment of Buju Banton and its construction of black transnational musical culture, I have not yet attended to an equally important visual motif that recalls the overlapping histories of slavery and Christianity in African diaspora communities. In what follows, I will suggest that this imagery of bondage and deliverance articulates the common struggles that unite black, gay, and black gay communities. Furthermore, I will argue that the invocation of the messiah and the persecution of slavery construct an alternate sense of time and history that contests Enlightenment notions of progress.

Throughout the film, Julien uses the image of a man with a Bible in his hands standing before a man with his legs in chains. At times this tableau works to suggest Christianity's role in the enslavement of African peoples, and at other times the image works to suggest Christianity's importance as a tool of liberation for Africans in the Americas. Julien also uses a black priest/messiah figure to suggest themes of persecution and liberation. Particularly in the third and final segment, these images are juxtaposed with statements about sexuality in order to suggest a parallel between homophobia and racism. This section is labeled "Faith," and it opens with the image of the Bible and the legs in chains. The narration discusses Christianity's complex role in both slavery and resistance in Jamaican history. The image appears again when the narrator explains the Catholic Church's opposition to the decriminalization of homosexuality. The recurring image and the narration link legalized, church-sanctioned slavery and legalized, church-sanctioned homophobia. Similarly, when an interviewee mentions Shabba Ranks's assertion that homosexuals should be crucified, the film cuts to a shot of the priest figure with his arms stretched out on either side of him. In suggesting an ironic parallel between the persecution of gay men and lesbians and the persecution of Christ, the film follows a trajectory that has already been mapped out by slaves who saw their own struggles reflected in the Christian story. Thus, although some of the film's representational strategies may have worked to suggest a fundamental difference between homophobic Jamaica and more enlightened communities in the U.S. and Britain, the use of these tableaux constructs a potential point of identification between gay men and lesbians and all people of the African diaspora, suggesting "that antiracist and antihomophobic politics are informed by a common corporeal interest in survival" (Thomas 65), and thereby creating the possibility of coalition across difference.

The visual invocation of common histories of persecution, struggle, and redemption unsettles some of the distinctions between a homophobic, patriarchal Jamaican popular culture and black gay speakers throughout the diaspora, suggesting a common ground for identification and dialogue. Similarly, rational, secular conceptions of progress are unsettled by the persistent references to the messianic, eschatological time, with its implication of alternative structures of judgment. However, it is the imagery of slavery that resonates the most critically with Enlightenment notions of civilization as progress and perfectibility. In histories, like Kenneth Clark's, which remain embedded in these assumptions, slavery can only be understood as an aberration in the history of modernity or, preferably, as the last gasp of a premodern era (Gilroy, *Black Atlantic* 46–58). Lord Clark himself refers in passing to the antislavery movement as "the first communal expression of awakened conscience" and notes proudly that it began in England (Vol. 13, "Heroic Materialism"). In contrast to those historians who treat slavery as a footnote to the history of civilization, in *The Black Atlantic*, Paul Gilroy argues that African-American artists, particularly writers, have persistently remembered and reimagined racial terror in their work as a means of undermining "the heroic narrative of western civilization" and "the monumental time that supports it" (*Black Atlantic* 197). What Gilroy calls "the repudiation of the ideology of progress by the racially subordinated who have lubricated its wheels with their unfree labour" highlights the omissions that have enabled a view of European cultures as the pinnacle of a history of human perfectibility and rationality (215). Furthermore, as I suggested in my analysis of the opening shot, references to slavery emphatically recall the violent exclusions that were the constitutive underside of universalizing Western humanism.

In his discussion of black music in *The Black Atlantic*, Paul Gilroy describes the critical power that derives from the doubleness of black musical forms, a doubleness that derives from "their unsteady location simultaneously inside and outside the conventions, assumptions, and aesthetic rules which distinguish and periodise modernity" (73). This kind of doubleness provides an appropriate framework for conceptualizing *The Darker Side of Black*, which mobilizes a rhetoric of "civilization" in order to create a remarkably effective critique of homophobia, even as it destabilizes the very assumptions on which that rhetoric rests. For a diasporic "double consciousness" to achieve its full critical potential, however, modernity, diversity, and cosmopolitanism must not remain the preserve of the Western metropolis. As the epigraph to this section suggests, to the extent that the film constructs and maintains a conventional differential between New York and London and their backwards, provincial margins, it cannot conceive of these diasporic locales in a mutually productive *dialogue* over homophobia.

NOTES

1. By emphasizing the ways in which Julien marginalizes Buju's voice, I end up downplaying the fact that Julien lets hostile voices be heard at all. I do, however, feel that there is something disingenuous about the claim that "Julien makes an effort to determine their [the rappers'] positions in order to initiate dialog" (Grundmann 28), because it ignores the effect that the medium of representation has on the message. Moreover, I am not sure that a pluralistic approach, which demands that all views be granted equal validity and opportunity, is necessarily achievable or desirable in efforts to combat homophobia.

2. Even in *The Black Atlantic*, where Gilroy is explicitly concerned with countering rigid definitions of black authenticity, he mainly discusses gender and sexuality in terms of the sense of community and identity that they offer: "Experiencing racial sameness through particular definitions of gender and sexuality has also proved to be eminently exportable. The forms of connectedness and identification it makes possible across space and time cannot be confined within the borders of the nation state and correspond closely to lived experience" (85).

For whom do these forms of gender and sexuality allow connectedness and identification? To whose lived experience do they correspond? To leave these questions unexamined is to ignore the ways in which such identities function as much
through exclusion as through "connectedness and identification." In his discussion of black music critics' defense of 2 Live Crew, Gilroy does address misogyny, but not in a way that acknowledges this dynamic. He suggests that such
critics need to "develop a reflexive political aesthetics capable of distinguishing
2 Live Crew and their ilk from their equally authentic but possibly more compelling and more constructive peers" (84). What seems to me to be missing here
is a recogition that certain formulations of identity might be both compelling
and productive (in the Foucauldian sense) in part because they operate through
the othering of queer and female bodies (Gopinath 121). Certainly misogynistic
rap has contributed to forms of black masculinity that have proven to be very
compelling to some audiences.

  3. See, for example, Lauren Berlant's *The Queen of America Comes to
Washington City* on the significance of homophobia to current configurations of
citizenship and the public sphere.

Works Cited

Berlant, Lauren, and Michael Warner. "Sex in Public." *Critical Inquiry* 24
  (1998) 547–566.

Clark, Kenneth. *Civilisation: A Personal View*. London: BBC Television, 1969.

Clifford, James. "Diasporas." *Routes: Travel and Translation in the Late Twentieth Century*. Cambridge, Mass.: Harvard UP, 1997.

Gilroy, Paul. *'There Ain't No Black in the Union Jack': The Cultural Politics of
  Race and Nation*. Chicago: U of Chicago Press, 1991.

——— . *The Black Atlantic: Modernity and Double Consciousness*. Cambridge:
  Harvard UP, 1993.

Gluckman, Amy, and Betsy Reed. "Introduction." *Homo Economics: Capitalism, Community, and Gay and Lesbian Life*. New York: Routledge, 1997.

Gopinath, Gayatri. "Funny Boys and Girls: Notes on a Queer South Asian
  Planet." *Asian American Sexualities: Dimensions of Gay and Lesbian
  Experience*. New York: Routledge, 1996.

Grundmann, Roy. "Black Nationhood and the Rest in the West: An Interview
  with Isaac Julien." *Cineaste* 21.1–2 (1995): 28–31.

Julien, Isaac, dir. *The Darker Side of Black*. Produced for Arena and Channel
  Four. Noon Films, 1993.

Lopate, Philip. "Introduction." *The Art of the Personal Essay: An Anthology from the Classical Era to the Present*. New York: Anchor-Doubleday, 1994.

Mercer, Kobena. *Welcome to the Jungle: New Positions in Black Cultural Studies*. London: Routledge, 1994.

Nichols, Bill. *Ideology and the Image: Social Representation in Cinema and Other Media*. Bloomington: Indiana UP, 1981.

——. *Blurred Boundaries: Questions of Meaning in Contemporary Culture*. Bloomington: Indiana UP, 1994.

Pratt, Mary Louise. *Imperial Eyes: Travel Writing and Transculturation*. London: Routledge, 1992.

Savage, John, and Isaac Julien. "Queering the Pitch: a Conversation." *Critical Quarterly* 36.1 (1994): 1–12.

Thomas, Kendall. "'Ain't Nothin' Like the Real Thing': Black Masculinity, Gay Sexuality, and the Jargon of Authenticity." In *Representing Black Men*, ed. Marcellus Blount and George P. Cunningham. New York: Routledge, 1996.

Titon, Jeff Todd. "Representation and Authority in Ethnographic Film/Video Production." *Ethnomusicology* 36.1 (1992): 89–92.

Wallerstein, Immanuel. *Historical Capitalism*. London: Verso, 1983.

Young, Robert J. C. *Colonial Desire: Hybridity in Theory, Culture, and Race*. London: Routledge, 1995.

CHAPTER EIGHT

Broadening Postcolonial Studies/ Decolonizing Queer Studies

Emerging "Queer" Identities and Cultures in Southern Africa

WILLIAM J. SPURLIN

Similar to a previous elision of queer analysis in studies of culture in the West, postcolonial inquiry has not sufficiently interrogated same-sex desire as a viable way of being positioned in the world. In its analyses of marginalization and subaltern experience, its emphasis on national identities and borders, and its attention to race, gender, and class, postcolonial studies have seriously neglected the ways in which heterosexism and homophobia have also shaped the world of hegemonic power. A parallel problem is that queer studies, most highly developed in the U.S., have shown little interest in cross-cultural variations of the expression and representation of same-sex desire; homosexualities in non-Western societies are, at best, imagined or invented through the imperialist gaze of Euroamerican queer identity politics, appropriated through the economies of the West, or, at worst, altogether ignored. If academic queer studies truly aim to politicize and to credibly intervene as an agent of social transformation, they must begin to look beyond the borders of North America and Europe and more seriously address how queer identities and queer cultural formations have taken shape and operate else-where. By remaining otherwise narrowly Eurocentric in perspective, the discipline helps to underwrite nationalist strategies at work in many colonial and postcolonial contexts that read homosexuality as foreign to non-Western societies.

Acknowledging that queer inquiry needs comparative, relational, historicized, and contextualized understandings of "queer," engaging *localized* questions of experience, identity, culture, and history in order to better understand specific processes of domination and subordination (Alexander and Mohanty xvii) so much at the heart of postcolonial inquiry, my chapter, through a specific focus on southern Africa, inves-tigates historical and cultural representations of same-sex desire in spaces outside of the Euroamerican axes of queer culture and political influence, and considers the ways in which queer cultural productions outside of the U.S. and Europe not only intersect with, but also resist, Western queer identity politics and cultural practices. In postapartheid South Africa, the major focus of this chapter, African National Congress (ANC) developments toward democratization have helped to create new spaces of "queer" visibility, identity politics, and literary/cultural prac-tice both in South Africa and in the neighboring region, thereby provid-ing an urgent opportunity not only for comparative studies of sexual identities, but for a critique of the *heterosexist* biases of postcolonial studies and the *Western* biases of academic queer theory.[1]

A critical problem in contemporary Western identity politics and cultural studies is that a unity or self-sameness is often projected onto identities and cultures without fully engaging the disputes and differ-ences within a particular social group about its identity and its relation-ship to the wider social world. Such an appropriation speaks to another problem whereby differences according to race, gender, class, and sexu-ality are articulated as if they are in parallel relation to one another without accounting for their differential structures and their intersecting and converging formations within the social field. "Queer" identities and cultural practices in the "new" South Africa are not merely forms of self-assertion and self-expression as they often are in the West, but are explicitly shaped by the resistance to fixed identities and fixed notions of culture previously imposed by the system of apartheid (1948–1990). The dismantling of the structures of apartheid has, in one sense, led to the de-racialization of South African political institutions, to other claims of identity and solidarity, and to the exposure and critique of other axes of domination including heteronormativity and homophobia. Though there is now a seriousness about lesbian and gay issues in South Africa and the neighboring region in ways that previously were not possible, one must acknowledge that material conditions still mitigate against the fullest realization of ANC-initiated democratic imperatives and that the status of homosexuality still remains a highly contradictory question.

With these preliminary thoughts in mind, the questions I raise in this chapter are the following: What is the role of the politics of (homo)sexuality in current debates on difference and democratic community in southern Africa, especially in the "New" South Africa where previously marginalized voices are now claiming subjectivity, cultural legitimacy, and political viability? How might a study of historical and cultural representations of sexual difference in southern Africa help further diversify representations of (homo)sexual identity as a social position that is always already *mediated* by race, gender, social class, and geopolitical spatialization? How might a study of queer cultural and political practices among Africans in southern Africa help (re)articulate a critique of nationalist claims in the region that read homosexuality as alien to Africa, and, at the same time, lead to a more self-reflexive critique of the colonizing gestures of queer identity politics in the West that rely on Euroamerican models of gay liberation (such as Stonewall) as paradigmatic for claiming a queer identity and reclaiming a queer past? How might recent efforts at (re-)reading queer identities, desires, and imaginaries transnationally help us to better question the "national" as self-evident and, as Povinelli and Chauncey note, more critically analyze how normative discourses interpellate individuals into hegemonically rendered social circles that produce subjects of gender and the trajectory of their desire (444)?

Though South Africa's new constitution contains a clause that expressly prohibits discrimination according to sexual orientation, discourses surrounding the status of homosexuality in South African culture, social life, and history remain nonetheless contested. To give a fairly recent example, in December 1997 Winnie Madikizela-Mandela appeared before South Africa's Truth and Reconciliation Commission (TRC) to speak about her role in the kidnappings and beatings of several black youths, one of whom, fourteen-year-old Stompie Moeketsi Seipei, was later found dead. Though she denied having had any part in the abductions or beatings, referring to the accusations and evidence

against her as "lunacy" and "ridiculous lies" (Daley A1), according to
her testimony at her trial in 1991 the kidnappings and beatings, for
which she was later convicted, were necessary to save the youths from
the homosexual advances of a white minister, Paul Verryn. As Rachel
Holmes has pointed out in an essay "Queer Comrades: Winnie Mandela
and the Moffies" published in *Social Text*, Mrs. Madikizela-Mandela's
defense generated a homophobic public discourse within the context of
preelection attempts to move toward a new political climate in South
Africa. Her defense team, with the help of the popular media, conflated
homosexuality with child sexual abuse at nearly the same time the ANC
formalized its commitment to equal rights for lesbians and gay men in
the draft bill of rights (168–69). Through implying, Holmes continues,
that homosexuality is antithetical to the "fraternity" of the nation, and
by casting it on the constitutive outside of the formative discourses of
new South African nationhood, the 1991 trial demarcated homosexuality by marking it racially as a form of deviance tainted with whiteness
(178). For many black gay men and lesbians in South Africa, then, Mrs.
Madikizela-Mandela's testimony to the Truth Commission evoked
memories of the homophobic discourse surrounding her trial that fed off
of social phobias about homosexuality already in place, perhaps best
summed up by many of her supporters at the trial who defended her
actions by carrying placards declaring "Homosex is not in black culture." Winnie Mandela herself, and others in southern Africa who argue
that black queer activists support "lifestyles" that are "imports" of
empire, have continued to play upon homophobically inscribed nationalist assertions that read homosexuality as inherently alien to indigenous
black cultures.

I also mention this because historical research in South Africa,
informed by Marxist/Althuserrian notions of the status of the subject in
history, was critical in writing the black working class back into history
and uncovering the mechanisms of its exploitation through addressing
colonialism, capitalism, and racism as intersecting and interrelated systems of power; yet, historical work on homosexuality among Africans
has not only remained woefully inadequate, but, as Zackie Achmat
argues, has strayed into history only as the "unnatural vice" of the
South African gold mines, thereby ignoring another possible lens for
reading the subject—through the production and history of desire (95).
In their search for the origins of exploitation and oppression, especially
in trying to understand the apartheid era through the perspective of

postapartheid politics, contemporary historiography in South Africa and postcolonial studies on South Africa largely done in the West have ignored the sexual and struggles for erotic autonomy as significant axes of analysis, that is, how "conquest and domination must also be understood as an inscription of power relations on the body" (Achmat 96). This elision is most evident in terms of how the dominant body of historical work in southern Africa on homosexuality among Africans still locates it within the normalizing structures of heteronormativity and dominant social relations, and reads it not only as a colonial import, but, in the specific context of South Africa, as a disorder brought about by the oppressive social structures of apartheid and the concomitant harshness of exploitative labor conditions.

For example, T. Dunbar Moodie's research on same-sex "marriages" among male migrant workers in the South African gold mines was one of the first major studies to address homosexual relations between African men in southern Africa. Yet his assumptions of same-sex desire remain circumscribed by traditional medical, juridical, and theological discourses that read it as a temporary aberration, practiced intermittently in labor compounds, prisons, and other spatial formations where men are forced to cohabit for extended periods of time. He and his colleagues write that most mine workers were not allowed to go back to visit women in the townships for long periods of time, and feared being robbed by the "town women" and getting venereal disease, both of which would be tied to the possible loss of one's rural identity (421). The "mine marriages," according to Moodie, et al., were a reliable social structure in the mines and a source of rural resistance to the wage economy (425). Because the marriages usually involved the "marriage" of young "boys" to more senior men, Moodie seems to suggest that the mine marriages were modeled on the gender norms of traditional, precapitalist rural marriages insofar as the "wife" performed domestic duties and personal services that the senior men were reluctant to forego, the major difference being that the younger male was given remuneration, which would help him to earn bride wealth ("lobola") and therefore help him to more rapidly become a "real" man back home. Moodie indicates that his research found that sexual activity seldom involved anal penetration, but took the form of "hlabonga" or nonpenetrative sex, more commonly known as "thigh fucking," in which the younger male played the more passive, receptive, and nonejaculatory role (413, 417).

Moodie's research has only recently come under attack in the context of contemporary queer politics in the "New" South Africa for helping to legitimate, whether intentionally or not, nationalistic claims that homosexuality, if it exists at all in African cultures, is solely the product of inhumane labor systems and apartheid capitalism, and for erasing any memory of insurgent sexualities, which radically disrupt dominant social relations rather than merely being subsumed under them. Achmat writes that Moodie's study attempts to "neutralise the *subversive* and *destabilising* effects of sex in the compounds . . . and, through this, to 'normalise' sexual activity, fix 'cultural' identity, and center monogamous, heterosexual relations" (108; emphasis added). In addition, Moodie's heteronormative perspective, because it assumes that after leaving the mines, the men returned to their presumed heterosexual destinies, causally links homosexuality to the forced conditions of racial oppression and overinscribes same-sex relations among African men with economic and biological determinism. More important, Moodie's study violently robs those being studied of the agency of their own desire and is misogynistic to the extent that it inscribes the "boy," who assumes the more "feminine" role in the marriage, as a transferred sexual object that fulfills otherwise uncontrollable male heterosexual desire.[2]

Recently, Hugh McLean and Linda Ngcobo reexamined the mine marriages, and subsequent assumptions that reduce same-sex relations among African men to "circumstantial homosexuality," through interviewing African men of a range of ages in the townships who have sex with other men, and report that they enjoy their erotic ties with other men and prefer them over heterosexual relations. McLean and Ngcobo question a completely separate and unrelated relationship between gay sexual practices in the townships and sexual practices between men in the marriages on the gold mines. Excerpts from their interviews and a discussion of their findings, published in the essay "Abangibhamayo bathi ngimnandi," or "Those Who Fuck Me Say I'm Tasty," acknowledge "hlabonga" (thigh sex) as a cultural precedent in sexual relations commonly practiced between young, unmarried heterosexual couples in traditional African societies, such as among the Zulus, which was not regarded as premarital sex per se since the female would retain her virginity and her parents would not have to settle for a lower "lobola." But McLean and Ngcobo strongly question the prevalence of "hlabonga" in the mines and see Moodie's study as an attempt to sanitize sex between men; their interviews show that for most African men who have sex with other men, sex is commonly understood *to mean* anal penetration (167). McLean and Ngcobo criticize Moodie for representing gay male sexuality "too much like a mechanical and necessary substitute for heterosexual life . . . [making] no real concession to the fact that some men may . . . have enjoyed sex with other men or might [have] even prefer[ed] it to having sex with women" (166). Why the elision?; why offread in favor of privileging heteronormativity as Moodie's study seems to do? Why not recognize that when the life histories of the miners were gathered, stronger social taboos and the illegality of sodomy under apartheid could possibly have prevented Moodie's informants from admitting to having had anal sex, much less having had enjoyed it? Rereading the mine marriages through an antihomophobic lens, Achmat argues that the labor compound regime created a new space of desire that fostered a number of practices—including male homosexuality—that did not simply help sustain social relations in the countryside, but in fact disrupted them, and exacerbated pre-existing class, gender, and age differences in indigenous social formations (106),[3] though for the most part, this new research has not had wide circulation and has not engendered much public debate in South Africa, as national attention is now focused on trying to gain perspective on testimonies given to the Truth and Reconciliation Commission, economic recovery, and the task of the deracialization of South Africa's institutions after apartheid.

More recently, in literary and cultural studies, despite the current political transformations in South Africa, there are still significant elisions of same-sex desire as a legitimate focus of inquiry. Chris Dunton's analysis of the treatment of homosexuality in the plays of Gibson Kente, in Bessie Head's novel *A Question of Power*, and in the work of other African writers has identified a stigmatization of same-sex desire as a rarity in traditional African societies; Dunton has also identified a lack of a fully characterized and nonjudgmental depiction of homosexual relationships between Africans in texts written as late as the 1980s ("'Wheyting Be Dat?'" 445). Despite the proliferation of lesbian and gay writing in South Africa since the late 1980s, particularly in the Afrikaans literary canon (such as works by Hennie Aucamp, Mark Behr, and Koos Prinsloo, to name a few), as well as the production of two major anthologies (*The Invisible Ghetto* and *Defiant Desire*), Michael Chapman, author of a comprehensive and critical work *Southern African Literatures*, published in 1996 by Longman, only devotes a couple of sen-

tences to lesbian and gay literature through an all-too-brief mention of
Stephen Gray's novels *Time of our Darkness* (1988) and *Born of Man*
(1989), both of which Chapman patronizes as "giving voice and sensibility to the *victims* of marginalised sexuality: the homosexual body
marked by the body politic" (400; emphasis added). The erasures of
insurgent sexualities from collective memory in any attempt at nation
building, or, in the case of South Africa, nation *re*building, and the
absence of a concomitant antihomophobic or other politicized perspective that reads homosexuality as subversive and as a site of resistance to
normalization when it is "recovered" from history, require queer analysis that takes into account historicized and contextualized understandings of "queer."

It is equally important in any analysis of same-sex desire in postcolonial contexts to ensure that the axis of sexuality not obscure and
overexceed that of gender so that the *specificity* of lesbian desire, which
questions any apparent parallels between lesbians and gay men, is not
rendered invisible. As Biddy Martin reminds us, queer theorists often see
gender differences as constraining, as if they can be overridden by the
greater mobility of queer desires. Yet, such representations of gender, she
argues, get "coded implicitly, when not explicitly, as female while sexuality takes on the universality of man" (102). As long as we continue to
privilege sexuality as the more avant-garde, or as the more volatile site
of resistance to normalization at the expense of gender when studying
same-sex desire in non-western locations, we remain complicit in reinventing the logic of masculinist privilege that has very much plagued not
only colonialist rule, but anticolonialist and postcolonial struggles.
Queer inquiry can most productively intersect with postcolonial work
and with emerging queer movements in postcolonial locations if it
engages in comparative exchange so that queer studies, as they have
developed in the West, do not become another master discourse of the
postcolonial, if it maintains gender and sexuality as intimately entangled
axes of analysis, and if it analyzes sexuality as always already mediated
by gender in addition to race, geopolitical location, and class.

Judith Gay's study of "mummy-baby" relationships among
women in Lesotho, originally published in the *Journal of Homosexuality* in 1985, provides another significant site for broader investigation
and further elaboration of these issues. As one may recall, Gay did an
anthropological investigation of same-sex relations among women in
Lesotho, and maintained that these relationships must be understood in

the socioeconomic context of male migrant labor, where nearly half of Lesotho's adult male labor force migrates to nearby South Africa to work for long periods of time, increasing female economic dependence and making marital relationships unstable insofar as the migrant system encourages not only prolonged separation, but nonsupport, desertion, and divorce (98). So while affectionate and erotic ties between women in Lesotho certainly need to be understood in terms of the effects of kinship structures, colonization, and the effects of the organization of labor on women, Gay is quite adamant that these relations *not* be understood in the same way that Moodie problematically characterized sexual relations among men in the South African mine compounds which I have just discussed, that is, as motivated primarily by sexual release when the opposite sex was not available (Gay 112). "Mummy-baby" relationships between women in Lesotho are always initiated and agreed upon voluntarily, usually beginning in adolescence but not limited to pre-adulthood, when one girl takes a liking to another and asks her to be her "mummy" or "baby," depending on their relative ages. The relationship develops through organized encounters and by material and emotional exchanges such as gift-giving and advice on having sex with men, and are a *recognized* means within Lesotho culture by which young women extend the range of their social relations (102–103). More important, not only do affectionate ties between women usually include an intense level of genital sexuality where women are able to exercise a great deal of initiative and autonomy, unlike the formal rules of marriage where they are constrained both by the male-dominated family system and the modern male-dominated economic system (107), the romantic and sensual bonds that women create and sustain often continue *alongside* and are *compatible with* conventional heterosexual marriage (111) and can become the basis for a lifelong support structure. Building somewhat on Gay's research, Limakatso Kendall has recently published a collection of autobiographical narratives *Basali!* by and about women in Lesotho, several of whom write about caring for the women they love. For instance, Mpho 'M'atsepo Nthunya, in her piece "Three Moments in a Marriage" recalls:

> When I was living in the mountains near Marakabei I got a special friend. She was living in another village, and I passed her house when I was going to church every month. One day she saw me and said, "What is your name?"

I told her it was 'M'atsepo Nthunya. So she said, "I always see you passing here. Today I want to talk to you. I want you to be my *motsoalle*." This is a name we have in Lesotho for a very special friend. She says, "I love you." It's like when a man chooses you for a wife, except when a man chooses, it's because he wants to share his blankets with you. The woman chooses you the same way, but she wants love only. When a woman loves another woman, you see, she can love with her whole heart.

I saw how she was looking at me, and I said, "*Ke hantle*." It's fine with me. So she kissed me, and from that day she was my *motsoalle*. She told her husband about it, and he came to my house and told my husband, and these two husbands became friends too. (4–5)

Attention to the axis of gender in analyses of same-sex desire in post-colonial locations, given that affectionate and erotic exchanges between women in Lesotho are common though not specifically named as "lesbian," enables further sites of theoretical elaboration. While Gay points out that the compatibility of intimate female relations with heterosexuality challenges Western insistences on the polarization of hetero- and homosexuality, her anthropological perspective is somewhat limiting politically, as one of her conclusions is that "mummy-baby" relationships point to the growing recognition of bisexuality in the psychosexual literature, which is specifically supported in studies of non-Western societies (111–12). But it seems simplistic to stop there; further theoretical investigation needs to analyze, as Chris Dunton and Mai Palmberg imply, whether women in Lesotho, and other parts of southern Africa where affectionate ties between women may be common, draw rigid divisions between their friendships with women that have an erotic component and those that do not, and between their erotic relations with other women and with men (21). Because rural women in southern Africa may engage in same-sex relationships without necessarily self-identifying, indeed often resisting being named, as "lesbian," it is important for queer studies to ask how these erotic exchanges between women help rearticulate and redefine lesbian, gender, and African identity, which need not necessarily include the positioning of oneself as "queer," but may nonetheless subvert (whether consciously or not) normative regimes of compulsory heterosexuality.

Related to my point about gender, as Judith Butler has pointed out that in regimes of compulsory heterosexuality the regulation of

sexuality is intimately tied to the *policing* and *shaming* of gender
(238), it seems necessary to fortify the relation between gender and
sexuality as linked axes of analysis in postcolonial spaces, since "good
citizenship" often acts as a site of recolonization if it undermines erotic
autonomy and is tied to both women's and men's "proper" *gender*
roles as procreating, and therefore (so the argument goes), heterosexual citizens. Erotic ties between women in Lesotho seem to get around
this and *both* participate in *and* resist the patriarchal imperatives of
compulsory heterosexuality legislated in the name of nation building.
At the same time, critical attention to these relationships provides a
crucial opportunity to investigate the colonizing tendencies of queer
studies and queer activism in the West. As Jacqui Alexander has
argued, the absence of visible lesbian and gay movements outside of
Euroamerican locations is often seen by the West as a defect in political consciousness and maturity, using the presence of publicly organized queer movements in the U.S. as evidence of their own originary
status and their superior political maturity. She points out that we
leave undertheorized not only the imperial within the national (i.e., the
postcolonial nation-state), but the colonial within the oppositional
(i.e., academic queer studies) (69). How might the erotic ties between
women in Lesotho and between rural women in other parts of southern Africa create new sites of political agency and resistance to fixed
identities, to the hetero/homo split, and to the imperialist impulses of
American queer identity politics?

On the other hand, it is important to note that attention to the axis
of gender cannot imply, as I have argued elsewhere, completely wiping
out the axis of sexuality altogether, since this would ignore the *erotic* significance of the identities of women who engage in sexual relationships
with other women and the radical potential of these relationships to
transgress the opposition between "true" (heterosexual) femininity and
lesbian specificity.[4] Same-sex relationships among Basotho women subvert heterosexuality as a political regime and expose its pretense to
reflect a natural order of "true" genders defined *exclusively* by heterosexual desire. This also points to a concomitant need for feminist studies of the postcolonial not to assume sisterhood on the basis of gender
alone, but, as Chandra Mohanty notes, to look at the ways in which sisterhood is *formed* in concrete, historical, and political practice and
analysis (262). One dimension of the study of sisterhood must include,
I would add, attention to erotic ties between women and the ways in

which these operate oppositionally as sites of decolonization and erotic autonomy, thereby constituting other forms of resistance to heteropatriarchy.

Finally, in considering homophobia as a significant vector of domination in contemporary southern Africa, rigorous theorizations of heteropatriarchy and its prohibitions against homosexuality must be foregrounded in African literary and cultural studies where it still remains significantly absent. In addition, Jacqui Alexander reminds us that the postcolonial nation-state often makes rhetorical use of classificatory systems that are reminiscent of colonial relations of rule to argue against homosexuality and to maintain what it perceives to be the moral boundaries of the closet and the basis for "true" citizenship. In such arguments, she points out, strains of "evidence" are conveniently and idiosyncratically borrowed from science ("laws of nature"), medicine (outdated psychiatric discourses on perversion), and "common" sense, all of which function to interpret important dimensions of self (84–85). Consider, for instance, Zimbabwean President Robert Mugabe's much publicized denunciation of gay men and lesbians at the official opening of the International Book Fair held in Harare in August 1995, ironically themed "Human Rights and Justice," from which a small exhibit by GALZ (Gays and Lesbians of Zimbabwe) was excluded by government order at the last moment:

> I find it extremely outrageous and repugnant to my human conscience that such immoral and repulsive organisations, like those of homosexuals who offend both against the law of nature and the morals of religious beliefs espoused by our society, should have any advocates in our midst and even elsewhere in the world.
>
> If we accept homosexuality as a right, as is being argued by the association of sodomists and sexual perverts, what moral fibre shall our society ever have to deny organised drug addicts, or even those given to bestiality, the rights they might claim and allege they possess under the rubrics of individual freedom and human rights, including the freedom of the Press to write, publish, and publicise their literature on them? (*New York Times*, August 2, 1995; qtd. in Dunton and Palmberg 9–10)

Indeed, nationalistic discourses, such as those articulated by Mugabe and frequently supported in other parts of the region (including the "new" South Africa), condemn homosexuality as "un-African" or as a bourgeois Western phenomenon, and such arguments are particularly underscored with reference to emerging lesbian and gay movements in black communities in the region. Two weeks after Mugabe's attack, *The Chronicle*, a Harare newspaper, played on nationalist and masculinist assumptions that white colonial power was emasculating for Africa and that homosexuality among blacks is a form of ideological penetration by whites that further "feminizes" the nation-state (conceived of as masculine):

> Painful experience reminds us Zimbabweans, and all other Africans on the continent, of moves orchestrated by colonialists to wipe out anything that had to do with African culture as constituted mainly by our customs and traditions. . . . Many years after decolonisation, attempts to wipe out what is left of our cultural values are still being made—and made with a vengeance in some cases, witness the *shrill* outcries over the refusal by the Government to allow the Gays and Lesbians of Zimbabwe to *peddle* its ideas by exhibiting at the recent Zimbabwe International Book Fair in Harare—a refusal that all Africans who cherish their cultural identity—or what remains of it—should support unflinchingly. (The *Chronicle*, Harare, August 9, 1995; qtd. in Dunton and Palmberg 12; emphasis added)

Ironically, then, nationalistic discourses and appeals to a natural precolonial, heterosexual African identity make use of and reinvent the same medicalized tropes of pathology and abject gender, and, in so doing, rearticulate a homophobic discursive grid and system of inscription with which to read same-sex desire not altogether different from the white colonialist legacy such discourses otherwise purport to resist. Readings of homosexuality by the nation-state, which conceives of itself as masculine and then as "feminized" by the imperial imprint of homosexuality, are also linked to gender oppression and misogyny in that power is reduced to the phallus. The nation-state's fantasy of itself as masculine similarly points to and extends the ambivalence at the site of authority, not between colonizer and colonized as articulated by Homi Bhabha, but by the production of differentiations through which discriminatory practices "map out" queers as "Other." In naming queerness as such, the nation-state, following Bhabha, both projects and masks difference through strategies of repetition and displacement, asserting mastery of the Other through its discourse and simultaneously finding its authority slipping away (Bhabha 81, 84). At the same time, nationalistic appeals to "authentic" African beliefs and ways of being positioned in the world, as Anthony Appiah notes, see Africa as culturally homogeneous and fail to account for the diversity of its people and its cultures. Such views of African homogeneity, Appiah continues, not only assume that there are characteristically African ways of thinking, but that there are characteristically African beliefs (24). Moreover, nationalist ideologies, fueled by nostalgic appeals to a precolonial authenticity, are not only flawed because they assume that cultural practices can return to some "pure" and unsullied condition (Ashcroft, et al. 41–42), they also further normalize domination, fail to acknowledge the multiplicity and fluidity of African identities and cultures shaped by historical, economic, and political influences, and maintain a problematic self/Other split between Africa and the West, all of which, in addition to the censure of homosexuality, are highly characteristic of the imperialist gesture.[5]

As queer and postcolonial scholars, it is important that we address seriously the psychic violence, effected through homophobic strategies of excessive codification and regulation, directed toward lesbians and gay men outside of the Euroamerican axes of queer politics so that we may more credibly work towards the liberatory imperatives of both fields of inquiry and help revise the heterosexist and other oppressive ways in which self, citizenship, community, and cultural identity and difference are presently configured and understood. Black lesbian and gay writers in South Africa have written on the psychic effects of heteronormativity on lesbians and gay men of African descent in the region who often assume that their only choices are to take their African heritage as primary, suppressing their gay sexuality as frivolous, or to openly identify as lesbian or gay while suffering a sense of wounded African identity. Hein Kleinbooi, for instance, writes of the intense alienation he experienced as a black gay student activist at the University of Cape Town, where his gay white colleagues simplistically equated the heterosexist and homophobic oppression they experienced with racism during apartheid, thereby trivializing the violence and poverty resulting from racial oppression, and where his black liberationist comrades told him he was "hijacking the struggle" for racial equality when he spoke to them of gay rights (264). Both positions, as long as one does not interrogate the other, foreclose discussion on how a variety of oppressions may intertwine and create an

oppositional logic that insists on fixed notions of identity, thereby further impeding the decolonization of the mind.

Lastly, since Foucault, we have come to understand that the sexual is not separate from regimes of power; yet in postcolonial analyses
of culture and in postcolonial societies the politics of sexuality, if and
when recognized as a viable site of decolonization, seems deferred from
serious analysis until the more urgent tasks of nation building and
development have begun and brought about tangible social and economic change. Yet can attempts at nation re-building, democratization,
and national reconciliation in South Africa, for instance, be fully understood without an analysis of the sexual, just as any analysis of the sexual needs to be theorized within specific material conditions? An
engaged analysis of the sexual, despite new scholarship that has been
written in the postapartheid era, remains to be done. As late as 1998,
Derek Attridge and Rosemary Jolly, in their introduction to their collection *Writing South Africa*, assert that "clearly postcolonial writing
desires to contest the power of the colonizer, and assert the authority of
the oppressed subject" (8). But their brief gloss (at the very end of the
introduction) of Michiel Heyns's essay, the only piece in the collection
that specifically addresses gay writing in South Africa, is telling in that
there is no real analysis of the sexual alongside the larger questions of
antiapartheid and postapartheid struggle that they discuss in most of
their introduction. After citing Heyns's analysis of the fiction of the late
Afrikaans writer Koos Prinsloo during South Africa's State of Emergency in the 1980s, the period of the country's most brutal repression
of human rights, where Heyns says "to read Prinsloo is not so much to
understand the Emergency as to experience it, and to see the gay writer
not as a marginalized observer but as a participant in a troubled society" (12; Heyns 121), Attridge and Jolly go on to say that, like
Prinsloo's narrative, their book does not aim to tell the story of South
Africa and have the final word on the decline of apartheid as this would
(re)produce South Africa as spectacle (12). But is there any real analysis of the sexual here vis-à-vis what they earlier describe as "the intricate relations among aesthetics, ethics, and politics" the (other) essays
in the volume are proffered to explore "in the light of a new freedom"
(1–2)? Anne McClintock reminds us that postcolonial feminist struggles have taught us that the insistence on silence about gender conflict
where it already exists is to cover and thereby ratify women's disem-
powerment and maintain the nation-state as a repository of male

hopes, male aspirations, and male privilege (385). Likewise, following the implications of McClintock's argument, for postcolonial theorists to posit queer struggles as less urgent (or, in the case of Attridge and Jolly, to tokenize them without any serious analysis) and not recognize the transformative power of the erotic, irresponsibly trivializes the demands of lesbian, gay men, and other sexual minorities, defers necessary retheorizations of nation, citizenship, sexuality, and identity, and enables heteronormativity, as a normalizing regime, to perpetuate its own ideological longevity.

Finally, comparative, and perhaps transnational, queer inquiry should enable Western queer studies to radically interrogate and transform the lenses through which it reads and appropriates desire, queer identity, and sexual difference, and to self-reflexively examine its own imperialist and homogenizing impulses made possible through globalization. New work on thinking about sexuality in transnational, circulatorial terms, whereby we question the nation-state as the proper object of analysis and shift our attention from culture as territorially based to culture as mediated and disseminated across wide distances, raises, for me, crucial questions pertaining to the democratization of articulation and access. Western cultures have had the capital means to circulate queerness as a commodity and the economic power to appropriate emergent forms of queer cultural production outside of the Euroamerican axis. Shifting the centrality of sexual identities and imaginaries from national to transnational contexts dangerously risks the elision of the local. We might ask, "global according to whom?" It may be more productive, as Elizabeth Povinelli and George Chauncey suggest in "Thinking Sexuality Transnationally," to address the tension between local sexual ideologies and subjectivities organized in different, often resistant terms (446). We might then more productively ask what new forms of queer identity, erotics, and community are opened up and the practices of citizenship these may imply.

NOTES

I would like to express my gratitude to the National Endowment for the Humanities for funding my travel to South Africa in the summer of 1996 and for financially supporting much of the research for this chapter. I am also grateful to Bernth Lindfors and David Attwell for their in-depth knowledge of South

African literature and culture, and for leading me to important libraries, archives, and resources in South Africa. The assistance of Vasu Reddy, Ronald Louw, Ann Smith, and Marcia Blumberg on all of my trips to South Africa has been invaluable. Finally, I would like to acknowledge the Centre for Rhetoric Studies, University of Cape Town, where I was Visiting Fellow in spring 1998. The Centre's Directors, Philippe-Joseph Salazar and Yehoshua Gitay, generously provided me with office space and research support for this chapter and the larger project out of which it comes.

1. I use the term "queer" here to denote an oppositional political praxis in the "new" South Africa which operates against the normalizing ideologies of nationality, race, gender, and class, *as well as* sexuality, that marked the apartheid era, and which, as I shall mention, have not been entirely eradicated despite juridical changes (hence my use of scare quotes to differentiate and simultaneously interrogate the "new" South Africa). As queer political and cultural practices in South Africa in particular have deliberately sought to resist what Phillip Brian Harper refers to as "'sexual orientation' as a primary identificatory principle, uninflected by the pressures of other subjectivizing factors" (26), the term "lesbian and gay," insofar as it is restricted to a politics of sexual identity and sexual practices alone, may not be sufficient to describe them. Certainly the use of "queer" is not an appropriative one; Mark Gevisser has pointed out that gay men, lesbians, and other sexual minorities in South Africa have identified as queers, "moffies," dykes, lesbians, gays, etc. (17). I enclose the term "queer" in scare quotes in my title, and here in its first usage referring to the specificity of South Africa as a reminder that the term, while influenced by and not entirely removed from Western queer identity politics and cultural practices, is not reducible to them.

2. Moodie's use of the term "boy" to describe the younger male partner in the marriage, who usually played the more submissive role both sexually and domestically, is also problematic largely because he doesn't account for its racist usage where whites in power often addressed black men of any age as "boy" during the apartheid era Its use also points to how several vectors of domination—racism, gender oppression, and homophobia—intersected in apartheid South Africa that are not altogether absent from the current postapartheid context. In Bessie Head's novel, *A Question of Power*, for example, the narrator's reflection on the racist usage of "boy" to refer to black men during apartheid is also illustrative of the term's homophobic underpinnings through the shaming of gender: "'How can a man be a man when he is called boy? I can barely retain my own manhood. . . . Another man addresses me as boy. How do you think I feel?'" (45).

3. Taking Achmat's critique of Moodie, et al, one step further, Ronald Louw has researched same-sex marriages between African men in Mkhumbane,

an informal settlement in Durban in the 1950s. Louw argues that, unlike the mine marriages, the marriages at Mkhumbane were *not* restricted to intergenerational couplings, and that they were not entered into strictly for financial reasons as was often a motivating factor for the younger male in the mine marriages. Like Achmat, Louw asks whether the city could have also represented "a new space of desire" that similarly disrupted heteronormative social relations (15–16). Louw's study further challenges several of Moodie's assumptions on same-sex relations among African men, as well as broader nationalist and cultural assertions that homosexuality was practiced among African men simply as a response to labor conditions.

4. For further discussion of this point, as well as my argument that gender and sexuality be interrogated as enmeshed categories of analysis against Sedgwick's claim for the analytic usefulness of disjoining them while acknowledging their relatedness, see my essay "Sissies and Sisters: Gender, Sexuality and the Possibilities of Coalition" in *Coming Out of Feminism?*

5. Along these lines, texts by southern African writers, while not expressly addressing same-sex desire, are beneficial to postcolonial queer inquiry insofar as they help debunk nostalgic myths about recuperating a monolithic, precolonial African authenticity. Bessie Head, in her later work *The Collector of Treasures and Other Botswana Village Tales*, for instance, points not only to the incongruities between precapitalist and postcapitalist societies, but to the ways in which traditionalist societies have oppressed women. She writes: "The ancestors made so many errors and one of the most bitter-making things was that they relegated to men a superior position in the tribe, while women were regarded, in a congenital sense, as being an inferior form of human life. To this day, women still suffered from all the calamities that befall an inferior form of human life" (92). Also important, Ezekiel Mphahlele's autobiography of his exile from South Africa, *Down Second Avenue*, illustrates not only the complexity of African identity through his reflectively written intervals, but subjectivity as radically decentered and as requiring a continual *repositioning* of oneself in the world and in one's history, which, in turn, may help to generate thinking, both in Africa and in the West, on new matrices of political agency and resistance for lesbians and gay men in southern Africa and in other postcolonial nations.

WORKS CITED

Achmat, Zackie. "'Apostles of a Civilised Vice': 'Immoral Practices' and 'Unnatural Vice' in South African Prisons and Compounds, 1980–1990." *Social Dynamics* 19.2 (1993): 92–110.

Alexander, M. Jacqui. "Erotic Autonomy as a Politics of Decolonization: An Anatomy of Feminist and State Practice in the Bahamas Tourist Economy." Alexander and Mohanty, 63–100.

Alexander, M. Jacqui, and Chandra Talpade Mohanty, eds. *Feminist Genealogies, Colonial Legacies, Democratic Futures*. New York: Routledge, 1997.

Appiah, Kwame Anthony. *In My Father's House: Africa in the Philosophy of Culture*. New York: Oxford UP, 1992.

Ashcroft, Bill, Gareth Griffiths, and Helen Tiffin. *The Empire Writes Back: Theory and Practice in Post-Colonial Literatures*. New York: Routledge, 1989.

Attridge, Derek, and Rosemary Jolly, eds. *Writing South Africa: Literature, Apartheid, and Democracy, 1970–1995*. New York: Cambridge UP, 1998.

Bhabha, Homi K. "The Other Question: Difference, Discrimination, and the Discourse of Colonialism." In *Out There: Marginalization and Contemporary Cultures*, ed. Russell Ferguson, et al., 71–87. New York: The New Museum of Contemporary Art, and Cambridge: MIT Press, 1990.

Butler, Judith. *Bodies that Matter: On the Discursive Limits of "Sex."* New York: Routledge, 1993.

Chapman, Michael. *Southern African Literatures*. New York: Longman, 1996.

Daley, Suzanne. "Winnie Mandela is Defiant, Calling Accusations 'Lunacy.'" *New York Times*. 5 Dec. 1997: A1+.

Dunton, Chris. "'Wheyting Be Dat?' The Treatment of Homosexuality in African Literature." *Research in African Literatures* 20.3 (1989): 422–448.

Dunton, Chris, and Mai Palmberg. *Human Rights and Homosexuality in Southern Africa*. Uppsala, Sweden: The Nordic Africa Institute, 1996.

Gay, Judith. "'Mummies and Babies' and Friends and Lovers in Lesotho." *Journal of Homosexuality* 11.3–4 (1985). Rpt. in *The Many Faces of Homosexuality: Anthropological Approaches to Homosexual Behavior*, ed. Evelyn Blackwood. New York: Harrington Park Press, 1986. 97–116.

Gevisser, Mark. "A Different Fight for Freedom: A History of South African Lesbian and Gay Organisation from the 1950s to 1990s." Gevisser and Cameron 14–86.

Gevisser, Mark, and Edwin Cameron, eds. *Defiant Desire: Gay and Lesbian Lives in South Africa*. New York: Routledge, 1995.

Harper, Phillip Brian. "Gay Male Identities, Personal Privacy, and Relations of Public Exchange: Notes on Directions for Queer Critique." *Social Text* 15.3–4 (1997): 5–29.

Head, Bessie. *A Question of Power*. London: Heinemann, 1974.

———. *The Collector of Treasures and Other Botswana Village Tales*. London: Heinemann, 1977.

Heyns, Michiel. "A Man's World: White South African Gay Writing and the State of Emergency." Attridge and Jolly, 108–122.

Holmes, Rachel. "Queer Comrades: Winnie Mandela and the Moffies." *Social Text* 15.3–4 (1997): 161–180.

Kleinbooi, Hein. "Identity Crossfire: On Being a Black Gay Student Activist." Gevisser and Cameron, 264–268.

Krouse, Matthew, ed. *The Invisible Ghetto: Lesbian and Gay Writing from South Africa*. Johannesburg: Congress of South African Writers (COSAW), 1993.

Louw, Ronald. "(Un)African Traditional Weddings: Same-Sex Marriage in Mkhumbane in the 1950s." Unpublished paper. 1993.

Martin, Biddy. "Extraordinary Homosexuals and the Fear of Being Ordinary." *Differences: A Journal of Feminist Cultural Studies*. 6.2–3 (1994): 100–125.

McClintock, Anne. *Imperial Leather: Race, Gender and Sexuality in the Colonial Contest*. New York: Routledge, 1995.

McLean, Hugh, and Linda Ngcobo. "Abangibhamayo bathi ngimnandi (Those Who Fuck Me Say I'm Tasty): Gay Sexuality in Reef Townships." Gevisser and Cameron, 158–185.

Mohanty, Chandra Talpade. "Under Western Eyes: Feminist Scholarship and Colonial Discourses." *Boundary 2* 12.3, 13.1 (1984). Rpt. in *The Post-Colonial Studies Reader*, ed. Bill Ashcroft, Gareth Griffiths, and Helen Tiffin. New York: Routledge, 1995. 259–263.

Moodie, T. Dunbar, et al. "Migrancy and Male Sexuality on the South African Gold Mines." *The Journal of African Studies* 14.2 (January 1988). Rpt. in *Hidden from History: Reclaiming the Gay and Lesbian Past*, ed. Martin Duberman, Martha Vicinus, and George Chauncey Jr. New York: Meridian, 1989. 411–425.

Mphahlele, Ezekiel. *Down Second Avenue*. Boston: Faber and Faber, 1959.

Nthunya, Mpho 'M'atsepo. "Three Moments in a Marriage." In *Basali!: Stories by and About Women in Lesotho*, ed. K. Limakatso Kendall. Pietermaritzburg, South Africa: U of Natal P, 1995. 1–16.

Povinelli, Elizabeth A., and George Chauncey. "Thinking Sexuality Transnationally." *GLQ* 5.4 (1999): 439–49.

Spurlin, William J. "Sissies and Sisters: Gender, Sexuality and the Possibilities of Coalition." In *Coming Out of Feminism?*, ed. Elizabeth Wright, Naomi Segal, and Mandy Merck. Oxford, UK: Blackwell Publishers, 1998. 74–101.

CHAPTER NINE

GLOBAL (SEXUAL) POLITICS, CLASS STRUGGLE, AND THE QUEER LEFT

DONALD E. MORTON

> The ideas of the ruling class are in every epoch the ruling
> ideas . . . the ruling ideas are nothing more than the ideal
> expression of the dominant material relationships.
> —Karl Marx, *The German Ideology*

EVADING DETERMINATE EXPLANATIONS OF THE GLOBAL

If one can judge from recent exchanges, there is a great deal of interest in Australasia (as elsewhere) in the question of "global" politics and in particular of "globalizing" queer theory. I was recently invited to participate in an online forum sponsored by the *Australian Humanities Review* (AHR), where these questions were opened up; however, they were not very fully elaborated in theoretical terms and certainly not exhausted. Hence I am devoting this chapter to a further critique-al inquiry into the issue of "globalizing" queer theory and write mainly to address the following questions: How must the "global" be theorized so as to enable social justice worldwide for all? How is the question of class being minimized and trivialized by the dominant queer left? Although I bring into my discussion a recent (queer) book about the fall of the Berlin Wall and consequent changes in Eastern Europe, I shall focus mainly on the U.S./Australia axis,[1] specifically on a cluster of recent texts by Dennis Altman: "On Global Queering" (and various cyberinteractive responses to it), "Dennis Altman Replies," and "Rupture or Continuity? The Internationalization of Gay Identities."[2]

The choice of Altman's texts as my tutor texts for the U.S./Australia axis is neither "personal" nor "voluntarist," but historical. For more than two decades, Altman has written extensively and consistently on/along the U.S./Australia linkage on global sexual politics, and his thoughts on the issues are still regarded as "authoritative"—as is suggested by the very structure of exchanges in *AHR* (which place his writings at the focal point); by the recent publication of an essay in *Social Text;* and, not least, by the recent reprinting of his "classic" 1971 book, *Homosexual Oppression and Liberation.* Indeed, his academic work has been devoted, he himself says, to teaching "American politics to Australian students" (Altman, Homosexual Oppression 255). More important, however, is the fact that by "questioning" the wisdom of importing EurAmerican queer theory into Australasia, Altman (a well-known member of the gay left) represents himself as in some sense "against" the transfer of the latest (supposedly newer "left") ideology. Altman's position on this question seems to stand in relief against that growing group of Australasian academics who are eagerly acquiring the new complex and sophisticated (post)modern theoretical discourses: the work of such writers as Elizabeth Grosz and Annamarie Jagose are increasingly well-known instances of queer writing emanating from Australia.[3] Altman seems to "oppose" (post)modernism and (post)modern (queer) theory. However, if we want to understand a person, we do not—as Marx says—base our understanding "on what he thinks of himself" (Marx 21). We must therefore inquire into and critique Altman's "leftist resistance" in order to test its meaning and its limits.

Readers can find elsewhere the responses other writers from Australia, the Philippines, and the U.S., and I have already made to "On Global Queering"; but it is important to expand on these exchanges.[4] Basically Altman lists a series of "factors" he believes have to be taken into account to explain a specific form of "global change," the reproduction of versions of U.S.-style "gay/queer identities/communities" in countries of the "south" or "third world": the world-wide AIDS epi-

demic, its impact on the relations of the "straight" and "gay" communities, the relation of a growing global gay culture to the spread of capitalist markets, the gap between the "older" gay studies and "new"
queer theory, the question of (post)modernism and its associated knowledges, and especially the "wisdom" of Australian acceptance of "queer
theory" (an American export) for understanding sexual politics, . . .
However, while calling for an analysis of "global" connections, Altman's
text fails to offer a coherent and rigorous theorization of the relations
between these conditions. "On Global Queering" therefore displays a
fundamental contradiction: on the one hand, it issues an urgent call to
analyze "global" connections, while on the other, by providing a "multifactorial" frame which fails to show the determinate connections
between the factors, it actually blocks the possibility of reaching its own
announced goal.

It is interesting to note the divergent responses to this article from
Altman's critics, most of whom are "friendly" in a conventional sense.
On the one hand, some of these "friends" try to help Altman "update"
his discourses by redefining what looks—in spite of his various references to (post)structuralist writers such as Judith Butler—like a form of
naive positivist "multifactorialism" as actually a kind of (post)struc-
turalist "indeterminacy." Christopher Lane, for instance, emphasizes
Altman's "multifactorialism" as a "queer" version of Bhabha-esque
"hybridization."[5] In other words Lane wants to push Altman in the
direction of (post)modern complexity and theoretical sophistication. On
the other hand, Chris Berry notes the absence of rigorous critique or
complex philosophical understanding in Altman's text (which "takes
cheap potshots at various targets") and Gary Dowsett recognizes the
association of Altman's writing not with philosophical and theoretical
awareness but with journalism.[6] Nevertheless, both Berry and Dowsett
express admiration for Altman's "insight" (that is, "intuition") into a
difficult issue. In my response I called attention to the way in which Altman's "innocent" antitheoreticism actually converges—in political outcome—with the "knowing" antitheoreticism of persons like Eve Sedgwick and David Halperin, who have absorbed their antitheoreticism
from (post)structuralism and Foucault, and whom Altman mistakenly
thinks he is "opposing." The reason Altman doesn't care if his theoretical "credentials" are in order with friends, opponents, or anyone else is
basically because what matters to him is a certain notion of "action,"
and he therefore champions "activists" against "theorists," as if

activists' actions were not informed by "theory" and as if "theory" itself is not a form of action. However, what Altman, like many others on the queer left, is actually championing is not "activism" (carefully thought-through practice guided by the test of theory) but an entrepreneurial "actionalism" (a gut reaction to events).[7]

In the end, it doesn't matter that much whether you read Altman as a journalist merely reporting the "facts," or a pre(post)modern social scientist offering a positivist "multifactorial" analysis, or an incipient (post)structuralist or Foucauldian: on the political and ideological plane, all these readings end up endorsing the idea that all "global" phenomena are so complex that no determinate or coherent explanation of them can be offered. Some respondents praise Altman's recognition of the complexity of the phenomena he discusses but urge him to yet greater levels of (post)modern "subtlety."[8] As in (post)modern theory generally, what is at stake behind the call for endlessly increasing "subtlety" and recognition of "complexity" is the desire to evade any form of determinate explanation of the global, for such determinate explanations are consistently rejected by bourgeois theorists today as "reductive," on the one hand, and "totalizing," on the other. Of course the main target of this rejection is classical Marxism (not post- or neo- but classical Marxism) with its inclusivist interest in the "social totality" (expressed in Marx's notion that until everyone is free, no one is free) and its "reductive" explanations of social phenomena in terms of economics (it posits, as is well known, a *determinate* relation of the superstructure to the base). As Mas'ud Zavarzadeh has recently shown, post-al theories, which supposedly reject reductionism and totalizing, are themselves reductive and totalizing theories. The Derridean declaration that "there is no outside the text" is a totalization (an inclusive generalization) and a reduction (everything is rendered as a mode of textuality). Thus our "choice" of theoretical perspective is never a choice between the totalizing/reductive theories and the nontotalizing/nonreductive theories, but a choice between modes of totalizing/reducing.

The point here is to re-stage the theoretical contestation over what is at stake in discussions of "globalism" and "sexual politics" among gay/queer theorists and critics in the 1990s. I am arguing that the relation of global sites is systematic, structural, and determinate and not a question either of positivist "multifactorialism" or (post)structuralist "hybridity," both of which cancel the possibility of determinate explanation of global relations. To reinforce this point, I call attention to the

sudden shift of tone in Altman's second text, "Dennis Altman Replies."[9]
Despite its eclectic diffuseness, "On Global Queering" had at least pro-
ceeded with "confidence." However, in the second round, when Altman
responds to his respondents (including Halperin), that "confidence" dis-
appears and Altman becomes strikingly "apologetic" and "defensive."
The defensiveness is shown in the foregrounding of the question of
(respect/disrespect for) personalities and in the effort to correct misreadings of his essay (as if "misreadings" are to be "corrected" rather
than "critiqued"). The shift from ideas to personalities is telling in the
light of Altman's explicit claim that "it is possible to have sharp dis-
agreements on these issues without personalising them." Thus the relative friendliness/conciliatoriness of his reply to (most of) his critics suggests that it is not personalizing per se that troubles Altman, only
personalizing that is perceived—by some—as "negative." Hence he off-
sets the impression of the initial essay's "negative personalizing" with
the reply's "positive personalizing" (with expressions of "friendliness"
and "respect"). Most important, Altman offers a long string of apolo-
gies—for seeming to suggest that his "resistance" to the uncritical
importation of queer theory from the U.S. to Australia can be read
inhospitably as resistance to the recent importation of queer theorist
David Halperin from MIT to the University of New South Wales (he
recalls that he had "rung David . . . to congratulate him when the
appointment was made"); for failing to correctly read the title of
Halperin's book (*Saint Foucault*) as "ironic" (as Halperin himself said
he does); for giving the impression that he has "attacked" Eve Sedgwick.

In other words, in Altman's reply the façade of supposed opposition to queer theory and queer theorists (Halperin, Sedgwick, . . .) completely collapses so as to reestablish what is basically a comfortable
bourgeois class solidarity. He abruptly shifts from the level of pretend-
ing to be engaged in a serious struggle over ideas to the level of
"friendly" and "personal" reassurance. One must note that Altman does
not apologize to/conciliate with all his critics. To my own critique challenging Altman's notion of the "global" as class interested, Altman
responded *completely unapologetically*: "I plead (cheerfully) guilty to
Donald Morton's delightful allegation that by refusing to enter into a
dispute about the governance of the English Department at SUNY,
Albany, I have apparently failed to support 'the worldwide solidarity of
the working class.'" Here, Altman—supposedly a staunch "left" advocate of the "global"—does not simply distance himself from the oppres-

sion of workers in a U.S. English department. No, he "cheerfully" and frankly dissociates himself from the fate of the great "unwashed" masses of working class gay/lesbian humanity worldwide, a group that doubtless comprises the largest fraction of the world's sexual margins and suddenly and, with a violence masked by "humor," decisively realigns himself with the lesbigay academy's bourgeois entrepreneurs. What is, of course, most telling in Altman's rejection of solidarity with the masses is that he could easily have expressed—as even many bourgeois queer writers routinely do—at least a "sexual solidarity" with them, while sidestepping the issue of "class." This move would have been quite readily and easily made by most EurAmerican queer academics. Altman's inability to do this should be read not in "personal" terms but in terms of the material differences between the different situatedness of subjects in global capitalism. Those bourgeois intellectual workers most distant from the EurAmerican metropole may indeed be less fully or quickly interpellated into the latest forms of EurAmerican bourgeois ideology: hence Altman's first *AHR* text appears not just "theoretically innocent" but also "critical" or at least "skeptical"—it offers no effective critique—of (post)modernism and queer theory, and he thus initially seems to assert his "difference" from such writers as Sedgwick and Halperin. In other words, those in "other" countries may proudly and defiantly announce their "difference" from those in EurAmerican metropoles. That is, they may announce the "autonomy of their desires" (is this supposed to be "different"?). Nevertheless, bourgeois intellectual workers in Australia and similar sites, with a greater material proximity to the "great unwashed masses" of the so-called underdeveloped/developing world, betray a sharper and more immediate anxiety to separate themselves from the fate of those masses. So as Altman's second text shows, when the global class difference has been seriously introduced into the discussion (in a way that determinately links global workplaces—connects what happens to Altman at LaTrobe, for instance, to what happens to others in the SUNY-Albany English Department), other "differences" (in Altman's case, between the older gay studies with which he "identifies" and the new queer theory, between Australia and the U.S., between himself and Halperin, Sedgwick, . . .) are jettisoned immediately and unapologetically. He says, "cheerfully." "Cheerfully" of course signifies the tremendous relief the bourgeois academic feels at (a) not himself sharing the fate of the masses and (b) acknowledging no responsibility whatsoever to provide a rigorous and systematic theory of the global that connects issues of (his) "desire" to issues of (their) "need." The "humorous" tone serves to "cover over" the sudden and violent remarginalization of the already marginalized great unwashed. The "humor," of course, is meant to have other effects as well: in spite of his denial of personalizing, Altman is basically discrediting me by turning me into a "figure of fun," by locating my theory of the "global" as evidently so "unreasonable" and "extreme" that he need not argue against it, but can merely make it the butt of humor and count on his readers to nod in ready agreement. Here Altman is by no means alone: there is a growing chorus of rejection of materialist queer theory on the grounds that it is, in one way or another, somehow "extreme" (too "x"): too "exaggerated,"[10] too "sweeping" (du Plessis 45 n. 20), too "monolithic" and "homogenizing" (Angelides 87 n. 48), too devoted to "broad conceptual categories" (Champagne, "A Feminist" 23), too "masculinist" (Champagne "Ethics" 178 n. 43), too full of "jargon,"[11] too much of a "desecration of literature" (McConnell 37), too "idealistic"(in fact "impossibly" so, [Haggerty 12]), too. . . .

Since the "too x" response to materialist queer theory has now become routine, it should be read back to those who deploy it, starting with the observation that it is not typically the response of those writers (such as Sedgwick, de Lauretis, Warner, Butler, Sinfield, Halperin, . . .) whom I have directly critiqued. Those writers can neither afford to engage the question of need nor deny its importance: hence they remain largely silent. The "too x" response comes mostly from those who, at one level, understand themselves as only tangentially involved "onlookers" viewing a struggle conducted between "others." They act rhetorically as "referees" in a fight where one side, they quickly conclude, is using "extreme" and unacceptable weapons—even the weapons of "terror." At another level, however, the "onlookers" know very well that they themselves are deeply implicated in the critiques being made of class positions; but rather than answering the critique with counter-critique (which may require extensive thoughtfulness about unfamiliar territory), they choose the simpler way of dismissing the critique by describing the critique-er as "too x."

In this connection, Altman's "reasonable" (non-"extreme") exchange with respondent David Halperin is of particular interest because it represents the negotiation between U.S. and Australian bourgeois ideologues (even if the U.S. writer, Halperin, has just moved "permanently" to New South Wales), who seem at first to have a lot of "differences," but whose "differences" quickly get "patched up," get rejoined, I argue, in ruling class ideology. Of course, their texts do not offer an explicit defense of ruling class ideas (these are representatives of a supposedly resistant "queer left"), but an implicit defense of ruling class theoretico-social premises. To clarify, it is necessary to dwell on some of the details of this "patch up." In engaging Halperin's response, Altman complains that Halperin writes as if "I had spent a great deal of the article attacking him,"[12] but then Altman repeats the same move and goes on to spend more than half of his second text on Halperin. In other words, Altman and Halperin collaborate by turning the *AHR* "exchanges" into a "family quarrel" between the gay/queer "insiders," one representing old-style modernist gay studies derived from Stonewall "movement" activism, the other representing sophisticated and complex (post)modern theory. It is, moreover, not simply an exchange between any "insiders," but specifically an exchange between gay/queer studies "icons," which makes their fencing over the "saintliness" of Foucault especially telling. Since they and everyone else are so deeply aware of their particular roles as "celebrities" of the dominant academic and intellectual establishment (Berry), Altman and Halperin must at least formally agree to "problematize" (ironize) "iconity" itself. Such agreement helps to distract attention away from the ideological function of the role they are enacting in the rapid "institutionalization" of gay/queer studies, a role overtly if "playfully" foregrounded by Halperin's canonization of Foucault. This distraction helps to mystify the fact that although they formally play the role of "outsiders," they have actually become "elder statesmen" in the rapidly changing bourgeois academy.

Again, at the theoretical level, what is of special interest is the concept through which they manage to "seal" their newfound agreement and "patch things up"—this is their shared notion of "irony." Altman—the "resister" who doesn't take (post)modern theory seriously—had complained in "On Global Queering" that the title of Halperin's recent book *(Saint Foucault)* was not "ironic" but straightforwardly worshipful[13]; yet as soon as Halperin reassures Altman that the title is indeed "ironic," everything is "settled." How can a single concept do so much? It can do so much because "irony" in the (post)modern world has become such an inclusive concept. For modernists like Altman, "irony" means saying one thing while meaning the opposite; thus, only specifically designated meanings are ("truly") "ironic." For (post)modernists like Halperin, all meanings are "ironic" in the (post)structuralist sense that meaning is "differential," and the relation between all words and concepts is not a relation of inclusion/exclusion but a relation of "supplementarity." At the political level, "irony" is an ideological code word; it is the trope signaling Altman's and Halperin's joint suspiciousness (even if the "suspiciousness" of each has a somewhat different philosophical basis) of all truth claims and their joint embrace of "skepticism." The U.S. pragmatist philosopher, Richard Rorty, has theorized the space in which Altman and Halperin find (consciously or not) their common ground. I have to emphasize the important role Rorty plays in contemporary politico-theoretical debates. Eugene Goodheart has recently called Rorty's work "the most significant expression of postmodern liberalism" (Goodheart 44) and John McGowan explains that Rorty's project has been to "appropriate the term postmodernism to describe . . . the true way of pragmatism" (McGowan 181). Rorty has retheorized irony—that is, updated it in (post)modern terms—in such a way as to renew the concept's ideological usefulness to the ruling class. In *Contingency, Irony, and Solidarity*, Rorty divides the world between two kinds of people, "ironists" and "metaphysicians." Ironists realize that "anything can be made to look good or bad by being redescribed" and so they renounce "the attempt to *formulate criteria* of choice between final vocabularies" (Rorty 101). Like the subjectivities envisioned in "queer theory,"[14] they are "meta-stable" people who are "never quite able to take themselves seriously because always aware that the terms in which they describe themselves are subject to change, always aware of the contingency and fragility of their final vocabularies, and thus of their selves" (Rorty 101). Ironists, in other words, are never committed to any "final vocabulary" (mode of explanation of the social) but are constantly shifting to a new one. Metaphysicians, by contrast, "assume that the presence of a term in [their] own final vocabulary ensures that it refers to something which has a real essence" (Rorty 102). Furthermore, "they do not believe that anything can be made to look good or bad by being redescribed—or, if they do, they deplore this fact and cling to the idea that reality will help us resist such seductions" (103).

Of course, by dividing the world up in this way and claiming that the decisive difference is that between "ironists" ("skeptics/doubters/redescribers") and "metaphysicians" ("believers") concerning objective reality, Rorty displaces the significance of a lot of other distinctions, say, the idealist/materialist distinction. Moreover, by championing the practice of "redescription" himself, Rorty cancels the objective difference between the world's poor and the world's rich (that difference, like all others, is just a matter of "redescription") and thus cancels also the historicity of the class struggle. Anyone, such as a Marxist, for example, who opposes such "redescriptions" as leading to an evasive "relativism," is cast as just a blighted "metaphysician" (Rorty 102). What this of course means is that anyone who does not accept Rorty's "pragmatic ironism" (going with the flow) is a "metaphysician." To accept the ironist's pragmatism, however, is to deny the possibility of radically transformative change; it is to install things-as-they-are rather than things-as-they-might-be as the measure of all one's practices.

For some it was once unthinkable to associate (post)modern theory and its antifoundationalist critiques with pragmatism at all; but as (post)modern knowledges (like the dominant queer theory) are becoming more and more institutionalized in the bourgeois academy and the culture industry, their "practical" usefulness is being increasingly recognized and celebrated. Thus while the University of New South Wales may have "officially" hired David Halperin as a "lecturer in queer theory" to bring its (sexual) knowledges "up-to-date," what this basically means is that the university is helping to institutionalize (post)modern theory so as to train Australian students (future workers) into the most advanced form of bourgeois ideology.[15] Indeed Richard Rorty's "pragmaticization" of (post)modern theory has been instrumental in its institutionalization as providing the most "useful" state of consciousness for today's global citizens. This is why Eugene Goodheart associates Rorty's "philosophical" work as crucial for "politics": for retheorizing liberalism in (post)modern terms (Goodheart 44). As evidence that Rortyan (post)modern pragmatism has moved into the mainstream, I cite *The Truth About the Truth: De-confusing and Re-constructing the Postmodern World*, published by Putnam in its "New Consciousness Reader" series. The editor, Walter Truett Anderson, argues that (post)modernism offers "practical tools for coming to terms with vast amounts of unsettling information, daily interactions with unfamiliar cultures and beliefs, and a continuous and overwhelming set of choices" (Anderson, back cover matter). In other words, it is time to recognize that (post)structuralist language games/Rortyan redescriptions are not just games for high culture elites alone but are knowledges capitalism needs to have transferred to the mainstream (ordinary workers) and that deconstruction can be rendered "affirmative" by understanding it as a

"reconstructive" mode of knowing useful to the prevailing mode of production. In terms of the argument I am developing here, Anderson's
book, which reprints a passage of Rorty's book on "ironists" and
"metaphysicians" (Anderson 100–106), is itself an ideological tool
through which the ruling class helps U.S. citizens, as well as citizens of
other countries, to achieve the "new consciousness" needed for today's
cybercapitalism. In other words, it helps them "accept" (post)modern
theories as somehow "practical" aids to living at the end of the twentieth century. As the sudden collapse of Altman's "opposition" to
(post)modernists and his own increasing use of (post)modern terminology shows, Altman can also be "brought around." Indeed, he was
already evidently long ago on the path to "bringing himself around": in
the afterword to the recent reprint of his *Homosexual Oppression and
Liberation*, Altman declares that "without fully understanding what [he]
was writing," he had been in the 1970s a "social constructionist without knowing the term" (Altman, Homosexual 253).

   From the Marxist perspective, however, pragmatism must be
implacably resisted and "the practical" historicized. As the onset of the
AIDS epidemic (which renders unsafe sex utterly "impractical") shows,
what is "practical" is never a transhistorical behavior but is instead
materially and historically conditioned. As for the question of "global
queering," it must be argued that no matter what materially privileged
EurAmerican sexual liberationists and queer theorists say, it is not self-
evident that "queer theory" and "sexual liberation" are indeed "practical" (in the Marxist sense of "praxical") in all societies under all material conditions. Not all the world's homosexual subjects can "afford" to
understand sexuality as "autonomous." When the Brazilian writer João
Trevisan made efforts to bring together gay university students in 1976
to discuss homosexuality, the question persistently arose: "Is it politically valid for us to meet to discuss sexuality, something generally considered secondary given the serious situation in Brazil?" "All movements," Trevisan goes on to say, "ran up against this question, without
reaching a clear answer" (Trevisan 247). Similar issues arise when
"Third World" subjects discuss the "everyday" reality of social practices
both in their home cultures and the various diasporas. For instance, in
the new anthology, *Asian-American Sexualities: Dimensions of Gay and
Lesbian Experience*, writers mention having to defend themselves
against the charge that the Asian-American gay community is "more
homophobic" (Leong 96) because of the lingering residue of the "per-

ceived conservatism" of their home cultures (77). Rather than confessing guilty to the charge and simply following in lockstep Western models of "queering the planet"/"making things perfectly queer,"[16] some of these writers are beginning to problematize "the silences surrounding homosexuality in Asian America" (Leong 27) by bringing sexuality into relation with race, ethnicity, and class, and by beginning to critique today's dominant (queer theory) notions of sexuality as a "colonial imposition" (114) and of "coming out" (breaking the silence) as a "very white model" (99). They thus refuse merely to take on passively dominant Western theoretical categories that mystify their historical conditions: as one of the writers remarks emphatically, rejecting (post)structuralism's mystifications, "We are not the other. We are who we are—complex human beings!"(89). Their resistance thereby challenges the simple assumption of the ready "exportability" of Western notions of sexuality to (post)colonial/Third World cultures/diasporas and begins to foreground queer theory's (First World) class politics based on privileging the category "desire" and marginalizing the category "need." The implication here is not that questions of sexuality have no significance or legitimacy or priority at all in Third World cultures and their various diasporas, but rather that material conditions affect social priorities in those cultures (as in all others). Such a notion is of course heretical in the dominant gay/queer establishment which declares desire "autonomous" for people the world over.

The Ideology of "Post-ality"

To repeat: from the perspective of the U.S. queer avant-garde, Altman's discourses on sexual politics appear rather underdeveloped. This is because they are fairly innocent of, even if they occasionally mention, the complexities of (post)modern theory, that is, innocent of the most advanced form of bourgeois ideology available today. Yet, for reasons that deserve still further comment, his discourses are not simply left on the margin, but are welcomed even into the "advanced" ideological sectors of global capitalism. The recent publication of Altman's two *AHR* texts was quickly followed by the publication of a related essay, "Rupture or Continuity? The Internationalization of Gay Identities" in *Social Text*, an academic left U.S. journal devoted to cultural materialism. *Social Text* prides itself on the intellectual sophistication of the essays it publishes. Furthermore, in the wake of the Sokal affair in the fall of 1996, that journal has itself become the subject of much discussion not only in academic journals like *The Chronicle of Higher Education* and *Lingua franca*, but also in the London *Times*, the *New York Times*, the *Los Angeles Times*, the *Nation* magazine, . . . and its editors have been represented as leading defenders of (post)modern knowledges.[17]

Again in *Social Text*, Altman raises the same urgent issues he raised before: the meaning of "global queering/gaying," the cultural imperialism behind interpreting emerging gay identities in countries outside EurAmerica according to the U.S. gay/queer model, the relation of changing sexual practices to the expansion of capitalism and the ongoing worldwide process of modernization. The problem is not so much in the choice of topics (which are indeed urgent ones), but with Altman's entrapment of his reader in an incoherent and deeply contradictory mode of analysis and in one that consistently separates the cultural from the economic. So again, immanent critique can show this text's internal contradictions. For instance, his titular invocation of the difference between "rupture and continuity" (Altman, Rupture 77) and his expressed wish to avoid falling into a "linear genealogy" (79) hints at an awareness of Foucauldian analytics. Furthermore, the text is studded with numerous examples of "specificity" in the form of quotations and anecdotes from friends, acquaintances, or informants from far-flung global sites. But these knowledges are treated completely uncritically and on a more or less equal "footing": a quotation on orientalism from Edward Said is no more intellectually or politically productive than a quotation on love between men from Christopher Isherwood couched in a humanist frame. Thus while on the one hand, some comments seem to render Altman a champion of Foucauldian "specificity," on the other hand they depend either on personal experience or on the authority of anthropological sources and have really nothing at all to do with rigorous discursive analysis or genealogy-as-critique. Altman uses the word "critique" in the essay (84), but his text is entirely descriptive and does not offer any sustained deployment of the concept either in terms of deconstruction as a critique of the Western metaphysics or Foucauldian genealogy as critique of the power/knowledge relations of discourses and the institutions allied with them or as Marxist ideology critique. Altman tries to cover over the incoherence of his quasi-modernist, quasi-(post)modernist discussion by proposing on the first page that "modern and postmodern can be used here interchangeably, for both terms rep-

resent the rapid reshaping of extensive areas of life and economy in previously underdeveloped parts of the world to fit the needs of Western
capitalism" (77). In other words, we are supposed to believe that he
takes economic materialist analysis (Marxism) seriously. But being an
"ironist" (in the way theorized by Rorty), he "ironizes" Marx and situates Marx not as a "believer" in revolution with a rigorous, reliable, and
determinate explanation of social injustice that could become a "material force" for transformative social change, but (in the usual bourgeois
fashion that blurs Marx with Nietzsche) as just another "master of suspicion," whose theories enable merely another form of "skepticism." It
is, again, skepticism towards all theories (he consistently "thematizes"
instead of "theorizing" issues) that marks Altman's writing: Christopher
Lane in fact applauds Altman precisely (not for critiquing queer theory
but) for bringing "a healthy skepticism to some of queer theory's
claims." Yet Altman is equally skeptical about "political economy."
There is of course a difference at the theoretical level between human-
ist/modernist "skepticism," in which "not knowing/being committed to
a particular truth" is a feature of the individual, and (post)modern
"skepticism," in which "not knowing" is the condition of all subjects in
a world where meaning has been rendered "undecidable." However, on
the political/ideological plane the result is the same—an unwillingness to
commit to and sustain a position based on arriving at a reliable knowledge of the social totality that can provide the ground for transformative social practices. Altman seems to feel, like all liberals, that the opposite of "relativism" is "dogmatism" and does not want to be viewed as
"dogmatic." To be so marked might not end his academic employment
but it would abruptly end his role as a celebrated "icon"/"elder states-
man" of gay/queer studies in the bourgeois academic establishment and
suddenly relocate him as an "extremist" and an unredeemable "outsider."

If Altman's text—riven by the obvious contradictions just mentioned—is welcome in a "sophisticated" metropolitan leftist journal
like *Social Text*, the "attraction" is not epistemological (not due to its
theoretical complexity) but ideological. It is because *Social Text,* as
Jennifer Cotter has recently demonstrated, is basically a post-Marxist
journal which also "ironizes" Marx by abandoning economic determinism and economic revolution as a goal: Cotter cites Stanley
Aronowitz, a leading theorist of the *Social Text* collective, who rejects
"economic change [as] . . . a guiding principle for . . . social emanci-

pation" (Cotter 314). We can see the kinship of Altman and Aronowitz in the arguments the latter puts forward, for example, in *The Crisis in Historical Materialism* (first published at the beginning of the 1980s and again at the beginning of the 1990s). In the preface to the second edition, Aronowitz rejects the idea that his title should have referred to the "crisis of, not in historical materialism," which would have suggested the complete irrelevance of Marxism for today. In rejecting this suggestion, Aronowitz remarks that he believes "that Marxism has asked the right questions" (Aronowitz xii), but then goes on to say they were the right questions for an earlier time. In other words, like other bourgeois apologists, he claims that historical change itself has rendered Marx's understanding of history "incomplete." If Marxism is still helpful (Aronowitz says it is "incomplete but not surpassed" [xviii]) for social theory and analysis, today new questions have to be asked about other relations and the project of emancipation seen in quite different and "plural" terms. "The proletariat," Aronowitz declares, ". . . no longer occupies, if it ever did, a privileged space in the social formation" (xii) but must simply be set alongside other new "oppositional" (143) segments of society, including women, the "racial underclasses," and "lesbians and gays" (143–44). Hence, writing long before the advent of queer theory (1981), Aronowitz articulated the position queer theory tenaciously rearticulates a decade later by declaring that the subjects of class, gender, race, sexuality, . . . constitute "autonomous" oppositional groups. His work, like that of Ernesto Laclau and Chantal Mouffe before him, becomes an enabling condition specifically of the separation of "sexuality" from "gender" that marks the birth of queer theory. In *Epistemology of the Closet*, we must recall, Eve Sedgwick declares the separation of sexuality from gender to be "axiomatic" for investigating sexual alterity: endorsing the hypothesis of Gayle Rubin, Sedgwick says, "the question of gender and the question of sexualtiy . . . are . . . not the same question" (30). Following Aronowitz's view of the social as the space of various autonomous "oppositional" groups, *Social Text* coeditor, Andrew Ross—not himself a gay/queer theorist—has written: "A politics of sexuality that is relatively autonomous from categories of gender may be needed to achieve and guarantee the full sexual rights of sexual minorities" (227). As with Aronowitz and Ross, so with Altman: if Marxism and class analysis are still somehow "useful," its concerns and explanations have no particular priority.

As these examples show, many global sites are increasingly dominated today by an advanced form of (post)modern bourgeois ideology—
what Mas'ud Zavarzadeh has theorized as the ideology of "post-
ality"—that proceeds by carefully localizing all cultural and social
phenomena, that is, by separating the racial, ethnic, national, gender,
sexual "identity" of all subjects from their class position. This mode of
analyzing sexuality that "refers to" Marx but basically de-links sexuality from class and routinely blurs the differences between Foucault and
Marx is now the standard bourgeois mode for analyzing sexual politics:
it informs not only countless essays (a recent instance is the essay on
"Semiotics and/as Social Theory" by Ki Namaste[18]) but also such
extended studies as David Evans's *Sexual Citizenship: The Material
Construction of Sexualities* and Gary Kinsman's *The Regulation of
Desire: Sexuality in Canada.*[19] The "post-alizing" of Marxism has been
a complex process going through many relays, and I have only been able
to address a small part of it here. Along another line of analysis, of
course, one would have to trace the genealogy (from Raymond
Williams, Stuart Hall, Richard Hoggart, . . . through Alan Sinfield and
Jonathan Dollimore and on to Scott Wilson) of texts in which cultural
materialism (and the materiality of sexual difference) has been "safely"
detached from economic materialism (see Wilson). Such detachment is a
completely routine gesture on the gay/queer left: writing about the
recent work of Jonathan Katz, for instance, Jim Marks reports that
"although he points to economic explanations for changes in concepts
about sexuality, Katz is opposed to any kind of determinism" and
quotes Katz as remarking: "I think any kind of social or biological determinism that leaves out the role of active subjects is really mistaken"
(Marks 7). Thus while Katz, like Altman, points to "political economy,"
his recent book *The Invention of Heterosexuality* is a discussion of the
history of an idea unrelated in any serious way to Marx or changes in
the mode of production (Katz). Defenders of the class system like Altman, Katz, . . . do not reject Marxism because they believe it has no theory of agency: they know Marx's view that "Men make their own history, but . . . not . . . under circumstances chosen by themselves . . . but
directly encountered, given, and transmitted from the past" (Marx 15).
What they reject is Marx's theory of *revolutionary* agency. The dominant gay/queer theory/studies is devoted to a completely idealist notion
of "agency" (whether envisioned as the "activism" of the modernist
movement or the "agitations" of a [post]modern autonomous desire),

an emphatically idealist notion of agency which Altman expressed a long time ago and still follows today: "a change in individual consciousness is a basic requirement for any qualitative social change" (Altman, Homosexual 113).

At a general level, then, Altman's essay is welcome to *Social Text* because of its "ironism," "skepticism," and theoretical "eclecticism" but especially because its "eclecticism" is broad enough to allow at least the mention of political economy. Being so thoroughly devoted to the pursuit of pleasure, *jouissance*, erotic satisfaction, most gay/queer theory/studies writers don't feel the need to mention class issues at all. Since *Social Text* has consistently shown its own libidinalist orientation, it has tried to "balance" libidinalism with texts that somehow refer to historical materialism (see, for instance, the anti-Marxist-but-pro-socialist essay by International Mr. Leather for 1986, Scott Tucker, who follows the *Social Text* program by arguing that "cultural struggle matters as much as any other kind" (Tucker 6), and see also the "Marxist" essay by Andrew Parker eroticizing the relation of Marx and Engels). Hence, Altman's invocation of "political economy" helps to make up for the general "neglect" of the gay/queer connection with class. If Altman's text is much less "libidinal" than Tucker's, this ideological readjustment away from *jouissance* is again not a voluntary "choice" on the part of *Social Text's* editors, but a historical necessity: current conditions dictate this "balancing." In recent times, there has been a sharp rightward swing in government and politics in the Western-style liberal democracies. EurAmerican capitalists and their supporters (whether of the Newt Gingrich hard-core variety or of the Bill Clinton "new democrat" variety) continue their attack on spending for the citizenry's needs (and decrease or cancel state health services/insurances, social security and welfare and housing programs, services of children and the elderly, . . .) in order to increase the concentration of capital for the demands of today's global market competition. By the mid-1990s, it had become increasingly clear to everyone that while citizens have been "distracted" in recent decades by the illusion of limitless freedom to consume (fulfill their "desires"), the difference of class ("need") in the U.S. and elsewhere had grown ever sharper. Given the stark evidence of these conditions, it was just too "embarrassing" to wholly neglect questions of class; but of course the kind of class analysis that is "allowed" is the kind of post-Marxist class analysis endorsed by such writers as Aronowitz, Altman, . . . , which robs it of its priority, rigor, and determinateness. As the current crisis of need breaks through to public consciousness once more today, it doesn't much matter whether post-Marxism is presented in the highly sophisticated and theoretically complex form of Laclau and Mouffe's *Hegemony and Socialist Strategy* (whom Aronowitz and *Social Text* are following in shifting attention away from economic determination to a radical, pluralist idea of democracy) or in Dennis Altman's "On Global Queering" and "Rupture or Continuity?" (which are marked also by an utterly "open" pluralism and eclecticism). In both these texts Altman proposes that he and his readers face an "impossible" choice of interpretive knowledges (difference theory/anthropology, on the one hand, and political economy, on the other), each of which is in his view "inadequate." But what Altman presents basically as a set of epistemological dilemmas or paradoxes (we are in his view "ironically" caught between humanist self-assertion, social scientific data, and postmodern critiques of the other two; we are caught between welcoming the insights of queer theory and wanting to defend the insights of the older gay studies; we are caught, as Michael Tan puts it, between "celebrating" and "fearing" the process of "global queering"[20]) are actually ideological contradictions determined by class interests. Even if to some extent Altman acknowledges our class interestedness (we are all, he acknowledges, "subjects of capitalism"), he denies that we can "do anything about it." In other words, in Altman's work, as in bourgeois writing in general, this acknowledgment of class takes the form of a guilt-tinged confession to interestedness rather than the form of political auto-critique that might enable new—and materially transformative—practices.

Although Altman keeps using the phrase "political economy" and thus keeps invoking some kind of Marxism, he is basically referring to a kind of nostalgic post-al Marxism (the kind invoked by Derrida in his recent book as little more than a "specter" [Derrida]). It is the kind of post-al Marxism that abandons fundamental concepts that give Marxism its explanatory power. I have already indicated how the texts I have discussed here show that Altman has no use for Marxism as a form of rigorous and determinate explanation. Let me add another. Early in 1994, when I was assembling texts for *The Material Queer*, I asked Altman for permission to reprint an excerpt from one of his books. Although he gave the permission with "enthusiastic agreement,"[21] he remarked "I'm not sure how I feel about being a 'foretext,'" referring to my placement of his piece in a section on the pre-history of the "queer."

Altman's discourses in his reply to me conflate his "self" with his "text" and by doing so leave little room for an auto-critique-al perspective that acknowledges the historicity of his own writings (that the effectivity of any text is not timeless but tied to its history). Such an acknowledgment of the historicity of all one's practices is fundamental to a serious view of "political economy."

The Fall of the Berlin Wall
and the Rise of Queer Theory

I want to elaborate more fully exactly what is at stake in Altman's theoretico-political moves and to show how those moves are part of a global pattern of knowledges by turning briefly to the current (queer left) fascination with Eastern European countries, which were until recently parts of the Marxist alternative visions of the social but which, in the wake of the fall of the Berlin Wall and the collapse of those socialist states, are now seen as parts of capitalism's newest potential market. The former socialist countries are now suddenly being transformed: what were once viewed as hostile forces standing in the way of, and in fact containing, capitalist expansionism are now seen as new markets with vast opportunities for capitalism's entrepreneurs. Anyone committed to a global understanding of the social, especially in relation to marginal sexualities, will have to ask a number of questions such as these: Why is it that the appearance of queer theory coincided historically with the fall of the Berlin Wall?[22] In other words, why did the appearance of bourgeois ideology's strongest declaration of the "autonomy of desire" (queer theory), with its emphatic endorsement of the shift from a conceptual economy to a libidinal economy model of culture, coincide with the collapse of the Soviet Union and the socialist countries of Eastern Europe? Isn't it because this collapse gives new legitimacy to the ever-expanding search for (commodified) pleasures? Doesn't queer theory actually celebrate the supposed liberation of the subject into the space of "unfettered consumption," "unregulated desire"? In other words, isn't queer theory, which at one level seems to be a socially harmless extension of "sexual liberation," actually an allegory of the "freedom of desire," which is little more than the celebration of the "triumph" of capitalist ideology?

As my tutor text for these questions, I take Stan Persky's recent book inquiring into the changes in Eastern Europe from a "gay" perspective, *Then We Take Berlin,* which has evidently been well received and has gone through more than one edition and been published under more than one title.[23] Persky is a U.S.-born writer who has lived in Canada for many years, writing poetry, teaching philosophy, reviewing and commenting for various Canadian newspapers including the Toronto *Globe and Mail* and the well-known, but now defunct, gay "socialist" newspaper, *Body Politic.* Persky has written extensively on local and international issues, from the provincial politics of British Columbia to the U.S. involvement in Central America and the Polish Solidarity movement. Persky sets out to inquire into the historic change emblematized by the fall of the Berlin Wall and to study the "end of Communism" (Persky 183, 394, 408). For many readers, however, Persky's new book has been something of a puzzle. Persky himself tells us that interviewers who had read an earlier printing thought it disjointed and asked him what his sexual adventures had to do with the politics of Eastern Europe. One reviewer, the gay historian Martin Duberman, for instance, praises the book's libidinal descriptions as "delicious," but then complains about its "unfocused purpose" and that it turns into "a mere stream of diffuse, laconic, sometimes pretentiously aimless vignettes, stitched together rather than linked together by any organizing vision or sustained political analysis" (12–13). Duberman indicates that Persky is "deft and economical" in "describing an erotic encounter" but not good at all at providing an understanding of "the political complexities of Eastern Europe." These puzzles are solved if one reunderstands the book as basically a symptom of the changes in contemporary knowledges—from conceptual "knowing" to libidinal "(un)knowing"—and the contradictions those changes represent.

Before he gets very far into his book, both Persky and his readers are left wondering "what happened" to his project of investigating political change (Persky 183), for it turns out that his study of the relation of interconnections of "*eros, logos,* and *polis*" (16) loses (if it ever had one) its analytic grasp on its topic (that is, its claim to conceptual rigor) and, though still haunted by questions of politics ("need"), becomes pretty exclusively a work of "eros" (desire). This loss of analytical grasp (especially notable in a writer who is also a professor of philosophy) is accompanied by Persky's own hesitant but gradual absorption—at a basic level—of (post)modern theory.

Again like Altman, Persky situates himself initially on both the political and sexual margins, calling himself a "leftist" (83) with "scant loyalty to the capitalist panacea of the marketplace" (89). From this "dual" vantage point, he initially sets himself the goal of putting the fall of the Berlin Wall on a serious historical footing to save it from being what he says it mostly was for North Americans, a media event with images "of celebrating youths atop the Berlin Wall or crowds in Prague looking into an unknown future" (408). He thus writes to preserve historical memory of the fact that the "Iron Curtain" was once a "compelling" "division," "a fact of life for me and everybody I knew" (2), a decided "binary political configuration" (25). History for gay leftist Persky, however, is not (as it is for Marx) the history of changes in the mode of production that have to be grasped conceptually, but instead an experiential global drama into which one can somehow imaginatively "insert" oneself by visiting the physical sites of historic events. So the book records Persky's travels to such cities as Berlin, Tirana, Warsaw, Vilnius, to interview participants in the historic changes. But side-by-side with this public and global history, he interweaves his personal history: his birth in Chicago into a working-class Jewish family with roots in Russia and Lithuania; his learning to read at an early age through lessons from his father, a "communist" sympathizer; his immersion in the sea stories of London, Verne, Dana, Melville; his awakening adolescent (homo)sexuality; his enlistment in the U. S. Navy; . . . All of these events are understood to be stages in a growing connectedness with the larger world, in the growing awareness "that there was a flow of events *out there* that affected our lives *here*" (3), in other words, a growing "awareness" of history. Persky's account of both his personal history and public history is associative, personalist, and experiential: he recounts early memories of homoerotic adolescent fantasies alongside memories of the Kefauver hearings into organized crime and the McCarthy hearings into the infiltration of communists and homosexuals into goverment. Persky thus understands history (and not just in his childhood or adolescent years but in adulthood and while writing the book itself) as just a sequence of events that "happen to" people, in other words, in traditional historicist fashion. In innocently absorbing this version of history, he fails to recognize that even history has a history, and while "aware" of the historic changes symbolized by the fall of the Berlin Wall is unaware of the historic changes in contemporary knowledges and thus cannot historicize his own understanding of history. Like Altman, Persky does not theorize his project in advance by critiquing contemporary knowledges. Hence he can neither consciously adopt, in a philosophically precise and intellectually effective manner, (post)modern knowledges for his project nor challenge those knowledges in the name of something else. Instead of rigorously taking those knowledges on (in either sense), Persky is—again like Altman—overtaken by them and is set in motion by their ideological force.

As a part of his personal ideological "drift," Persky has basically "drifted" into a way of writing that turns his book into a performance (in the queer sense) of the autonomy of desire and an "innocent" instance of the new genre of "intimate critique," which intersperses descriptions of his various encounters with Eastern European "rent boys" with discussions of the changes taking place after the fall of the Wall. In other words, Persky's book is yet another instance of the increasing popularization of (post)modern theory as a "practical" understanding for living. Thus he follows (without acknowledgement) Roland Barthes in writing for the "pleasure of the text," Jane Gallop in "thinking through the body," and Elizabeth Grosz and Elspeth Probyn in exploring "strange carnalities."[24] In Persky's popular version, the complexities of (post)modern desire-theory are rendered in such aphorisms as "Desire is the body's first epistemology" (Persky 173, 188) and "desire is my most reliable epistemology" (188). Thus everything, not just the sexual encounters, becomes a matter of "desire." Those he interviews in Eastern European countries who lived under the socialist regimes describe those regimes basically in terms of "repression," which suggests that the only alternative to an unacceptable socialist "repression" is what passes as capitalist "freedom." Evidently unaware of the pervasiveness of (post)modern libidinalism, Persky and many of his readers seem to think it a novelty to mix discussions of politics with descriptions of sexual encounters. In an "Afterword" written for a new edition of the book, Persky expresses surprise that interviewers treated his discussions of political issues so cursorily but were fascinated—he says "disproportionately" (398)—by the description of his sexual adventures. Having written seductively about seduction, Persky expresses "surprise" that his readers are seduced! And when those interviewers moved out of the erotic frame of mind and asked him what his sexuality had to do with the political events he was ostensibly writing about, Persky says he "'dutifully explained exactly' . . . just what [his] sex life had to do with history, while thinking to himself all along that the real answer to that question was, 'Gee, probably very little.'" (399). Thus, while Persky purports to be giving a "gay male account" of the political events he is discussing, no one is buying this idea (not even Persky himself): the book is simply an account of political events that is only incidentally written by a gay male. In other words, Persky is unable to offer a rigorous theoretical account in any terms—(post)modern or other—of the operations of "desire" in the texts of culture, including his book (although he too occasionally uses some current terminology). He has basically "drifted" into writing "intimate critique." Hence, in some "sober" moments he writes in a modernist vein as if "experience" precedes "knowledge" unproblematicallly, while much of the time, he writes as if the entire book were a "dream" or—in (post)modern terms—neither "fictional" (desire) nor "factual" (history) but "fictual" (something in between). Having stumbled into the (post)modern fictualist manner of writing about politics, Persky also situates Marxism, with which he avows some sympathy, as a failed utopianism, a nostalgia for a lost and impossible future. What he puts in place of Marxism's conceptual grasp of the social totality is the libidinal: whereas communism was a just "dream that didn't come true," his various sexual encounters (of a middle-aged man with teenaged boys) are "dreams that do come true." We are left with the very "queer" conclusion that unlike Marxism, eros can fulfill your dreams. On the one hand, the book is an elaborate nostalgic description of the "failed utopia" of Eastern European communism, and on the other, a paean to a homosexual utopia (from this viewpoint, the central chapter is the one that turns Berlin into Boyopolis). When challenged during the writing of the book by a straight leftist about the economic conditions enabling the "fulfillment of his erotic dreams" (that he pays the Eastern European sex workers hard cash for the pleasure they provide him), Persky first evades the economic issue by diverting attention to subsidiary issues (the relative differences between heterosexual and homosexual prostitution, the fact that he was not engaged in pedophilia, . . . [204ff]) before finally confessing that he is indeed exploiting the young men (212). Like Altman's then, Persky's awareness of "political economy" finally leads to nothing more than a confession of guilt. And, in the end, the "we" of Persky's title (*And Then We Take Berlin*)—a nostalgic citation of the 60s utopianism of Leonard Cohen—turns out to designate nothing more than capitalist commercial—and queer sexual—entrepreneurs.

It is important to note that in his postcommunist Eastern European travels, Persky not only encounters in person Richard Rorty, who has been imported to Hungary as the main speaker for the inaugural meeting of the Budapest Kollegium (his topic is "Universality and Pragmatism" [275]), but also praises Rorty's book *Contingency, Irony, and Solidarity*. Because he is having so much trouble providing a coherent theoretical account that connects his personal practices with his "left" politics, Persky is therefore very relieved to encounter an eminent philosopher who assures him that while there may be "justificatory arguments for one course of action over another" (276), none of these arguments has any priority over the others.

Persky speaks repeatedly of the "epistemology of desire" and thus, like Altman, seems to posit both modernist theory (which grounds itself on concepts and reason) and (post)modernist theory (which sees desire as ungrounding everything) as two epistemological alternatives, two different and competing ways of "knowing" the world. Yet such a representation produces a significant distortion. Especially in its (post)structuralist and queer forms, ludic (post)modern theory is actually hostile to theory, to conceptuality, and to the very possibility of reliable knowledges. (Such is the very implication of the Lyotardian shift from a conceptual economy model to a libidinal economy model.) This "antitheory" dimension of ludic (post)modernity takes several distinct forms: one is the disruption of the signified (conceptuality) by the signifier (textuality) (which is basically the form it has in the texts of Derrida and Butler, where—as Derrida says—we are not talking about the sensuous per se but only about "something like the sensuous" [Derrida, *Margins* 250]) and another is the disruption and displacement of conceptuality by erotics (thought by sensation) (as exemplified in such "queer"—especially lesbian—writings say in Diane Chisholm's text, "The 'Cunning Lingua' of Desire" or the recent book *Her Tongue on My Theory*).[25] Whatever the differences, what is fundamentally at stake in both modes of disrupting conceptuality is the erasure of the possiblility of a sustained "knowing," a reliable "knowledge" on which a political agenda could be based. Indeed the theory of the performative that Butler elaborates is precisely a theory meant to "pre-vene" and "pre-vent" the possibility that one's behavior is grounded on a "reliable knowledge" of any kind. It is in fact this very commitment to an "unknowing" rather than "knowing" that lies behind Halperin's argument (in *Saint Foucault*, the book Altman pretends to critique) that the most important elements that Foucault offers marginal groups is not a reliable knowledge of anything but bundles of "strategies," various theoretico-political "moves," the conceptual content of which is—as Halperin vigorously argues—ultimately beside the point. Along a different global axis, Persky's queerly accented text too shows the subject of desire "on the move" away from a conceptual grasp of the world's historicity and towards the search for pleasure.

SEXUAL IDENTITY *AND* CLASS IDENTITY

While the most overt and obvious efforts to undermine historical materialism come obviously from the right, I am mainly concerned in this text with the undermining of historical materialism by the (queer) left. As Mary-Alice Waters has argued writing about Marxist feminism, the decisive difference among leftists is that between "revolutionary and reformist currents . . . between those committed to a class struggle perspective and those following a line of class collaboration."[26] The "cultural left," of which the dominant gay/queer theory/studies is an advanced element, can lead only to a reform of the existing structures of inequality, not to the overthrow of the structures themselves. As a leading gay/queer studies writer, Dennis Altman has maintained a position from the 70s to the 90s as a significant figure in *left reformism*. In the 1970s he followed the Freudo-Marxist version of reformism theorized by Herbert Marcuse, who believed that capitalism did not have to be overthrown in the advanced democracies because it had reached a stage where liberation could be achieved by getting rid of "surplus repression." In the 1990s Altman was following—if somewhat reluctantly and at a distance—the "Foucauldian Marxist" version of reformism theorized by the queer left, who believe that social change will come about by declaring unconscious desire "autonomous." Again we have an uncritical amalgamation of Freudian and Marxist theoretical elements. Yet as Ann Foreman has argued:

> . . . to accept Freud's theory of the unconcious and the instincts would in effect require abandoning the marxist theory of revolution. For marxism's central premise was that a development in consciousness not simply at an individual level, but at the level of a whole class, the working class, was possible; and the concept of socialism took its meaning from the idea of collective and conscious control. In short, to synthesise marxism and psychoanalysis was an impossible task. (Foreman 105)

Even if Foucault rejected Freudian notions of the "repression" of desire (for the idea of desire as "produced,") his genealogical critique eventually rejoins desire-theory and separates decisively from Marxism (Morton, *Material* 9–19).

The reformists of the dominant academy and the culture industry serve capitalist interests by promoting theories and analyses that systematically detach—as Altman's and the overwhelming majority of gay/queer texts do—sexual identity (gay/queer) from class identity (bourgeois/proletarian) so that discussions of sexual oppression can be detached from discussions of class exploitation. It serves the interests of capitalist bosses to keep workers divided along the lines of race, gender, ethnicity, sexual orientation, nationality, . . . rather than united for radical change. As Bob McCubbin *(The Roots of Lesbian and Gay Oppression: A Marxist View)* wrote two decades ago: "Anti-gay prejudice is an instrument of bourgeois class rule . . . the . . . capitalist class uses every means at its disposal to divide the international working class." With an awareness of the situation of the 1990s, Nicola Field makes a similar argument against a fragmenting identity politics today.[27] While ad hoc coalitions may form from time to time allowing various divided worker groups to jointly struggle temporarily for various limited goals, no lasting solidarity can form between workers divided by "suspicion" of each other. Furthermore, no solidarity can form between workers in the absence of a theory (a reliable knowledge) that both sets forth the urgent need of worker solidarity (in spite of recognized differences of race, ethnicity, gender, sexuality, . . .) and points to the path for achieving that solidarity. It is in the name of socially transformative practices that not only Nicola Field but also such writers as Teresa Ebert (*Ludic Feminism and After*), Robert Nowlan (*Queer Theory, Cultural Studies, Marxism*), and Peter Ray ("Determined to be Different") effectively reconnect gender and sexuality with class for the political contestations of the 1990s and beyond.[28]

Complaining in a tone of false frustration about the contradictory criticisms of him offered by his respondents ("Dennis Altman Responds"), Altman—whose writings, I must once again emphasize, naturalize contradictions as "inevitable" and "irresistible," promote "skepticism" and not "praxical knowledges," and thereby support reform not revolution—remarks, "I guess I can't win." The frustration is "false" (and not simply "ironic") because Altman has of course "won" at the level that "counts": the class position he and other reformists defend remains today the safely dominant position.

NOTES

1. I want to separate my understanding of the Australia/U.S. axis from the dominant queer studies understanding. In the dominant queer studies, U.S. interest in Australia is most likely to be deeply subjective in the new ways made possible by (post)modern theory, which is to say, imaginary, fetishistic, libidinal, and erotic, rather than rational, collective, objective, and historical. In a recent post on the U.S.-based Queer Studies Mailing List, for instance, the U.S. theorist John Champagne announced that he is "working on an essay in which [he] refer[s] to the fantasy Australia represents for (some) U. S. gay men" and inquires about "titles of any porno films that specifically promise to feature Australian men" (John Champagne, JGChampgne@aol.com "Island Fantasies." 9 Nov. 1996. QSTUDY-L@UBVM [10 Nov. 1996]). Champagne's eroticization of "Australia" here is consistent with his prioritization of the (post)structuralist emphasis on "desire" that marks his recently published book, *The Ethics of Marginality: A New Approach to Gay Studies* (Minneapolis: University of Minnesota Press, 1995). That book is an exemplary instance of the most advanced form of bourgeois U.S. queer theory, which proceeds from the assumption that "desire" is "autonomous" (that is, is unconditioned by other forces) and that "desire-theory" is the proper mode of social and cultural understanding. His book exemplifies the role of queer theory as the ultimate realization of that shift, heralded by Jean-François Lyotard, as the displacement of a conceptual economy model of culture by a libidinal economy model, which also entails the displacement of politics by ethics. But as I have already argued extensively elsewhere (*The Material Queer: A LesBiGay Cultural Studies Reader*, Boulder, Colo.: Westview Press, 1996), "desire"—far from being autonomous—is always conditioned by the question of "need," and sexual politics must be consistently brought into connection with class politics. Thus, today's dominant desire-based queer theory/queer studies must be displaced by a historical materialist queer theory/studies that prioritizes need and situates desire in relation to it. For a Marxist critique of Champagne's book, see Donald Morton, "The Class Politics of Queer Theory," *College English* 58.4 (April 1996): 471–482; for Champagne's reply to my critique and my response, see the March 1997 issue of *College English*.

2. The first two were published in the online journal *AHR* (URL: http://wwwlib.latrobe. edu.au/AHR/home.html) and the third in the U.S.-based *Social Text* 48 (Fall 1996): 77–94.

3. See Elisabeth Grosz, *Volatile Bodies: Toward a Corporeal Feminism,* Bloomington, Indiana University Press, 1994; Elisabeth Grosz and Elspeth Probyn, eds *Sexy Bodies: The Strange Carnalities of Feminism,* London and New York, Routledge, 1995; Annamarie Jagose, *Lesbian Utopics,* New York and London, Routledge, 1994.

4. Again, the relevant URL on the Web is http://wwwlib.latrobe.edu.au/ AHR/home.html.

5. Christopher Lane "Christopher Lane Responds." *Australian Humanities Review* 2 (July–September 1996) (http://www.lib.latrobe.edu.au/AHR/ home.html); see Homi Bhabha, *Nation and Narration,* London and New York, Routledge, 1990, and Homi Bhabha, *The Location of Culture,* London and New York, Routledge, 1994.

6. See Chris Berry, "Chris Berry Responds to Dennis Altman" and Gary Dowsett, "Gary Dowsett Replies to Dennis Altman," *Australian Humanities Review* 2 (July–September 1996) (http:wwwlib.latrobe.edu.au/AHR/home.html).

7. For further clarification of this issue, see Donald Morton, "Reply" *PMLA* (111) (1996): 472–73.

8. See Fran Martin, "Fran Martin Responds to Dennis Altman." *Australian Humanities Review* 2 (July–September 1996). (http://www.lib.latrobe. edu.au/AHR/home.html).

9. Dennis Altman, "Dennis Altman Replies," *Australian Humanities Review* 2 (July–September 1996) (http://wwwlib.latrobe.edu.au/AHR/home.html).

10. Dennis Altman, "Rupture or Discontinuity?" p. 93, n. 30.

11. William B Hunter, "To the Editor," *PMLA* 111 (1996): 133; Susan Balée, "To the Editor," *PMLA* 111 (1996): 470–471; Chidsey Dickson, "To the Editor," *PMLA* 111 (1996): 471–472.

12. Dennis Altman, "Dennis Altman Replies" *Australian Humanities Review* 2 (July-September 1996) (http://www.lib.latrobe.edu.au/AHR/home.html).

13. For a materialist critique of Halperin's book, see Donald Morton, "The Class Politics of Queer Theory," *College English* 58 (April 1996): 471–482.

14. As Lynda Hart has written, "One of the most important things that queer theory has to contribute to discussions of subjectivity formations is that not only are the identities fluid across and between categories but they are also always unstable and shifting *within* the categories themselves" *(Fatal Women: Lesbian Sexuality and the Mark of Aggression,* Princeton, N.J., Princeton University Press, 1994, p. 91).

15. On the pedagogical dimensions of the issues, see Chapter 6, "A Very 'Good Idea' Indeed: The (Post)Modern Labor Force and Curricular Reform," in Mas'ud Zavarzadeh and Donald Morton, *Theory as Resistance: Politics and Culture after (Post)structuralism,* New York, Guilford, 1994.

16. For the elaboration of these tropes, see Michael Warner, ed *Fear of a Queer Planet : Queer Politics and Social Theory,* Minneapolis, University of

Minnesota Press, 1993; Alexander Doty, *Making Things Perfectly Queer: Interpreting Mass Culture*, Minneapolis, University of Minnesota Press, 1993.

17. Regarding this controversy, see the Sokal web page at http://weberu.washington. edu/~jwalsh/sokal.

18. Ki Namaste, "Semiotics and/as Social Theory: AIDS/HIV Treatment Information and Semantic Intervention," *The American Journal of Semiotics* 101–2 (1993): 177–200. Namaste follows the pattern specifically by stressing the need to "move beyond . . . determinism," p.186.

19. David T Evans, *Sexual Citizenship: The Material Construction of Sexualities*, London and New York, Routledge, 1993; Gary Kinsman, *The Regulation of Desire: Sexuality in Canada*, 2d ed., rev., Montreal and New York, Black Rose Books, 1987.

20. Michael Tan "A Response to Dennis Altman from Michael Tan in the Philippines." (http://www.lib.latrobe.edu.au/AHR/home.html).

21. Dennis Altman polda@lurelatrube.edu.au, "Queer anthology," 27 April 1994. Personal e-mail (28 April 1994).

22. I have addressed this question also in *The Material Queer*, p. 29.

23. It has been published not only by Knopf but also by Overlook Press as *Boyopolis: Sex and Politics in Gay Eastern Europe*.

24. Roland Barthes, *The Pleasure of the Text*, trans Richard Miller, New York, Hill & Wang, 1975; Jane Gallop, *Thinking Through the Body*, New York, Columbia University Press, 1988; Grosz and Probyn, *op. cit.*

25. See Diane Chisholm, "The 'Cunning Lingua' of Desire: Bodies-Language and Perverse Performativity," in *Sexy Bodies: The Strange Carnalities of Feminism, ed Elisabeth Grosz and Elspeth Probyn*, London and New York, Routledge, 1995. See also Kiss and Tell Collective, *Her Tongue on My Theory*, Vancouver, Press Gang Publisher, 1994. For a more sustained discussion, see Donald Morton, "The Politics of Queer Theory in the (Post)Modern Moment," *Genders* 17 (Fall 1993): 121–150.

26. Mary-Alice Waters, *Feminism and the Marxist Movement*, New York, Pathfinder, 1972, p. 8. Waters also points out that one of the most common strategies reformists use to undermine the revolutionary position is to associate revolutionaries with reformists of the past—for instance, with "the right wing of the pre-World War I American socialist party," with "Stalinists," with "sectarians and ultra-leftists who refuse to recognize the complexity of class struggle or the need to fight for democratic rights," p. 8. This kind of blurring of lines between reformist and revolutionaries on the left is part of the agenda of this recent book: *Gay Men and the Sexual History of the Political Left*, ed. Gert Hekma, Harry Oosterhuis, and James Steakley, New York and London, Haworth Press, 1995.

27. Nicola Field, *Over the Rainbow: Money, Class and Homophobia* London: Pluto Press, 1995. See especially chapter 4.

28. Teresa L Ebert, *Ludic Feminism and After: Postmodernism, Desire, and Labor in Late Capitalism,* Ann Arbor, University of Michigan Press, 1996; Robert A. Nowlan, *Queer Theory, Cultural Studies, Marxism,* Urbana and Chicago, University of Illinois Press, 1997; Peter Ray, "Determined to Be Different: Social Constructionism and Homosexuality," in *Marxism, Mysticism and Modern Theory*, ed. Suke Wolton, London, Macmillan, 1996, pp. 135–161.

WORKS CITED

Altman, Dennis. *Homosexual Oppression and Liberation*. New York and London: New York UP, 1971.

Anderson, Walter Truett, ed. *The Truth About the Truth: De-confusing and Reconstructing the Postmodern World*. New Consciousness Reader series. New York: Putnam, 1995.

Angelides, Steven. "The Queer Intervention: Sexuality, Identity, and Cultural Politics." *Melbourne Journal of Politics* 22 (1994).

Aronowitz, Stanley. *The Crisis in Historical Materialism: Class, Politics and Culture in Marxist Theory*, 2nd ed. Minneapolis: U of Minnesota P, 1990.

Champagne, John. *The Ethics of Marginality: A New Approach to Gay Studies*. Minneapolis: U of Minnesota P, 1995.

———. "'A Feminist Just Like Us?' Teaching Mariam Ba's So Long a Letter." *College English* 58 (1996).

Cotter, Jennifer M. "'Left' Journals after the 'Post' and the Construction of the Political 'Everyday.'" *Transformation: Boundary Work in Theory, Economics, Politics and Culture* 1 (Spring 1995): 314.

Derrida, Jacques. *Margins of Philosophy*. Trans. Alan Bass. Chicago: U of Chicago P, 1982.

———. *Specters of Marx: The State of the Debt, the Work of Mourning, and the New International*. Trans. Peggy Kamuf. New York: Routledge, 1994.

Duberman, Martin. "Wander Lust." *Lambda Book Report: A Review of Contemporary Gay and Lesbian Literature* 5.4 (October 1996): 12–13.

Foreman, Ann. "Marxism and Psychoanalysis." In Donald Morton, *The Material Queer*.

Goodheart, Eugene. *The Reign of Ideology*. New York: Columbia UP, 1997.

Haggerty, George E., and Bonnie Zimmerman, eds. *Professions of Desire: Lesbian and Gay Studies in Literature*. New York: Modern Language Association of America, 1995.

Katz, Jonathan. *The Invention of Heterosexuality*. New York: Dutton, 1995.

Leong, Russell, ed. *Asian American Sexualities: Dimensions of the Gay and Lesbian Experience*. New York and London: Routledge, 1995.

Marks, Jim. "From Freud to Friedan: Jonathan Ned Katz Looks to a World in which Neither Heterosexuality Nor Homosexuality Exists." *Lambda Book Report* 4.9 (March/April 1995): 7.

Marx, Karl. *The Eighteenth Brumaire of Louis Bonaparte*. [1898]. Reprint, New York: International Publishers, 1964.

———. *A Contribution to the Critique of Political Economy*. [1904]. Reprint, New York: International Publishers, 1970.

McConnell, Frank. "Desecrating Literature." *Commonweal* (January 1, 1996): 37.

McCubbin, Bob. *Roots of Lesbian and Gay Oppression: A Marxist View*. 1976. Reprint, New York: World View Forum Press, 1993.

McGowan, John. *Postmodernism and its Critics*. Ithaca, N.Y. and London: Cornell UP, 1991.

Morton, Donald E., ed. *The Material Power: A LesBiGay Cultural Studies Reader*. Boulder, Colo.: Westview P, 1996.

Parker, Andrew. "Unthinking Sex: Marx, Engels and the Scene of Writing." *Social Text* 29 (1991): 28–45. Reprinted in Warner.

Persky, Stan. *Then We Take Berlin: Stories from the Other Side of Europe*. Toronto: Knopf, 1995.

Plessis, Michael du. "Blatantly Bisexual, or, Unthinking Queer Theory." In *Representing Bisexualities: Subjects and Cultures of Fluid Desire*, ed. Donald E. Hall and Maria Pramaggiore. New York and London: New York UP, 1996.

Rorty, Richard. *Contingency, Irony, and Solidarity*. Cambridge: Cambridge UP, 1989.

Ross, Andrew. "The Popularity of Pornography." In *The Cultural Studies Reader*, ed. Simon During. London and New York: Routledge, 1993.

Sedgwick, Eve Kosofsky. *Epistemology of the Closet*. Berkeley: U of California P, 1990.

Trevisan, João B. "A Delayed Start." In *Coming Out: An Anthology of International Gay and Lesbian Writings*, ed. Stephan Likowsky. New York: Pantheon, 1993.

Tucker, Scott. "Gender, Fucking, and Utopia: An Essay in Response to John Stoltenberg's Refusing to Be a Man." *Social Text* 27 (1990).

Warner, Michael, ed. *Fear of a Queer Planet.* Minneapolis: U of Minnesota P, 1993.

Wilson, Scott. *Cultural Materialism: Theory and Practice.* Oxford: Blackwell, 1995.

Zavarzadeh, Mas'ud. "Post-Ality: The (Dis)Simulations of Cybercapitalism." *Transformation 1: Post-ality: Marxism and Postmodernism.* Washington, D.C.: Maisonneuve P, 1995.

CHAPTER TEN

QUERYING GLOBALIZATION

J. K. GIBSON-GRAHAM

It was an article on rape by Sharon Marcus that first "drove home" to me the force of globalization. The force of it as a discourse, that is, as a language of domination, a tightly scripted narrative of differential power. What I mean by "globalization" is that set of processes by which the world is rapidly being integrated into one economic space via increased international trade, the internationalization of production and financial markets, the internationalization of a commodity culture promoted by an increasingly networked global telecommunications system. A forceful visual image of this present and future domain is the photograph of Spaceship Earth which is increasingly used to advertise the operating compass of global banks or businesses, promoting the message that "we" all live in one economic world.[1]

Heralded as a 'reality' by both the Right and the Left, globalization is greeted on the one hand with celebration and admiration, on the other with foreboding and dismay. This chapter focuses initially upon left discussions in which globalization is represented as the penetration (or imminent penetration) of capitalism into all processes of production, circulation, and consumption, not only of commodities but also of meaning:[2]

> The distinctive mark of late capitalism, underpinning its multinational global reach, is its ability to fuse and obliterate the boundaries of production and consumption through the *pervasive domination* of all levels of consumer culture and everyday life. (Deshpande and Kurtz 1994, 35 emphasis mine)

> Multinational capital formation . . . no longer makes its claims through direct colonial subjugation of the subject, but rather by the hyperextension of interpellative discourses and representations generated with and from a specifically new form of capital *domination*. Thus, it is important to recognize that *domination* occurs intensively at the levels of discourse, representation, and subjectivity. (Smith 1988, 138 emphasis mine)

> The prodigious new expansion of multinational capital ends up *penetrating* and colonizing those very precapitalist enclaves (Nature and the Unconscious) which offered extraterritorial and Archimedean footholds for critical effectivity. (Jameson 1991, 49 emphasis mine)

Fueled by the "fall of socialism" in 1989, references are rampant to the inevitability of capitalist penetration and the naturalness of capitalist domination. The dynamic image of penetration and domination is linked to a vision of the world as already or about to be wholly capitalist—that is, a world "rightfully owned" by capitalism.

It was in the light of this pervasive discourse of capitalist penetration and of assertions that the Kingdom of Capitalism is *here* and *now* that Marcus's argument about rape spoke to me so directly. Marcus challenges the inevitability of the claim that rape is one of the "real, clear facts of women's lives" (1992, 385). She draws attention to a "language of rape" which assumes that "rape has always already occurred and women are always either already raped or already rapable" (1992, 386). Reading her analysis of the positioning of women in the language of rape, I found myself replacing her object of study with my own—rape became *globalization*, men became *capitalism* or its agent, the *multinational corporation (MNC)*, and women became *capitalism's "other"*—including economies or regions that are not wholly capitalist, noncommodified exchanges or commodities that are not produced by capitalist production, and cultural practices that are conducted outside the economy.

When Marcus expressed her concern that feminist activism to make rape visible in communities had also produced a politics of fear and subjection, I thought of the industry activism I had participated in that had generated a knowledge of globalization and capital flight, and the way in which a politics of fear and subjection had emerged from it. When she made reference to the ways in which women limit their activities—for example, avoiding or thinking twice about being out in public spaces alone or in the evening, for fear of being accused of "asking for" rape—my mind turned to the way in which workers have limited their demands for higher wages or improved working conditions, given the knowledge about capital mobility and the operations of the MNC, for fear that they might be "asking for" capital abandonment.[3]

But how, Marcus prompted me to ask, was this message of fear conveyed by analyses of globalization? How had globalization become normalized so as to preclude strategies of real opposition, as in Marcus's view the normalization of rape has hindered feminist strategies for real and active resistance within the rape event itself? Within the discourse of globalization fear of capital flight and subjection to heightened exploitation are positioned as legitimate responses to the so-called realities of globalization[4]—just as fear of violation, and passivity or paralysis in the face of violence become legitimate responses to the "realities" of rape. As Marcus notes, "(w)e are taught the following fallacy—that we can best avoid getting hurt by letting someone hurt us" (395). She argues that unquestioned acceptance of rape as a fact of life limits the political efficacy of feminist actions that could be taken to prevent it. Accepting men's capacity to rape as a self-explanatory "fact" encourages activism in the areas of litigation and reparation "after the fact," rather than in the form of direct challenges to the victim role prescribed by the "rape script."

Parallels can be drawn here with the 1970s industrial activism that accompanied the widespread acceptance of capitalist globalization as a "fact." Some unions within national labor movements were tempted into aggressive bids for their piece of the action—a role in the World Car plan, for example. Others accepted globalization by pressing for state assistance to regions hardest hit by capital flight. Rather hollow-sounding calls for the "international workers of the world" to unite were revived;[5] but while the polemic was inspirational for a time (in a nineteenth-century kind of way), efforts to realize such a movement were largely thwarted by the discursive positioning of capital's globalization as a more powerful force than labor's internationalism.[6]

In her suspicion of claims about "reality" and the unmediated nature of women's "experience," indeed, in her refusal to recognize "rape as the real fact of our lives" (1992, 388), Marcus is led to explore the construction of rape as a linguistic artifact and "to ask how the violence of rape is enabled by narratives, complexes and institutions which derive their strength not from outright, immutable, unbeatable force but rather from their power to structure our lives as . . . cultural scripts" (1992, 388–89). A language shapes the rape script—"the verbal and physical interactions of a woman and her would-be assailant"—permitting the would-be rapist to constitute feelings of power and causing the woman to experience corresponding feelings of terror and paralysis. But the language also "enables people to experience themselves as speaking, acting, embodied subjects" (390), offering the potential for new words, different feelings and unexpected actions to emerge. By invoking the metaphor of a language, something that has rules of grammar but rules that can be used to say many different things, Marcus suggests that we might begin to imagine an alternative script of rape (1992, 387).

I could see in Marcus's project the contours of an argument very similar to the one I was constructing to challenge the dominant discourse of capitalist globalization. And what began as a simple game of seeing how far the comparisons and analogies between rape and globalization might take me ultimately developed into a rather complex form of play—the project of reading the globalization literature through the lens of poststructuralist feminist and queer writings about bodies, sexuality, and gender. In pursuing this project I hoped to gain some purchase on globalization discourse, to become more active in the face of it, less prey to its ability to map a social terrain in which I and others were relatively powerless and inconsequential.

Rape Script/Globalization Script

Marcus conveys many different meanings through her idea of a rape script. She does not use the metaphor literally to invoke a set of preconstituted parts—victim and rapist—in which actors play out fixed roles. Instead she employs the more fluid image of a script as a narrative—"a series of steps and signals" (390)—whose course and ending is not set. Her notion of a script involves the continual making and remaking of social roles by soliciting responses and responding to cues, and in this sense she highlights the self-contradictory nature of any script and the ways in which it can be challenged from within (391, 402). When she narrates the common rape script she draws our attention to the choices that are made, through which unset responses become set and woven into a standardized story.

The standardized rape script goes like this: men are naturally stronger than women, they are biologically endowed with the strength to commit rape. In the gendered grammar of violence, men are the subjects of violence and aggression. Their bodies are hard, full, and projectile.[7] Women are naturally weaker than men. They can employ empathy, acquiescence, or persuasiveness to avert (or minimize the violence of) rape, but they cannot physically stop it. In the gendered grammar of violence, women are the subjects of fear. Their bodies are soft, empty, vulnerable, open.[8]

There are many obvious points of connection between the language of rape and the language of capitalist globalization. Feminist theorists have drawn attention to the prevalence of shared key terms, for instance—"penetration," "invasion," "virgin" territory—in commenting on the phallocentrism of most "developmentalist" theory (Fee 1986). But beyond the by now familiar gender coding of the metaphors of economic development, there are interesting resonances in the ways a scripted narrative of power operates in both the discursive and social fields of gendered and economic violence.

> The most appropriate metaphor for modernity is rape—rape of nature, of the body politic, of vulnerable minorities, as much as that of women, both literal and metaphorical. . . . This is happening to me and I feel violated. (Banuri 1994, 7)
>
> . . . capital's history is aleatory because of its endless ability to *overcome* particular material conditions and obstacles, extending its reach ever further into all domains of discourse and, indeed, of existence . . . (Smith 1988, 141, emphasis mine)

In the globalization script, especially as it has been strengthened and consolidated since 1989, only capitalism has the ability to spread and invade. Capitalism is represented as inherently spatial and as naturally stronger than the forms of noncapitalist economy (traditional economies, "third world" economies, socialist economies, communal experiments) because of its presumed capacity to univeralize the market for capitalist commodities. In its most recent guise, "the market" is joined by the operations of MNCs and finance capital in the irreversible process of spreading and spatializing capitalism. Globalization according to this script involves the *violation* and eventual death of "other" noncapitalist forms of economy: "Capitalist production destroys the basis of commodity production in so far as the latter involves independent individual production and the exchange of commodities between owners or the exchange of equivalents" (Marx 1977, 951).

The globalization script normalizes an act of nonreciprocal penetration. Capitalist social and economic relations are scripted as penetrating "other" social and economic relations but not vice versa. (The penis can penetrate or invade a woman's body, but a woman cannot imprint, invade, or penetrate a man.) Now that socialism is no longer perceived as a threat (having relinquished its toehold on strategic parts of the globe), globalization is the prerogative of capitalism alone. After the experience of penetration—by commodification, market incorporation, proletarianization, MNC invasion—something is lost, never to be regained. All forms of noncapitalism become damaged, violated, fallen, subordinated to capitalism. Negri's vision of "real subsumption" in the current phase of capitalist production and accumulation evokes the finality of this process:

> With the direct absorption by capital of all the conditions of production and reproduction, capital, through its command over the logic of social cooperation, envelops society and hence becomes social: capital has to extend its logic of command to cover the whole of society . . . (Footnote: It is not being claimed here that "real subsumption" precludes the existence of noncapitalist formations. Rather, in "real subsumption" a form of social cooperation exists that enables even noncapitalist formations to be inserted into a system of accumulation that renders them productive for capital.) (Surin 1994, 13, interpreting Negri)

To paraphrase Marcus (399), the standardized and dominant globalization script constitutes noncapitalist economic relations as inevitably and only ever sites of potential invasion/envelopment/accumulation, sites that may be recalcitrant but are incapable of retaliation, sites in which cooperation in the act of rape is called for and ultimately obtained.

For the Left, the question is, how might we challenge the dominant script of globalization and the victim role it ascribes to workers and communities in both "first" and "third" worlds? For, as Marcus suggests, to accept this script as a reality is to severely circumscribe the sorts of defensive and offensive actions that might be taken to realize economic development goals.

In connection with the dominant rape script, Marcus proposes two quite different courses of action. One is to change the script from within, to challenge it by refusing to accept the victim role. The other is to challenge the discourse of sexuality that the rape script inscribes and from which it draws its legitimacy and naturalness. Both challenges offer potential for thinking through alternative responses to globalization.

BECOMING SUBJECT, UNBECOMING VICTIM

> Rapists do not prevail simply because as men they are really, biologically, and unavoidably stronger than women. A rapist follows a social script and enacts conventional, gendered structures of feeling and action which seek to draw the rape target into a dialogue which is skewed against her. (Marcus 1992, 390)

To break from the victim role, Marcus suggests, a woman might change the script, use speech in unexpected ways, "resist self-defeating notions of polite feminine speech as well as develop physical self-defence tactics" (389). She might remember that an erection is fragile and quite temporal, that men's testicles are certainly no stronger than women's knees, that "a rapist confronted with a wisecracking, scolding, and bossy woman may lose his grip on his power to rape; a rapist responded to with fear may feel his power consolidated" (396).

Reading this I found myself asking, how might we get globalization to lose its erection—its ability to instill fear and thereby garner cooperation? I was drawn to an alternative reading of the globalization script that highlights contradictory representations of MNCs and their impacts upon "developing" economies.

The MNC[9] is seen as one of the primary agents of globalization in part because it provides an institutional framework for the rapid international mobility of capital in all its forms. Like the man of the rape script, the MNC is positioned in the standard globalization script as inherently strong and powerful (by virtue of its size and presumed lack of allegiance to any particular nation or labor force):

> TNCs are unencumbered with nationalist baggage. Their profit
> motives are unconcealed. They travel, communicate, and transfer
> people and plants, information and technology, money and
> resources globally. TNCs rationalize and execute the objectives of
> colonialism with greater efficiency and rationalism. (Miyoshi 1993,
> 748)

In "global factories" the MNC coordinates multiphase production
processes in different countries and regions, seeking the cheapest combination of labor with appropriate skills to perform requisite tasks. But
is this representation of a powerful agent able to assert and enact its will
the only possible picture? Could we see the MNC in a different light—
perhaps as a sometimes fragile entity, spread out and potentially vulnerable?

In the face of images of the all-pervasive global spread of MNC
activity comes the contrary evidence that three of the four major *source*
nations of transnational investment (the U.S., U.K., and West Germany,
but not Japan) are also the major *hosts* of foreign direct investment
(Dicken 1992, 87) and that "only perhaps 4 or 5 percent of the total
population of TNCs in the world can be regarded as truly *global* corporations" (49, emphasis in the original).[10] *Multi*national corporations,
as Dicken points out, are more likely to be bi- or at the most quatrina-
tional in their scale of global operation.[11] And in light of the finding that
most international productive investment flows between the so-called
developed nations,[12] the much publicized orientation of MNCs to areas
of low-wage costs bears reexamination. Most productive investment by
U.S. firms, for example, is market oriented, hence its focus upon Europe.
Even investment in poorer countries may not be motivated by cost considerations but more by concern about access to final markets.[13] The representation of an all-encompassing global network of MNCs with a
voracious appetite for cheap labor begins to crack in the light of these
alternative illuminations, suggesting that the script of "capital flight"
that dominates the political calculus of many activists in older industrial
areas may be susceptible to revision.

The power of the MNC might also be open to discursive contestation. Corporate globalization is often constrained by language, law, and
business culture to certain national partnerships and not others.[14] When
it does reach beyond the safe channels between North America and
Europe and selected countries around the Pacific Rim, it may be spread

quite thin across national boundaries, vulnerable to being punched in the underbelly by changes in political leadership or trade policy or to being denied access (given the risk factor) to cheap venture capital. Increasingly, too, the MNC has become the prey of corporate raiders, the new knights of the global order. In the battle for ownership and control, size is no longer a protection. Small groups of individuals or relatively small firms organized into loose networks now lead takeover bids for much larger targets, and in most of these cases "the 'junk bond' financing arranged by these bidders necessitates that they liquidate a substantial portion of the target's assets to amortize these short-term bonds" (Coffee 1988, 116). Almost overnight large MNCs may experience a change in control as shareholders exercise their "right" to mobilize and redesign their corporate possessions, forcing management to restructure and sometimes dismantle the company (Useem 1993). If the spatial spread of many or even most MNCs encompasses only a handful of countries, then projects of "multinational" labor coordination might not be as difficult and daunting as they have sometimes appeared. Moreover, since institutional shareholders have begun to exercise their power over the operations of MNCs, there might be room for the institutional investment arms of the labor movement (pension and superannuation funds) to exercise their muscle in the corporate marketplace. It would seem possible, therefore, to offer different (nonstandard) responses to the set cues of the globalization script:

> And I grabbed him by the penis, I was trying to break it, and he was beating me all over the head with his fists, I mean, just as hard as he could. I couldn't let go. I was determined I was going to yank it out of the socket. And then he lost his erection . . . pushed me away and grabbed his coat and ran. (Bart and O'Brien, quoted by Marcus 1992, 400)

A nonstandard response to the tactics of globalization was offered by the United Steel Workers of America (USWA) during the early 1990s when Ravenswood Aluminum Company (RAC) locked members of Local 5668 out over the negotiation of a new contract (Herod 1995). Research into the new ownership of RAC (which had been brought about by a leveraged buyout) established that the controlling interest was owned by a global commodities trader who had been indicted by the U.S. Department of Justice on 65 counts of tax fraud and racketeering and was now residing in Switzerland to avoid his jail sentence (350). The union surmised that the "key to settling the (contract) dispute . . . lay in identifying (the trader's) vulnerabilities and seeking to exploit them internationally" (351). They decided (amongst other strategies) to allege that the company was a corporate outlaw "thereby potentially damaging its public image and encouraging government examination of its affairs" (351–2) and, through the channels of several truly international labor organizations, persuaded unions in a number of countries to lobby their own governments against dealing with such a corporate operator. Their interventions ended up ranging from Switzerland, Czechoslovakia, Rumania, Bulgaria, and Russia to Latin America and the Caribbean, all in all 28 countries on five continents. This international strategy—combined with a domestic end-user campaign to boycott RAC products—resulted (20 months after initiating the action) in the approval of a new three-year contract and in placing restrictions on the trader's expansion into Latin America and Eastern Europe.[15] Terrier-like, the USWA pursued the company relentlessly around the globe yanking and pulling at it until it capitulated. Using their own globalized networks, workers met internationalism with internationalism and eventually won.[16]

If one way to challenge the rape script is to diminish the power of the penetrator, another is to rescript the effects of the rape on the victim. Marcus suggests that feminists question the representations of rape as "theft," as "taking," as "death"—an event that is final and lasting in terms of the damage it does to self.[17] How might we challenge the similar representation of globalization as capable of "taking" the life from noncapitalist sites, particularly the "Third World"? In the standard script the MNC conscripts Third World labor into its global factories, setting it to work in highly exploitative assembly plants, often located in export processing zones where production takes place for the world market, sealed off from the "local economy." The intervention of MNCs in the productive economy of the "host" country not only violates the "indigenous" economy, robbing it of its capacity for self-generation, but also sterilizes it against future fecundity. In this sense it is a death ("We absorb the following paradox—that rape is death, but that in a rape the only way to avoid death is to accept it" [Marcus 1992, 395].) Yet is this representation the only one available? Could we not see MNC activity in Third World situations in a slightly different light, as perhaps sometimes unwittingly generative rather than merely destructive? In concocting this different story, there are a large number of industry studies to draw upon, of which studies of the semiconductor industry are perhaps the most numerous and compelling.

The semiconductor industry has become a well-known instance of the global factory. The most famous product of this industry is the integrated circuit, which is produced in a multiphase process that is often spatially dispersed. Assembly work, or the application of microscopic circuitry to silicon chips, is frequently performed in Asia by young women at low wages. The assembled chips are then re-imported to the "home" country where they are used in the production of electronic products like computers and computerized equipment. Labor relations and working conditions in the export processing zones where chips are assembled have often been described as repressive and barbaric.[18] But it is important that we not accept this model of economic sterility and social violence as the "inevitable" outcome of MNC operations in the Third World.

Recent developments in the international semiconductor industry indicate that the penetration of Asia by foreign MNCs has borne unexpected fruit. In Hong Kong, Singapore, and Thailand, complexes of local firms have emerged to supply specialized services and inputs to U.S.-owned semiconductor assembly plants (Scott 1987; Scott and Angel 1988). This development counters the image of the sterile branch plant in poor countries, which repatriates profits and contributes only to underdevelopment rather than industrial growth. The development of the locally-owned semiconductor industry in Southeast Asia has been extremely dynamic and relies increasingly on highly skilled local workers.[19] It appears that the economic "rape" wrought by globalization in the Third World is a script with many different outcomes. In this case we might read the rape event as inducing a pregnancy, rather than initiating the destruction and death of indigenous economic capacity.

Of course, one might be concerned that penetration by the MNCs has instigated the reproduction of many more rapists, indigenous capitalists eager to enact their own sinister scripts. But there are other indications that the effects of MNC capitalist activity in the Third World has had implications for noncapitalist activity as well. Recent feminist research has emphasized the dynamic and conflictual interactions between capitalist factory employment, households, the state, and "Third World women," supplanting the mechanistic narrative of women's subsumption to the logic of capital accumulation with multiple stories of complexity and contestation (Elson and Pearson 1981; Pearson 1986; Ong 1987; Kondo 1990; Lim 1990; Cameron 1991; Wolf 1992; Mohanty et al. 1991).[20]

The proletarianization wrought by globalization has created, for many Third World women, a more complex social formation, one which is not dominantly or only capitalist. Participation in the capitalist class process of surplus value production and appropriation in global production sites has interacted in a variety of ways with women's participation in class processes in their households.[21] For some women, involvement in capitalist exploitation has freed them from aspects of the exploitation associated with their household class positions and has given them a position from which to struggle with and redefine traditional gender roles. Strauch (1984), for example, writes of the abandonment by women factory workers from rural Chinese families in Malaysia and Hong Kong of the traditional patriarchal custom of living with their husbands' families and of their success in establishing independent households or moving conjugal families back to their childhood villages or homes. Urban employment has unsettled traditional domestic class practices in which their surplus labor was destined to be appropriated by their husbands' families.[22]

In addition to the changed insertion of women into the traditional household, the emergence of factory employment has been associated in certain households with the rise of nontraditional domestic class processes. Women are now often the only income earners in their households and may live on their own as single women or as single mothers whose husbands have abandoned the family or migrated in search of work (Cameron 1991; Heyzer 1989). With no male head of household present to appropriate their surplus labor, these women are engaged in the independent domestic class process of producing, appropriating, and distributing their own surplus labor. Their example, while still relatively uncommon, may encourage other women to participate in household struggles for class transformation, leaving their husbands' families or even their husbands to establish new households along independent class lines. Communal households in which household members jointly produce and appropriate their surplus labor also may be emerging as one of the consequences of factory employment options for Third World women.[23] Globalization can be seen, then, as overdetermining the emergence of different noncapitalist class processes in the household.[24]

Reading globalization as Marcus reads rape, as a scripted series of steps and signals, allows me to see the MNC attempting to place regions, workforces, and governments in positions of passivity and victimization and being met by a range of responses—some of which play into the standard script and others that don't. It helps me to challenge representations of the superior power of the MNC, to recognize how that power is constituted through language as well as in action, or more importantly, in a complex interaction between the two. As Ernesto Laclau has argued, we do ourselves an injury, and promote the possibility of greater injury, by accepting a vision in which "absolute power has been transferred . . . to the multinational corporations":

> A break must be made with the simplistic vision of an ultimate, conclusive instance of power. The myth of liberal capitalism was that of a totally self-regulating market from which state intervention was completely absent. The myth of organized capitalism was that of a regulatory instance whose power was disproportionately excessive and led to all kinds of wild expectations. And now we run the risk of creating a new myth: that of the monopoly corporations' limitless capacity for decision-making. There is an obvious symmetry in all three cases: one instance—be it the immanent laws of the economy, the state or monopoly power—is presented as if it did not have conditions of existence, as if it did not have a constitutive outside. The power of this instance does not therefore need to be hegemonically and pragmatically constituted since it has the character of a ground. (Laclau 1990, 58–9)

> His belief that he has more strength than a woman and that he can use it to rape her merits more analysis than the putative fact of that strength, because that belief often produces as an effect the male power that appears to be rape's cause. (Marcus 1992, 390)

INSCRIBING SEXUAL/ECONOMIC IDENTITY

Rewriting the script of gendered violence so that women are no longer subjects of fear and objects of violence but become subjects of violence (and therefore capable of real opposition) in their own right is enabled by discussions and evidence that challenge the unquestioned capability of male bodies to rape, and that question their superior strength and the impossibility of resistance. Stories of resistance, of cases where women averted rape or fought back, provide empowering images that might help women to "rewrite" the standard rape script. But Marcus is concerned to go beyond the tactics of reversal and individual empowerment. This leads her to another kind of interest in the metaphor of a script.

One of the powerful things about rape in our culture is that it represents an important *inscription* of female sexual identity. Marcus argues that we should

> view rape not as the invasion of female inner space, but as the forced *creation* of female sexuality as a violated inner space. The horror of rape is not that it steals something from us but that it *makes* us into things to be taken. . . . The most deep-rooted upheaval of rape culture would revise the idea of female sexuality as an object, as property, and as inner space. (Marcus 1992, 399 emphasis mine)[25]

The rape act draws its legitimacy (and therefore the illegitimacy of resistance) from a very powerful discourse about the female body and female and male sexuality. Thus the subject position of victim for the woman is not created merely by the strength and violence of the rapist but also by the discourse of female sexuality that the rape script draws upon in its enactment: "Rape *engenders* a sexualized female body defined as a wound, a body excluded from a subject-subject violence, from the ability to engage in a fair fight. Rapists do not beat women at the game of violence, but aim to exclude us from playing it altogether" (Marcus 1992, 397 emphasis mine). In Marcus's view, the creation of alternatives to the standard rape script is predicated upon a significant revision of the very powerful discourses of sexual identity that constitute the enabling background of all rape events. "New cultural productions and reinscriptions of our bodies and our geographies can help us begin to revise the grammar of violence and to represent ourselves in militant new ways" (400).

The feminist project of rewriting and reinscribing the female body and sexuality has born much theoretical fruit in recent years, prompted especially by the work of French philosophers Irigaray, Kristeva, and Cixous. Marcus's challenge and encouragement to marry this rethinking with strategizing a new (poststructuralist) feminist politics of rape prevention has prompted me to further thoughts about globalization and the politics of economic transformation. In particular, they have led me to consider how a rewriting of the male body and sexuality might affect views of capitalism and its globalizing capacities. "Men still have everything to say about their sexuality, and everything to write. For what they have said so far, for the most part, stems from the opposition activity/passivity, from the power relation between a fantasized obligatory virility meant to invade, to colonize, and the consequential phantasm of woman as a "dark continent" to penetrate and 'pacify'" (Cixous 1980, 247).

Feminist theorists have generated many new representations to replace that of the vacant, dark continent of female sexuality. However, as Grosz remarks, the particularities of the male body that might prompt us to challenge its naturalized hard and impermeable qualities have largely remained unanalyzed and unrepresented (1994, 198). Discussion of bodily fluids, for example, is rarely allowed to break down the solidity and boundedness of the male body: "Seminal fluid is understood primarily as what it makes, what it achieves, a causal agent and thus a thing, a solid: its fluidity, its potential seepage, the element in it that is uncontrollable, its spread, its formlessness, is perpetually displaced in discourse onto its properties, its capacity to fertilize, to father, to produce an object" (Grosz 1994, 199).

Grosz's suggestive words offer a brief glimpse of how we might differently conceive of the body of capitalism, viewing it as open, as penetrable, as weeping or draining away instead of as hard and contained, penetrating, and inevitably overpowering. Consider the seminal fluid of capitalism—finance capital (or money)—which has more traditionally been represented as the lifeblood of the economic system whose free circulation ensures health and growth of the capitalist body.[26] As seminal fluid, however, it periodically breaks its bounds, unleashing uncontrollable gushes of capital that flow every which way, including into self-destruction. One such spectacle of bodily excess, a wet dream that stained markets around the globe, occurred in October 1987, when stock markets across the world crashed, vaporizing millions of dollars in immaterial wealth (Wark 1994, 169). The 1987 crash was for many the bursting of a bubble of irrationality, "a suitable ending, fit for a moral fable, where the speculators finally got their just deserts" (Wark 1994, 171–2). But the growth of activity on international financial markets represents an interestingly contradictory aspect of the globalization script.

One of the key features of globalization has been the complete reorganization of the global financial system since the mid 1970s: "The formation of a global stock market, of global commodity (even debt) futures markets, of currency and interest rate swaps, together with an accelerated geographical mobility of funds, meant, for the first time, the formation of a single world market for money and credit supply" (Harvey 1989, 161). On the one hand this growth has been seen to facilitate the rapid internationalization of capitalist production, and the consolidation of the power of finance capital is seen to represent the "supreme and most abstract expression" of capital (Hilferding, quoted in Daly, 1991, 84). On another, this growth has unleashed money from its role as a means of circulation and allowed the rampant proliferation of global credit: "Now detached from its necessity to abide by the laws of capital accumulation the finance sector oversees and facilitates capital movement into speculation, mergers, acquisitions—'financial gamesmanship'" (Harrison and Bluestone 1988, 54). Money has become

> a kind of free-floating signifier detached from the real processes to which it once referred. Through options, swaps and futures, money is traded for money. Indeed since much of what is exchanged as commodities are future monetary transactions, so what is traded in no sense exists. (Lash and Urry 1994, 292)

The globalization of credit and financial markets has created an "opening" for capital to transcend its own limits: "The economy is an ensemble of movements and flows, mostly tied more or less to the physical space of fixed assests that persist in time. The financial vector is a dynamic development that seeks to escape from commitment to such permanence" (Wark 1994, 176).[27]

For those interested in historical periodizations of capitalism, this development signifies the demise of capitalism in its "second nature" (Debord 1983), when the productive base anchored the movements of credit and money.[28] Today, the whole relation between signifier, signified, and referent has been ruptured thereby unleashing capitalism's "third nature," "the spectacle" (Debord 1983), "the enchanted world" (Lipietz 1985) in which the "economic real" is buried under the trade of risk, information, image, futures, to be revealed only in momentary displays such as occurred when stock markets crashed in October 1987 (Wark 1994). At such orgasmic moments the body of capitalism undergoes a spasm of uncontrollability and unboundedness, to be brought back to itself and recontained within its own limits during the little death that follows.

> Capital pushes the development of the [finance] vector so hard and fast that it bursts through its own limit, as it did in October 1987. Like a meltdown, the crash was an accident programmed in advance to happen as the system pushed against its own limits. . . . In attempting to increase its power over itself and the world via the vector, capital encounters obstacles within itself. . . . Third nature is both the means by which capital extends itself, and the symptom of its inability to do so. . . . The event [the crash] is a privileged moment in which to see third nature for what it really is, stripped of its myths and kitchen gods. (Wark 1994, 192)

Globalization, it seems, has set money free of the "real economy" and allowed capital to seep if not spurt from the productive system, but the implications of this unboundedness, this fluidity, for the identity of capitalism remain unexplored. Having set the signifier free from the referent, theorists of the global economy are loath to think about the effects of seepage, porosity, uncontrollability, that is, to feminize economic identity (Grosz 1994, 203). The global economy may have been opened up by international financial markets, but nothing "other" comes into or out of this opening. It would seem that the homophobia that pervades economic theorizing places a taboo on such thinking.[29]

> Part of the process of phallicizing the male body, of subordinating the rest of the body to the valorized functioning of the penis, with the culmination of sexual activities occurring ideally at least, in sexual penetration and male orgasm, involves the constitution of the sealed-up, impermeable body. Perhaps it is not after all flow in itself that a certain phallicized masculinity abhors but the idea that flow moves or can move in two-way or indeterminable directions that elicits horror, the possibility of being not only an active agent in the transmission of flow but also a passive receptacle. (Grosz 1994, 200–201)

How might we confront the economic "unthinkable," engendering a vision of the global economy as penetrable by noncapitalist economic forms? Perhaps the very same financial system that is represented as both the origin of seepage and the agent of capital's assertion of identity might yield a further surplus of effects. It might, for example, be possible to see the proliferation of credit and deregulation of financial markets as creating opportunities for the growth of noncapitalist class relations as well as capitalist ones. The huge expansion of consumer credit (including credit card financing with large maximum limits, home equity loans, and a variety of other instruments almost forced upon "consumers") is often assumed to promote personal indebtedness associated with a culture of consumption. Yet, given the growth in self-employment and of home-based industries—some of which is associated with the downsizing and streamlining of capitalist firms—it is clear that much of what is seen as consumer credit is actually (or also) producer credit, in other words it is used to buy means of production (including computers and other equipment) and other inputs into the production processes of self-employed workers. Historically such loans have been notoriously difficult to obtain from traditional financial institutions like local and regional banks, but with the growth of new international credit markets they have become quite instantaneous and straightforward. This has contributed to an increase in small businesses that are sites of noncapitalist class processes of individual and collective surplus appropriation (as well as providing a source of credit to small capitalist firms). From this perspective, then, the financial sector can be seen as an *opening* in the body of capitalism, one that not only allows capital to seep out but that enables noncapitalism to invade.

The script of globalization need not draw solely upon an image of the body of capitalism as hard, thrusting, and powerful. Other images are available, and while we cannot expect the champions of globalization to express pleasure in leakage, unboundedness, and invasion, it is important to draw upon such representations in creating an anticapitalist imaginary and fashioning a politics of economic transformation. If the identity of capitalism is fluid and malleable, able to penetrate and be penetrated, then the process of globalization need not constitute or inscribe "economic development" as inevitably *capitalist* development. Globalization might be seen as liberating a variety of different economic development paths. In fact, the script of globalization may already (without explicit instances of opposition) be engendering economic differences.[30]

Marcus encourages a rejection of the fixed sexual identity that is *inscribed* upon the body of women by the rape script. Given that this

identity is rooted in a dominant discourse of heterosexuality (in which
the bodies of men and women are distinguished by rigid and fixed gender differences and in which male and female behavior can only be
understood in terms of opposition, complementarity, or supplementarity), one of the implications of Marcus's argument is that rape (along
with marriage) is a recognized and accepted (if not acceptable) practice
of heterosexuality. Challenging the legitimacy our culture implicitly
grants to rape becomes, in this formulation, a challenge to heteronormativity itself.

My desire to reject globalization as the inevitable inscription of
capitalism prompts me to take Marcus's implication one step further
and to explore the ways in which discourses of homosexuality might liberate alternative scripts or inscriptions of sexual/economic identity:

> many gay men . . . are prepared not only to send out but also to
> receive flow and in this process to assert other bodily regions than
> those singled out by the phallic function. A body that is permeable,
> that transmits in a circuit, that opens itself up rather than seals itself
> off, that is prepared to respond as well as to initiate, that does not
> revile its masculinity . . . or virilize it . . . would involve a quite rad-
> ical rethinking of male sexual morphology. (Grosz 1994, 201)

QUEERING GLOBALIZATION/"THE UNIVERSALITY OF INTERCOURSE"

Rethinking capitalist morphology in order to liberate economic development from the hegemonic grasp of capitalist identity is indeed a radical project. Yet resources for such a project are already available in the
domain of social theory, especially within queer theory, where a rethinking of sexual morphology is taking place. For queer theorists, sexual
identity is not automatically derived from certain organs or practices or
genders but is instead a space of transitivity (Sedgwick 1993, xii): "one
of the things that 'queer' can refer to [is] the open mesh of possibilities,
gaps, overlaps, dissonances and resonances, lapses and excesses of
meaning when the constituent elements of anyone's gender, of anyone's
sexuality aren't made (or *can't be* made) to signify monolithically"
(Sedgwick 1993, 8, emphasis in original).

Sedgwick's evocation of the way in which things are supposed to
"come together" at certain social sites—she speaks of the family, for

example, where a surname, a building, a legal entity, blood relationships, a unit in a community of worship, a system of companionship and
caring, a sexual dyad, the prime site of economic and cultural consumption, and a mechanism to produce, care for, and acculturate children[31] are "meant to line up perfectly with each other" (1993, 6)—captures the oppressiveness of familiar identity-constituting/policing
discourses and provides a glimpse of the productiveness of fracturing
and highlighting dissonances in seemingly univocal formations. Through
its challenges to such consolidities of correspondences and alignments,
queer theory has encouraged me to attempt to rupture monolithic representations of capitalism and capitalist social formations.

One key conflation or "coming together" that participates in constituting a capitalist monolith is the familiar association of capitalism with
"commodification" and "the market." When it is problematized, which is
not very often, the presumed overlap between markets, commodities, and
capitalism will often be understood as the product of a capitalist tendency
to foster what Marx calls "the universality of intercourse" (1973, 540).
This tendency is central to the representation of the capitalist body as
inherently capable of invading, appropriating, and destroying:

> while capital must on one side strive to tear down every spatial bar-
> rier to intercourse, i.e. to exchange, and conquer the whole earth for
> its market, it strives on the other side to annihilate this space with
> time, i.e. to reduce to a minimum the time spent in motion from one
> place to another. . . . There appears here the universalizing tendency
> of capital, which distinguishes it from all previous stages of pro-
> duction. (Marx 1973, 539–40)

> When the "market" is invoked today, nearly fifty years after the
> construction of the post-war order, the main referent must be to the
> world market—to the markets for goods and services, capital (or
> "loci of production"), money and credit. The world market is the
> site of economic reproduction of the global capital relation, as well
> as of the political organization of hegemony. An opening to the
> world market is thus synonymous with integration into the global
> process of economic reproduction and a historically determined sys-
> tem of hegemony. (Altvater 1993, 80–81)[32]

In discussions of the bodily interactions (that is, market transactions) between capitalism and its "others," the metaphor of infection

sometimes joins those of invasion and penetration: "capital is the virus of abstraction. It enters into any and every social relation, corrupts it, and makes it manufacture more relations of abstraction. It is a form of viral relations which has a double aspect. It turns every qualitative and particular relation into a quantitative and universal one" (Wark 1994, xii).

It is perhaps not surprising that capitalism is represented as a body that invades and infects, but is not itself susceptible to invasion or infection. In the shadow of the AIDS crisis, queer theorists have shed light upon the homophobia that pervades social theory (if not the specific heteronormativity of economic theory) (Sedgwick 1993). The infection metaphor suggests an "immensely productive incoherence" (to use Eve Sedgwick's phrase [1993, xii]) that may help to disrupt the seamlessness of capitalist identity, reconfiguring capitalism's morphology in ways that our earlier rethinking of heterosexual rape and penetration could not.

The locus and agent of universalizing intercourse is "the market," which continually seeks new arenas/bodies in which to establish a medium, or circuitry, through which contamination by capitalism may flow. Globalization discourse highlights the one-way nature of this contamination and the virtual impossibility of immunity to infection. But markets/circuits cannot control what or who flows through them. The market can, in fact, communicate many diseases, only one of which is capitalist development. Consider as an example the increasingly international labor market, another character in the standard script of globalization. The huge increase in international migration and the establishment of large immigrant "underclasses" in the metropolitan capitals (world cities) of the global economy since the 1960s is attributed both to economic and political destabilization in "donor" countries and to the voracious appetite of "first world" capitalism for cheap labor, particularly in the growing service industries and low-wage manufacturing (Sassen 1988). The loss of labor from source countries is usually portrayed as yet another outcome of the penetration of capitalism, via a process in which "the market" or "commodification" has destroyed the traditional, often agricultural, economy and forced people into proletarianization.

When incorporated into a script of globalization, the extraordinary economic diversity of immigrant economies in "host" countries is subsumed to, or depicted as an "enclave" within, the capitalist totality, located on a trajectory of homogenization or synthesis with the host society. The noncapitalist nature of immigrant entrepreneurial activity is documented for its cultural interest, but is rarely allowed the autonomy afforded to "capitalist enterprise." Yet immigrant economies made up of self-employed, feudal, and communal family-based enterprises (as well as small capitalist enterprises) operate their own labor and capital markets, often on a global scale (Collins et al. 1995; Waldinger 1986). They maintain complex economic as well as political and cultural connections with other diasporic communities as well as with their "home" countries.

Even immigrant workers who may be wage laborers in metropolitan capitalist economies cannot be seen as "subsumed" in any complete sense. Rouse (1991) documents how Mexican immigrants working as wage laborers in the service industries of U.S. cities manage two distinct ways of life, maintaining small-scale family-based farms or commercial operations in Mexico. Money received as wages in the U.S. is siphoned into productive investment in noncapitalist activity in the Mexican economy.[33]

> Aguilillans have come to link proletarian labor with a sustained attachment to the creation of small-scale, family based operations. . . . Obliged to live within a transnational space and to make a living by combining quite different forms of class experience, Aguilillans have become skilled exponents of a cultural bifocality that defies reduction to a singular order. (Rouse 1991, 14–15)

Globalization, it would seem, has not merely created the circuitry for an increased density of international *capital* flows: "Just as capitalists have responded to the new forms of economic internationalism by establishing transnational corporations, so workers have responded by creating transnational circuits" (Rouse 1991, 14). Labor flows have also grown, and with them a variety of noncapitalist relations.

This case is a small but suggestive example of the productive incoherence that can be generated through a metaphor of infection—an infection whose agent is the market (in this instance the international labor market). It challenges the imperial nature of capitalism, depriving capitalism of its role as sole initiator of a spatially and socially expansive economic circuitry of infection. If capitalist globalization is an infection, it can be said to coexist with many other types of infection. Were we not bedazzled by images of the superior morphology of global capitalism, it might be possible to theorize the global integration of noncap-

italist economic relations and noneconomic relations and to see capitalist globalization as coexisting with, and even facilitating, the renewed
viability of noncapitalist globalization.

Another productive incoherence introduced by the metaphor of
infection arises from the possibility of immunity. Lash and Urry note
that "(g)oods, labour, money and information will not flow to where
there are no markets" such as into eastern Europe after the devastation
of state economic governance or into the "black ghetto in the USA"
(1994, 18). The globalization of the capitalist market is a spotty affair—
characterized by cobweb-like networks of density and sparseness (24),
areas of infection and areas of immunity. Within the areas of sparse-
ness/immunity the economic transactions that take place are seen to be
of no consequence, and yet it is easy to imagine that in the interstices of
the (capitalist) market, other markets do exist. And in these interstices
noncapitalist commodities are exchanged.[34]

But the market is notoriously catholic in its tastes and desires for
the exotic, the noncapitalist, the unclean. And, so goes the standard
script, sooner or later, these areas of immunity, of capitalist vacuity, of
noncapitalist commodity production, will come under the power of capitalism. It is only a matter of time before capitalism reaches out via "the
market" into the unknown, infecting subjects with the desire for capitalist commodities and gathering to itself objects for exchange.

> Capitalist culture industries typically seek out the "new" in the cul-
> tures of various "others." . . . African American, Third World, gay
> and lesbian, working-class, and women's (sub)cultures frequently
> serve the function of research and development for cultural capital-
> ists. (MacNeill and Burczak 1991, 122)[35]

> It is not the people who have nothing to lose but their chains, but
> the flow of qualitative information about people, their places, and
> the things they produce, in short their "culture." Culture . . . ceases
> in the process to be culture, and becomes instead a postculture or a
> transculture. . . . Culture is something that will be overcome—
> whether we like it or not. (Wark 1994, xiii)

Contact, via the market, with noncapitalist commodities or "other cultures" never permits the transmission of infection back into the capitalist body. Instead, in the wake of the capitalist market, comes the commodification of culture and the death of "authentic culture."

The homogenizing claims made for the global market and capitalist commodification are, in the eyes of Grewal and Kaplan, insufficiently
interrogated:

> What is not clear in such debates is what elements of which culture
> (including goods and services) are deployed where, by whom, and
> for what reason. Why, for instance, is the Barbie doll sold in India
> but not the Cabbage Patch doll? Why did the Indian Mattel affili-
> ate choose to market Barbie dressed in a sari while Ken remains
> dressed in "American" clothes? . . . Which class buys these dolls
> and how do children play with them in different locations? . . . Get-
> ting away from . . . "transnational centrism" acknowledges that
> local subjects are not "passive receptacles" who mechanically
> reproduce the "norms, values, and signs of transnational power."
> (1994, 13)

The market is not all or only capitalist, commodities are not all or only
products of capitalism,[36] and the sale of Barbie dolls to Indian girls or
boys does not at all or only presage the coming of the global heterosexist capitalist kingdom. A queer perspective can help to unsettle the
consonances and coherences of the narrative of global commodification. That there need not be a universal script for this process is suggested by Mary Gossy's discussion of the use to which a Barbie-like
doll is put in a series of photographs entitled "Gals and Dolls":[37] "Barbie is not a dildo, not a penis substitute, but rather a figure of lesbian
eroticism, a woman in the palm of a woman's hand. In fact, playing
with Barbies and Kens teaches girls lesbian butch/femme roles—and
thus in puberty the doll becomes a representative of lesbian desire"
(1994, 23).

In the same spirit, might we not wonder exactly what is being
globalized and how infection is moving when Barbie dolls are marketed
in India or, for that matter, Indiana?[38] What power and potentialities do
we relinquish when we accept the univocality of the market/commod-
ity/global capitalist totality?[39]

If we create a hegemonic globalization script with the MNC, the
financial sector, the market, and commodification all set up in relations
of mutual reinforcement, and we then proclaim this formation as a
"reality," we invite particular outcomes. Certain cues and responses will
be seen as "normal," while others will be seen as unrealistic or quixotic.

By querying globalization and queering the body of capitalism we may open up the space for many alternative scripts and invite a variety of actors to participate in the realization of different outcomes.

CONCLUSION: GLOBALIZATION AND ITS "OTHER" OR GLOBALIZATION AS "OTHER"

> To treat rape simply as one of . . . "the realities that circumscribe women's lives" can mean to consider rape as terrifyingly unnameable and unrepresentable, a reality that lies beyond our grasp and which we can only experience as grasping and encircling us. (Marcus 1992, 387)

The discourse of globalization that I have been discussing in this chapter presents capitalism as something that is certainly "grasping and encircling us." Against the force of globalization many have focused upon the "local" (or localization) as its only "other." Localization invokes the way in which "global processes can in a sense be pinned down in certain localities and hence can become the basis for self-sustaining growth in those places" (Lash and Urry 1994, 284). "As spatial barriers diminish so we become much more sensitized to what the world's spaces contain" (Harvey 1989, 294). Theorists such as Haraway have been concerned to make visible the many and heterogeneous globalized organizations that build alliances across situatednesses and establish "webs of systematicity" between locales (Harvey and Haraway 1995).

But while localization may involve certain resistances to global processes, there is no room for the penetration of globalization/capitalism by the local. Localization, it seems, is not so much "other" to globalization as contained within it, brought into being by it, indeed part of globalization itself.

Marcus's discussion of the rape script has prompted me to explore the ways in which we might resist and rethink the representation of globalization as the social disciplinarian that polices all economic transactions—forcing them into line, into direct competition and equilibration—and thereby establishes a Kingdom on earth in which the local is humbled. Her rethinking of rape has inspired me to imagine the repositioning of subjects in the globalization script, and to think differently about globalization (based upon a differently constituted morphology of capitalist identity) as itself "other."

The strategies suggested by Marcus involve first rewriting the globalization script from within, denying the inevitability and "reality" of MNC power over workers and communities, and exploring ways in which the hard and penetrating body of the MNC can be seen as soft, fragile, and vulnerable. Making global capitalism lose its erection becomes a real possibility if we reject the naturalization of power and violence that is conferred upon the MNC by the globalization script. It also becomes possible to challenge the representation of economic penetration as necessarily inducing sterility or causing death in the Third World body economic.[40] Both these rewritings attempt to generate a vision of alternative scripts and outcomes for economic transformation without challenging the naturalness of (capitalist) globalization itself.

The second strategy for querying globalization entails identifying the larger discourse of economic identity and development that grants "reality" and legitimacy to global capitalism, and exploring the inscription by the globalization script of a hegemonic capitalist identity upon the world body economic. Drawing upon feminist retheorizations of sexual identity, the naturalness of capitalist identity as the template of all economic identity can be called into question. We may attempt to make globalization less genital, less phallic, by highlighting various points of excess in its inscriptions—places where the inscription can be seen as uncontrollable or indeterminate, or as potentially inscribing noncapitalist identity.

Finally, the severing of globalization from a fixed capitalist identity is enabled by a queering of economic identity, a breaking apart of the monolithic significations of capitalism (market/commodity/capital) and a liberation of different economic beings and practices. A space can be made for thinking globalization as many, as other to itself, as inscribing different development paths and economic identities. Globalization need not be resisted only through recourse to the local (its "other" within) but may be redefined discursively, in a process that makes room for a host of alternative scriptings, capable of inscribing a proliferation of economic differences.

> Rape does not happen to preconstituted victims; it momentarily makes victims. The rapist does not simply *have* the power to rape; the social script and the extent to which that script succeeds in solic-

iting its target's participation help to create the rapist's power. The
rape script pre-exists instances of rape but neither the script nor the
rape act results from or creates immutable identities of rapist and
raped. (Marcus 1992, 391)

NOTES

We gratefully acknowledge the helpful comments of Will Milberg and David
Ruccio on an earlier draft of this chapter.

1. The photographs of "Spaceship Earth" taken during the Apollo space
mission from 1968–1972 have played a powerful role in envisioning one world.
They ushered in the eras of both "environmental crisis" and "global capitalism"
and have been deployed to popularize environmental concerns for "life on a
small planet," on the one hand, and to celebrate the technological and economic
triumphs of global corporate integration on the other. Geographers Cosgrove
(1994) and Roberts (1996) provide interesting readings of the uses of these
images in discourses on globalization.

2. Where globalization is seen in terms of penetration, the parallels with
rape are obvious. I wish to argue that celebratory admiration of globalization is
not limited to the Right and that, despite the criticisms of globalization that
emanate from the Left, there is an undercurrent of leftist desire for "penetration." Consistent with the often expressed view that the one thing worse than
being exploited by capital is not being exploited at all, there is a sense that not
to be penetrated by capitalism is worse than coming into its colonizing embrace.
The ambivalent desire for capitalist penetration is bound up with the lack of an
economic imaginary capable of conceiving economic development that is not
capitalist development (with its inherent globalization tendency), just as conceptions of sexuality that are not dominated by a phallocentric heterosexism (in
which the act of penetration, whether called rape or intercourse, defines sexual
difference) are difficult to muster.

3. It is not hard to see how the knowledge of interior wages and working conditions in a distant industrial setting, conjoined with the pervasive belief
in the driving force of international competition, global economic integration,
and the power of multinational corporations, could have a disciplining and
dampening effect upon local workplace struggles.

4. And here, it might seem, the analogy between rape and global economic processes could be seen to founder. For women, in this argument, the fear
is of bodily penetration while, for workers in the case I alluded to, the fear is of
capital withdrawal. I would argue that in the discourse of globalization, capital

flight is simply the flip side of a process of increasing capitalist penetration and integration on a global scale. Withdrawal of capital from one productive site at one geographical location does not leave that space empty of capitalism—it does not, for example, rule out capitalist activity in that same location at another economic site, such as the service sector—and thus does not indicate any less penetration.

5. Kayatekin and Ruccio (1996) situate these calls *within* the discourse of globalization: "there is an imperative for individuals and groups to shed their previous (false?) national identities and to recognize the (true?) global subjectivity which corresponds to the worldwide basis and reach of capital. This subjectivity is often announced in attempts to move trade unions from their traditional national organizational structures to adopt a more 'internationalist' approach, for example, by engaging in international solidarity and other forms of global cooperation" (8). In their view this political subjectivity "remain[s] inscribed within the totalizing vision of globalization" (8), subject to its logic and its capitalocentrism.

6. Herod documents this positioning in the industrial restructuring literature, commenting that "[t]here is little sense that workers are themselves capable of proactively shaping global economic landscapes through their direct intervention in the geography of capitalism. They are portrayed as the bearers of global economic restructuring, not as active participants in the process" (1995, 346). The close relationships between many left political economic theorists of globalization and labor unions suggest that the hegemonic representations of globalization were not unimportant in shaping the rather constrained politics of opposition that emerged in response.

7. Marcus, paraphrasing Brownmiller: "The instrumental theory of rape . . . argues that men rape because their penises possess the objective capacity to be weapons, tools, and instruments of torture" (1992, 395).

8. "The rape script describes female bodies as vulnerable, violable, penetrable, and wounded" (Marcus 1992, 398).

9. Also known as the transnational corporation. We prefer the term "multinational" because it suggests that the corporation is subject to the jurisdiction of several nations, whereas "transnational" implies transcendence of national jurisdiction.

10. What is more, the magnitude of foreign direct investment compared to domestic investment for these major investors is relatively small. Taking the example of the United States, from 1960 to 1988, 95.5 percent of total U.S. investment was invested domestically. And if the eight nations that are the major sources of direct foreign investment are included, the ratio of foreign direct investment to total investment is less than 4 percent (Koechlin 1989, as quoted in Graham 1993, 238).

11. And even when they are active in other countries, their assets and activities tend to be concentrated in their countries of origin (Chang 1995, 5).

12. "Between 1983 and 1989, only 19.7% of world FDI went to developing countries" (Chang 1995, 5, citing Hirst and Thompson 1992).

13. Gordon estimates that much of the 25 percent of U.S. foreign investment that does go to poorer countries is attempting to access markets that are closed by tariff and nontariff barriers to foreign imports (1988, 50). And Tim Koechlin calculated that well over half the output of U.S. multinational corporations in the Third World is sold locally (1991; personal communication).

14. In the words of Chang, "TNCs do not have unambiguously superior bargaining power in all industries in relation to all countries. Their bargaining power ranges from being almost absolute (e.g., Nike looking for an investment site for shoe production) to being close to zero (e.g., automobile TNCs groveling at the feet of the Chinese government for the people's car project). Conversely, some countries have large bargaining power at least in some industries, while others have very little in most industries for which they qualify as reasonable investment sites. Thus, whether TNCs or the national governments have the upper hand depends on the industry and the country" (1995, 19).

15. Herod notes that the success of this dispute partly rested upon the financial resources that could be drawn upon from the international union and upon the ability to personalize the action—the trader made "an easy target for the locked out workers to vilify, which arguably strengthened their resolve to continue the corporate campaign against RAC" (1995, 354).

16. In this case the internationalism was ad hoc, partial, and realizable, quite different from the remote fantasy of a single worldwide workers' organization commensurate in scale with the gargantuan "global capital." When "global capital" is reduced to a set of corporations operating under different circumstances and constraints, successful opposition becomes a strategic process involving specific projects and alliances.

17. "The rape script strives to put women in the place of objects; property metaphors of rape similarly see female sexuality as a circumscribable thing. The theft metaphor makes rape mirror a simplified model of castration: a single sexual organ identifies the self, that organ is conceived of as an object that can be taken or lost, and such a loss dissolves the self. These castration and theft metaphors reify rape as an irrevocable appropriation of female sexuality" (Marcus 1992, 398).

18. Spivak (1988, 89), for example, draws attention to the way in which the government, male workers, and company management conspired to violently quash union activity among women workers in a South Korean semiconductor plant owned by Control Data.

19. Many of whom are trained in local technical schools and training facilities. Scott (1987) found indigenous producers engaged in all phases of the production process from design to testing, though assembly subcontracting was the major activity at the time. To challenge the globalization script and point out the local "vitality" of the industry is not, however, to deny or dismiss the importance of the conditions under which many women labor in these firms.

20. The standard globalization script highlights the employment of cheap, docile, and compliant female wage-labor in Asia and Latin America by industrial corporations eager to escape the expensive, organized, and predominantly male labor forces of the industrial capitalist world (Armstrong and McGee 1985; Fröbel, Heinrichs, and Kreye 1980). Actually, though, the industries that use female labor in the Third World are usually the ones that employ women in their home countries, such as textiles, garments, and electronics (Porpora, Lim, and Prommas 1989). In the standard script the patriarchal household has a non-contradictory relation to capitalist exploitation, facilitating and deepening it. Patriarchy plays the support role to capitalism, enforcing women's participation in wage-labor, as families drive them into the labor market in order to get access to a wage that will be dutifully remitted by their daughters. It also enhances exploitation, as employers take advantage of the devaluation of women's labor and the female docility that is patriarchally induced.

21. See Resnick and Wolff (1987) and Gibson-Graham (1996) for an introduction to a poststructuralist Marxist conceptualization of class and class processes. In this conceptualization, capitalist class processes are usually understood to involve the appropriation of surplus labor from wage labor as surplus-value. In any particular economy capitalist class processes may, and usually will, coexist with a variety of other forms of appropriation of surplus labor (slave, communal, individual, feudal, etc.), which may take place both within and outside the household.

22. Under their new circumstances, they were expected to contribute labor to their natal families if proximity allowed; but the degree of exploitation associated with these new transfers of labor—though not explicitly assessed by Strauch—was apparently much less than that experienced by the traditional daughter-in-law, both because the transfer of surplus labor was not enforced by longstanding tradition and because of other householding options available to the women themselves.

23. Whereas the state is often theorized as promoting capital accumulation by "liberating women's labour to capital" (Pearson 1986, 93), it is less often seen as overdetermining a class transition in the household. In Singapore, however, where there was a shortage of labor, women's labor was seen as crucial for an export-oriented development strategy. As industrialization has progressed, the state has encouraged men to play a greater role in child care and housework

in order to make it possible for more women to work outside the home (Phong-paichit 1988). The Singaporean state can thus be seen not only as facilitating the extension of capitalist class processes but as fostering the development of communal class processes as well.

24. Even in cases where the class nature of the traditional household is unchanged, women's exploitation at home may stand in contradictory relation to their exploitation in the factory. Rather than merely constituting a woman as less militant and more exploitable in the capitalist workplace, the woman's double day may also be a condition of her activism. In a certain Thai factory, for example, the women were not able to take advantage of management invitations to socialize after work. They developed a view of these social events as a "management ploy" and were much less likely to be co-opted by management than were their male coworkers (Porpora, Lim, and Prommas 1989). Over time, their suspicions of management developed into a more organized and ultimately successful struggle for improved working conditions. Ironically, then, for the married women at this factory, successfully changing their conditions of capitalist exploitation was an overdetermined and contradictory effect of their continued exploitation in a feudal domestic class process at home (Cameron 1991, 22).

25. Marcus continues: "Thus, to demand rights to ourselves as property and to request protection for our vulnerable inner space is not enough. We do not need to defend our 'real' bodies from invasion but to rework this elaboration of our bodies altogether" (399).

26. See Chapter 5 of Gibson-Graham (1996) for an extended discussion of organicist economic metaphors and their implications for politics and policy formulation.

27. Many have drawn attention to the detrimental effects such developments have upon the productive "base." Share trading can dissolve corporations overnight, productive investments can be milked for cash to play the currency markets, and managers of corporations can be asked to trade themselves out of a job (Coffee, Lowenstein, and Rose-Ackerman 1988). Mitchell (1995, 369) refers to the credit system characteristic of "casino capitalism" as a "feral credit system" running wild and uncontrolled, which "seems completely disconnected from the productive economy: in which the movement of goods has become "more and more negotiated and regulated" throughout the 1980s (Thrift 1990, 1136).

28. That is, capitalism as we knew it under the names of, for example "organized capitalism" (Lash and Urry 1987) or Fordism.

29. Indeed, as Whitford suggests, "(t)he house of the male subject is closed . . . whereas one characteristic of woman's sexual bodies is that they are precisely not closed; they can be entered in the act of love, and when one is born

one leaves them, passes across the threshold. (One might argue that men's bodies can be entered too, but no doubt Irigaray would argue that the massive cultural taboo on homosexuality is linked to men's fear of the open or penetrable body/houses)" (1991, 159).

30. Kayatekin and Ruccio (1996, 14) point to the many forms of noncapitalist production and provisioning that are enabled by revenues that could be said to "flow out of global capitalism." These include wages paid by multinational corporations that are used to pay for inputs to "family" businesses which may be organized within individual, communal, feudal, or even slave relations of surplus appropriation (not to mention wages that support the household itself, which is a major locus of noncapitalist production).

31. All these features and more are listed in Sedgwick (1993, 6).

32. By contrast, Daly notes: "There is nothing . . . which is essentially capitalist about the market. Market mechanisms pre-exist capitalism and are clearly in operation in the socialist formations of today. It is clear, moreover, that a whole range of radical enterprises exist within the sphere of the market" (1991, 88).

33. Here we are making the not fully warranted assumption that family-based enterprises are noncapitalist (i.e., that family members are not hired as wage-laborers by a family capitalist who appropriates surplus-value from his/her family members). Presumably when Rouse speaks of "different forms of class experience" he is referring to the communal, feudal, and even slave relations that may characterize family businesses; but since he does not actually specify the forms of class relations, we cannot exclude the possibility of capitalist exploitation nor can we assume that noncapitalist family relations are necessarily less exploitative than capitalist ones. The point is simply that capitalism does not necessarily breed capitalistm.

34. Commodities (goods or services for sale) can of course be produced within a variety of class relations—slaves may produce commodities as may independent and collective commodity producers who appropriate their own surplus labor.

35. Businesses that anchor their identities upon the appropriation of "Third World" or "tribal" artifacts and knowledges are good examples of this new trend: "The tribal world, it turns out, is full of traditional wisdom, especially in providing recipes for products that can be sold at The Body Shop. The urge to 'globalize' a society for its own purposes may not be entirely a new phenomena [sic] in the corporate world. However, in the case of The Body Shop, it is being done as a practice integral to the very identity of that corporation" (Deshpande and Kurtz 1994, 47).

36. See n. 34.

37. The photographs show a Barbie-like doll emerging from or entering a vulva.

38. Rand concludes her fascinating queer exploration of Barbie memories and practices within the United States with this reflection: "Surprisingly often, the stories I heard were about how Barbie turned people into cultural critics and political activists—about how seeing activists queer Barbie, or remembering their own Barbie queerings, or hearing about my Barbie work, induced them to move from Barbie anecdotes to thinking about cultural politics, ideology, oppression, and resistance, and sometimes to political plotting and practice" (1995, 195).

39. Daly points to some other ways of destabilizing the capitalist totality: "There has been a corresponding shift towards more politically aware forms of lifestyle consumerism–emphasis on local produce, environmentally sound products, anti-apartheid, anti-vivisectionist goods, etc. And these new developments cannot be thought within the classical identification of the new economic space as a fixed capitalist totality, or as a homogeneous milieu" (1991, 88).

40. This representation draws its force from the conceptualization of national economies as self-contained organisms that compete for survival (see Gibson-Graham 1996, Chapter 5).

Works Cited

Altvater, E. *The Future of the Market: An Essay on the Regulation of Money and Nature After the Collapse of "Actually Existing Socialism."* Trans. P. Camiller. London: Verso, 1993.

Armstrong, W., and McGee, T. *Theatres of Accumulation: Studies in Asian and Latin American Urbanisation.* London: Methuen, 1985.

Banuri, T. "Rape as a Metaphor for Modernity." *Development: Journal of the Society for International Development* 1 (1994): 6–9.

Bluestone, B., and B. Harrison. *The Deindustrialization of America.* New York: Basic Books, 1982

Cameron, J. "Women and Factory Employment in South East Asia: Liberating the Theory." Unpublished manuscript, Department of Geography, University of Sydney, 1991.

Chang, H.-J. "Transnational Corporations and Strategic Industrial Policy." Paper presented to the WIDER Conference on Transnational Corporations in the Developed, Developing, and Transitional Economies, Cambridge, U.K., September 1995.

Cixous, H. "The Laugh of the Medusa." In *New French Feminisms*, ed. E. Marks and I. de Courtivron, 245–64. Amherst: U of Massachusetts P, 1980.

Coffee, J. C. "Shareholders versus Managers: The Strain in the Corporate Web." In *Knights, Raiders and Targets: The Impact of the Hostile Takeover*, ed. J.C. Coffee, L. Lowenstein, and S. Rose-Ackerman, 77–134. New York: Oxford UP, 1988.

Coffee, J., L. Lowenstein, and S. Rose-Ackerman. *Knights, Raiders and Targets: The Impact of the Hostile Takeover*. Oxford: Oxford UP, 1988.

Collins, J., C. Alcorso, S. Castles, K. Gibson, and D. Tait. *A Shopful of Dreams: Ethnic Small Business in Australia*. Sydney: Pluto, 1995.

Cosgrove, D. "Contested Global Visions: One-world, Whole-world, and the Apollo Space Photographs." Annals of the Association of American Geographers 84.2 (1994): 270–94.

Daly, G. "The Discursive Construction of Economic Space: Logics of Organization and Disorganization." *Economy and Society* 20.1 (1991): 79–102.

Debord, G. *Society of the Spectacle*. Detroit: Black and Red, 1983.

Deshpande, S., and A. Kurtz. "Trade Tales." *Mediations* 18.1 (1994): 33–52.

Dicken, P. *Global Shift: The Internationalization of Economic Activity*. New York: Guilford P, 1992.

Elson, D., and R. Pearson. "'Nimble Fingers Make Cheap Workers': An Analysis of Women's Employment in Third World Export Manufacturing." *Feminist Review* 7 (1981): 87–107.

Fee, E. "Critiques of Modern Science: The Relationship of Feminism to Other Radical Epistemologies." In *Feminist Approaches to Science*, ed. R. Bleier, 42–56. New York: Pergamon P, 1986.

Fröbel, F., J. Heinrichs, and O. Kreye. *The New International Division of Labor*. New York: Cambridge UP, 1980.

Gibson-Graham, J. K. *The End of Capitalism (As We Knew It): A Feminist Critique of Political Economy*. Oxford: Blackwell, 1996.

Gordon, D. "The Global Economy: New Edifice or Crumbling Foundations?" *New Left Review* 168 (1988): 24–26.

Gossy, M. "Gals and Dolls: Playing with Some Lesbian Pornography." *Art Papers*, November and December (1994): 21–24.

Graham, J. "Multinational Corporations and the Internationalization of Production: An Industry Perspective." In *Creating a New World Economy: Forces of Change and Plans for Action*, ed. G. Epstein, J. Graham, and J. Nembhard, 221–41. Philadelphia: Temple UP, 1993.

Grewal, I., and C. Kaplan, C., eds. *Scattered Hegemonies: Postmodernity and Transnational Feminist Practices*. Minneapolis: U of Minnesota P, 1994.

Grosz, E. *Volatile Bodies: Toward a Corporeal Feminism*. Bloomington: Indiana UP, 1994.

Harrison, B., and B. Bluestone. *The Great U-Turn: Corporate Restructuring and the Polarizing of America*. New York: Basic Books, 1988.

Harvey, D. *The Condition of Postmodernity*. Oxford: Blackwell, 1989.

Harvey, D. and D. Haraway. "Nature, Politics and Possibilities: A Debate and Discussion with David Harvey and Donna Haraway." *Environment and Planning. D, Society and Space* 13 (1995): 507–27.

Herod, A. "The Practice of International Solidarity and the Geography of the Global Economy. *Economic Geography* 71.4 (1995): 341–63.

Heyzer, N. "The Internationalization of Women's Work." *Southeast Asian Journal of Social Sciences* 17.2 (1989): 25–40.

Hirst, P., and G. Thompson. "The Problem of 'Globalisation': International Economic Relations, National Economic Management and the Formation of Trading Blocs." *Economy and Society* 21.4 (1992.): 357–96.

Jameson, F. *Postmodernism, or the Cultural Logic of Late Capitalism*. Durham, N.C.: Duke UP, 1991.

Kayatekin, S., and D. Ruccio. "Global Fragments: Subjectivity and Politics in Discourses of Globalization." Paper presented at the Allied Social Science Association Meetings, San Francisco, January 1996.

Koechlin, T. "The Globalization of Investment: Three Critical Essays." Ph.D. dissertation, University of Massachusetts, Amherst, 1989.

Kondo, D. K. *Crafting Selves: Power, Gender and Discourses of Identity in a Japanese Workplace*. Chicago: U of Chicago P, 1990.

Laclau, E. *New Reflections on the Revolution of Our Time*. London: Verso, 1990.

Lash, S., and J. Urry. *The End of Organized Capitalism*. Madison: U of Wisconsin P, 1987.

———. *Economies of Signs and Space*. London: Sage, 1994.

Lim, L. "Women's Work in Export Factories: The Politics of a Cause." In *Persistent Inequalities: Women and World Development*, ed. I. Tinker, 101–19. New York: Oxford UP, 1990.

Lipietz, A. *The Enchanted World: Inflation, Credit and the World Crisis*. London: Verso, 1985.

MacNeill, A., and T. Burczak. "The Critique of Consumerism in 'The Cook, the Thief, His Wife and Her Lover.'" *Rethinking Marxism* 4.3 (1991): 117–24.

Marcus, S. "Fighting Bodies, Fighting Words: A Theory and Politics of Rape Prevention." In *Feminists Theorize the Political*, ed. J. Butler and J. Scott, 385–403. London: Routledge, 1992.

Marx, K. *Grundrisse: Foundations of the Critique of Political Economy*. [1857]. Trans. M. Nicolaus. New York: Random House, 1973.

Marx, K. *Capital*. Vol. 1. Trans. B. Fowkes. New York: Random House, 1977.

Mitchell, K. "Flexible Circulation in the Pacific Rim: Capitalisms in Cultural Context." *Economic Geography* 71.4 (1995): 364–82.

Miyoshi, M. "A Borderless World? From Colonialism to Transnationalism and the Decline of the Nation State." *Critical Inquiry* 19 (1993): 726–51.

Mohanty, C. T., A. Russo, and L. Torres, eds. *Third World Women and the Politics of Feminism*. Bloomington: Indiana UP, 1991.

Ong, A. "Disassembling Gender in the Electronics Age." *Feminist Studies* 13 (1987): 609–26.

Pearson, R. "Female Workers in the First and Third Worlds: The 'Greening' of Women's Labour." In *The Changing Experience of Employment*, ed. K. Purcell, S. Wood, A. Waton, S. Allen, 75–94. London: Macmillan, 1986.

Phongpaichit, P. "Two Roads to the Factory: Industrialisation Strategies and Women's Employment." In *Structures of Patriarchy: The State, the Community and the Household*, ed. B. Agarwal, 150–63. London: Zed, 1988.

Porpora, D., M. Lim, and U. Prommas. "The Role of Women in the International Division of Labour: The Case of Thailand." *Development and Change* 20 (1989): 269–94.

Rand, E. *Barbie's Queer Accessories*. Durham, N.C.: Duke UP, 1995.

Resnick, S., and R. Wolff. *Knowledge and Class*. Chicago: U of Chicago P, 1987.

Roberts, S. "The World is Whose Oyster? The Geopolitics of Representing Globalization." *Society and Space*, 1996.

Rouse, R. "Mexican Migration and the Social Space of Postmodernism." *Diaspora* 1.1 (1991): 8–23.

Sassen, S. *The Mobility of Labor and Capital: A Study in International Investment and Labor Flow*. Cambridge: Cambridge UP, 1988.

Scott, A. "The Semiconductor Industry in South East Asia: Organization, Location and the International Division of Labor." *Regional Studies* 21.2 (1987): 143–59.

Scott, A., and D. Angel. "The Global Assembly-Operations of US Semiconductor Firms: A Geographical Analysis." *Environment and Planning A* 20.8 (1988): 1047–67.

Sedgwick, E. K. *Tendencies*. Durham, N.C.: Duke UP, 1993.

Smith, P. "Visiting the Banana Republic." In *Universal Abandon: The Politics of Postmodernism*, ed. A. Ross, 128–48. Minneapolis: U of Minnesota P, 1988.

Spivak, G. C. *In Other Worlds: Essays in Cultural Politics*. New York: Routledge, 1988.

Strauch, J. "Women in Rural-urban Circulation Networks: Implications for Social Structural Change." In *Women in the Cities of Asia: Migration and Urban Adaptation*, ed. J. Fawcett, S. Khoo, and P. Smith, 60–77. Boulder, Colo.: Westview P, 1984.

Surin, K. "Reinventing a Physiology of Collective Liberation: Going 'Beyond Marx' in the Marxism(s) of Negri, Guattari, and Deleuze." *Rethinking Marxism* 7.2 (1994): 9–27.

Thrift, N. "The Perils of the International Financial System." *Environment and Planning A* 22 (1990): 1135–40.

Useem, M. "Shareholder Power and the Struggle for Corporate Control." In *Explorations in Economic Sociology*, ed. R. Swedberg, 308–34. New York: Russell Sage Foundation, 1993.

Waldinger, R. *Through the Eye of the Needle: Immigrants and Enterprise in New York's Garment Trades*. New York: New York UP, 1986.

Wark, M. *Virtual Geography: Living with Global Media Events*. Bloomington: Indiana UP, 1994.

Whitford, M. *Luce Irigaray: Philosophy in the Feminine*. London: Routledge, 1991.

Wolf, D. *Factory Daughters: Gender, Household Dynamics and Rural Industrialization in Java*. Berkeley: U of California P, 1992.

CHAPTER ELEVEN

COLONIAL FANTASIES AND POSTCOLONIAL IDENTITIES

Elaboration of Postcolonial Masculinity and Homoerotic Desire

HEMA CHARI

The sixteenth and eighteenth centuries were inexhaustible on the subject of Turkish and Persian mores when it came to the world of the seraglio. . . . What is remembered about the harem, however, are the sexual excesses to which it gives rise and which it promotes. A universe of *generalized perversion* and of the *absolute limitlessness of pleasure,* the seraglio does appear as the ideal locus of the phantasm in all its contagious splendor. . . . It underscores its polysexuality: to male homosexuality, to zoophilia and other vices, one can now add female homosexuality.

—Malek Alloula, *The Colonial Harem* (95–96)

Not only are the travel narratives of the voyages to the East replete with erotic fantasies of aberrant and illicit sexuality practiced in the Orient, but Western literature is overwhelmingly saturated with a plethora of aphrodisiac pleasures offered by the East, and Western literary writers relentlessly seek "the Orient on the flying-carpet of Orientalism" (Kabbani x). In fact, one could unequivocally claim that perhaps nowhere else are the sexual dynamics of same-sex desire so powerfully underwriting questions of identity and subjectivity as within the cultural politics of colonialism. For most Western writers the fabulous Araby is not merely an erotically torrid imaginative geography, but a psychic space on which deviant sexuality is projected, fantasized, explored, and fulfilled. As Said argues, "the Orient was a place where one could look for sexual experience unobtainable in Europe" and procure "a different type of sexuality" (1979, 190).

Yet, the powerful dynamics of interracial desires of same-sex and of homoerotic colonial fantasies continue to be elusive and contradictory in most commentaries on colonial narrative including the works of Alloula and Said.[1] What Said terms as "a different type of sexuality" (1979, 190), the "sexual promise and threat" that the Orient enticed Western tourists with, refers to what is now commonly understood in the West as male homosexual practice. Said argues that the Arabic Orient was consistently gendered as feminine, and Orientalism is a "male perception of the world," "a male power-fantasy," and an "exclusively male province," in which the Orient is penetrated, silenced, and possessed (1979, 207), so much so that the Orient is sexually available to be penetrated, rationalized, and controlled (1979, 36, 40, 41, 44, 45, 137–138). However, though Said explicates how the two terms "orientalism" and "masculinity" are interchangeable signifiers in colonialist orientalist discourse, he analyzes these aspects strictly within a heterosexist framework and completely disregards how the specter of the homoerotic masculine body haunts the colonial project in its politics of masculinity and masculine identity. Said examines the sexual and political dynamics of race by consistently investigating the feminization of the Oriental races and cultures. However, as several of his critiques point out, Said analyzes the feminization of race and culture as a discrete category and does not connect colonial politics of race to that of gender and sexuality (Boone, Lowe). Similarly, in his "Orientalism Reconsidered," while comparing the discourse of Orientalism to patriarchy, Said ponders on the incongruity of yoking together the "despotic—*but curiously attractive*—ruler" when he comments on how the "Orient was routinely described as feminine, its riches as fertile, its main symbols the sensual woman, the harem . . ." (emphasis added, 1986, 225).

I would like to draw attention to Said's phrase, the "despotic—but curiously attractive—ruler," because I contend that what is evoked here is specifically the male body, and the "despotic but curiously attractive ruler" *is* the object of European male desire fulfilling the powerful erotic fantasies of the colonizers in its project of subordination *of men by men*.[2] I also insist that the gaze of the imperial voyeur is directed elsewhere, not necessarily or always on the female, but glancing askance on the colonized men. In this process of appropriation, the East is not only projected as the other, but, more importantly, as the aberrant other to fulfill Western psychosexual needs and to sanction the phenomenon Said terms as "orientalism." Colonial power sustained its domination and status by appropriating a contradictory but systematic process of avowal and disavowal of sexual desire between men in the colonies. Further, the ambivalence of colonialist masculine erotics, which is simultaneously a promise and a threat, powerfully substantiates my claims that discursive practices of deferred and displaced homoeroticism underwrite colonial rule, and in fact continue to dominate the politics of postcoloniality. We find such conflicting depictions of the politics of homoerotic desire in Salman Rushdie's novel *The Moor's Last Sigh*, and its portrayals of colonial masculinity, homosociality, and homosexuality put into crisis the postcolonial politics of masculine identity and representation. In order to delineate these discursive and deferred homoerotic narratives in the novel, this chapter investigates three interrelated thematic strains that complicate the politics of homoerotic desire in postcolonial India: questions of colonial masculinity and emasculation; nationalism and the image of the nation as Mother; and finally the disjunctures of postcolonial diaspora and globalization. By correlating these three themes to the homosocial, homophobic, and homoerotic strains, I contend that the novel portrays how the appropriated and projected aberrant sexuality of the East during colonialism continues to transfer its profound masculine anxieties to postcolonial narratives of empire, race, gender, sexuality, and ethnicity, and questions the dynamics of the postcolonial nation with neocolonialism, nationality, and nationhood. Finally, I would like to suggest that if we accept the premise that colonialism is predominantly a male project between and of men, then this violative penetration and control that operates as the predominant trope within which the colonial enterprise is executed is that of male rape (Sedgwick, 1985). Subsequently, my reading of Rushdie's novel attempts to uncover the consequences of the violence of colonial male rape on postcolonial India.

The question of appropriation is crucial, and one needs to carefully interrogate not merely the literary representations of same-sex desire or the lack of such portrayals when analyzing colonial narratives, but more importantly examine the predominantly heterosexual frameworks of postcolonial theory. Several postcolonial theorists besides Edward Said, such as Sara Suleri, Homi Bhabha, and Gayatri Spivak, for example, have provided sophisticated analyses of the complexities of colonial discourse and subjectivity.[3] However, none of these theorists articulate the impact of colonial ambivalence in terms of same-sex desire, which has also caused great male anxiety and terror within the Empire and has intruded upon its project of Empire building. The question of male sexuality either as a covert goal influencing the conquering mission of the Empire or as a voyeuristic spectacle impacting the dynamics of colonial appropriation, knowledge and control remains largely silent or tangential for these theorists.[4]

Some of the works in gay and lesbian studies have taken into account the significance of colonialism and race on the discursive formation of same-sex desire.[5] As Teresa de Lauretis suggests "[n]either race nor gender nor homosexual difference alone can constitute individual identity or the basis for a theory and a politics of social change" (148). A sustained focus on the imperial constitution of colonial masculinity, race, gender, and sexuality will refine our understanding of the complexities of the modernist production of the discourse of sexuality on a global level. For though recent studies on the politics of masculinity, same-sex desire, and homophobia have achieved ground-breaking theoretical sophistication, their broader sociological and literary analyses have remained ensconced within a predominantly Western metropolitan frame of reference. Similarly, there is a marked reticence in engaging the complexities of the imperial structures of power and knowledge that were undeniably influencing the discursive complexities and practices of same-sex desire in modern societies in groundbreaking studies on sexuality such as those of Michel Foucault and Eve Sedgwick, and especially Jeffrey Weeks's account of the historical construction of gender and the regulation of sexuality in the late nineteenth century. Only one chapter in Sedgwick's *Between Men: English Literature and Male Homosocial Desire* (1985) pertains to the analysis of homosexuality and race. Her reserve is notable, as Victorian literature is particularly obsessed with the colonizing project of the Empire. However, although Sedgwick's analysis of the impact of heterosexual rivalries on gender and sexuality is crucial to the point of departure of my paper, my analysis of colonial masculinity and homosexuality is not based on how homophobia and misogyny have consequences on male bonding and on heterosexual men, which in turn affect women's relationships and positions in heterosexuality; instead this paper concentrates on those liminal and contradictory cultural spaces that constantly expose the ambivalence of colonial masculinity where the colonial male becomes not merely an object of derision but also an item of exchange and a subject for erotic desire and/or voyeuristic pleasure.[6]

The discursive sites of colonial masculinity and homoerotic desire are complicated when issues of race and gender affect the complexities of heterosexuality, homosociality, and homophobia. Sedgwick's triangular formulation describing the relationship of men and women in heterosexuality is problematic when seen within a colonial context.[7] Several times the issue of race splits male identity, so much so that women of the colonizing cultures 'bond' with the colonizers against the colonized men. European women in the colonies are themselves fragmented in terms of their own identities. Their status was equivocally divided as subordinates to their own colonizing men due to their gender, but they were also active agents of the imperial power. In addition, in colonial situations the homoerotic desire further segregated women of the colonizing culture from that of the colonized men. Indian psychiatrist Ashis Nandy associates white women's racism to the homosexual desire of the white men: "the white women in India were generally more exclusive and racist because they unconsciously saw themselves as the sexual competitors of Indian men, with whom their men had established an unconscious homo-eroticized bonding" (9–10). As the colonized male was perceived as a rival by the women of the colonizing culture, in the colonial situation then the homosocial triangle of Sedgwick is reversed to some extent, where the colonized male becomes the item of exchange in highly charged political imbroglios.[8]

Correspondingly, contributions to the understanding of sexuality and masculinity oftentimes elide issues related to the colonial rule. For example David Halperin maintains that the publication of Michel Foucault's *History of Sexuality* in 1978 was the most distinctive contribution made to the study of sexuality (7). According to Foucault, the discourse of sexuality, which is a modernist production, enabled the construction of the homosexual other by carefully distinguishing in nineteenth century discourse normal and aberrant sexuality. However, Western orientalism painstakingly constructed the colonial other by differentiating their sexual deviancy or abnormality from accepted Western sexual practices.[9] Foucault's analysis of the construction of homosexual identity in nineteenth-century discourse, as I have argued elsewhere, is analogous to the Empire's construction of the sexually deviant and decadent racial other in colonialist discourse even though Foucault does not account for the influence of colonization on the discourse of sexuality (see Chari 217–218).[10] For the Victorians these contaminated cultures of the colonies were bastions of sexually deviant and abnormal behavior continually in need of European refinement. For example, in his terminal essay of 1885–86 edition of the *Thousand and One Nights*, Richard Burton concludes that "perverse" and "unnatural" sodomitic vices were endemic to the "Sotadic Zone": "Running eastward the Sotadic Zone narrows, embracing Asia Minor, Mesopotamia and Chaldea, Afghanistan, Sind, the Punjab and Kashmir" (qtd. in Sedgwick, 1985, 183). In fact, the most defiling aspect of the colonized culture according to the Empire was its homosexual practices, and aberrant sexuality combined with the flawed and emasculated colonial masculinity endorsed the continual need for colonial intervention specifically for its civilizing mission. As a matter of fact, the eternal anathema of deviant sexuality on the colonies exonerated the larger contentious global and colonial interests of the Empire.

The ambiguous and contradictory sites of homoerotic desire in colonial discourse are further complicated by questions of colonial and postcolonial masculinity.[11] "Postcolonial masculinity" denotes in this essay the politics of masculinity as practiced during the imperial British rule during which a particular variety of masculinity or a masculinized ideal was established. The discourse of colonial masculinity differentiated the cultured and superior Western masculinity from the effeminate and flawed masculinity of the colonies. Recapitulating Ashis Nandy's argument, Partha Chatterjee claims that "[t]he 'hyper-masculinity' of imperialist ideology made to figure of the weak, irresolute, effeminate babu a special target of contempt and ridicule" (1991, 61). Subsequently, colonial masculinity does not refer to a single pattern of control but to specific practices of male domination. Implications of colonial masculinity impacted not only the politics of colonialism but also the dynamics of nationalism and neo-colonialism in postcolonial India.

Colonial masculinity not only established stereotypes such as the powerful, manly, and virile Englishman as against the effeminate, impotent, unmanly 'native,' but also discursively shifted definitions to "virile" Sikh, "militant" Pathan or Maratha, or the slight and weak Madrasi.[12] Colonial masculinity contributed to the establishment of a specific discourse and genealogy of masculinity that was further reinforced in post-coloniality in which the virile male body legitimated political and cultural supremacy. Stereotypes of unmanliness during colonialism reinforced the images and implications of anomalous sexual practices and vice versa. Significantly, the exotic tropics became signifiers for same-sex perversions, homosexual licenses, male pornographic fantasies, and male libidinous anomalies. Cultural practices, especially those markers of sexual orientation such as gender bending, cross-dressing, female impersonation, and androgyny, are consistently associated with the Orient, and the burden of oriental homosexuality plagues Anglo-Indian literature (Behdad, Boone, Garber, Lowe, Silverman). In fact, even an early mystery novel like Wilkie Collins's *Moonstone* attributes sexual and racial anomalies to the Orient (Chari). In Anglo-Indian fiction, the imperial narrative of Rudyard Kipling, the portrayal of Kim is haunted by the problematics of homoeroticism and is obscured by Kim's participation in the "Great Game" of colonization (Lane, Sedgwick, Suleri).

The androgynous aspects of oriental cultures particularly attracted modernist writers, such as James Joyce, T. S. Eliot, E. M. Forster, and Virginia Woolf, among others. Modernist writers were strongly influenced by and inclined towards the philosophy of the East. These writers were particularly reacting to the masculinist ideologies of their own culture and some of them found consolation and relief in the androgynous philosophy of the East. So, according to Raymond Williams, the Bloomsbury group identified itself emotionally and intellectually with the androgynous aspects of the Orient (1989, 160–166). Interestingly enough several of the modernist writers who explored the issue of androgyny investigate the transgressions of gender boundaries and of the seductions of homoeroticism by consistently setting their scenes for gender impersonations in the East within an oriental setting. For example, Virginia Woolf's explorations of Orlando's sex-changes are situated behind the oriental veil, eventually eroticized and unveiled within the textual fantasies of Oriental abduction, seduction, and titillation. The lifting of the "veil" to "unveil" Orlando's sexuality is orientalized within

the Eastern trope of veiling and unveiling the colonized oriental woman
(*Orlando*, 134–137). The novel dresses the East in the feminine/mascu-
line garb of androgyny to display an alternative physiognomy. While
costuming, adorning, and dragging the narrative through various suggestions of sexual alternatives, the novel substantially depends on systematic cultural and racial veils. The narrative's significant event of gender crossing and fantasy of transsexual desire is located *outside* the
imperial boundaries of the English soil, but only to be significantly situated *inside* the libidinous terrain of the Orient.

Similarly, the postcolonial novel *The Moor's Last Sigh* presents a
blend of sexual repression, homosocial conflicts, and heterosexual complexities of postcolonial India.[13] In this novel, Rushdie writes from the
borderlands of the migrant condition even though the novel is set in
India. This novel can be seen as a sequel to his earlier novel *The Satanic
Verses*, as Rushdie continues to articulate the anguish of the migrant
male and of his ambivalent relationship to the postcolonial nation and
nationality. While in *The Satanic Verses* homoerotic desire is implied but
buried, in *The Moor's Last Sigh* one of the characters, Aires da Gama,
is gay. However, homoerotic desire and the complexity of gay identity
are constantly deflected and diverted to be regulated and calibrated
within a heterosexual paradigm, and the complexities of Aires's homosexual desire are developed through three interrelated and overlapping
themes: the trauma of colonial emasculation, "native" effeminacy or
flawed masculinity counteracted with hyper-colonialist masculinity; a
fetishized obsession with the nation as mother and the phobia of the
motherland emasculating her sons (the love for the motherland is relocated as the theme of nationalism which is nuanced as erotic nationalism); and finally, the anxiety of alienation from home, nation, and ethnic community in which estrangement is portrayed as the fundamental
condition of the postcolonial, diasporic, globalized ethnic male identity.
Together these themes reflect, deflect, resist, and displace the intense politics of same-sex desire as homophobia, homoeroticism, and homosocialism within the dynamics of colonialism as well as within the politics
of multinationalism, nationalism, globalism, and postcolonialism.

The three thematic strands of the novel form a nexus around
which homosexual epistemologies of both Western and oriental cultures
are encountered, identified, practiced, regulated, and speculated upon.
Male desire is simultaneously represented as both object and subject; as
the same and the other; as a contradictory and unresolved site of identi-

fication and difference that not only reinforces the binarisms of homosexuality and heterosexuality but also reveals how the encounters of the East and West are imbricated by issues of colonialism, race, nation, nationalism, and class in postcolonialism. By accentuating the hybridity of postcolonial India, the narrative underscores not merely the diversity of its race, culture, and religion, but also of its divergent sexual practices, "[c]ircular sexualist India" (166).

The novel is a saga of the da Gamas; especially of the rise and fall of the half-Jewish, half-Catholic four generations of the da Gama-Zogoiby family whose father might have been an illegitimate descendant of Boabdil, the last Muslim Sultan of Granada, who was driven from Spain in 1492 (72, 79–81). His Catholic mother, Aurora da Gama, comes from a Christian spice-trading family that proudly claims illegitimate descent from Vasco da Gama, the Portuguese navigator who brought European trade and colonialism to India: "English and French sailed in the wake of that first-arrived Portugee, so that in the period called Discovery-of-India . . . we were 'not so much sub-continent as sub-condiment,' as my distinguished mother had it" (4–5). The chief narrator of the novel is their son, Moraes Zogoiby, who symbolizes the hybrid racial, cultural, and religious melange of modern India.[14] Nicknamed the Moor, he is heterosexual and embodies literally and allegorically the trauma of colonial emasculation. As for his physical features, he is described as grotesque with a deformed hand: "a deformed right hand like a club" with "[m]y right hand: the fingers welded into an undifferentiated chunk, the thumb a stunted wart" (146). He also suffers from a genetic disorder which ages his body twice as fast as a normal individual's (144–146, 153–154), in spite of his premature birth— "[f]our and a half months in the wet and slimy felt much too long to me" (144).[15] The Moor's physical deformity underscores another inadequacy; he is racially flawed due to his hybrid racial heritage, consequently reinforcing and continuing the masculinist colonial anxiety of miscegenation in postcolonial India. Inasmuch as he inherits a diverse mixture of races and creeds that are constitutive of modern India, a secular nation, his racial potpourri also accentuates the crisis of modern India, which is fundamentally divided into Muslims and Hindus, especially after colonization, in spite of the numerous other minority communities and myriad religious faiths and belief systems that form a palimpsest of races and subcultures on the Indian subcontinent: "I, however, was raised neither as Catholic nor as Jew. I was both, and nothing:

a jewholic—anonymous, a cathjew, a stewpot, a mongrel cur. I was . . .
a real Bombay mix. *Bastard*: . . . a smelly shit; like, for example, me"
(104). While the Moor represents the hybridization of modern India, he
also uncovers the colonialist and masculinist phobia for racial impurity,
contamination, and homophobia in postcolonial India. Postcolonial
India not only imbibes the imperialist ideology and its hypermasculinity—the racial homosocial conflicts of colonialist India—but also pre-
serves the colonialist policies of divide and rule.

In addition, the intricacies and intense familial bonding and rivalries of the da Gama family in postcolonial India duplicate the homosocial politics of colonialism, especially in the manner in which the novel
resorts to family disputes and differences in order to defer same-sex
desire, which allows the narrative to calibrate male desire within a heterosexual paradigm. The intricacy of the da Gama family replicates the
homosocial conflicts of colonial India in several ways: on a personal
level it reflects the collapse of the family as a social unit while also mir-
roring on the political level the disintegration of the secular state in postcolonial India. Homosocial inimity jeopardizes the masculine identity,
catastrophically threatening to undo both familial and national history,
and the emasculated male identity becomes the predominant trope echoing the cataclysmic partition of the nation into India and Pakistan by the
British:

> Disharmony and discord have been introduce-o'ed everywhere by
> appointees of Aires, whether direct or indirect does not signify;
> business circumstances clearly dictate the company integrity is
> impossible to maintain. If the Gama Company remains a single cell,
> then the shame of these atrocities will finish it off. Divide, and
> maybe the sickness can be contained in one half only. If we do not
> live separately then we will die together. (41)

The nation, like the family, has to endure the curse of eternal rifts
because "[o]nce divided, always divided; in that household it was a fight
to the bloody finish" (49).[16] The history of the da Gama family also
divulges the continental history of the subcontinent, replicating in its
own familial schisms, the homosocial divide, and rule practice and economics of the empire in colonialism (40, 42, 46, 55, 56). The intense
prominence of personal and political rivalries were indicative of private,
psychic fear and anxiety about manhood, as well as of a collective polit-

ical panic about masculinity and potential loss of manhood on national and global levels; the personal and the public were profoundly afflicted by the continuing intricacies of colonial masculinity and neocolonialism in postcolonial India. In addition, both colonial and postcolonial India are underscored by a fetishistic obsession for male dominance. However, by accentuating intense male rivalry and homosociality of the family, and in this case the da Gamas in postcolonial India, the novel stifles the unfolding of an intricate and complex portrayal of masculine desire.

The homosocial paradigm of colonialism becomes not merely the basis for the da Gama family and for the conflicts of postcolonial India, replicating colonial manipulation of divide and rule in its portrayal of male bonding and unbonding, but also contentiously shapes neocolonialism and fundamentalism in contemporary India. For example, one of the central anxieties in the novel is the rise of Hindu fundamentalism, which is portrayed by commenting on the celebration of the Ganesh festival or the elephant God. Every year during this festival the Zogoiby family is ripped apart as the various members of the family allege their alliances to the various factious groups of either Hindu fanaticism, the secular moderates, or other religious groups of the Islamic faith. The novel exposes the valorization of the male heterosexual religious narratives (Hinduism, Islam, Christianity, etc.) in postcolonial India, but only to uncover the different layers of hybridity and to dismantle the homosocial conflicts of race, ethnicity, class, caste, religion, gender, and sexuality. The primary catalyst inciting these dissentions is a relentless fundamentalist moral and political view of hypermasculinity, ethnocentricism, and homophobia that denies any ruptures in the globalized, hybrid, postcolonial Indian identity. The traumatic "ruinous climax of divide-and-rule" of colonial India—"two nations in the subcontinent, one Hindu, the other Mussulman. Soon the split will be *irreversible*" (emphasis added, 87)—is traced in the novel from colonial to postcolonial religious and ethnic dissentions. However, even after independence, the rift continues to split deeper the confines of the already ruptured nation, and the scourge of Hindu fundamentalism afflicts the nation especially during the Ganesh festivals in Bombay: "Ganesha Chaturthi had become the occasion for the fist-clenched, saffron-headbanded young thugs to put on a show of Hindu-fundamentalist triumphalism, egged on by bellowing 'Mumbai's Axis' party politicos and demagogues such as Raman Fielding, a.k.a. *Mainduck* ('Frog')" (124). As the homosocial politics of nationalism and Hindu fundamentalism consoli-

date to confront colonial politics, both nationalism and Hindu fundamentalism imbibe and promote the very colonial politics they challenge;
in its core both anticolonialist and Hindu fundamentalist postcolonial
politics divulge male discourses that are haunted by a homophobic and
paranoiac masculine anxiety.[17] In addition, just as the colonial Empire of
the mid-nineteenth century was plagued by a dreadful fear of homosexuality and virulently fostered homophobia, especially as England was
losing its global and national power, similarly, postcolonial India confronts its national and racial threats of destabilization with homophobia
and frenzied attacks on secularism. Any manifestation of weakness or
compromise, either on a personal or political level, is perceived as effeminate, and feminization as a threat to national identity (125, 133, 293,
295, 300).[18]

The Moor's heterosexual but deformed body becomes the site of
intense anxiety about male identity and masculinity. However, in addition to being physically deformed, the protagonist is also religiously and
spiritually maimed as he is a racial and ethnic hybrid blending together
different religions (he is half-Jewish, half-Catholic). The Moor declares
"[m]ine is the story of the *fall from grace* of a high-born cross-breed: me,
Moraes Zogoiby, called 'Moor,' for most of my life the only male heir to
the spice-trade-'n'-big-business crores of the da Gama-Zogoibydynasty
of Cochin, and of my banishment from what I had every right to think
of as my natural life by my mother Aurora" (emphasis added, 5). This
condition of being banished by his mother, about which the Moor
relentlessly wails throughout his narrative, becomes a predominant
trope in the novel, and, within this context of exile, different aspects of
masculinity, including male identity, homophobia, homosocialism, and
homoeroticism, are problematized. The condition of exile and banishment is subsequently related to themes of nationalism and homophobic
fundamentalism; the burden of expatriation becomes a predicament for
the postcolonial country that is banishing its inhabitants. The novel is a
narrative of intense betrayal where postcolonial India, or "Mother
India," as the novel suggests, has emasculated and deceived her sons and
has not lived up to its promise of a secular state. Due to this betrayal,
postcolonial India continues to engender profound anxieties about racial
desire, sexual desire, masculinity and masculine desire, heterosexuality,
and femininity. However, what is at stake is the question of masculinity
and virility. Homoerotic desire is consistently displaced and deferred
into various categories of homosocial conflicts, sexual ambivalence,

political contention, and national and racial dispute. By carefully ascribing the genealogy of the Moor's family to Portuguese, Jewish, Spanish, Arabic, and Indian roots, the novel reveals how racial splits question the homogeneity of race and sexual desire in postcolonial India. Subsequently, masculine desire along with racial desire rupture national unity; diasporic dispersals fracture male identity and the notion of "nation" uncovers the construction of masculinist power and knowledge.

While the Moor symbolizes the physical, spiritual, and racial deformation of the nation, his uncle's sexual identity questions the heterosexual conformity of male desire in India. The Moor's genealogy is further flawed by his uncle's masculine desire, and Aires, the gay character in the novel, is portrayed as a flamboyant Victorian dandy: "brilliantine struggling to keep slicked-down his thick, wavy, white hair premature whitening . . . how my great-uncle postured! . . . what a ridiculous figure he cut in his monocle, stiff collar, and three-piece suit of finest garbardine" (12). Aires is the typical "preening Anglophile dandy" (198). Dandyism, as Richard Dellamora suggests, was associated in the nineteenth century with a "eunuch strain" and with effeminacy, which often connotes male-male desire (199)[19]. Similarly, Ashis Nandy explains that colonial masculinity and culture in India revolved not so much around the opposition between masculinity and femininity, but rather between masculinity and effeminacy which was in turn associated with homoeroticism (8). Aires's narrative constructs his gayness through his dandyism, and his dandyistic pose combined with his luxurious, indolent, leisurely, and aristocratic lifestyle undercut the significance of his role as a gay man in postcolonial India. His ostentatious Wildean dandyism, while delineating the multiplicity of masculine identity, reduces the complexity of Aires's gay sexuality. To a large extent, Aires's dandyism deflects the significance of his struggle to confront both colonial and neocolonial masculinist tendencies in postcolonial India, and Aires becomes a comic caricature. In addition, Aires's dandyism promotes a certain amount of indifference in him towards his wife Carmen's distress, and he comes across as a misogynist. His treatment of Carmen further stereotypes and weakens the depiction of gay identity and sexuality (46, 49). Aires's homosexual identity becomes ineffectual, and his "closet" lifestyle is largely held responsible for Carmen's loneliness and oppression: "And Carmen in her solitary bed, her fingers reaching down for solace below her waist, entwined herself in herself, drank her own bitterness and called it sweet . . . excited herself with fantasies

of seductions . . . of seducing Aires's lovers . . . *O God think how many
new men he will find is finding has found in jail*" (47). However, when
Aires returns from imprisonment, he is confronted by an "altered wife"
who threatens to kill him: "'If you do not give up your shame and scandal then, Aires, I will kill you while you sleep.' He bowed to her . . . the
bow of a Restorations dandy. . . . He did not give up his adventures; but
became more circumspect . . . in a rented Ernakulam apartment. . . .
Through the chick-blinds thin blades of daylight fell across his body and
another's, and the cries of the market rose up to him and mingled with
his lover's moans.'" (49–50)

We are introduced to Aires when he marries Carmen but is
rumoured to have dressed himself in her wedding gown and spent the
night with his lover Henry, the Navigator:

> on her wedding night her husband had entered her bedroom late,
> ignored his terrified and scrawny young bride who lay virginally
> quaking in the bed, undressed with slow fastidiousness, and then
> with equal precision slipped his naked body (so similar in propor-
> tions to her own) into the wedding-dress . . . and left the room . . .
> Carmen . . . saw the wedding-dress gleaming in moonlight as a
> young man rowed it and its occupant away, in search of whatever it
> was that passed, among such occult beings, for bliss. (13)

The homoerotically charged encounter between Aires and Henry on the
wedding night figures as an unspeakable scene of desire between two
male lovers and more significantly as a voyeuristic spectacle which is at
once a discreet "secret" of the closet as well as a knowledge that is public:[20]

> The story of Aires's gowned adventure, which left great Aunt
> Sahara abandoned in the cold dunes of her unbloodied sheets, has
> come down to me in spite of her silence. Most ordinary families
> can't keep secrets . . . but then again, perhaps the whole incident
> was invented, a fable the family made up to shock-but-not-too-
> much, to make more palatable—because more exotic, more *beauti-
> ful*—the fact of Aires's homosexuality?(13)

This voyeuristic spectacle of the gay male body is exposed and displayed
for consumption on the wedding night and is displaced to uncover

secrets, aberrant liaisons, betrayals as well as to disclose Aires's lifestyle: "the story . . . put Aires's secret wildness into a pretty frock, hiding away the cock and arse and blood and spunk of it, the brave determined fear of the runt-sized dandy . . . but by no means faithful liaison with the fellow of the wedding-night boat, whom Aires baptized 'Prince Henry the Navigator.'" (14)[21] While the narrative allows the reader to decipher the subtle signs of gayness, to recognize the gay male body, the "secret" lifestyle of the gay character is constructed as a problem to simultaneously deflect and to make the homosexual more conspicuously visible to the public. However, Aires's gayness and promiscuous life eventually disintegrate; he is castigated for his transgressive behavior when Prince Henry is diagnosed with "a particularly pernicious strain of syphilis, and it soon became clear that Aires, too, had been infected" (117). Further, Aires attempts to shape a compromise between the masculine ideals of colonial India and the bourgeois marriage structure of postcolonial India. In this conflict Carmen, his wife, is caught in between, and the unspeakable display of desire between the two men is represented as a familiar scene of deceit when Aires's homosexual desire wrecks the heterosexual familial structure and bourgeois domesticity. As the Moor in the novel mourns: "Aires and Carmen's lives were painful and twisted, because they were living out a lie, and so sometimes their behaviour came out twisted too" (103). However, while for both Carmen and Aires the bourgeois fantasy of family crumbles, Carmen steps in not as an item of exchange but to nurse both Aires and Prince Henry: "'We better get you well,' she said, 'or who am I going to dance with the rest of my life? You,' and here she made the briefest of pauses . . . 'and your Prince Henry, too'" (117). After nursing them back to health she insists that "there was no need for Prince Henry to move out. 'Too many wars in this house and outside it' . . . 'Let us make at least this one three-cornered peace'" (117). She does not want Aires to masquerade and lead a double life.

Nonetheless, in Aires's case there is a certain anxiety of pretense and falseness in relation to his identity, an aberration between his lifestyle and his gender and sexuality as identity (epistemological and ontological), and the ways in which that gender and sexuality are masqueraded by the homosexual individual in society. Nevertheless, it is the outside heterosexual society that affirms Aires's male body as gay and culturally reifies his "homosexual" identity. From the onset of Aires's narrative, homosexuality functions as a "secret," an identity that necessitates exposure as well as concealment (13, 28, 49, 103, 117). Aires's homosexuality is portrayed as inauthentic and his homosexual difference as anxiety ridden, which is potentially identifiable as well as unidentifiable. In the process, Aires's sexual desire becomes more visible to the society.

However, in postcolonial India it is the construction of the "nation" that becomes the site of a particular heterosexual anxiety, about the inscriptions of postcolonial Indian masculinity, which in turn discloses homophobic paranoia. Neocolonial and fundamentalist movements reassert not only a heterosexual identification with the nation but reveal an epistemological crisis and paranoiac homophobic anxiety about what constitutes an Indian/Hindu/masculine nation:[22]

> I had seen India's beauty in that crowd with its soda-water and cucumber but with that God stuff I got scared. In the city we are for secular India but the village is for Ram. And they say *Ishwar and Allah is your name* but they don't mean it, they mean only Ram himself, king of Raghu clan. . . . In the end I am afraid that the villagers will march on the cities and people like us will have to lock our doors and there will come a Battering Ram. (55–56)[23]

The assertion of a vitriolic and virulent Indian/Hindu/masculine nation, "that corrosive acid of the spirit, that adversial intensity which poured into the nation's bloodstream" (351), culminated in the cataclysmic and tragic episode, when, due to the fundamentalist/religious/nationalist paranoia, the Babri Masjid was destroyed in Ayodhya by the insistent and brutal ramming of the "Battering Ram" (363–365). Further, this divisive construction of a postcolonial Indian nation that denies its own hybridity (in fact the fundamental philosophic tenet of Hinduism is metamorphosis) becomes the site of further ruptures and struggles where issues of nation, nationalism, gender, ethnicity, and sexuality are confronted and contested. The fundamentalist national reaction is no different from the colonialist construction of virulent hyper-masculinity and sexuality; both uncover an intense male anxiety about the integrity of male bodies, masculinity, and the nation-state (260, 262, 293, 299, 300, 365). The fundamentalist dogma is obsessed with a paranoic terror of the imbrication of nationalism and sexuality and in particular of homosexuality in the dominant cultural expression of postcolonial India (298–300). Whereas nationalism itself was dependent upon a Eurocentric tradition and on Western forms of knowledge and power,[24] therefore, the nationalist schema was already cathected by colonial politics, defiled as well as contaminated by Western sources. Consequently, the relation of nationalism to colonialism was one of homosocial avowal and disavowal, almost an erotic pursuit. If one denies the male desire of colonialism and nationalism, then the novel pursues the possibility of the bastardization of nationalism. Interestingly, the novel projects this racial and sexual contagion on the first Prime Minister of India—Jawaharlal Nehru—who is portrayed as an elite anglophile dandy rumoured to have had affairs with Lady Edwina Mountbatten (176). In addition, the Moor is supposedly the illegitimate son of Nehru and Aurora (175–178). (Aires names his dog "Jawahar.") At every stage of its narration, the novel questions the claims of legitimacy and purity of the nationalist movement, especially in terms of its native/Hindu/religious/nationalist schema. In postcolonial India, both nationalism and sexuality are in flux, a crisis precipitated by the conflicting displacement and insecurity of masculinity and masculine identity in colonialism, nationalism, globalism, and in neocolonial fundamentalism.

Nationalism endorses a distinct form of homosocial male bonding and male fraternity, and as the novel portrays, certain types of homosocial bondings are essential to the perpetuation of nationalistic jingoism. Masculine privilege is sustained by male friendships, alliances, or rivalries, irrespective of whether the characters involved are Aires, his brother Cameons, Aurora, her husband Abraham, the Moor, or Raman Fielding. Fielding, known as "mainduck" or "frog," was a "full time communalist politician one of the founders of 'mumbai Axis,' the party of Hindu nationalists named after the mother-goddess of Bombay" (230). Fielding is the ultimate embodiment and signifier of homophobic hyper-masculinity. In addition, the masculinity urged by Fielding and the Hindu fundamentalists he represents has a twofold project: it demands a disavowal of the feminine identification that colonialism implicated on Indian men, and also paradoxically embraces the hyper-masculinity of colonial identity, the brand of masculinity that underscores virility and masculine power (230, 231, 298, 299, 308, 309, 312). The novel exemplifies the epidemic national anxiety about masculinity, especially that of Hindu fundamentalism, as *the* fundamental crisis of postcolonial India, an apprehension that has spiralled since India's independence and its desire ergo to prove its own "masculine" prowess, not merely across its own borders but globally. Additionally, the anxiety of masculinity in postcolonial India exemplifies the modernist crisis of individual identity; an identity that is discursively imbricated by the sexual, national, and imperial definitions of masculinity and continually intersected by the postcolonial politics of nation, nationhood, and nation state.

Significantly in the novel, the theme of nationalism is predicated by a fetishized obsession with the Nation-as-Mother and the Mother-as-Nation to the extent that the difference between the mother and the nation is collapsed. This infatuated eros for the motherland, configured as the theme of nationalism and obsessive patriotism, is exemplified as erotic nationalism, inasmuch as the erotics of nationalism and sexuality are sustained by the image of the dominant, controlling, and powerful mother-as-nation and nation-as-mother. With reference to the Jenkins's homosexual affair and scandal during Lyndon B. Johnson's presidential term, Lee Edelman exposes the threat posed to national security when male sexual desire is brought to the forefront of society: the "mobilization of this figure places homosexuality in a conceptual space contiguous with, and impinged upon by, an anxiety-producing image of the power that women wield as mothers" (276). Similarly, in Rushdie's novel the symbolic power of woman-as-mother and mother-as-nation, especially as the "anxiety-producing" and castrating mother/land, is embodied in the figure of Mother-India, Epiphania, Carmen, Aurora, including Indira Gandhi, one of the Prime Ministers of India: "Motherness—excuse me if I underline this point—is a big idea in India, maybe the biggest: the land as mother, the mother as land . . . I'm talking *major* mother country" (137). The mother's relation to the son is incestuous, which is reinforced by Rushdie's use of *Mother India*, the famous cinematic representation of nationalism: "Aurora could not refrain from raising the subject . . . of mother-son relations. . . . And now look—you have gone and marry-e'ed him! . . . to marry your own son, I swear, wowie." (137) In the novel, due to the incapacitating abilities of mothers towards their sons, the mother is condemned for emasculating, castrating, and effeminizing her sons. The Moor's sterile feelings of inadequacy and impotency are compounded by a sense of betrayal by his "mothers," which increasingly leads him to doubt his "manhood" (223, 235, 288, 316). Aires and Moraes are both stifled by their mothers, "Mother India who loved and betrayed and ate and destroyed and again loved her children" (60–61). As for Aires, his conflicted identity along with the void created by an absent father (his own father committed suicide) compounded by an impotent Fatherland, entangle him in a widening web of homoerotic desire (28). Aires's homosexuality is further blamed on the overarching figure of the dominant and controlling mother who usurps the role of the father (18, 26, 33). His homosexual desire is triggered by his crisis of paternity, on both personal and political levels: he is deprived of both personal and political paternal legacies. Additionally, it is within this setting and constraints of a generic patriarchy in colonial and postcolonial contexts that the crisis of male homosexuality, effeminacy, and male emasculation are portrayed.

However, another constraint is enacted in the novel that I want to interrogate; and that is the figure of the mother who is convicted of strangling her child and annihilating the family and the nation: "And maybe I'm right; or maybe this attitude, too, is a part of my complaint, maybe this-what?—this fucked-up dissident mind-set, too, is all my mother's fault" (206). The novel's portrayal of the mother figure is extremely problematic. While the figure of the mother is condemned for emasculating and effeminizing her sons, she is also burdened with the guilt of pushing her son to homosexuality. A predominant concern of paternity is that the suffocating and overpowering mother coerces her son to be more dependent on her than on the father-figure, which in turn leads to homosexuality (Edelman 276–277, Kristeva 13). However, by making the figure of the mother the site for the conflicts of postcolonial India, the complexities of Aires, the gay identity, are also weakened.

The novel ends with the following invocation to his mother "[s]he, too, had gone beyond recall, and she never spoke to me, never made confession, never gave me back what I needed, the certainty of love" (432). As the Moor finds reconciliation in the art of narration, "[a]s for me, I went back to my table, and wrote my story's end" (432), he also captures a moment to pause and discontinue, if possible, his traumatic extirpation from his mother/land and to ruminate on "his" story from the land of his ancestors in Spain from where his Jewish ancestors were expelled in 1492 (72). He returns to Benegeli with a "last sigh for a lost world" (4) to recount how his ancestor, the Sultan Boabdil of Granada, was evicted by Catholic monarchs Fernando and Isabella (80). This moment of banishment, 1492, set into motion the long line of exile due to which all the male inheritors of the Sultan, including the Moor, are diasporic or "wanderers of the earth":

> He departed into exile with his mother and retainers, bringing to a
> close the centuries of Moorish Spain; and reining in his horse upon

the Hill of Tears he turned to look for one last time upon his loss, upon the palace and the fertile plains and all the concluded glory of al-Andalus . . . at which sight the Sultan sighed, and hotly wept— whereupon his mother, the terrifying Ayxa the Virtuous, sneered at his grief. Having been forced to genuflect before the omnipotent queen, Boabdil was now obliged to suffer a further humiliation at the hands of an impotent (but formidable) dowager. *Well may you weep like a woman for what you could not defend like a man*, she taunted him . . . she despised this bubbling male, her son, for yield- ing up what she would have fought for to the death. (80)

The Moor acknowledges to Sultan Boabdil, "*I too am thy mother's son*" (80) and is able to find consolation by reclaiming his lost paternity and male heritage. While he gains solace in narration and gains a sym- bolic "home," Aires, his gay uncle, is not granted any such consolations; he is left without a "home." For a postcolonial gay subject, such as Aires, issues of estrangement and alienation are further exacerbated by the trends of global diaspora; and issues of nation, nationhood, ethnic nationality, and "home" are particularly conflicted. In Aires's postcolo- nial India, fundamentalism, especially Hindu fundamentalism, compli- cates the condition of exile and home. The notion of home in the nation state is a formation that is in flux even within normative heterosexual- ity, whereas, when uprooted by issues of colonialism, nationalism, and neocolonialism, the notion of "home" for gay identities questions not merely racial and gender complexities but sexual multiplicity. The sense of rootlessness is further complicated when queerness and diaspora intersect to question postcolonial global contexts, especially as they influence transnational culturalism.

While the novel represents gay identity through a minor character, there is no evidence of a possibility of change in the parameters of the role of gay identity in postcolonial India. Amongst all the chatter of colonialism, postcolonialism, nationalism, and fundamentalism there is an engulfing stripping away of male sexuality as a political necessity, a distillation that can potentially fatigue the reader. The portrayal of Aires' gayness remains a weak depiction of alternative sexuality as it is caught within the intricate web of colonialism, postcolonialism, funda- mentalism, and nationalism. Aires's membership in the upper echelon of Indian society instills in him a confidence that is grounded in his wealth rather than in his sexual identity; his alternative sexuality fails to deter- mine his selfhood. In several ways the novel entertains the colonial phobia for sexuality and shows an unwillingness to avail itself of the lessons of history, and the stereotypes of sexuality prevail. Filtered through a fundamentalist anxiety (a fundamentalism that attempts to assert cohesion through a negation of differences), the use of sexuality as an identity easily erupts into a parody that is denied and choked of any cultural representation or of multivarious coterminous possibilities. The disjunctive norms of alternative sexuality are caught within the dichotomy of East/West, colonizer/colonized, homosexual/heterosexual, female/male, with the West signifying modernism/progress and the Orient a symbol of paganism/crude practices. My concern is with the space of sexuality as an identity in postcolonial India that Aires leaves and the manner in which he avoids or fails to express the totality of his hyphenation as a postcolonial-gay-man and that of his other margins. My goal is not to define or limit Aires as a character. He deserves the freedom to define himself. Instead, this chapter aims to clarify the manner in which the portrayal of Aires's gay subtext, while attempting an independent vista, ultimately authorizes homosexuality solely as a specter reinforcing the existing colonial structure.

NOTES

1. For a complex analysis of the sexual politics in colonialism I am indebted to both Joseph Boone, "Vacation Cruises; or, The Homoerotics of Orientalism," and Marjorie Garber, *Vested Interests: Cross-Dressing and Cultural Anxiety*. Both these works have influenced my understanding of the politics of sexuality in colonialism.

2. For a more detailed analysis of the connections between colonialism, masculinity, and decadence see my article, "Imperial Dependency, Addiction, and the Decadent Body."

3. Most of the critical theories in colonial and postcolonial studies tend to overlook the issue of same-sex desire. Several of these theories elaborate on the effect of colonial or postcolonial contexts with respect to gender or class but almost always neglect the question of homoeroticism. Similarly, certain theoretical frameworks fleetingly mention the issue of homoeroticism but do not engage in this issue in a sustained manner with a detailed analysis.

4. However, recently Anne McClintock carefully analyzes how social categories of race, gender, ethnicity, class, and sexuality powerfully implicated the colonial project and rule, especially pages 75–180.

5. I am particularly indebted to the following works: Joseph Boone, "Vacation Cruises; or The Homoerotics of Orientalism"; Marjorie Garber, *Vested Interests*; Christopher Lane, *The Ruling Passion* and *The Burdens of Intimacy*; Kaja Silverman, *Male Subjectivity at the Margins*; Steve Neale, "Masculinity as Spectacle"; Eve Sedgwick, *Between Men* and *The Epistemology of the Closet*; Teresa De Lauretis, "Sexual Indifference and Lesbian Representation."

6. See Tania Modleski, *Feminism Without Women: Culture and Criticism in a "Postfeminist" Age* (New York and London: Routledge, 1991), where she mentions the criticisms that are levelled against Sedgwick's analysis for "driving a wedge between gay men and straight men" (12). See also Lane (1995), 8–9.

7. My analysis moves away from Sedgwick's model, especially in her analysis of the positioning of women, to use her phrase "between men." Sedgwick maintains that women's identity is affected in homosociality especially when men exchange women to bind themselves in relationships of kinship and reciprocity. In Sedgwick's framework homosociality is a triangular desire where woman's identity is caught within the politics of male allegiances and binding of male society. Woman becomes an exchange item and, as Gayle Rubin contends, it results in the "traffic in women." The role of women, to a large extent, is in fostering and nourishing positive bonds between men and in bringing them together. According to Sedgwick, women regulate men's desire and function as cohorts of a "potentially erotic" relationship of men for men. Further, Sedgwick also argues that patriarchal cultures, which are based on male coalitions, are also intensely homophobic. So men will be compelled to direct their desire and intimacy through women, and women mediate men's desire for each other.

8. European women to a large extent reinforced white solidarity and demarcations of racial boundaries. Further, several scholars of Lesbian and Gay studies have examined the difficulty of Sedgwick's term "homosocial," and these critiques are extremely useful for colonial and postcolonial contexts.

9. See also Homi Bhabha, "The Other Question," p. 19. Similarly, Sander Gilman claims that the Hottentots, especially the black female, prevailed as the essence of the black in the nineteenth century. Gilman also argues that the sexuality of the black becomes an icon for deviant sexuality during the colonial period, and "deviant sexuality" is the most notable marker of decadence and of "otherness" (209).

10. It is astonishing that Foucault in *The Order of Things* attributes the constitution of the "other" to the beginning of the nineteenth century and investigates how the negative aspects of Western culture was transferred to the "other" but does not analyze the discourse of colonization (see Chari, "Imperial Dependency," 219). For an analysis of how Foucault's examination of sex eludes colonial politics of race, see Ann Laura Stoler, pgs. 1–94.

11. For questions of masculinity see Maurice Berger, Brian Wallis, and Simon Watson, eds., *Constructing Masculinity*; Harry Stecopoulos, and Michael Uebel, eds., *Masculinities;* Anne Stoler, *Race And The Education of Desire*. See also, Mrinalini Sinha, *Colonial Masculinity: The 'Manly Englishman' and the 'Effeminate Bengali,'* which draws connections between colonialism and masculinity. Sinha does not take into consideration issues of same-sex desire and passingly refers to homosexuality.

12. For more detailed analysis of colonial masculinity, especially for differentiations of cultural value systems between the "manly" Englishman and the "effeminate" Bengali babu, see Mrinalini Sinha. She also provides a detailed analysis of the impact of colonial masculinity on the course of Indian history and the legal systems.

13. The term "homosocial" is used catachrestically throughout this essay to analyze the ambivalence of either rivalry or intense male bonding amongst men and to examine male relationships that can be perceived as erotic or potentially erotic.

14. Rushdie's fascination with Islamic culture and religion continues to haunt this novel even though it is not as overtly concerned with Islam as is his earlier novel, *The Satanic Verses*. However, one cannot help but register the embedded reference to Islam when he traces the religious and cultural genealogy of the Moor; the Moor is the offspring of Judaism and Catholicism analogously reflecting the religious lineage of Islam.

15. Rushdie, however, does point out that his Moor was handsome: "I must say without false modesty that, for all my South Indian dark skin . . . and with the exception of my crippled hand, I did indeed grow up good-looking; but for a long time that right hand made me unable to see anything but ugliness in myself" (162).

16. Interestingly enough at this point of the narrative the two da Gama brothers—Camoens and Aires—are arrested echoing the imprisonment of the Indian nationalists by the British:

> In June 1925 the da Gama brothers were sentenced to fifteen years' imprisonment. The unusual severity of the judgement led to some speculation that the family was being paid back for Francisco's involvement with the Home Rule Movement. . . . Many Menezes and Lobo men, and some women, were jailed or condemned. . . . (40)

17. Partha Chatterjee, noting the importance of history as a source of nationhood, points out that "Hindu nationalism" is synonymous with "Indian nationalism" and is a modern concept. He also argues that the seeds for the Hindu fundamentalist movement in postcolonial India were sown during the

Indian nationalist movement's struggle for independence against colonial Britain. "The majority 'community' is Hindu; the others are minorities. . . . This view, which today is being propagated with such vehemence in postcolonial India by Hindu-extremist politics, actually originated more than a hundred years ago, at the same time Indian nationalism was born" (1993, 110). Rushdie refers to the rise of Hindu fundamentalism, especially the Bharatiya Janata Party (BJP) and its election slogan to achieve "Ramrajya," or Rama's rule, which was synonymous with ideal rule. Ramrajya never implied a "Hindu" rule other than a just rule. However, the ruling BJP party, synonymously interchanged "ideal" with "Hindu" and denied the inherent pluralism of Hinduism (55–56, 351) The "battering ram" refers to the "ramming" of one single religion and to the violent destruction of the Babri Masjid in Ayodhya, considered as Rama's birthplace, by Hindu fanatics in 1992. Countrywide communal riots followed after the attack in which several hundreds died. Further, for Indian nationalism's dependence on colonialism see, Ashis Nandy, 1983, and Partha Chatterjee, 1986, 1993.

18. I am particularly referring to the portrayal of homophobia, homosexuality, and masculinity in literary works such as Wilkie Collins, *The Moonstone*; Charles Dickens, *The Mystery of Edwin Drood*; Oscar Wilde, *The Picture of Dorian Gray*, etc.

19. "In the nineteenth century, 'effeminacy' as a term of personal abuse often connotes male-male desire, a threat of deviance that seems to haunt gentlemen should they become too gentle, refined, or glamourous" (Dellamora, 199). Similarly, James Eli Adams argues that in attacks on the Tactarians during the Victorian period what emerged was a "gendered rhetoric that facilitated the subsequent sexualizing of gender transgression, in which 'effeminacy' was seen not as a public failure . . . but as the outward manifestation of a private, sexual deviance" (17). Further, Adams with reference to Carlyle argues that "his writings are incessantly preoccupied with the dandy as a figure of masculine identity under stress" (24). The analysis of the dandy as "a figure of masculine identity under stress" is relevant to Aires's position in postcolonial India. However, both Richard Dellamora and James Eli Adams point out that the Victorian dandy did not belong to the aristocratic classes but was instead predominantly middle class. They also argue that Reginia Gagnier misplaced the "dandy" in high society because the dandy is a middle-class phenomenon in the Victorian age. Nonetheless, in *The Moor's Last Sigh*, Aires belongs to the leisurely upper aristocratic class, fashioned after the flamboyant Wildean dandy. However, neither Dellamora nor Adams connects his analysis of the role of the dandy to colonial or postcolonial masculinity; their analyses pertains to the role of the dandy in the Victorian age and how it affected different aspects of Victorian masculinity.

20. Sedgwick notes that as a result of the Wilde trials the new public discourse on male homosexuality was simultaneously "minoritizing" and "univer-

salizing." The discourse pertaining to male homosexuality she describes as "the occluded intersection between a minority rhetoric of the 'open secret' or glass closet and a subsumptive public rhetoric of the 'empty secret'" (164). Sedgwick's analyses of the discursive complexities of the "secret" and of the "secrecy" of the gay closet, which are simultaneously private as well as public knowledge, are pertinent to Aires's homosexual lifestyle (1990, 164–165).

21. Steve Neale's analysis of the spectacle of masculinity and of spectatorship in Hollywood cinema is relevant to Aires's display of his gay identity as spectacle on his wedding night. Neale defines and differentiates between three psychic functions that influence the male as object of the look—identification, voyeurism, and fetishism—and demonstrates how all of these attempt to disguise or deflect homoeroticism: "in a heterosexual and patriarchal society the male body cannot be marked as explicitly as the erotic object of another male look: that look must be motivated in some other way, its erotic component repressed" (281). These three aspects—identification, voyeurism, and fetishism are exhibited; however, Aires's display of the gay male body is clearly marked by male desire.

22. Contemporary Hindu revivalists and members of the Bharatiya Janata Party claim that the only manner in which India can achieve some recognition as a world power is by asserting its "Hindu" identity and masculinity. This affirmation was particularly revived when India recently conducted a series of nuclear tests. On hearing of the tests, Bal Thackeray, a chauvinist leader of the Shiv Sena Party exclaimed: "We have to prove that we are not eunuchs" (qtd. from Los Angeles Times, Tuesday, May 17, 1998, p. B7). Rushdie's portrayal of Mainduck or Raman Fielding is based on Bal Thackeray.

23. It must be pointed out that Hindu fundamentalism is very much an outgrowth of postcolonial globalism, largely supported and financed by expatriate Indians and their network and sites in cyberspace, especially in the United States. One could almost say that the "patriarchy" and "masculinity" of the Hindu fundamentalist movement are the main concern of postcolonial India and are predominantly prompted and supported by globalism and by corporate fundamentalism. The Hindu fundamentalist movement began with the rural to urban migration, was connected to nationalism, but has currently become a part of the metropolitan fabric of postcolonial India and is strongly affiliated to and influenced by postcolonial globalism, the global economy, and global politics.

24. Nationalism's dependence on colonialism and on Western forms of knowledge has been extensively researched and chronicled to establish that nationalism was cathected by colonialism and discursively implicated by the colonial process. See Ashis Nandy (1983), Partha Chatterjee (1986), and Gayatri Spivak (1988).

Works Cited

Adams, James Eli. *Dandies and Desert Saints: Styles of Victorian Masculinity.* Ithaca, N.Y.: Cornell UP, 1995.

Alloula, Malek. *The Colonial Harem.* Trans. Myrna and Wlad Godzich. 1981. Minneapolis: U of Minneapolis P, 1986.

Behdad, Ali. *Belated Travellers: Orientalism in the Age of Colonial Dissolution.* Durham, N.C.: Duke UP, 1994.

Berger, Maurice, Brian Wallis, and Simon Watson. eds. *Constructing Masculinity.* New York: Routledge, 1995.

Bhabha, Homi. "The Other Question . . . Homi K. Bhabha Reconsiders the Stereotype and Colonial Discourse." *Screen* 24 (1983): 18–36.

——— . *The Location of Culture.* London: Routledge, 1994.

Boone, Joseph. "Vacation Cruises; or, The Homoerotics of Orientalism." *PMLA* (110:1): 89–107.

Chari, Hema. "Imperial Dependency, Addiction, and the Decadent Body." *Perennial Decay: On the Aesthetics and Politics of Decadence.* Ed. Liz Constable, Dennis Denisoff, and Mathew Potolsky. Philadelphia: U of Pennsylvania P, 1999: 215–232.

Chatterjee, Partha. *Nationalist Thought and the Colonial World.* Delhi: Oxford UP, 1986.

——— . "A Religion of Urban Domesticity: Sri Ramakrishna and the Calcutta Middle Class." *Subaltern Studies* VII, ed. Partha Chatterjee and Gyanendra Prasad. Delhi: Oxford UP, 1991.

——— . *The Nation and its Fragments: Colonial and Postcolonial Histories.* Princeton, N.J.: Princeton UP, 1993.

Connell, R. W. *Masculinities.* Berkeley: U of California P, 1995.

Dellamora, Richard. *Masculine Desire: The Sexual Politics of Victorian Aestheticism.* Chapel Hill: U of North Carolina P, 1990.

De Lauretis, Teresa. "Sexual Indifference and Lesbian Representation." In *The Lesbian and Gay Studies Reader,* ed. Henry Abelove, Michele Aina Barale, and David M. Halperin, 141–158. New York and London: Routledge, 1993.

Edelman, Lee. "Tearooms and Sympathy, or, The Epistemology of the Water Closet." In *Nationalisms and Sexualities,* ed. Andrew Parker, Mary Russo, Doris Summer, and Patricia Yaeger, 263–284. New York: Routledge, 1992.

Foucault, Michel. *The Order of Things: An Archaeology of the Human Sciences*. New York: Vintage, 1973.

———. "The Deployment of Sexuality." *The History of Sexuality*. Vol. I: An Introduction. New York: Random House, 1980.

Garber, Marjorie. *Vested Interests: Cross-Dressing and Cultural Anxiety*. New York: Routledge, 1992.

Halperin, David. *One Hundred Years of Homosexuality and Other Essays on Greek Love*. New York and London: Routledge, 1990.

Kabbani, Rana. *Europe's Myths of Orient: Devise and Rule*. London: Macmillan, 1986.

Kristeva, Julia. *Powers of Horror: An Essay on Abjection*. Trans. Leon Roudiez. New York: Columbia UP, 1982.

Lane, Christopher. *The Ruling Passion: British Colonial Allegory and the Paradox of Homosexual Desire*. Durham, N.C. and London: Duke UP, 1995.

———. *The Burdens of Intimacy: Psychoanalysis and Victorian Masculinity*. Chicago and London: U of Chicago P, 1999.

Lowe, Lisa. *Critical Terrains: French and British Orientalisms*. Ithaca, N.Y.: Cornell UP, 1991.

McClintock, Anne. *Imperial Leather: Race, Gender and Sexuality in the Colonial Context*. New York and London: Routledge, 1995.

Nandy, Ashis. *The Intimate Enemy: Loss and Recovery of the Self Under Colonialism*, Delhi: Oxford UP, 1983.

Neale, Steve. "Masculinity as Spectacle." In *The Sexual Subject: A Screen Reader in Sexuality*. London and New York: Routledge, 1992.

Rushdie, Salman. *Satanic Verses*. New York: London and Viking, 1988.

———. *The Moor's Last Sigh*. New York: Random House, 1995.

Said, Edward. *Orientalism*. New York: Vintage, 1979.

———. "Orientalism Reconsidered." In *Literature, Politics and Theory: Papers from the Essex Conference, 1976–84*, ed. Francis Barker, Peter Hulme, Margaret Iversen, and Diana Loxley. London: Methuen, 1986.

Sedgwick, Eve Kosofsky. *Between Men: English Literature and Male Homosocial Desire*. New York: Columbia UP, 1985.

———. *Epistemology of the Closet*. Berkeley: U of California P, 1990.

Silverman, Kaja. *Male Subjectivity at the Margins*. New York: Routledge, 1992.

Sinha, Mrinalini. *Colonial Masculinity: The "Manly Englishman" and the "Effeminate Bengali" In The Late Nineteenth Century*. New York: St Martin's P, 1995.

Spivak, Gayatri Chakravorty. "Subaltern Studies: Deconstructing Historiography." *Selected Subaltern Studies*. Ed. Ranajit Guha and Gayatri Chakravorty Spivak, 3–32. Oxford: Oxford UP, 1988.

Stoler, Ann Laura. *Race and The Education of Desire: Foucault's History of Sexuality and the Colonial Order of Things*. Durham, N.C. and London: Duke UP, 1995.

Stecopoulos, Harry, and Michael Uebel, eds. *Race and the Subject of Masculinities*. Durham, N.C.: Duke UP, 1997.

Suleri, Sara. *The Rhetoric of English India*. Chicago: U of Chicago P, 1992.

Weeks, Jeffrey. *Sexuality and Its Discontents: Meanings, Myths and Modern Sexualities*. New York: Routledge, 1985.

Williams, Raymond. *The Politics of Modernism: Against the New Conformists*. London: Verso, 1989.

Woolf, Virginia. *Orlando: A Biography*. New York: Harcourt Brace Jovanovich. 1973, c. 1928.

CHAPTER TWELVE

By Way of an Afterword

SAMIR DAYAL

In this Afterword, my aim is to highlight some of the important issues raised by the contributors to this collection and to identify elements of an ongoing project for queer studies that emerges from a consideration of these issues. The collection traverses several disciplinary borders, including those that define literary studies, gender studies, cultural studies, and postcolonial studies. Such a cross-disciplinarity is required if one wishes, as many contributors here evidently do, to situate queer studies in a global frame. The chapters appeal to a general audience, recognizing that queer studies must address a wider readership than gay, lesbian, bisexual, and/ or transgender (GLBT) communities as such. And John Hawley, in his introduction, briefly traces the traveling of "queer theory" from the terrain previously demarcated by terms such as "gay" and "lesbian." The shared premise here is that "queerness" entails a queering of the pitch, a displacement of colonial, heteronormative, or otherwise hegemonic stratifications, and that a queer perspective constitutes an interrogation, implicitly at least, of the way in which all subjects, not only GLBT subjects, are interpellated as gendered bodies within a given social space. For what often causes discomfort is when these bodies refuse to stay within disciplined, normative categories. This broadening of the critique of normativity (call it "queering") is as great a political imperative as ever, and is certainly a live issue in the public sphere—witness the recent debates on the question of the legal status of same-sex couples in Vermont or, further afield, the debates in France around the issue of granting full partner rights to unmarried partners, in the case of either heterosexual or same-sex couples. I suggest that what emerges as a still underdeveloped dimension of queer theory is the frame it proffers for a rethinking of normalizing heterosexuality and its more liminal practices, particularly having to do with a disavowed but pervasive (if sometimes only fantasmatic) homoeroticism. The greatest promise for a postcolonial queer theory may be in participating, at the level of public discourse, in an ongoing reeducation of desire. This is a project through which queer theory could make itself a powerful and more broadly influential force.

This collection takes as diacritical the distinction between terms such as "gay" or "lesbian" on the one hand and "queer" on the other. Michael Warner, in the introduction to *Fear of a Queer Planet*, suggests that this distinction really came to the fore in the 1990s. As he indicates, the embrace of "queer" over "gay" represents a commitment to a more systematic and thoroughgoing critique of and resistance to heteronormativity in all its guises (xxvi). Queering would entail not merely adding to an existing mainstream of gay and lesbian discourse but a radical reconstitution of the panoply of cultural discourses, including the discourse of sexuality as well as aesthetic or socioeconomic theory or medical (and more generally) scientific discourse. Warner maintains that the insistence on the term queer "has the effect of pointing out a wide field of normalization, rather than simple intolerance, as the site of violence"; for him, its "brilliance as a naming strategy lies in combining resistance on that broad social terrain with more specific resistance on the terrains of phobia and queer-bashing, on the one hand, or of pleasure, on the other" (xxvi).

As Joël Dor reminds us, it was in the wake of Darwinism and subsequent developments in embryology that the notion of bisexuality, a "third sex," emerged; Freud's crucial contribution, a contribution in which the ideas of Wilhelm Fliess had a part, was to have dissociated psychic from biological bisexuality ("*De la différence des sexes*" 29). But the emergence of gay sexual identity as a *psychic* alternative was also overdetermined by the advent of capitalism. John D'Emilio's "Capitalism and Gay Identity" here develops the thesis that capitalism is what made possible the emergence of gay identity—not homosexual acts, but a political identification. And capitalism is what needs to be critiqued. Such concerns animate much of D'Emilio's work. His book, *Sexual Politics, Sexual Communities*, first published in 1983 and then republished in a second edition in 1998, traced the emergence of not only gay identity but of the gay movement and of what he calls a "homosexual minority" between 1940 and 1970 (the great watershed moment of course being the Stonewall riot of 1969). In it D'Emilio argued that since Stonewall gay resistance, including AIDS activism, has been "exceptional and sporadic rather than typical and sustained" (*Sexual Politics* 261) and it is only in a systemic sense—as part of a wider critique of sexuality as produced by capitalist cultural formations—that homophobia can be combated. What D'Emilio calls "homophile activism" can and should take as a part of its project not only a critique and a shaping of gay liberation, but a critique of and participation in the larger public sphere, including the global sphere.

Among the major emphases of many pieces collected here is the necessity to rethink the meaning of gay identities, or of gay identifications, in the era of globalization. If queering implies an oppositional edge, then the "cut" is most visible in the constructionist and antiessentialist theory of the subject. But while this queering is a useful counter to a simplistic identity politics, for many minorities it remains an imperative to assert an ethnic identity grounded in material specificity, in the everyday and the local—an identity that is firmly historicized. Besides, there is some suspicion of "performativity" as a liberal, elitist, or Eurocentric construct, even when that suspicion does not rest on the quicksand of a mistaken understanding (only too common) of performativity theory. These suspicions should not be whitewashed out of a postcolonial queer perspective. Given these caveats, however, it is important to note, in this retrospective overview, that many of the contributors to this collection conceive gay, lesbian, and bisexual identities as productively dissident, not just minority, identifications. Non-normative sexualities are emblematic of resistance against the onrushing homogenization of many facets of public life and private desire—a homogenization that is often globalization's byproduct. The Eurocentrism of the project of modernity makes rethinking of heteronormativity a sine qua non; but the wider theoretical implications of such a rethinking for understanding old and new subjectivities are also worth considering. Implicitly in agreement with the main argument of D'Emilio, Dennis Altman emphasizes in his contribution that as a sociological category, the concept of

gay or lesbian identity as a sociological category is of quite recent prove-
nance, and reminds us that its "survival even in Western developed
countries cannot be taken for granted." Freud had recognized in his
"Three Essays on the Theory of Sexuality" that object choice was independent of what he termed "inversion"—an invert being someone who
chooses as his or her object someone of the same anatomical sex. Only
in the twentieth century has the hetero-/ homosexual divide, along with
the rigid understanding of what makes someone "homosexual," come to
be naturalized in the Western mind. As early as 1971, in *Homosexual:
Oppression and Liberation*, Altman was already calling for an end of
"the homosexual," for an evacuation of the category "homosexuality."

Another important caveat in queer theory is presented by William
J. Spurlin's reminder (in his contribution to this collection) that "the axis
of sexuality [should not be allowed to] obscure and overexceed that of
gender so that the specificity of lesbian desire, which questions any
apparent parallels between lesbians and gay men, is not rendered invisible" and that gender should not be subordinated in the discursive privileging of sexuality as "the more avant-garde or . . . more volatile site of
resistance to normalization." In the wake of Judith Butler's popularization of "performativity"—and in the aftermath of the misapprehensions
and confusions of performativity with performance, even with cross-
dressing—Spurlin's caution also points out a direction in which gender
theory (and the theory of subjectivity too) needs fuller elaboration. Like
D'Emilio, as well as Spurlin and Gaurav Desai in this volume, Altman
too emphasizes the need to distinguish between homosexual acts and
gay identity. The guiding question of Altman's chapter is whether a uni-
versalist approach to gay identity can be "linked to modernity." Clearly,
he would want to insist on a plurality of gay identities, and of different
gay *communities* instead of *community*, for there looms always the danger that gay people are lumped together into a homogenous *and pathologized* group, just as in the case of racism. Paige Schilt also sounds the
caution in her chapter in this volume that "a belief in the theoretical universality of human experience does not necessarily dislocate European
culture's position as the pinnacle of that experience," and this holds even
more strongly if one is talking about normative sexual experience, about
homophobia and racism as analogous and sometimes intimately linked.

What is also represented in the collection is an important internal
critique of and *within* queer studies, and I consider this at some length
below as a symptom of a salutary self-consciousness, of a necessary con-

cern with the future of queer studies. This too is more than a gesture at the political. Almost all the essays point to the necessity of an ongoing engagement with the forms of GLBT identifications *and the constitutive contradictions—or difference* of queer subjectivities not only among geographical locations but also among cultural or ideological positions. Given my aim to highlight the achievements of the chapters and to point up future directions for such inquiry, I will argue that one crucial territory that remains undertheorized, even in these pages, is the psychic or psychoanalytic dimensions of desire in an exploration of those subjectivities, and through that exploration a quickening or freeing up of the erotic itself, which sometimes gets lost or ghettoized (or worse, pathologized) within a narrow cultural zone.

One way of going beyond the easy binarisms on which heteronormativity (and *a fortiori* homophobia) relies is to insist on the liminality of gender. Thus Altman in his chapter refers to the broad range of commentators who speak of a "third gender" or of a "third sex"—sometimes confusing the two terms. But as he points out, it was not until the flowering of the contemporary gay movement in the West that this confusion was even noticed. In Asia and the societies of the Pacific, the etiology of the conflation of a third gender and a third sex has been somewhat different. Many alternatives to the presumed binaries of Western sexual identity have emerged there, and if the transnational flows of globalized culture have done nothing else to challenge heteronormativity, they have complicated the understanding of modern sexualities in the West as well as posing a threat to traditional sexual norms in the East. Altman cites studies that document "four or five categories of sex/gender" in Thailand, and others that describe in Brazil an erotic economy different from the one that structures Western heteronormativity, hinging on the question of who penetrates whom. In Pakistan, sex acts and actual intimacy between males may exist in the absence of any sense of gay identity.

The destabilization of Western categories of normative sexuality (but also the panic and frisson that accompany such destabilization) is the motivating interest of Joseph Boone's chapter. An example of queer theory's method of testing the porosity of cultural, geographical, and sexual boundaries, this chapter rejects the presumed universality of Eurocentric definitions of homosexuality by counterposing these definitions with non-Western understandings of homosexual and heterosexual practices. In doing so, Boone highlights the instability of categories of identity but also points up the considerable anxiety occasioned by the fact that for many "white gay male [and, we might add, middle-class] subjects" the inscrutable non-Western "object of desire remains simultaneously same and other, a source of troubling and unresolved identification and differentiation." At the same time heterosexuality itself is rendered unstable in the non-West and especially in the "Orient."

That non-Western performatives may predate Western discourses of gay or queer *identity*, and may trouble the stability of these Western categories, is a case made by Desai in this collection. Desai avowedly borrows the frame of his critique from standard texts of Western queer studies, particularly D'Emilio, but the specifics of his argument point to another geopolitical space, namely Africa, as represented in the work of Ifi Amadiume. Amadiume shows, according to Desai's account, that in precolonial Nnobi culture, there was "a certain fluidity in the gender-sex system so that biological sex did not necessarily determine social gender," and that the contemporary fixing of gendered identities in this society "was not a precolonial legacy but rather a consequence of British colonial practices aimed at regulating the possible gender options available."

In his chapter Desai, like Boone, reintroduces the category of the raced other, a category that so often gets marginalized even within a body of work, such as queer theory, which is constituted in large measure by the struggle against marginalization at various levels and on several fronts. The category of the raced other is also central to Hema Chari's chapter; it takes as its point of origin the by now classic Saidian observation, also fundamental in Boone's chapter, that "the Orient" was the *locus classicus* for an exotic, "excessive" sexuality, full or irregular promise for Western travelers constrained by contemporary Western mores. The Orient then represents not only a geographic remoteness but a structural otherness, against which the Western subject can define itself. The Orient also functions as a "Sotadic Zone," in Richard Burton's phrase, as the zone proper to the "despotic" or dissolute other, who was at the same time dangerously seductive (Said 207). Chari's aim is to redirect attention to the dynamic of desire between European men and non-European men, precisely because such attention is rare in both queer studies and postcolonial studies; Chari hopes particularly to situate the figure of "male rape" within the lexicon of tropes representing the project(ion) of imperialism in the East. Her chapter draws together three strands of thought about the construction of homoerotic desire in

India, through a reading of Salman Rushdie's *The Moor's Last Sigh*—the issue of colonial masculinity and its imperilment, the counterposed image of the nation as Mother (without forgetting the rise of a patriarchalist Hindu fundamentalism), and finally the contemporary frame of diaspora in a global era.

Reading same-sex desire back into the colonial calculus certainly adds a dimension to the understanding of the traveling discourse of empire. The promise of this approach, probably not fully realized even in this collection, is that it could radically restructure the understanding of desire and its ambivalences in the colonial primal scene, where the structure of affiliation, we are told, yielded to the shuttling of affiliation. What would be required for such a radical restructuration of the analysis of colonial relations (between men and men, as well as between men and women, and relations between men that were themselves mediated by relationships with women—as well as between women)? Certainly more than the relatively surface-level analysis offered by Chari, of "male anxiety and terror." Because she takes stock of a fairly small slice of colonial reality, Chari cannot fully account for the erotic charge of the homosociality and even homosexuality as it drove the colonial adventure in South Asia. Nor can she account for the relative importance of the homosexual eros over against the more straightforward heterosexual eros (and ethos?) that pervades the more standard analyses, and even informs the otherwise nuanced work of Kenneth Ballhatchet, Ronald Hyam, or Ashis Nandy (whom Chari herself mentions). Rushdie's book, the focus of Chari's chapter, acknowledges that even postcolonial Indian culture has been able to tolerate only a highly sanitized picture of non-heteronormative desire, "hiding away the cock and arse and blood and spunk of it" (*The Moor's Last Sigh* 14). But Chari's chapter also erases much of the complexity of homoeroticism in the colony. It must be acknowledged then that it stops short of truly queering hegemonic approaches to colonial history, presumably the unspoken grail for such an enterprise. But this is really to say that the shortfall underscores the large ambition of the project in which it participates. Indeed, a major contribution of this collection as a whole is that it points powerfully to the need to develop (and make more sophisticated) queer theoretical approaches to colonialism that could illumine the relative *significance* of homoerotic desire in the annals of colonialism and area studies.

Like Desai, Boone, and Chari, Spurlin is interested in (what he terms) the "cross-cultural variations of the expression and representation of same-sex desire," and he too tries to link the registers of a post-colonial analysis with queer critique. For Spurlin the proliferation of non-Western queer identities and cultural production give the lie to the presumptive and presumptuous universalism that informs the practices and discourses of mainstream Western queer as well as heterosexist discourses. His reference to work describing homosexual practices in South Africa (such as "hlabonga" or non-penetrative sex) turns on a conceptual distinction between "homosexual" practices and sexual identity (or gender). Like Desai's chapter, Spurlin's seeks not only to question the "nationalistic" assertion that homosexuality is a Western export but also to "diversify representations of (homo)sexual identity as a social position that is always already *mediated* by race, gender, social class, and geopolitical politicization." He specifically ties in postcolonial theory to highlight the ways in which for instance the queer academic left sometimes betrays its own colonizing impulses, and the ways in which the West disavows its continuing cultural imperialism. This line of thought is especially promising, and more needs to be said about it. The authors in this volume reintroduce the connections between postcolonial and queer theories, but the linkages are only beginning to be explored. But if this collection is premised on the existence of such linkages between postcolonial and queer theories, it would nevertheless be wrong to suggest that these theories themselves presume or subtend a level, continuous terrain.

The asymmetries between the images of (GLBT) culture emerging from metropolitan locations in Euroamerica and the reality of (GLBT) life in the postcolonial non-West are the main subject of Altman's chapter in this collection. Altman calls attention to the internal contradictions in the "internationalization of gay identities." The emergence of a "commercial gay world" should not, he notes, obscure the "relative overrepresentation" of Latin America in this imagined market "as against the underrepresentation of Chinese East Asia." He stresses the political and cultural factors that impinge on the everyday life of GLBT people in the non-West who may be profoundly influenced by Western consumerism and elite gay discourse, but his ultimate concern is to suggest that these "other" gay people's interests may not be best served by a unipolar "internationalization" of the "gay world." One of his most persuasive arguments in favor of remaining open to the ongoing evolution of gay identity in the increasingly globalized world is that the "contemporary world is simultaneously experiencing the creation/solidification of identities and their dissolution: we don't know yet if identities based on sexuality will be as strong as those based on race or religion." This is intended to register a dissent against a hasty cognitive mapping of race, gender, and other identity-defining categories onto one another that has become customary in recent multiculturalist discourse. To Altman's critique we might add D. A. Miller's caution that we need to be careful even about the term "homosexual"; for terms such as "homosexual men" and "male homosexuals" are "redolent of psychiatry, the police, and social science, and historically assisting in the attempt . . . to stigmatize those so named (as sick, criminal, or just 'other')" (Miller 214).

For Donald Morton, however, it would seem that Altman's explicitly left-leaning rhetoric is finally no more than a pretty gesture. What is needed, writes Morton in this volume, is a weightier commitment to a global politics with the goal of social justice worldwide. Morton's focus is unswervingly on how members of the queer left, for whom Altman is an influential figure, have reneged on the issue of class after making the right overtures. Altman's announced goal is leftist resistance. But, according to Morton, while on the one hand Altman calls for an analysis of "global" connections, he on the other hand fails to "offer a coherent and rigorous theorization" of such connections. As Morton sees it, Altman's innocent antitheoreticism depends on a simplistic opposition of theory and activism, although perhaps some would want to defend Altman from the charge of being uninterested in theory. Jeffrey Weeks, for one, has suggested that Altman was the author of the inaugural study offering a "framework" precisely for a "new sexual politics" (Weeks 4). Actually, says Morton, what Altman and many others on the queer left are championing is not activism but (entrepreneurial) actionalism—a gut reaction to events. This visceral reaction "converges" with an enfeebled politics: "the 'knowing' anti-theoreticism of persons like Eve Sedgwick and David Halperin, who have absorbed their anti-theoreticism from (post)structuralism and Foucault and whom Altman mistakenly thinks he is 'opposing.'" Morton's claim is that behind the "call for an endlessly increasing 'subtlety' and recognition of 'complexity' is the desire to evade any form of determinate explanation of the global." The main target of this rejection is classical Marxism. As in (post)modern theory generally, such determinate explanations are consistently rejected by bourgeois theorists today as 'reductive,' on the one hand, and 'totalizing,' on the other. Morton wants to "re-stage the theoretical contesta-

tion over what is at stake in discussions of 'globalism' and 'sexual politics' among gay/queer theorists and critics in the 1990s."

What galls Morton is that under the guise of the easy "sexual solidarity" of many bourgeois queer writers, class gets elided or side-
stepped as an issue:

> What is . . . most telling in Altman's rejection of solidarity with the
> masses is that he could easily have expressed—as even many bour-
> geois queer writers routinely do—at least a 'sexual solidarity' with
> them, while side-stepping the issue of 'class.' This move would have
> been quite readily and easily made by most EurAmerican queer aca-
> demics. Altman's inability to do this should be read not in 'personal'
> terms but in terms of the material differences between the different
> situatedness of subjects in global capitalism. Those bourgeois intel-
> lectual workers most distant from the EurAmerican metropole may
> indeed be less fully or quickly interpellated into the latest form of
> EurAmerican bourgeois ideology.

Morton presents himself as a rare and brave defender of a materialist
queer theory. Yet there is also the opposite danger, that the catechism of
"resistance" as codified class critique can become a soporific alternative
to a careful attention to the nuances of gay identification. Such a catechism of resistance is not difficult to find, and at times even the most
self-aware critics can have recourse to it in such a way that it becomes a
crutch.

Morton objects to the "growing chorus of rejection of materialist
queer theory on the grounds that it is, in one way or another, somehow
'extreme.'" This objection is made, usually, by onlookers viewing class
struggle as a struggle by others, distanced from themselves. One of the
most obvious examples of this distancing is the "attitude" of postmodern irony. Irony, says Morton, has become a major trope in (post)mod-
ern queer theory. Irony is thought of in this theory as a suspicion of all
truth claims, the opposite, in a Rortyian language, of a metaphysics.
This suspicion of truth claims is one more instance of the antimaterial-
ist bias which Morton is attempting to describe. He writes that "Rorty
has retheorized irony—that is, updated it in (post)modern terms—in
such a way as to renew the concept's ideological usefulness to the ruling
class." Rorty displaces other distinctions than the metaphysical/ironic
distinction, according to Morton, such as the idealist/materialist divi-

sion. Morton's objection is that "[t]o accept the ironist's pragmatism . . . is to deny the possibility of radically transformative change; it is to install things-as-they-are rather than things-as-they-might-be as the measure of all one's practices." Rorty's irony has become mainstream and now serves as an "ideological tool" in the service of "cybercapitalism." Morton's declared project, therefore, is almost to *will* (or should that be *wish*?) queering into bearing a transformative potential; yet he seems to be less open to solidarism with queer theorists of a different stripe than his noble utopianism might lead one to expect.

After careful attention to Morton's important rehearsal of this internal critique, one still asks, Is it always necessary to declare one's left credentials before one can participate in the critique? It is one thing to suggest that the critique be made more complex, and I do so myself. It is quite another to paint the entire body of existing queer critique as being in denial of the realities of material class differentials. The question for Morton then is whether all theory that does not explicitly thematize a materialist analysis is by definition inferior to any critique that does. Is class analysis the only game in town when it comes to thinking about issues of queer and straight sexuality in contemporary global culture? Couldn't an analysis that focused on a careful account of the politics of health care for same-sex partners be quite valuable even if it neglected to provide a fully developed class analysis, which is admittedly part of the total story of health care and who gets it? Is it bourgeois bad faith to say that it is sometimes a matter of emphasis? One can certainly acknowledge the need for a wider *range* of emphases, including a class analysis, even if one does not perform such an analysis.

In fact one could argue that there is already such a range of analytic approaches within queer studies. There are many writers and cultural critics, such as Kobena Mercer and Isaac Julien, who could be mentioned as producing queer critique from within metropolitan spaces but without echoing the "completely routine gestures" of disavowal of economic materialism Morton imputes to metropolitan gay critique. Even among the contributors to this volume, a range of analysis is perceptible. The authors are sometimes more and sometimes less attentive to class difference. (This is admittedly not a reliable index to the quality or comprehensiveness of their chapters.) Chong Kee Tan, for instance, suggests that Taiwanese "*kuer*" or "*tongzhi*" negotiations of the global and the local, of "American homosexuality" and "local circumstances," provide examples of existing forms of queer thinking and writing; "hybrid

homosexualities" are not exactly rare in this globalized cultural landscape. In her contribution to the volume, Paige Schilt expressly suggests
one way in which such a critique might operate. She develops the ways
in which Julien's film, *The Darker Side of Black* (1993), queers the
"style and narrative voice" of British high culture as represented by the
BBC, not to mention the traditional humanism of which that style and
that voice speak: in the very appropriation of the narrative of the for-
merly imperial nation resides a queer critique that is neither oblivious to
the workings of capitalism nor insensitive to the socioeconomic differ-
entiae of culture. And Jarrod Hayes in his contribution to this collection
productively complicates the cultural location of Western homosexuality itself by suggesting that "the increasing conformity of same-sex
desire to the so-called Western paradigm might have as much to do with
a resistance to neo-colonial, late capitalist economic expansion as with
something imported by it." Hayes's reading, if correct, does not endorse
a picture of a simple bipolar hegemony of an elite Western gay/queer discourse that is oblivious to issues of political economy or disavows structural "difference." At least Hayes explicitly avows his desire to "nuance
our paradigms of globalizations." All of these approaches turn on a
recognition of class-stratified society.

It may indeed be, as Morton puts it, that "[n]ot all the world's
homosexual subjects can 'afford' to understand sexuality as
'autonomous.'" Yet Morton himself notes the challenge to dominant
white queer theory from some Asian-American quarters, and frequently
the refractions of queer identity in non-Western performatives. By the
same token, Morton's trenchant prose seems to be itself too narrowly
focused on one, hegemonic, elite metropolitan/Western queer discourse
as though it were *representative* of queer thinking *tout court*. Does not
Altman himself speak of a "small elite" who "see themselves as interconnected with a global network . . . and an international commercial
scene in which they participate"; and does he not say that many others
from similar class positions are sensitive to "cultural imperialism" and
the perils of an elite perspective on the role of sexual identification? It is
safe to say, the above notwithstanding, that Morton's critique points one
way forward for queer theory, one—but not necessarily the only—way
to maintain a necessary eternal vigilance against the policing of sexualities, against the construction of sexual normativity in the public sphere,
and against the distortions of mass-cultural, antiacademic, *and* high
intellectual understandings of sexual performativity.

While it is understandable that GLBT or queer studies may be hostile to any suggestion that they might aim at a wider public sphere than GLBT audiences, it is certainly worth considering whether a broader conversation might not further their causes. As Weeks has noted, the "cutting edge of gay radicalism in the early 1970s" had already questioned the "existing 'gayworld' for its 'ghetto mentality,' its emphasis on sexuality to the exclusion of wider cultural issues" and indeed of the exclusion of a more general eroticization. Likewise queer studies, particularly the edgier theoretical work informed by a Lacanian understanding of the subject, sometimes takes itself too seriously, or finds itself too embattled in the academy and its adjunct spaces such as the broadly defined psychoanalytic community, to allow the erotic to emerge in its full vigor. The project for queer theory and cultural intervention can be an ongoing reeducation and interminable retheorization of *desire* in response to found conditions, to actual material conditions, recognizing that they are indeed traversed by global cultural flows of desire, just as desire itself is mass-mediated in the global circulation of images. I am not proposing the celebration of a free-floating libido. Rather, a queer project could potentially set its sights ambitiously on the interminable reeducation of heterosexual desire as well—a kind of erotic *Bildung*. Or at least that is the promise of the future for the kind of work this collection seeks to represent.

Where to begin? And how to proceed? It is clear from Freud's work that the human being is fundamentally bisexual and polymorphously perverse, and only later acquires accretions and sedimentations of culturally approved sexual formations. The importance of this point has rarely been recognized by queer studies. Among the exceptions is Judith Butler's *The Psychic Life of Power*, which develops Freud's insight by arguing that people who grow up heterosexual do so by sacrificing a more primordial bisexuality or homosexuality—which sacrifice generates melancholy. Butler concludes that the heterosexual subject is constituted in part by a lost object (23, 133). My argument is that what a collection such as this one suggests is that the wider culture might be persuaded to think not of the exceptionality or freakishness of a GLBT sexual orientation, identity, or aesthetic formation, nor of the special interests represented by queer theory/practice, but rather of a certain universality of that constitutive loss.

Thus, outside this collection, in his chapter "Conclusion: The End of the Homosexual," Altman writes that "[a]s homosexuals come out they lead heterosexuals into a greater acceptance of their own sexuality, in part perhaps because many homosexuals are more aware of sexuality than are straights" (*Homosexual* 242)—they are more aware, he would say, of the significance of the lost object, and they could remind us all of this significance. "Gay liberation," he suggests therefore, will also entail straight liberation, and even lead to the liberation of a "new human" that follows from the disappearance of the homosexual as we know him or her (247). While the language may seem dated and the generalizations rather broad, Altman's point is well taken, I believe, because it calls for a wider horizon to what thirty years after Altman's book was first published has come to be called queer studies. And on occasion, Altman's language seems, even in this relatively early book, to have a contemporary freshness, as when he writes that "To see the total withering away of the distinction between homo- and heterosexual is to be utopian. I suspect however, it will come before the withering away of the state and may indeed be a necessary prelude to that" (246). Since at least the McCarthyite 1950s, there has been a pattern of "labelling . . . lesbians and homosexuals as moral perverts and national security risks" (D'Emilio, *Sexual Politics* 49). But the disjunctures between nation and queerness have also been a central preoccupation of a more recent generation of scholars and remain today a vexed issue (see for instance Duggan, Berlant and Freeman, Ratti, Gopinath, and Hardt and Negri). Even today there remains a tendency to deny membership of GLBT people the unconditional citizenship that is implied by a full sense of "belonging" to a nation, so one has to be cautious even today about drawing analogies between the citizenship status of African Americans or immigrants or other minority constituencies and that of GLBT people who identify as queers: they may even see differences between their concerns and those of feminists, and may be more reluctant than other groups to endorse the antistatist or postnational stance than other progressive groups steeped in postcolonial theory. This distinction needs to be respected now and in the foreseeable future, and writers represented in this collection could do worse than keep such differences before themselves and their readers. Queer theory, in any case, must maintain a critical tension with postcolonial theory.

To put it differently, cultural understandings of heterosexuality (which is often seen as "sexuality" *tout court*, against which other forms of erotic expression are seen as distortions or departures) can be "redressed" continually by advances in thinking about homosexuality.

Can queer studies offer a stage where the erotic can sport and, dare I say, play a part in regenerating the sense of the erotic even of heterosexual readers, so that queer studies can speak not only to the choir? The sometimes recherché verbal *jouissances* of Lacan's labyrinthine lexicon on the one extreme and the exclusivity of the sometimes too stridently pornographic GLBT "erotic" literature and cultural production equally leave one wishing there were some more public, even somewhat more communitarian mode of achieving a broader sentimental reeducation of desire. Drawing on Foucault, Jonathan Katz has written that "we need to focus . . . on the ways eroticism is produced, now and in the past, noting how . . . social-sexual systems regulate and control individuals and populations" (171). Katz wants a recognition of the fact that there would be "no reason for the hetero/homo division if heteros did not stand above homos in a social hierarchy of superior and inferior pleasures" (187). But Katz also rightly cautions against any utopian or oracular projections about the future of pleasure. He argues for a more reactive model: "we construct the shape of future sex as we act up in the present in response to AIDS, gay and lesbian rights, domestic partnership benefits. . . . As we struggle to create a society less productive of pain, more productive of pleasure, we invent the sexuality of tomorrow" (189). He echoes Altman's call for a destruction of the categories of homosexual and heterosexuality, but ultimately seems to end up, despite his own reservations, endorsing an individualist, we-are-one-world kind of universal "future pleasure system"—a kind of exaggeratedly American embrace of "life, liberty, and the pursuit of happiness" (190–91). My own preference would be for a greater suspicion of the libertarian predilection to seek individualist pleasure. Alongside a greater freeing of desire, a postcolonial queer studies can enable a greater cultural and theoretical sophistication about the construction of sexualities along with a greater commitment to the agonistic politics and practices of pleasure.

Morton mocks the "thorough devotion" of "most gay/queer theory/studies writers" to "the pursuit of pleasure, jouissance, erotic satisfaction" at the expense of class, but his recommendations are quite different from my own. In support of his preference for the Marxist over the Freudian paradigm (to say nothing of a Lacanian paradigm), he invokes Ann Foreman's rejection of "the unconscious" in favor of "consciousness." Altman, by marked contrast, writes in this collection that "[t]here is a need to examine emotional as much as sexual fantasies." There certainly are other alternatives than a reductively aestheticized notion of desire on the one hand and on the other a global understanding of the local "especially in relation to marginal sexualities," which Morton calls for. It is precisely a developed theory of desire, I would submit, that could respond to this call. Such a developed theory would need to have as one of its components an aesthetic theory, along with a theory of class—and I think this needs to be said here even if it sounds like precisely what seems suspect to Morton.

Morton's call for a more or less traditional class analysis is a head-on challenge to queer studies. But there may be other ways of entering or engaging the broad, radical project to which Morton would want to subscribe, which are at least latently inscribed within the discursive and conceptual paradigms implied by a "queering" of status quo social formations. J. K. Gibson-Graham propose in their chapter in this volume that a rethinking of masculinist sexual and "capitalist morphology" can be initiated not as a brute frontal attack but in terms of precisely the "attack" or approach that I have suggested defines "queerness"—that is to say a true querying or queering of the scripts of this capitalist morphology (assuming that it is a single continuous morphology) from within. This would entail undermining its naturalizing and legitimizing claims in the same way as would an undermining of the affective and hegemonic structures that make rape *possible*. Gibson-Graham thus want to effect a productive homomorphism, to coin a phrase, between the strategic goal of queering heteronormativity and that of queering capitalist hegemony in the era of globalization. One of the merits of this approach is that it moves us beyond the obvious or customary understandings of the workings of capitalism. Drawing upon Sharon Marcus's provocative reconceptualization of the possibility of fighting against rape, and founding their argument on the analogy with global "penetration," "domination," and "colonization," Gibson-Graham argue that the usual victim rhetoric need not be seen as the only response to rapacious global capitalism: there are other ways of bringing capitalism to detumescence. If it is not necessary for women (or men) to subscribe to the customary notions of the rape victim as helpless (knees being harder than testicles), and if it is possible to see the outcome of rape, for instance, then it is possible to think of the withdrawal of phallic capital as being not necessarily the most desirable goal for underdeveloped regions of the globe.

Besides, to mix metaphors, Gibson-Graham point out that an "immunity" to infection by capitalism is not always what "pre-capitalist" regions necessarily want. But we cannot forget that there is a difference in modalities of *desire*, as well—a difference between wishing that capital does not withdraw itself from one's local economy, and wishing not to be the victim of rape. For all Gibson-Graham's care, these different modalities are relegated to a footnote. Gibson-Graham's argument, and this collection as a whole, points beyond itself to the need of an even more sophisticated articulation of queer theory, the critique of globalization, and a (psychoanalytically informed) theorization of desire.

Whatever its faults, Altman's chapter, in a different way from Morton's, helps to point to what such a sophisticated theory of desire—and therefore of subjectivity—would require. It would require a thematization of sexual difference in the psychoanalytic sense (so that we could understand whether or how women negotiate desire differently from men), as well as a fuller exploration of the lent, borrowed, or learned forms of love that circulate in public discourse. It would also mean a fuller understanding of global flows of labor and capital, and of the interactions among nations at the level of trade and diplomatic relations—but in terms of sexuality itself, even the most sophisticated queer theory must actively look in the future for the ways in which Western and non-Western discourses of *love*, and not just of *sexuality* might be freshly opened to exploration. This project can reveal its difficulty only in the still uncharted flows of global, mass-mediated flows. This collection should leave the reader with a renewed sense that the waters of cultural difference remain both perilous and promising.

I have argued that what is imperative for a sophisticated theory of desire, of subjectivity (and that is to say, not *only* queer subjectivity) is a closer attention to psychoanalysis. Some academic queer theory, such as the work of Tim Dean or some of the work of Christopher Lane, does address itself to psychoanalysis, but as this collection itself demonstrates, there is a need to develop the scope and appeal of psychoanalytic approaches. I would maintain, therefore, *pace* Morton that it is not just an analysis of class that could enrich queer theory but a more systematic and fully fledged engagement with psychoanalysis, despite the frequent association of such engagement as an elite mode. Queer studies need to be more and not less attentive to the construction and policing of fantasmatic desire. Spurlin seems to recognize the productivity of a psychoanalytic approach when he notes that nation-statist constructions of homosexuality, in which queering is tantamount to feminization, "are also linked to gender oppression and misogyny in that power is reduced to the phallus." Yet the reference to the phallus, even in Spurlin's informed prose, could benefit from far greater sophistication. Spurlin's usage masculinizes the phallus. But the phallus is not just a metaphor for the penis, nor just a symbol of masculine political power: this common misperception, arising from a less-than-thoroughgoing engagement with psychoanalytic terminology, does more harm than good, because it confuses the terms, and leads some feminists for instance to discount psychoanalysis prematurely as a productive site for developing an understanding of desire and subjectivity in contemporary global culture, especially turning upon the way the body is represented. To offer a couple of examples, the work of critics such as Charles Shepherdson and Paul Verhaeghe suggests some of the promise of this line of inquiry for queer studies. This understanding, I have been at pains to argue, is a critical project of the utmost significance, and queer theory can contribute powerfully to it owing to the nature of its central concerns.

This invocation of psychoanalysis brings us back to a question I raised at the outset, the question of the domination of Western or Eurocentric discourses of queer subjectivity, which persists despite the vaunted globalization of our era. Psychoanalysis emerged from theories of the modern Western mind and could be applied only to it—or such was the insistence, as Joël Dor reminds us, of the figure whose work most eminently represents the contemporary period's most radical developments in psychoanalysis, Jacques Lacan (33). Are there then *no* substantial universal problems of sexual identification or is there no universal language within which to theorize precisely the differences in sexual practice? Perhaps one can project a universal frame within which we can recognize cultural difference and the differences in sexual behavior. For otherwise we could be reduced to theoretical silence before the fact that in some countries sexual acts between people of the same anatomical structure historically have not been seen as perverse or determinant of gender identification, contrary to the story of Western sexuality.

This is why I would stress the need to work towards a sophisticated theorization of psychic structures that takes into account cultural difference. Postcolonial queer studies must perennially ask whether the Oedipus complex is a universal structure within which subjectivity emerges (Feher-Gurewich 79), and whether, or how psychoanalysis, a Western formation, can contribute to an understanding of global identity shifts, to the analysis of the persistence of cultural difference in the face of the transnational economy of the images around which identifications condense as accretions within an economy of desire—the economy, precisely, of subjectivity. André Green has called for a "reformulation of the theory of sexuality" in order to comprehend cultural variations in sexuality, especially non-Western variations that have been neglected—"*notoirement peu étudié*" (46–47). How do we think modernity in terms of contemporary gender theory, in terms of the advent of specifically twentieth century "neosexualities"?

One of the significant implications of queer studies is that marginality can be a general condition of critical and intellectual purchase on contemporary life. Queer subjects by definition have a marginal perspective on capitalism and the West. But one can argue, without betraying the specific commitment to gay, lesbian, and bisexual issues, that there are analogies between the struggles of queer subjects and other peripheral or subordinated groups, and such analogies enrich the critique of globalization. There are possibilities for new solidarisms, as I have tried to suggest, between gay activists and others who may identify themselves with "minority" perspectives—perspectives that are not powerless but interstitial, an example of which is postcolonial discourse. The world system today has reduced distance in many ways ranging from the Internet's disregard to borders to finance capital and a truly transnational market, where neither capital nor labor nor raw materials are limited within national borders. But the distance between the haves and the have-nots often grows proportionately as well—so lip service to "class analysis" is certainly not going to suffice. But on the other side of the ideological fence too, there is a need for more than celebration of the opportunities of the global marketplace: there is a need for attention to those at the margins who bear the cost disproportionately. This imperative coheres with postcolonial and subaltern critiques, especially.

There are many issues of justice that one cannot afford to overlook even if one's primary focus is on the injustice meted out to queer subjects in many cultures. If sexuality is among the most "obvious" modes by which minorities are constructed as marginal, then race is no less potent a division. What many of the chapters in this volume suggest is that the articulation of race and sexuality, as in the work of Robert Mapplethorpe most obviously, requires serious attention. Desai, Spurlin, Chong Kee Tan, and other contributors to this collection take this charge seriously. Minority as a critical position, then, is a keystone of this book. The prospects before queer theory are no less grand than the prospects were for feminism after it had made its first inroads into the academy. If queer studies remain on the peripheries of both academic and popular discourse, this is also a moment of opportunity.

Works Cited

Altman, Dennis. *Homosexual: Oppression and Liberation.* 1971. Reprint, New York: New York UP, 1993.

Ballhatchet, Kenneth. *Race, Sex, and Class under the Raj: Imperial Attitudes and Policies and Their Critics, 1793–1905.* London: Weidenfeld and Nicolson, 1980.

Berlant, Lauren, and Elizabeth Freeman. "Queer Nationality." *Boundary 2* (Spring 1992): 149–80.

Butler, Judith. *Bodies That Matter: On the Discursive Limits of "Sex."* New York: Routledge, 1993.

———. *The Psychic Life of Power: Theories in Subjection.* Palo Alto, Calif.: Stanford UP, 1997.

Dean, Tim. "Transsexual Identification, Gender Performance Theory, and the Politics of the Real." *Literature and Psychology* 39.4 (1993): 1–27.

D'Emilio, John. *Sexual Politics, Sexual Communities.* Second Edition. Chicago: U of Chicago P, 1998.

———. "Capitalism and Gay Identity." In *The Lesbian and Gay Studies Reader*, ed. Henry Abelove et al., 467–476. New York: Routledge, 1993.

Dor, Joël. "De la différénce des sexes à l'indifférenciation sexuelle." *Logos Anankè* 1 (Spring 1999): 29–33.

Duggan, Lisa. "Queering the State." *Social Text* 39 (Summer 1994): 1–14.

Feher-Gurewich, Judith. "Lacan sous sa forme inverseé." *Logos Anankè* 1 (Spring 1999): 75–82.

Freud, Sigmund. *The Freud Reader.* Ed. Peter Gay. New York: W.W. Norton, 1989.

Gopinath, Gayatri. "Funny Boys and Girls: Notes on a Queer South Asian Planet." In *Asian American Sexualities: Dimensions of the Gay and Lesbian Experience*, ed. Russell Leong. New York and London: Routledge, 1996.

Green, André. "La clinique psychanalytique du sexuel aujourd'hui et ses relations avec certaines disciplines connexes." *Logos Anankè* 1 (Spring 1999): 35–48.

Hardt, Michael, and Antonio Negri. *Empire*. Cambridge: Harvard UP, 2000.

Hyam, Ronald. *Empire and Sexuality: The British Experience*. New York: St. Martins, 1990.

Julien, Isaac, dir. *The Darker Side of Black*. Produced by Arena and Channel Four. Distributed by Noon Films, 1993.

Katz, Jonathan. *The Invention of Heterosexuality*. New York: Penguin, 1995.

Lane, Christopher, and Tim Dean, eds. *Homosexuality and Psychoanalysis*. Chicago: U of Chicago P, 2001.

Mercer, Kobena. *Welcome to the Jungle: New Positions in Black Cultural Studies*. London: Routledge, 1994.

Miller, D. A. "Sontag's Urbanity." In *The Lesbian and Gay Studies Reader*, ed. Henry Abelove et al., 212–220. New York: Routledge, 1993.

Nandy, Ashis. *The Intimate Enemy: Loss and Recovery of the Self Under Colonialism*. Delhi: Oxford UP, 1983.

Ratti, Rakesh, ed. *A Lotus of Another Color: An Unfolding of the South Asian Lesbian and Gay Experience*. Boston: Alyson Publications, 1993.

Said, Edward. *Orientalism*. New York: Columbia UP, 1979.

Shepherdson, Charles. "The Intimate Alterity of the Real: A Response to Reader Commentary on 'History and the Real.'" *Postmodern Culture* 6.3 (May 1996).

———. "The Epoch of the Body: Need, Demand and the Drive in Kojève and Lacan." *Perspectives on Embodiment: Essays from the NEH Institute at Santa Cruz*, ed. Honi Haber and Gail Weiss. New York: Routledge, 1996.

Verhaeghe, Paul. "The Subject of the Body." Unpublished paper.

———. *Does the Woman Exist?* New York: The Other Press, 1999.

Warner, Michael, ed. *Fear of a Queer Planet: Queer Politics and Social Theory*. Minneapolis: U of Minnesota P, 1994.

Weeks, Jeffrey. Introduction to 1993 Printing of Altman, *Homosexual: Oppression and Liberation*.

CONTRIBUTORS

Dennis Altman teaches at La Trobe University in Australia. He is the author of nine books, including *Power and Community: Organizational and Cultural Responses to AIDS* (Taylor and Francis, 1994), *Homosexual: Oppression and Liberation* (NYU, 1993), and *The Homosexualization of America: The Americanization of the Homosexual* (Beacon, 1983).

Joseph Boone is professor of English at the University of Southern California. Among his many publications is *Libidinal Currents: Sexuality and the Shaping of Modernism* (U of Chicago P, 1998).

Hema Chari is associate professor of English at California State University at Los Angeles. She has published on Nuruddin Farah and on gender and the nation state.

Samir Dayal teaches English at Bentley College. He is on the editorial board of *Genders*, and among his essays are "Postcolonialism's Possibilities: Subcontinental Diasporic Intervention" (*Cultural Critique*) and "Style is not the Woman: Sara Suleri's *Meatless Days*" (Temple, 1996).

Gaurav Desai is an assistant professor in the English Department at Tulane University and associate director of its African and African Diaspora Studies Program. He serves on the MLA's executive committee on Anthropological Approaches to Literature and has published articles in *Research in African Literatures, Cultural Critique, English Today*, and *Genders*. He is currently working on a book on colonial discourses in Anglophone Africa.

Jillana Enteen is assistant professor of English at the University of Central Florida. She has spent several years in Bangkok, including one as a Fulbright junior researcher. While there, she taught at several colleges and worked with women-centered nongovernmental organizations.

J. K. Gibson-Graham is the pseudonym for Katherine Gibson, of Monash University in Melbourne, and Julie Graham, of the University of Massachusetts at Amherst. Together they have published *The End of Capitalism (As We Knew It): A Feminist Critique of Political Economy* (Cambridge: Blackwell, 1996).

John C. Hawley is associate professor of English at Santa Clara University. He is the editor of eight other books, including *Christian Encounters with the Other* (NYU, 1998), *Cross-Addressing: Resistance Literature and Cultural Borders* (SUNY, 1996), and *Writing the Nation: Self and Country in Postcolonial Imagination* (Rodopi, 1996). *The Encyclopedia of Postcolonial Studies* is forthcoming from Greenwood Press.

Jarrod Hayes is assistant professor of French at the University of Michigan and is the author of *Queer Nations: Marginal Sexualities in the Maghreb* (University of Chicago, 2000). He has published most recently on "Rachid O. and the Return of the Homopast: Reading the Autobiographical as Allegory in Childhood Narratives by Maghrebian Men" in the journal *Sites*, on Proust in *PMLA*, and on Baudrillard in the *Literature Film Quarterly*.

Donald E. Morton is professor of English at Syracuse University. He has published in *Cultural Critique, PMLA, College English, diacritics, Genders, Social Text, Textual Practice, The Journal of Urban and Cultural Studies*, and *New Literary History*. In the area of queer theory, he writes a regular essay-column for the Melbourne-based journal *Critical inQueeries* and among his forthcoming texts are "Queer Theory as Pathos" and "Pataphysics of the Closet: The Political Economy of 'Coming Out.'" Among his books are *Theory / Pedagogy / Politics: Texts for Change; Theory, (Post)Modernity, Opposition: An "Other" Introduction to Literary and Cultural Theory; Theory as Resistance: Politics and Culture After (Post)Structuralism;* and *The Material Queer: A LesBiGay Cultural Studies Reader*. He is now completing a book, *Red-ing the Queer*, on the class politics of sexualities. He is founding coeditor of *Transformation: Marxist Boundary Work in Theory, Economics, Politics and Culture*.

Paige Schilt is visiting assistant professor of English at Allegheny College, concentrating on racialized sexualities in contemporary documentary film. She has recently written on Richard Rodriguez for *Texas Studies in Literature and Language.*

William J. Spurlin teaches twentieth century literature and queer studies at Cardiff University in Wales. He has coedited *Reclaiming the Heartland: Lesbian and Gay Voices from the Midwest* (Minnesota, 1996) and *The New Criticism and Contemporary Literary Theory: Connections and Continuities* (Garland, 1995), and has recently edited *Lesbian and Gay Studies and the Teaching of English: Positions, Pedagogies, and Cultural Politics* (National Council of Teachers of English, 2000). His numerous essays in queer studies have appeared in scholarly collections and in journals, most recently in *Decentring Sexualities* (Routledge, 2000); *James Baldwin Now* (New York University Press, 1999); *Mourning Diana: Nation, Culture, and the Performance of Grief* (Routledge, 1999); South Africa's *Journal of Literary Studies* (June 1999); and *Coming Out of Feminism?* (Blackwell, 1998). The essay that appears in this volume comes out of his current book project, *Imperialism within the Margins: The Cultural Politics of Queer Identity in Post Colonial Contexts.*

Chong Kee Tan has degrees from Cambridge, the National Taiwan University, and most recently from Stanford University in Chinese literature. He is the founder of a highly acclaimed web site (http://www.sintercom.org) that features Singapore politics and society from an alternative point of view. He has several articles forthcoming on Chinese homosexuality.

Index